Partial Reason

Recent Titles in
Contributions in Philosophy

Self-Construction and the Formation of Human Values: Truth, Language, and Desire
Teodros Kiros

Diogenes of Sinope: The Man in the Tub
Luis E. Navia

Simone de Beauvoir Writing the Self: Philosophy Becomes Autobiography
Jo-Ann Pilardi

Stalking Nietzsche
Raymond Angelo Belliotti

The Transient and the Absolute: An Interpretation of the Human Condition and
of Human Endeavor
Mordecai Roshwald

The Adventure of Philosophy
Luis E. Navia

Intentionalist Interpretation: A Philosophical Explanation and Defense
William Irwin

Natural Law Ethics
Philip E. Devine

Anglo-American Idealism, 1865–1927
W. J. Mander, editor

Two Views of Virtue: Absolute Relativism and Relative Absolutism
F. F. Centore

Liberty: Its Meaning and Scope
Mordecai Roshwald

Buddhist Epistemology
S. R. Bhatt and Anu Mehrotra

Partial Reason

Critical and Constructive Transformations of Ethics and Epistemology

Sally E. Talbot

Contributions in Philosophy, Number 78

GREENWOOD PRESS
Westport, Connecticut • London

Library of Congress Cataloging-in-Publication Data

Talbot, Sally E., 1953–
    Partial reason : critical and constructive transformations of ethics and epistemology /
Sally E. Talbot.
        p.   cm.—(Contributions in philosophy, ISSN 0084–926X ; no. 78)
    Includes bibliographical references and index.
    ISBN 0–313–31273–7 (alk. paper)
    1. Caring—Moral and ethical aspects.   2. Feminist ethics.   3. Liberalism.   I. Title.   II.
Series.
    BJ1475.T35 2000
    170—dc21   99–088622

British Library Cataloguing in Publication Data is available.

Library of Congress Catalog Card Number: 99–088622
ISBN: 0–313–31273–7
ISSN: 0084–926X

First published in 2000

Greenwood Press, 88 Post Road West, Westport, CT 06881
An imprint of Greenwood Publishing Group, Inc.
www.greenwood.com

Printed in the United States of America

The paper used in this book complies with the
Permanent Paper Standard issued by the National
Information Standards Organization (Z39.48–1984).

10 9 8 7 6 5 4 3 2 1

Copyright Acknowledgment

The author and publisher wish to acknowledge the Country Women's Association of Australia for per-
mission to use the poem from the *C.W.A. Cookery Book and Household Hints*, Western Australia: Wigg,
1978.

For David Talbot and Wendy Fatin

Contents

Preface ix

Acknowledgements xi

Introduction 1

1. People Standing Alone: A Critique of Liberal Moral Theory 9

2. A Necessary Corrective? Responses That Fill the Gaps 37

3. Theorising Connection as Primary: Understandings of Selves-in-Relation 63

4. Seeing Together: Care as Disposition 91

5. Understanding Partiality: Problematising Conceptions of Knowledge and Knowing 121

6. Partial Reason: The Epistemological Imperatives of Partiality 157

7. Care: The Ethical Imperatives of Partiality 187

Bibliography 219

Index 231

Preface

Too many versions of the ethic of care miss what I consider to be the crucial insight of the original work of both Carol Gilligan and Nel Noddings: that the concrete, everyday response of care provides the grounds for a radical critique of prevailing liberal moral theory and for a transformed understanding of both ethics and reason. Liberal moral theory, I argue, explores the ethical potential of a form of rationality that celebrates the capacity to think in an abstract, universal, and impartial way. The ethic of care, like liberal ethics based on duty, utility, and contract, is also grounded in a set of epistemological assumptions. My assertion is, however, that the epistemological assumptions grounding care are not those privileging abstraction, universality, and impartiality. Liberal moral theory insists on the notion of truth as a universal and unitary regulatory ideal, on the autonomy of separate knowing individuals, and on the establishment of a common language. The moral understandings of care, by contrast, locate truth in the elaboration of the particular contexts in which we function as knowers, identify knowers as selves-in-relation, and seek out particular shared interests as the basis of a commonality in which to see together.

The moral understandings of care entail a radical critique of the ethical and epistemological axioms of liberalism. From this critique, I draw an account of the ethic of care that both informs and is informed by partial reason. Although the sufficient conditions for caring are not quantifiable, I show that a number of ethical and epistemological imperatives can be drawn out of the endeavour to know and to care well. These imperatives suggest that creating and sustaining shared belief systems, mutual understandings, and intersubjective agreements might be understood as the processes of selves-in-relation, for whom neither ethics nor epistemology is immutable. Drawing insights from feminist and nonfeminist critics of liberal moral theory, from feminist moral theorists and epistemologists, and from feminist postcolonial writings, my discussion establishes that the elaboration of an ethic of care can be a transformative project.

Acknowledgements

As well as my immediate family, to whom this book is dedicated, many other people have nurtured and sustained me during the decade it has taken to arrive at this point. Two must be singled out: Patsy Hallen for showing me that philosophers can change the world, and Christina Chandler for helping me summon up the courage to try.

Introduction

During the years following my first philosophical encounter with the ethic of care in the mid-1980s, I have become increasingly interested in trying to develop care as both a critical and a constructive resource for feminist theory. This interest has been generated from two sources. On one hand, it has arisen from my own exhilaration after reading the original work of Carol Gilligan[1] and Nel Noddings[2] at finding myself engaged intellectually both as a moral philosopher and as a feminist. My experience of seeing colleagues and students across the academic disciplines stimulated by their first encounters with theories of care has been shared by many over the past decade. As Monique Deveaux has pointed out: "[T]he suggestion that an ethic of care is central to morality has generated controversy in sociology, ethics, moral and political philosophy, and political science, as well as in such professional fields as nursing, medicine, and education."[3]

On the other hand, like many feminist philosophers who have turned their energies to developing theories of care, I have found myself caught up in the controversies to which Deveaux alludes. Debates about the assumptions and implications of care ethics have elicited responses not only from those working in a variety of disciplines and professions but also from those belonging to various political persuasions and schools of thought. Susan Hekman notes the diversity of reactions to Gilligan's early work:

[In a Different Voice] has been both criticized and praised by feminists, moral philosophers, and moral psychologists. Gilligan's work has been hailed both as the harbinger of a new moral theory and as the final blow to the exhausted masculinist tradition of moral philosophy. It has also been condemned as methodologically unsound, theoretically confused, and even antifeminist. Gilligan's critics and defenders have cast her, respectively, as either villain or saviour in the ongoing intellectual debate of the 1980s and 1990s.[4]

As the debates about the relevance of care to different feminisms and to various feminist and non-feminist moral theories have unfolded, I have found it increasingly difficult to endorse unequivocally either the critics or the defenders of Gilligan. Too many versions of care have seemed to me to be missing the point that I had taken to be central to the original work of both Gilligan and Noddings. This point, which I perceive to have both critical and constructive aspects, is that the concrete, everyday response of care provides the grounds for a radical critique of prevailing liberal moral theory and for a transformed understanding of both ethics and reason.

"Any discussion of a care ethic," according to Gilligan, "has to begin with the issue of framing."[5] My thinking about care has taken shape within the framework suggested by Moira Gatens' identification of three feminist approaches to theory.[6] Following Gatens' terminology, I refer to these approaches as separatist-radical, extensionist-equality and critical-interrogative. For me, situating various versions of ethics, epistemology and feminism within this framework has been a way of clarifying both my criticisms of some approaches to caring and my own understanding of the assumptions and implications of a care ethic.

Gatens starts by distinguishing a separatist-radical approach to theory. Here, all theoretical intellectualising is dismissed as being essentially male and therefore either irrelevant or actually antithetical to the interests of women. On this view, feminist analysis "needs to dissociate itself from traditional theory,"[7] not only in terms of the content of its theses but also by specifically rejecting the methodology of traditional philosophical approaches.

The second account offered by Gatens is of an extensionist-equality approach, which involves reworking masculinist theory to accommodate women. This is the "neutral framework, sexist content"[8] claim that separates the sexist language, metaphors and examples used by philosophers from the sex-neutral kernel of truth they aim to convey. It is the assumption that this is a legitimate distinction which leads feminists to locate themselves within a liberal, Marxist or psychoanalytic paradigm and define their task as the "completion" of philosophy[9] by "subtract[ing] the surface sexism"[10] in what they see as otherwise universally relevant theories.

Gatens' third model, which reflects a critical-interrogative approach, identifies feminists as engaged in a confrontation with philosophy, asking questions that threaten the very framework of the traditional philosophical enterprise. This third approach evolves directly from the first two. It shares the perceptions of the first about philosophy's hostility to women. Its response, however, is to transform, rather than sever, the connections between the feminist and the philosophical enterprises. It does this by inverting the methods of the second approach, taking feminism as a base from which to evaluate philosophy.[11] Its method is summarised by Gatens: "By *self-consciously* demonstrating that any philosophical paradigm is *not* neutral, these feminists make themselves, both as philosophers and as women, *visible*. By making themselves visible, they in turn throw into question the legitimacy of claims and assumptions in philosophy that have been taken as axiomatic."[12]

It is Gatens' third model, the approach of the critical-interrogative feminist philosopher, that I want to endorse in this investigation of the ethic of care. It seems to me that both the first and second strategies do not necessarily challenge the philosophical status quo.[13] The separatist-radical approach, by equating theory with maleness and praxis with femaleness, serves to consolidate the dichotomous construction of human existence. Furthermore, I think that this approach implicitly accepts the transcendental claims of philosophy by refusing to engage in the project of philosophically deconstructing those claims. Thus, the abstract, impartial concepts of truth, reason and knowledge, on which philosophy's claim to transcendence is based, are allowed to flourish in the male province of theory while women proceed to construct a reality grounded in the practical domain of care, partiality and concrete particularity.

The extensionist-equality approach also avoids confronting philosophy's established wisdom. In fact, here the endorsement of traditional methodological assumptions is explicit, with the task being defined as the insertion of women into existing philosophical paradigms.[14] The account of female experience here appears as a postscript, an addendum that rectifies the bias in the traditional conflation of the male and the human. The practice of privileging concepts that are not associated with women is assumed to be accidental rather than designed, an error occasioned by historical circumstance rather than by philosophical fiat.

In the approach of the critical-interrogative feminist philosopher, however, feminists stop taking "philosophy and its overt pronouncements at face value."[15] The claim here is not just that the exclusions of traditional philosophy are oppressive to women but that such exclusions are crucial to, and endemic in, the way certain conventional philosophical approaches constitute themselves. This point is important, encapsulating as it does the suggestion that the privileging of certain styles of thinking, certain ways of accounting for human existence, is not simply a neutral methodological device.

The critical part of my discussion starts in Chapter 1 by looking at liberal moral theory and the assumption that ethics is properly the domain of thinking that is abstract, universal, and impartial. There is, of course, a significant body of literature, both feminist and nonfeminist, addressing the shortcomings of liberal ethics based on duty, utility, or contract and challenging ethical assumptions about abstract, universal, and impartial reasoning.[16] The critique that I develop in Chapter 1 investigates the possibility that liberal moral theory not only restricts the realm of moral relation but also gives an account of that realm that is less than adequate.

In Chapter 2, I consider various understandings of how concepts of care stand in relation to liberal moral theory. According to Virginia Held, certain important issues debated during the last decade are now all but resolved. Feminist discussion, she claims, has made it clear that "neither [justice nor care] can be dispensed with: both are highly important for morality. . . . What remains to be worked out . . . is how justice and care and their related concerns fit together."[17]

I am wary of such resolutions.[18] The danger, it seems to me, is that an ethic of care conceived on this basis will only fill the gaps conceded by liberal moral theory.[19]   I argue in Chapter 2 that approaches that understand care as complementing or supplementing the ethic of duty, utility, or contract do not necessarily disrupt the axiomatic assumptions of liberal moral theory. Neither do such approaches necessarily challenge the idea that accounts of relation in liberal moral theory are accounts of individuals who are not otherwise related.

Chapter 3 forms a bridge between the critical and the constructive parts of my argument. Without venturing directly into the realm of ontology, my argument here is that selves are more adequately described as selves-in-relation than as separate, autonomous, and impartial. In this chapter I discuss some of the ways in which understandings of ethics and epistemology are transformed when presumptions about selves are altered.

An aspect of approaches to care that serve only to fill the gaps conceded by liberal moral theory is the construction of care as irrational or as opposed to reason. One of my central concerns in the constructive part of my argument is to show that the ethic of care, like liberal ethics, maintains a nexus between ethics and reason: that care, like duty, utility, and contract, is grounded in a set of epistemological assumptions.   As the first step toward bringing the epistemological assumptions or understandings of care to the surface, I develop, in Chapter 4, a particular reading of care as both action and disposition. Importantly, this reading moves care away from the confines of the irrational and also from the "needs-based," instrumental versions of caring espoused, for example, by Joan Tronto.[20]

The reasoning that I associate with care understood as both action and disposition is based on the concept of *seeing together.*[21]   I contrast seeing together with "seeing the same thing."[22] This latter is the possibility ensured by impartial reason, which privileges abstraction and universalisation. *Partial* reason, on the other hand, takes account of the concrete and particular contexts in which we respond as selves-in-relation. The concept of partial reason, however, depends on an understanding of partiality that is not immediately available, even in feminist critiques of impartiality. In Chapter 5, I show that, where the understanding of partiality is confined to bias, feminist theory is left without a means of critiquing liberal concepts of reason in their own terms. I develop the points raised in this chapter into three central epistemological assumptions that sustain the concept of partial reason. These assumptions, which I establish as a grounding for the ethic of care, distinguish partial reason from the abstract, universal, and impartial thinking privileged by liberal moral theory. They involve locating truth in the elaboration of the context in which we function as knowers, identifying knowers as selves-in-relation, and seeking out particular shared interests as the basis of a commonality in which to see together. The elaboration of these assumptions forms the content of Chapter 6.

Having reworked the concepts of both care and reason, my final chapter brings together an account of the ethic of care that both informs and is informed by partial reason.   My objective here is to show that, although the sufficient conditions for caring are not quantifiable, nevertheless a number of ethical and epistemological imperatives can be drawn out of the endeavour to know and to care well.

Throughout this discussion, my arguments are premised on the assumption that creating and sustaining shared beliefs systems, mutual understandings and intersubjective agreements are ethical as well as an epistemological undertakings. Building on the insights of both feminist and nonfeminist critiques of liberal moral theory, gleaning ideas from the work of feminist ethicists and epistemologists, and stimulated by the writings of postcolonial feminists, what I have shown is that the elaboration of an ethic of care can be a transformative project. Linking the ethic of care and partial reason with the concept of seeing together leads to the suggestion that shared understandings and agreements are better understood as the processes of selves-in-relation than as the principled products of autonomous individuals. When neither ethics nor epistemology is taken to be immutable, both can be established as resources informing the thoughtful practice of ethical care.

A final word needs to be said about the spirit in which I have written this book. Working as a feminist philosopher on the development of care as both a critical and a constructive resource, I have found myself growing increasingly aware of the ambiguity entailed in situating care within a philosophical framework. Can the actual lived practices of caring and the abstract conceptual thought processes of philosophy be mutually informing? Can care be theorised or formalised while yet retaining a grounding in concrete practices of caring? Can the practices of philosophy themselves become practices of care? I have been encouraged to give affirmative (albeit tentative) answers to these questions by a range of insights drawn from other feminist theorists and writers. As well as the explicit acknowledgment I have already made of Gatens' notion of a critical-interrogative approach by feminists to theory, I want to cite three other sources that have shaped the writing of this book. The first is Janice Moulton's paper on the adversarial tradition, in which she raises the possibility that philosophy might be done on bases other than those that privilege deductive reasoning and adversarial argument.[23] Moulton argues:

Under the Adversary Paradigm, it is assumed that the only, or at any rate, the best, way of evaluating work in philosophy is to subject it to the strongest or most extreme opposition....If one wants philosophy to be objective, one should prefer the Adversary Method to other, more subjective, forms of evaluation that would give preferential treatment to some claims by not submitting them to extreme adversarial tests....If [the Adversary Method] were merely *one* procedure among many for philosophers to employ, there might be nothing worth objecting to except that conditions of hostility are not likely to elicit the best reasoning. But when it dominates the methodology and evaluation of philosophy, it restricts and misinterprets what philosophic reasoning is.[24]

That there might, as Moulton concludes, be "other ways of evaluating, reasoning about and discussing philosophy"[25] is one of the prospects that have guided my thinking.

A second idea that has influenced my thinking is contained in the reminder by Sara Ruddick that the range of resources that contribute to feminist philosophical work is perhaps greater than those taking more traditional approaches have conceded. When asked about her philosophical methodology, Ruddick identifies herself as a "participant-observer," an engaged, interested, active reflector on her own and others' practices. She describes her process in these terms:

I begin by remembering as honestly and deeply as I can my own experience as a mother and a daughter and that of my closest friends. I then extend my memory as responsibly as I am able, by reading, by eavesdropping, by looking at films, and, most of all, by mother-watching. . . . But finally, as mother, reader, and observer, . . . I make it up.[26]

Finally, in developing both the critical and the constructive aspects of my understanding of care, I have remained keenly aware of the salience of Minnie Bruce Pratt's words. It is in the spirit she advocates that I submit the ideas in this book for consideration:

We each have only a piece of the truth. So here it is: I'm putting it down for you to see if our fragments match anywhere, if our pieces, together, make another larger piece of the truth that can be part of the map we are making together to show us the way to get to the longed-for world.[27]

NOTES

1.   Gilligan, *In A Different Voice*.
2.   Noddings, *Caring*.
3.   Deveaux, 'Shifting Paradigms,' 115.
4.   Hekman, *Moral Voices, Moral Selves*, 1.
5.   Gilligan, 'Hearing the Difference: Theorizing Connection,' 125.
6.   Gatens, 'Feminism, Philosophy and Riddles without Answers'; Gatens, *Feminism and Philosophy*, especially Chapter 5.
7.   Gatens, 'Feminism, Philosophy and Riddles without Answers,' 15.
8.   Ibid., 18.
9.   Gatens, *Feminism and Philosophy*, 89.
10. Ibid., 91.
11. Gatens, 'Feminism, Philosophy and Riddles without Answers,' 24.
12. Ibid., 25.
13. Although they may do so.
14. Gatens, 'Feminism, Philosophy and Riddles without Answers,' 20, suggests that feminists taking this approach may, in practice, make significant alterations to existing paradigms. However, because the critical element of their methodology is restricted to the content rather than the structure of the paradigm, this aspect of their work tends to go unrecognised by the Establishment, and its significance may be lost to the feminist enterprise.
15. Ibid., 27.
16. Throughout the chapters that follow, I cite the works with direct relevance to my arguments. Such citations cannot fully acknowledge the extensive critical work that has paved the way, however indirectly, for my arguments to take shape. Some works must be mentioned here. While distinctions are not absolute, I have found the following to be valuable critiques of traditional moral theorising: Baier, 'What Do Women Want in a Moral Theory?' and 'The Need for More than Justice'; Calhoun, 'Justice, Care, Gender Bias'; Friedman, 'The Impracticality of Impartiality,' and 'The Practice of Partiality'; Held, *Feminist Morality*; Meyers, 'Moral Reflection'; Okin, 'Reason and Feeling in

Thinking about Justice'; Walker, 'Moral Understandings' and 'Partial Consideration.' For critiques focused on traditional epistemological methodology and the metaphysical assumptions of rationalism, see Bordo, 'The Cartesian Masculinization of Thought'; Code, *What Can She Know?*; Flax, 'Why Epistemology Matters' and 'Postmodernism and Gender Relations'; Fox Keller, *Reflections on Gender and Science*; Grimshaw, *Feminist Philosophers*; Harding, 'The Instability of the Analytical Categories of Feminist Theory' and *Whose Science?*; Jaggar, *Feminist Politics and Human Nature*; Lloyd, *The Man of Reason*; Moulton, 'A Paradigm of Philosophy: The Adversary Method'; Nelson, 'Epistemological Communities'; Ruddick, *Maternal Thinking*. Relevant nonfeminist critiques of traditional approaches to moral theory include Levinas, 'Philosophy and the Idea of Infinity' and 'Ethics as First Philosophy'; MacIntyre, *After Virtue* and *Whose Justice? Which Rationality?*; Murdoch, *The Sovereignty of Good*; Sandel, *Liberalism and the Limits of Justice*; Taylor, 'Cross-Purposes'; Williams, *Ethics and the Limits of Philosophy*. For more general critiques of traditional philosophical approaches, I have, among others, turned to Bernstein, *Beyond Objectivism and Relativism* and *The New Constellation*; Foucault, *Power/Knowledge*; Rorty, *Philosophy and the Mirror of Nature*.

17. Held, 'The Meshing of Care and Justice,' 128.

18. Although the view that care and justice can be integrated is common. As I note in Chapter 2, it is explicitly endorsed by Noddings in *Caring* and, on some readings (which I suggest may be misreadings), to Gilligan in *In a Different Voice*. In both these cases, the integration of justice and care is associated with the idea that care is irrational or unreasoned. Friedman, *What Are Friends For?*; Okin, 'Reason and Feeling in Thinking about Justice'; and Walker, 'Moral Understandings' and 'Feminism, Ethics, and the Question of Theory,' all either canvass or endorse the meshing of care and justice. So do Baier, 'A Note on Justice, Care, and Immigration Policy'; Narayan, 'Colonialism and Its Others'; and Tronto, 'Care as a Basis for Radical Political Judgements.' These are contributions to a Symposium on Care and Justice. See Deveaux, 'Shifting Paradigms'; Gilligan, 'Hearing the Difference'; and Held, 'The Meshing of Care and Justice,' for other contributions.

19. I focus my critique on liberal moral theory and read the general references to "justice" in care and justice debates as having a similar focus. Certainly, Gilligan develops the concept of her different voice in a context in which "justice" is synonymous with a train of thought in moral philosophy that extends directly from Kohlberg, through Rawls, to Kant.

20. Although I focus on Tronto's views, particularly as they are expressed in *Moral Boundaries*, this view is, of course, widely held. As Jaggar notes in 'Caring as a Feminist Practice of Moral Reason', in Justice and Care,' 180, "[d]escriptions of care thinking often take as paradigmatic situations in which the other is in need." Interestingly, although Ruddick, 'Remarks on the Sexual Politics of Reason,' 240, has said that for carers "[the] moral aim is to respond to people's real needs," she has subsequently noted (in personal correspondence with Jaggar, which Jaggar notes in 'Caring as a Feminist Practice,' 180) that "participants in caring relations also strive to delight and empower each other."

21. I draw the concept of "seeing together" from Haraway, 'Situated Knowledges,' 586. Here she talks of the possibility of "join[ing] with another, to see together without claiming to be another."

22. Once again, the citations in the chapters that follow of works with direct relevance to my arguments cannot fully acknowledge the extent to which my working out of the concept of seeing together is indebted to the writings of postcolonial feminist theorists. While it is important to emphasise that the distinction between postcolonial and more

mainstream feminist theorising is necessarily somewhat provisional (so that Haraway, e.g., from whom I take the notion of seeing together, might be acknowledged here as well as in note 16), the following writers are major contributors to the debates about difference and identity, sameness and otherness, self and other within which my notions of selves-in-relation and seeing together have developed: Braidotti, *Patterns of Dissonance*, 'Embodiment, Sexual Difference, and the Nomadic Subject,' 'The Politics of Ontological Difference,' and 'On the Female Feminist Subject'; Butler, 'Gender Trouble, Feminist Theory and Psychoanalytic Discourse'; Cornell, *Beyond Accommodation*; Diprose, *The Bodies of Women*; Irigaray, *Speculum of the Other Woman* and *This Sex Which Is Not One*; de Lauretis, *Alice Doesn't*; Lorde, *Sister Outsider*; Lugones, 'Playfulness, "World"-Travelling, and Loving Perception'; Scheman, *Engenderings*; Spelman, *Inessential Woman*; Spivak, *In Other Worlds*; Young, 'The Ideal of Community and the Politics of Difference.'

23. Although Moulton's paper is regarded as germinal, other feminist philosophers have taken up these themes. See, e.g., Code, 'Responsibility and Rhetoric.'

24. Moulton, 'A Paradigm of Philosophy,' 9–10.

25. Ibid., 18.

26. Ruddick, *Maternal Thinking*, 62.

27. Pratt, 'Identity: Skin Blood Heart,' 32.

Chapter 1

People Standing Alone:
A Critique of Liberal
Moral Theory

The extent to which deontological, utilitarian, and contract ethics discount or devalue the experiences of people who are not male and/or not white and/or not affluent is well documented in the literature of feminist moral theory.[1, 2] But equally well documented is the fact that, important as such a revelation is, it lends itself to several very different interpretations and, consequently, to widely diverging accounts of feminist ethical practice.[3] While feminist moral philosophy is certainly richer, rather than poorer, for this diversity, my suggestion is that some approaches are more productive than others, both in terms of sustaining a critique of liberal moral theory and in terms of generating more adequate accounts of our moral responsiveness.

In this chapter, I develop a critical approach that concentrates on two particular aspects of liberal moral theory: the nature of the nexus between ethics and reason and the capacity of liberal moral theory to account adequately for the experiences it claims are paradigmatic. This approach draws attention to the rational heart of the liberal moral subject and to the particular kinds of connection that are established by proceeding from a rational ideal to an ethical theory answering the demands of that rational ideal. This approach also reveals as problematic aspects of liberal moral theory that may be taken for granted by theorists who assume that the failures of liberal ethics are primarily failures to take account of relations that are not public and formal.

My objective in concentrating on these two aspects of liberal moral theory is to establish a framework for problematising the axiomatic association of ethics with autonomous, impartial reasoners and of care with the irrational, unreasoned, or purely instrumental response.[4] For the critical, interrogative approach with which I have identified my argument, the undermining of such axioms is crucially important. What I mean to clarify in this initial stage, however, is my understanding of how these axioms operate: what assumptions they sustain, what privileges they legitimate, what claims they disallow. Within this critical framework, traditional liberal moral philosophy is revealed as constructing an ethics in the service of, or subservient to, reason, so that the reasoning of the liberal moral agent is bound to and by the constraints of a rationality that privileges abstract, universal, and impartial thinking. Within this framework I build my case for arguing that liberal moral theory not only begs the question about how the nexus between reason and ethics is sustained but also provides an inadequate account of formal, public encounters. These insights lead to the suggestion, explored in later chapters, that the concepts of care and partial reason effectively undermine some of the central elements of liberal moral philosophy.

ETHICS IN THE SERVICE OF REASON

The moral subjects whose identities are secured by the categorical imperative or the principles of utility or contract are white, affluent, and male. The critical approach that I develop here, however, starts with the recognition of another, but not unrelated, attribute of liberal moral subjects as these subjects emerge out of the ethical structures established by Immanuel Kant, John Stuart Mill, and John Rawls. What I focus on are these liberal moral subjects as quintessential impartial *reasoners*. I explore the extent to which their ideal moral responses can be understood as the most perfect embodiment of the principles of rationality. My suggestion is that behaving ethically is seen by liberal moral philosophers as a way of embodying the principles of an impartial, formal reason, so that rational behaviour is equated with the ethical, while immoral behaviour can be judged and condemned on the grounds of its irrationality.

Working through an example helps to clarify what I mean by identifying liberal moral subjects as impartial reasoners. By taking each approach in turn, I show how deontologists, utilitarians, and contractarians might argue that lying is unethical. What emerges is a picture of the moral agent as bound by a rationality that is as immutable as it is impartial.

For Kant, the categorical imperative is an epistemological statement identifying reason as one of the active ingredients that turn an action into a moral action.[5] The discussion into which Kant enters with Benjamin Constant about what Constant sees as an apparently unethical implication of the categorical imperative illustrates this point.[6] Constant asks Kant whether it might be deemed ethical, according to the principles of deontology, to lie to someone of murderous intent about the whereabouts of his or her quarry. It seems to me that, in order to keep the categorical imperative intact, Kant has to allow that people acting ethically according to the morality of truth-telling (i.e., people who do not lie) are at least accessories to acts of blatant *immorality* in the case where their truth-telling allows murderers access to their potential victims. We might say that Kant is prepared to tamper with his notion of what is ethical (so that what is ethical might also be unfair or at least in some important way contrary to some kind of ordinary belief about the proper way to act) in order to keep intact the notion of reason as consistency. The idea of a rational principle that is not consistent, not universal, cannot, for Kant, be entertained: an ethical action the principle of which is not universalisable is self-contradictory. You cannot, for example, advocate lying by appeal to reason, since such an argument renders meaningless what are trying to advocate. To say that lying is justified must, according to the rational principle enshrined in the categorical imperative, be to say that everyone is justified in lying. But the implication of this is that the distinction between lying and telling the truth is no longer valid. If lying is universalised (i.e., if "everyone ought to lie" becomes a universal maxim of action), then the whole rationale for lying disappears because nobody will consider that any response might be truthful.[7] Such a maximum is self-contradictory, since it negates the distinction between lying and truth-telling. Lying can exist only if we expect to hear the truth; if we expect to be told lies, the motive for lying disappears. To identify lying as ethical, then, is to be inconsistent. It is to try to sustain two contradictory premises ("everyone ought to lie" and "everyone ought to tell the truth") and is therefore not rational. For Kant, the commitment to consistency is the commitment to reason (to be rational is to be consistent), and we understand and respect the necessity to be consistent to the extent that we are rational.

Kant's response to Constant draws attention to a particular understanding of the connection between reason and ethics. The ideals governing my action when I am asked whether I am hiding the murderer's potential victim are, ultimately, rational ideals. The dictates that govern my action are the dictates of reason. The connection between the truthful answer ("Yes") to the murderer's question ("Are you hiding your friend?") and the death of my friend may be unambiguous. Kant still wants to say that I should never lie, that it remains my duty, according to the dictates of reason, to tell the truth.

But Kant's is a reason without context, and its imperatives are categorical rather than circumstantial, impartial rather than interested. Kant may insist that I might rescue my friend by means other than lying, or he may justify my lying as a matter of expediency (in which case it is not a moral action), but the important thing is his determination that an ethical response to Constant must uphold the original rational principle, which operates without reference to interest, particularity, or concrete circumstances.

My point is not that a rethinking of the ethical and epistemological assumptions that rule the concrete, particular, and partial out of philosophical consideration was, in reality, open to Kant. Clearly, his whole theory of knowledge[8] would have collapsed with the admission of context (and consequence) into his ethical system. My point is that in the process of satisfying the ultimate rational principles of universality and consistency, the categorical imperative may become paradoxical (or even ambiguous or nonsensical). For Kant, moral responses are manifestations of the human capacity to reason; but the paradox, to which Constant draws attention, is that the Kantian mode of rationality may sanction the immoral response.

For the utilitarian, there might be no clear-cut answer as to whether lying is ethical. What is important to my argument, however, is that the deliberations that go into making the utilitarian calculation are deliberations about reason, about whether it is rational to lie. Here, reason is the key to the assessment of utility.[9] Applying the standards of reason, the utilitarian can be "as strictly impartial as a disinterested and benevolent spectator."[10] Whether utilitarians tell lies or the truth will depend on a rational assessment of how the greatest happiness is brought about. To lie (or to be truthful) is irrational if, as a consequence of lying (or telling the truth), there is a decrease in happiness or an increase in unhappiness.[11] Again there are two contradictory premises at stake: "it is ethical to lie (or tell the truth) and decrease happiness" and "the ethical act increases happiness." As in the Kantian moral framework, for utilitarians the unethical response relies on contradictory premises and is, therefore, irrational.

An ethic of contract places a similar emphasis on the rationality of ethical activity. According to Rawls, participants in the original position discussion have only two characteristics: they are free, and they are rational.[12] What is just and unjust is the choice of "rational men"[13] who, in bringing their powers of reason to the task of fashioning a moral system, will choose to sanction nothing that could possibly be detrimental to their own personal interests. Now one of the prerequisites of participating in the original position discussion is that I have neither a philosophical nor a psychological conception of the good.[14] Here is a crucial difference between utility and contract-based ethics. The utilitarian works all the time with a firm conception of the good in terms of happiness or well-being. Looking always at outcome rather than intent, the utilitarian judges moral substance by constantly referencing levels of happiness or unhappiness. In the original position, however, I can have reference to nothing other than my own interests, but with no indication of what these interests are or what would serve them. This is the nucleus of Rawls' concept of justice as fairness. The Rawlsian moral imagination has only one track: I cannot sanction lying without placing myself at risk of being lied to. I am not supposed to gamble on the possibility that you or I might benefit from telling or being told a lie. I am not supposed to be able to distinguish between white and black lies or between contexts in which lying might be an option. Hence, in the process of making up my ethical mind, I am led to a logical contradiction, since I cannot rationally sustain the notions that "what is fair disadvantages (or is unjust to) nobody,"[15] "lying is fair," and "being lied to may disadvantage (or be unjust to) me." What emerges from behind the veil of ignorance are principles that meet the demands of the only qualities admitted into the original position: a sense of reason and a sense of freedom (expressed as mutual disinterest).[16]

What happens if we test the case of lying not in the original position but in real life? Here we find a conception of ethics that casts the device of the original position in quite a new light. Comparing the moral philosopher's task to that of the grammarian, Rawls says:

There is no reason to assume that our sense of justice can be adequately characterized by familiar commonsense precepts, or derived from the more obvious learning principles. A correct account of moral capacities will certainly involve principles and theoretical constructions which go much beyond the norms and standards cited in everyday life; it may eventually require fairly sophisticated mathematics as well.[17]

What Rawls seems to be suggesting is that "everyday" moral operatives will be unable to give "a correct account" of their moral capacities, beyond perhaps referring the questioner to the principles handed down by those whose superior faculties enable them to grasp matters beyond the obvious and familiar. By explicitly identifying the sense of justice as "a mental capacity...involving the exercise of thought,"[18] Rawls is clearly expecting ordinary moral workers to fail to give a correct account of their work and is attributing this failure to a deficiency in their capacity to *reason* rather than their lack of ethical sense.[19] The featureless creatures participating in the original position discussion begin to take on the aspect of Plato's Philosopher Kings or, at least, of Hare's archangels.[20]

These three examples illustrate two points central to my argument. First, they show the rational heart of the Enlightenment moral subject, the essential *rationality* of ethical activity. Second, they illustrate the way ethics defers to reason in the philosophical pursuit of a foundational account of moral truth. Ethics is not about the real world where we watch expressions, listen to inflections, remember experiences of happiness and sadness, where our hopes are satisfied and disappointed and our passions aroused and dampened. It is not concerned with the ambivalences of intimate relationship or the ambiguities of self-reflexive consciousness. In the liberal ethical project no consideration is unique, no quandary original. What cannot be subsumed under some existing maxim or principle is ruled irrelevant or insignificant or outside the project of ethics. Ethics is the process of distilling the essence out of actual human experience on the understanding that what is concrete rather than abstract, particular rather than universal, partial rather than impartial, obfuscates the task of the moral philosopher, which is to account for morality in terms of rationality and thus confine ethics inside the fold of reason.

THE IMPARTIAL MORAL REASONER

Up to this point, I have talked about liberal moral subjects as quintessential impartial reasoners, where reason is grounded in the ideals of abstraction, universalisability, and impartiality. To strengthen my claim that, for the liberal moral philosopher, ethics is subservient to reason, I now look more closely at the question of what reason grounded in this way actually does. What kind of activity is the impartial moral reasoner engaged in?

For Kant, there are two ways to account for human experience. The first refers to the information we receive through the senses. The second refers to the information we receive "immediately," that is, not mediated through the senses. The first is related to the "sensible" world governed by the laws of nature, and the second to the "intelligible" world governed by laws that, Kant says, are "not empirical but have their ground in reason alone."[21] But, crucially, we are not to infer from this division of experience into mind and matter, thought and feeling, that reason's domain is confined to the nonempirical or the nonsensual, for Kant goes on to say, indeed to emphasise, that *"the intelligible world contains the ground of the sensible world and therefore also of its laws."*[22] As rational beings (or, to use Kant's terminology, *"qua* intelligence"), then, we experience both the sensible world and the intelligible world under the laws of reason.

It is a characteristic of reason that it "unrestingly seeks the unconditionally necessary."[23] It seems, then, that although there is an acknowledgment in the Kantian system of the particular, concrete, and partial realm of human experience, its significance is limited to providing the raw data for reason— abstract, universal, and impartial reason—to process. Kant conveys his notion of reason as being "scrupulously cleansed"[24] of everything empirical. Despite the attractiveness of the formula of the end in itself, with its emphasis on the integrity of reason, we find in the formula a reason purged of the very things that discriminate one human encounter from another.

What is it, then, that Kantian reasoners do? The most straightforward answer is the one most relevant to my argument: they celebrate their status as rational beings. It is as rational beings that they have intrinsic value. In other words, to the extent that they are rational, they are valuable in themselves. They are, as Kant says, "exalted above all price,"[25] and because of this they are prohibited from treating either themselves or other rational beings as anything other than ends in themselves. But the central point of Kant's argument is that it is in moral deliberation that reason is best celebrated. As H. J. Paton notes in his commentary on Kant, human beings are "imperfectly rational agents."[26] Indeed, their imperfection is the catalyst for the formulation of the categorical imperative, since a perfectly reasonable being would not need maxims to mediate between "I will" and "I ought."[27] In moral deliberation exists the possibility of overcoming or at least compensating for this flaw because to act morally (e.g., to be faithful or kind[28]) is to act in accord with pure reason, which dictates "the practical law that maxims should be universally valid."[29]

For Kant, reason is an end in itself, and it is in the process of reasoning that individuals claim their full humanity. They are reasoning (rather than feeling or sensing) when their thoughts and actions transcend the empiricism of the particular, the concrete, and the partial to focus on the universal and the abstract. The mien of reasoners is disinterested. They connect with those other individuals affected by their thoughts and actions only to acknowledge those others' membership of the class of autonomous, rational beings able, as reasoners, to inhabit a realm where individuals are "free in respect of all laws of nature" and bound only by reverence for the "sublimity of a maxim" in which their autonomy as rational beings is secured.[30]

For the utilitarian and the proponent of contract-based ethics, reason is conceived in a strictly instrumental sense. It is a way of making effective, efficient decisions about means in a context where questions about ends are already resolved.[31] Rawls is explicit about this point: "The concept of rationality must be interpreted as far as possible in the narrow sense, standard in economic theory, of taking the most effective means to given ends."[32] Likewise, for the utilitarian, "the end is given, and the role of reason is to minimise the costs of achieving that end."[33]

For the utilitarian, then, it is not rational to incur any more cost than is necessary to maximise happiness or minimise pain. If I can prevent my mother's being unhappy by writing to her once a fortnight, it is irrational of me to write to her weekly. The assumption here is that doubling my letter writing presents an additional cost to me (in terms of time, energy, and postage) that is not balanced by an increase in my mother's happiness (in terms of the reduction of her anxiety about my well-being). What is factored out of this calculation (which correlates inefficiency with irrationality) are the particular, concrete, contextual considerations that distinguish writing to my mother from, say, choosing whether to eat mollusks or crustaceans.[34] Utilitarians reason in abstract, universal terms. In their demeanour with respect to other human beings, they are as disinterested as Kantian reasoners.

Given Rawls' remarks about the mathematical prerequisites needed to give a "correct account" of reasoning, it is perhaps unsurprising to find him drawing his notion of reason from economics. The veil of ignorance might be a hypothetical construct, but it reveals an assumption at the heart of Rawlsian rationality about how reason works. Reasoning in the original position is a matter of eliminating extraneous factors. According to economic rationalism,[35] the provision of a service like child care is justifiable in terms of profit: parents who would otherwise be caring for children can return to the workforce, costing the economy less in welfare payments and returning more to the economy by way of their increased disposable incomes. By a similar reasoning process, native forests might be protected because there is more profit in forest tourism than in wood chips. The point is that in each case the process of reasoning is concerned with serving only one end: economic efficiency.

Now, the objective of efficiency is specifically engaged by Rawls to service his notion of reason. When they move behind the veil of ignorance, Rawlsian reasoners relinquish not only their own interests but the interest they might take in one another's interests.[36] In this state of mutual disinterest, others exist for them only as fellow reasoners entitled to press claims against each other with a minimum of personal disadvantage. The principles that emerge from behind the veil of ignorance are, according to Rawls, "the result of leaving aside those aspects of the social world that seem arbitrary from a moral point of view."[37] Things that are deemed arbitrary include my own specific interests and the specific interests of others as well as knowledge about my own and others' strengths and weaknesses and the self-consciousness knowledge on which a sense of location (or dislocation) depends. It seems, then, that Rawlsian reasoners perform best[38] in circumstances where their rationality is informed by nothing that tells them about themselves, others, or the world. Like economic rationalists, their subject matter consists only of certain aspects of reality: aspects that return an efficiency dividend in the currency of a strictly instrumental rationalism.

THE EXCLUSION BY LIBERAL ETHICS OF THE PRIVATE SPHERE

It may seem that the critique I am developing here generates a reactionary reimposition or reinforcement of the private-public distinction rather than new insights into the ethics-reason nexus. After all, the kind of moral theory to which Kant, Mill, and Rawls are major contributors has never claimed to be dealing with anything other than the public realm, the realm of the market, of contract, of bureaucracy, of rights, where other people are experienced only as the objects of what Ross Poole calls "transferable emotions."[39] Given this focus, it is unsurprising that their morality fails in the private sphere. If, as I am suggesting, morality is conceived in terms of impartial reason, and the private sphere is constituted in terms of emotion, then human experience is neatly bifurcated into what is rational, which equates with what lies within the moral sphere, and what is emotional, which lies outside morality.[40]

This distinction is enforced by Kant's division of experience into sensible and intelligible, with the first category consisting of feelings, emotions, and "ideas given to us from without, we ourselves being passive" and the second being informed by the power of reason or ideas "which we produce entirely from ourselves."[41] It is not simply that there is no place in the private realm of feeling for a categorical imperative. It is rather that such a notion is nonsensical: an imperative is categorical precisely because it is consonant with the notion of reason as consistency. It cannot be disobeyed without contravening reason. The realm of feeling is marked by its inconsistency[42] and is therefore not to be looked to as yielding maxims, principles, or examples of morality.

Similarly, the utilitarian calculus is for use by people who are strictly impartial and disinterested.[43] Clearly, it makes sense to expect people to adopt this kind of attitude only in the public sphere, since impartiality and disinterest would be signs of dysfunction in private relations. This leaves two possibilities open. On one hand, utilitarians might be said to be acting morally in the private sphere only to the extent that they can demonstrate their impartiality. So, for example, I have acted in accord with utilitarian ethics if I can show that I have not valued the happiness of my own child more highly than that of a child I have not met or not taken into account the fact that the person who is asking me to guarantee a financially risky project is my brother.[44] On the other hand, and this possibility seems to me to be more likely, utilitarians might consider morality as removed from the private sphere so that the calculation of utility in the public sphere is separated from the incalculable play of attachment and devotion in the private. In that case, neither the advantages I may bestow on my child nor the risky ventures I may underwrite to help my brother are subject to the utilitarian moral principle.

For Rawls it is clearly not in the realm of intimacy that the principles of justice as fairness are cultivated. He refers specifically to the "public conception of justice," which constitutes "the fundamental charter of a well-ordered human association."[45] He cautions against assuming that his system of justice will work for "private associations," "less comprehensive social groups," "informal conventions and customs of everyday life," and "voluntary cooperative" contractual agreements.[46] Whether they represent ideally rational selves or selves expressing an a priori sense of justice, the original position deliberators are unequivocally *public* selves. It turns out that the aspects of the social world that Rawls has decided are ethically arbitrary are precisely those aspects that are evoked, sustained, and inspired in the private sphere.[47] The noninstitutionalised realm of personal and particular (i.e., nontransferable) relations is regarded as unimportant to Rawls' scheme, just as the ability to be passionate, emotional, and attached is regarded as dispensable by the original position debaters.

The private sphere, then, lies outside the focus of liberal morality. With this in mind, I can elaborate on the question of whether acknowledging the failure of liberal morality in the private sphere necessarily leads to a strengthening of the public–private distinction. In fact, nothing in my reading of Kant, Mill, and Rawls suggests that they perceive any such failure. If, as I have argued, their approach to moral philosophy places ethics in the service of reason, then it becomes unnecessary to explore the realm of irrationality or nonrationality for its ethical significance.[48] As a feminist philosopher, there are two ways I might move to counter this idea. I consider both options by uncovering two different, but related, assumptions on which such distinctions between public and private are based.

First, there is the assumption that the private realm is generated and sustained in opposition to reason. This argument opposes reason and emotion, thought and feeling, knowledge and belief and then conflates reason, thought, and knowledge with masculinity and emotion, and feeling and belief with the feminine. For some care ethicists, this has proved to be a tempting assumption to endorse. The assumption that the irrational or nonrational nature of the sphere of private relations is indicative of an absence of moral capacity or ethical sense in women has been well documented.[49] One way to counter this, it seems, is to talk about women's moral capacity in terms not of a *lacking* but of a *different* ethical sense. Hence, one version of the ethic of care endows women with a moral sense that celebrates emotion and feeling. Caring becomes the morality of the private sphere, with justice characterising public morality. The private sphere is the realm of responsibility; the public, the realm of duty and obligation.[50]

I cannot see that either Kant, classical utilitarians, or Rawls would need to object to such a version of care. If I am right in suggesting that the limitation of their ethical theorising to the public realm is not perceived by them as a failure but as an entirely appropriate and inevitable omission, then the discovery of a morality that accounts for the private sphere without disputing the significance of the ethics of duty, utility, and contract in the public sphere will surely be accommodated. I am not suggesting that such accommodation would necessarily be accompanied by an unequivocal endorsement of this version of the ethic of care in particular or of the feminist ethical project in general. While the nexus between reason and ethics remains grounded in the understanding that moral reasoning is ultimately subject to the dictates of a reason that is both impartial and immutable, this version of caring will always be vulnerable to certain charges by defenders of liberal ethics. Because care deals with the particular, the partial, and the concrete (i.e., supposedly, with the irrational) rather than with the universal, the impartial, and the abstract (i.e., supposedly, with reason), the ethic of care will be regarded as a theory about psychological dispositions rather than morality. At best, if care is presented as the morality of the private sphere, it will be assumed to be a useful supplement to the repertoire of moral responses and suitable for acknowledgment in a pluralistic moral framework. This, I think, is the spirit in which several commentators on feminist ethics endorse the feminist ethical project.[51] At worst, this presentation of care confirms not only the moral but also the metaphysical inferiority of women, whose confinement in the realm of the emotional is guaranteed by their failure to couch their morality in the universal, abstract terms that are assumed to elevate reason above emotion. Both this best- and worst- case scenario seems to me to cement in place a rigid distinction between public and private, between reason and emotion, and between the rational and the non-rational. This suggests, I believe, that the approach that tries to accommodate the construction of the private realm in opposition to reason is not necessarily a fruitful approach to countering the liberal exclusion of the private sphere (understood as the sphere of concrete, particular, and partial considerations) from the realm of ethics. More strongly, I submit that the version of the ethic of care that confines caring to the private sphere is fundamentally flawed in that it cannot but endorse a system of opposing dichotomies, albeit with the possibility of developing differently valued hierarchical weightings. These points I develop in detail in Chapter 2.

However, what is relevant to my argument here is a second assumption sustaining the idea that the irrational or nonrational nature of the private sphere puts it outside the realm of ethics and makes it unnecessary to explore the private sphere for its ethical significance. This is the assumption that the model of the moral subject offered by liberal moral theory has a legitimacy that places it above challenge. It may be that both Kant and Rawls want to challenge the doctrine of utility. There may be volumes devoted to arguing the pros and cons of intentionalism and consequentialism, ethical naturalism, duty, rights, and justice. But stable at the heart of all this disputation is the moral subject: male, white, affluent, and, above all, rational. This assumption, while obviously related to the first, at least to the extent that they are used compatibly, forms an implicit common currency among exponents of deontological, utilitarian, and contract-based theories of morality. To the extent that it remains implicit, it generates a subtext that ensures that the sex of the moral subject *is* ethically significant,[52] even while the moral theory that it sustains loudly proclaims its gender-neutrality.[53]

It would seem that, unlike the first assumption (which, as I have shown, *is* endorsed by some versions of care), the construction of, and confidence in, the moral subject as impartial reasoner asserted in this second assumption are utterly antithetical to the project of care in particular and feminist theory in general. An interrogation of this second assumption forms the starting point of my critique of ethics. This critique, as I will show, turns the scepticism generated by an awareness of the gender, race, and class exclusiveness of established liberal moral theory into a critical transformation of ethics and reason. An interrogation of the concept of the moral subject as impartial reasoner is linked, I believe, to the realisation that the problem with liberal ethics is not only that it fails in the *private* sphere—a weakness that is perceived as a strength by its proponents—but also that liberal ethics fails to give an adequate account of human relationships in the *public* sphere. It is to a verification of this latter proposition that I now turn.

THE FAILURE OF LIBERAL ETHICS IN THE PUBLIC SPHERE

It seems to me that one of the features of liberal morality that has proven attractive to philosophers and nonphilosophers alike is that, in addition to prescribing and proscribing modes of thought and courses of action suitable for consideration by the moral subject, it defines which situations, which relationships are to be thought of as constituting the proper subject matter of morality. It tells us, in short, where and when our dilemmas are accurately perceived as moral dilemmas rather than dilemmas that are appropriately resolved by recourse to something other than moral deliberation. In some circumstances, according to liberal ethical theories, we look in vain for a moral code and might instead turn our attention to other decision-making procedures like coin tossing, accepting the advice of an authority, or following our inclinations.[54] The place where dilemmas that are appropriately resolved by moral deliberation are found is the public sphere.[55] Now, the point I want to make is that by confining morality to the public sphere, liberal ethics also confines morality to formal relationships. In other words, the only concept of relation with which liberal theory can deal is where the particularity of "the other" is irrelevant. To the extent that the other features in liberal ethics, it is as an exchangeable entity experienced as the object of transferable emotions.

Some examples will help to clarify what I mean. When I open the door and find someone with obviously murderous intentions asking whether I have seen the person on whom these intentions are focused, Kant's recommendation that telling the truth constitutes the moral response contains an insistence that I treat both the person I have hidden and the person at the door as abstractions. The person at the door might be my mother, but this aspect of the situation must be ruled out of my ethical deliberation. The person I have hidden might be my daughter, but this is similarly irrelevant.[56] In excluding their particularity from consideration, I have to set aside the history of my relationships with these people. I must overlook the memories of the shared happinesses and sadnesses that we have sustained, our mutual hopes and fears, the concrete details of the circumstances that have led the three of us to such a terrible impasse. In an abstract sense, none of this is relevant to my submission before the categorical imperative of rational consistency in which the moral response is grounded. Kant's insistence that we must always treat others as ends in themselves appears to be extremely ambiguous, given his confinement of morality to the public realm of reason where others are always treated ethically only in abstraction, as exchangeable objects.[57]

The contract ethicist makes similar demands of the moral subject. If I imagine myself applying to be one of the ideal deliberators behind the hypothetical veil of ignorance, then any indication that my recommendations might be based on particularity would rule me ineligible for a place in the original position. The particularistic or personal interest I might take in the well-being of my mother or daughter is regarded as a manifestation of a bias that can lead only to unfairness and is therefore potentially subversive of just social arrangements. My stance as a deliberator about rights or justice, then, has to be disinterested, detached from the hopes and fears I hold for particular others, and indifferent to the responsibilities placed on me by particular relationships. In the Rawlsian moral imagination, I am assumed either to have morally significant particular relationships with nobody (in the sense that my attachment to my mother and daughter is regarded as arbitrary from the point of view of justice as fairness) or to have particular relationships with everyone (in the sense that serving the interests of everyone by the disinterested construction of just and fair social arrangements is assumed to be the rational way to serve the interests of my mother and daughter). In other words, any distinction between my personal relationships and my relationships with strangers appears to be superfluous to the Rawlsian ideal of justice, in which relation is acknowledged only in the context of the homogeneous formality that choreographs the steps involved in conveying justice as fairness.

For the utilitarian, both the particularity of the other and the particularity of other interests are irrelevant. If my son is being bullied, the two grounds on which I *cannot* intervene are, first, that he is my son (and his pain is my pain) and, second, that the pleasure gained by the bully is unworthy (because it is gained by inflicting pain) of being weighted against my son's pain. Utilitarianism looks neither at the particularity of the other nor at the particularity of the context in which pleasure and pain are brought about. This latter charge is more properly laid against Benthamite utilitarianism than it is against Mill, whose move to distinguish qualitatively between pleasures may allow us to say that the pleasure obtaining, for example, to the acts of bullies and sadists is not to be counted in the utilitarian calculus. Nevertheless, even the modification of the crude Benthamite quantitative calculation of utility with Mill's qualitative measures universalises particular pleasures and pains into an abstract hierarchy of utility. In the utilitarian calculus, the introduction of intimacy or special attachment in relationships impairs the moral subject's capacity to act in the role of impartial spectator.

It seems to me that there are two equally important and equally fruitful arguments to be mounted against the confinement of ethics to formal, public relationships. The first takes as its focus the claim of liberal morality to deal successfully with moral activity. The second looks at the role of reason in the liberal ethical model and questions the presumptions made by liberal moral philosophers about what their project involves. I consider each of these points in turn.

I have already noted that the failure of liberal moral theories to account for relationships and events in the private sphere is regarded by proponents of those theories as a strength rather than a weakness. With this in mind, I suggest that it is worthwhile examining how effectively liberal approaches deal with the subject matter they claim as their own. As I have developed it, the idea that liberal moral theories deal with relationships where emotions are transferable means that their aim is to account morally for relationships where the actual identity of the other is secondary to the role that person is playing.[58] For example, it is not necessary for me to have a specific person in mind when I talk about my bank manager or my dentist. By this, I do not mean that I can simply revert to stereotypes when I refer to these people as mean and menacing or generous and gentle. Rather, I am saying that it literally does not matter whom I encounter when I walk into the office of my bank manager or dentist. Someone who experienced the difficulty of adjusting to a new bank manager or dentist on an *emotional* level would, I suggest, be regarded as behaving inappropriately in the context of the moral entailments of this relationship.

This notion of its not mattering whom I encounter captures the whole point I have been making about the factoring out of the particular, the concrete, and the partial. It applies to the morality of keeping promises, of fulfilling contracts, of regulating the obligations and rights around which encounters in the public sphere are structured. In all these cases, those with whom we engage in moral activity are not encountered ethically as specific, particular people but as promisers and promisees, contractors and contractees, or the objects of some other obligation on our part.

This construction of "the other" contrasts with relationships where emotions are *non*transferable. It is nonsensical to suggest that I can talk about my son or my father without having a specific person in mind.[59] Of course, these people may also be promisers and promisees or contractors and contractees. As such, they may be the objects of my moral deliberation, but as people in particular relationships they are not the individuals or at least they are not playing the roles in which the liberal moral theorist is supposed to be interested.[60]

The question about how effectively this kind of moral philosophising deals with its subject—the public, formal, transferable aspects of relations—is itself approachable from two directions. On one hand, I think serious objections can be made to the proposition that the place from which morality is generated is found in those aspects of relations where the specific identity of the other is irrelevant. It is not obvious to me why we need an *ethical* code to govern the formal aspects of our relationships, and why we need to refer to a *moral* code for insight into how we should behave with, for instance, our bank managers. Neither do I find it clear why we should classify dilemmas arising in the course of the formal aspects of our relationships as *moral* dilemmas, especially when the dilemmas we encounter in the personal aspects of our relationships are regarded as non-moral. Responding to these doubts, Kantians, utilitarians, and rights or contract theorists alike refer to the necessity to avert the social and political chaos that would ensue if there were no constraints placed on formal encounters. It is, I suggest, of significance that this social and political chaos is conceived in terms of the public sphere: broken contracts, disrespect for property rights, and renegation of market rituals. I think that it is also significant that when liberal moral philosophy tries to move into the private sphere, it sees a "personal" issue like abortion in terms of property and rights and is blind to "private" forms of violence like rape in marriage. The point I am making is that, in claiming its ground in the public realm, liberal morality effectively eliminates areas of human experience from moral consideration, thereby confining moral inquiry to nothing other than the ethical restraint of public and formal relations.

The other way of assessing how effectively this kind of moral philosophising deals with the morality of encounters of the abstract, impartial kind is to consider more closely how such exchanges are transacted. My suggestion is that the portrayal of any encounter or exchange between human beings as abstract has the effect of removing something that is so intrinsic to the actual encounter that what we are left with is a parody of human engagement rather than a paradigmatic ethical statement. Let me explain what I mean. The way of talking about our public, formal relationships as impersonal certainly captures the sense in which we distinguish between the levels of intensity or involvement we are prepared or find appropriate to bring into various encounters. I do not celebrate my dentist's birthday or expect to receive commiserations from my bank manager when my cat is run over. I am not taking issue with the notion that the degree of intimacy varies according to both the nature of the relationship and the individual personalities involved. What I am questioning is the suggestion that it is only legitimate to characterise an encounter or an action or a deliberation as moral when its particular and concrete aspects are relegated into insignificance and its abstract, universal features are granted prominence. More strongly, I am disputing whether there are *any* human encounters[61] that are appropriately and adequately accounted for morally *solely* in terms of generalised, abstracted rules and formulas, knowledge of which is supposed, by liberal moral theorists, to characterise the competent moral subject.

This is a point, I believe, on which a major section of feminist moral philosophy has yet adequately to interrogate existing ethical systems. Although it is a standard canonical point in the feminist literature that men as well as women are not well served by the assumption that particularity, concreteness, and partiality are morally insignificant, there is a certain taken-for-grantedness in sections of feminist theory about the adequacy of liberal ethics in the public realm. The presumption seems to be that, although liberal moral theory is impoverished by its exaltation of abstraction and generalisability, it might be effective in situations where intimacy or emotion are not involved. Margaret Urban Walker makes the point specifically: "Preoccupation (whether in deontological, consequentialist, or contractarian theories) with equality and autonomy, uniformity and impartiality, rules and reciprocity fits relations of nonintimate equals and transactions or contracts among peers."[62] On this view, one of the objectives of feminist theory is to make liberal moral theory indictable for its failure in the private sphere or at least to recast this failure as a weakness rather than a strength. But is it not possible that feminist theorists might be able to lay an even more serious charge at the door of liberal ethicists? It seems to me that there might be ethical dimensions even to encounters between nonintimate equals and peers that undermine the possibility that such encounters can be primarily conceived in terms of impartiality, the abstract following of rules or formulas and the irrelevance of the particularity of "the other." Let me offer two examples of situations involving nonintimate equals and transactions among peers that indicate how the flaw in such a conception of formal relations might be discerned. The point I want to illustrate is that the moral aspects of a situation might not be exhausted in the factors that can be formalised in terms of abstract principles and rules. Even in encounters between strangers, I remain ethically open to the particularity of "the other" in a way that seems to be neglected by liberal moral theory's emphasis on privileging abstract, universal, and impartial considerations.

Imagine that I am driving along the road when a car approaching from a side street fails to give way and collides with my car. It transpires that the other driver is not known to me, and the damage sustained affects the cars rather than people. In one sense, of course, I can follow the clear moral rules established for such situations. Such rules tell me that, from an ethical perspective, it does not matter whom I have encountered, beyond some abstract details that have to be entered onto insurance forms. But in another sense, in the sense in which this is an encounter between human beings rather than (or as well as) cars, the *only* thing that matters, in that it determines what I do next, is whom I have encountered. In establishing whom I have encountered, I look at the particular, concrete person who emerges from the other car. My ethical perspective if the person is a drunken youth will be different from my ethical perspective if she is heavily pregnant and in tears. In neither case do I have to assume anything other than the parameters specified by Walker (that the person is a nonintimate equal or a peer). In both cases (the youth or the pregnant woman) we can be described as nonintimate equals or peers, but in neither case do I continue in the situation with the abstract impartiality with which the morality of such public encounters is supposedly associated.

Imagine a second scenario where I am interviewing and being interviewed by the principal of a school to which I am considering sending my child. In what sense can I abstract the moral dimensions of the interview from the particularity, the concrete circumstances, of the encounter? Perhaps in one sense, if I am prepared to conduct my assessment of the interview on the basis of satisfying a number of points about the procedures and practices relating to, for example, discipline and homework, I might be able to factor out the specificity of the encounter. But what if I am unable to make eye contact with this person? What if she has obviously been crying, or if her hands are shaking? What if she turns out to belong to the same political party that I belong to or to live next door to my best friend? My point, as in the first example, is that, in determining the dimensions of an ethical response, who the other person is is *not* irrelevant. What I do is directly contingent on the particularity of the other.

In both these examples I have conceded that there is a sense in which I might be able to factor out the specificity of the encounter. Indeed, some might argue that it is precisely the *moral* dimension of the encounter that is *not* affected by the specific circumstances that shape other dimensions. So, it might be said that emotional or psychological responses, for example, are contingent on the concrete particularity of the other in a way that moral responses are not. This argument, it seems to me, begs the question about whether the moral response is contingent by refusing to grant moral coherence to the sense that what I do depends on contextual factors. The question, as I see it, is whether it is legitimate to assume that the sense in which how I proceed is *not* dependent on context should be given priority in characterising the moral dimensions of a situation, in accounting for an experience from an ethical perspective, or in arriving at a moral understanding of what is happening. Liberal moral theory wants to argue that it *is* the sense in which we meet each other as abstractions, as examples of general principles and rules, that distinguishes the human encounter from the collision of atoms and the rational from the irrational response. I want to suggest that what this overlooks is the difference between referring to an abstract set of rules or principles and referring to a concrete demand for a moral response.

THE RATIONAL IDEALISATION OF ETHICS

The elaboration of this distinction leads me to the second argument I want to mount against the confinement of ethics to formal, public relationships. It seems to me that another aspect of liberal moral theory that has not always been subjected to close scrutiny by feminist moral philosophers is the question of what the project of ethics involves. In one construction of the problem, this question is simply about the difference between descriptive ethics and normative ethics or about distinctions between sociological or anthropological analysis and moral philosophy. In another and, to me, more significant construction of the issue, however, it is about the legitimacy of distinguishing moral thinking through a series of rational idealisations, of transposing the ideals of impartial reason into a moral register. As I read it, part of the debate between Lawrence Kohlberg and Gilligan is about contesting this approach. Kohlberg's insistence on the legitimacy of equating rational and ethical ideals, where these ideals promote abstraction, universalisation, and impartiality, is challenged by Gilligan's critique of the ubiquity and utility of these ideals. The distinction between the abstract and concrete, the universal and particular, and the impartial and partial response is therefore firmly embedded not only in the conclusions advanced by Kohlberg and Gilligan but also in the fundamental methodological premises that each espouses.[63]

Some contemporary moral philosophers seem to assume that controversy around this point no longer exists. According to Keith Burgess-Jackson: "What we know, morally speaking or otherwise, is a function of how we live, not of how we *would* live if we were to allow reason alone to dictate our beliefs and actions."[64] I believe that both Kant and Rawls are talking about ethics in the sense rejected by Burgess-Jackson. For Kant, it is rational nature that exists as an end in itself.[65] Rawls makes a similar assumption in setting out what he calls the main idea of the theory of justice:

Men are to decide in advance how they are to regulate their claims against one another and what is to be the foundation charter of their society. Just as each person must decide by rational reflection what constitutes his good, that is, the system of ends which it is rational for him to pursue, so a group of persons must decide once and for all what is to count among them as just and unjust. *The choice which rational men would make* in this hypothetical situation of equal liberty . . . determines the principles of justice.[66]

In the case of utility, it is perhaps not so clear which approach the utilitarian adopts to the ethical project. As an ethical naturalist, Mill, for example, considers himself entitled to claim support for his theory from the empirical verification of the principle of utility: the interest in increasing happiness or pleasure is a function of how people live. It is what people actually want rather than something people might aspire to if they were endowed with archangelic moral capacities.[67] On the other hand, as I have shown in my earlier argument about how Kant, Mill, and Rawls place ethics in the service of reason, utilitarianism needs to appeal to nothing *other* than reason to confirm the principle of utility. The utility from which the utilitarian paradigm emerges may have concrete, empirical dimensions. The utilitarian calculation, however, is *not* an empirical project. Rather, it is a way of formalising moral responses according to a formula in which actual human happiness is regarded only in the abstract. There is no necessity for the utilitarian to refer to anything other than reason or rational insight in the assessment of moral worth. To refer to human happiness in any concrete, particular sense would undermine the impartial, disinterested stance of the utilitarian spectator. In other words, in the process of abstracting and rationalising from concrete and particular utilities to the paradigm of utility, concrete and particular considerations are relevant only to the extent that they confirm utility as a product of reason, as a product of rational insights that are abstract, universal, and impartial. To be sure, a utilitarian might argue that empirical evidence can be collected without sacrificing impartiality and disinterestedness (i.e., that one can be impartial and disinterested in concrete and particular things). But my point is that, for the utilitarian, such empirical evidence is admissible only to the extent that it confirms the paradigmatic nature of utility as a product of rational insights. The utilitarian is a man of reason no less than the Kantian or Rawlsian moral philosopher. As such, the utilitarian is the impartial judge of the application of principle, tempering interest in the process by which particular people resolve moral uncertainty in order to maintain the commitment to the impartial moral stance.

This conflation of the ethical and the rational (i.e., the abstract, universal, impartial) stance propagates other assumptions about what the project of ethics involves. In Chapters 5 and 6, I take three particular assumptions as the basis of a critique on which my concept of partial reason is based. One of these assumptions, which I call the premise of unpremisedness, is relevant to my discussion here. It is apparent in Kohlberg's theory of moral development, where we see assumptions about both reason and ethics being worked out under the guise of an assumption-neutral epistemology.[68] The important point is that Kohlberg's hierarchical stages of development reflect not only the growth of ethical sense but also the maturation of rationality itself.[69] To progress morally, according to Kohlberg, is to move from engulfment in the particular and the concrete toward a sense of the universality of human experience and an appreciation of a reality abstracted from the practical and material world. Such moral progress is presented by Kohlberg as an intrinsic part of a developing rationality in which the superiority of the abstract over the concrete and the universal over the particular promotes the impartial application of principles as more valid than partial considerations. Kohlberg's stages of moral development are strongly dichotomised, not only in terms of the opposition of the abstract, universal, and impartial and the concrete, particular, and partial but also in terms of self- versus other-orientations and cognitive skills versus practical experience. Underlying these stages of moral development are a concept of reason that both divides and confers value and a definition of what it is to be rational conceived in strongly dichotomised, hierarchically arranged terms.

Kathryn Pyne Addelson writes perceptively about the kind of critical questioning that exposes the pretences sustained by such an apparently assumption-neutral epistemology. Kohlberg's method, she says, is based on the understanding: "that a single individual can guarantee that his decisions are morally proper by reasoning all by himself. Or that a single individual can decide what is just or right for all of us by reasoning all by himself. Without reaching group understanding. Without working it out in practice."[70]   The assumptions identified by Addelson both sustain, and are sustained by, the endorsement of abstraction, universalisation, and impartiality as the basic premises of rationality.   Kohlberg's most ethically and rationally mature respondents demonstrate the superiority of a mind that reasons on its own (prompting the reasoner to act ethically in order to avoid self-condemnation) over the mind that involves others in its processes (prompting the reasoner to act ethically in order to avoid condemnation by others). Rational autonomy is secured by factoring out considerations that would undermine that autonomy: considerations of particular details, of relation, of promises made, of expectations raised and experiences interpreted, of what matters to a person, a family, a community. If none of this is relevant to the decision about what is just or right, then, of course, Kohlbergian logic can equate morality with mathematics ("sort of like a math problem with humans"[71]) in a series of ethical equations (demonstrating, e.g., that the injunction against stealing, which protects property, is overridden by the greater principle involved in the rule: property<life). If the voice of the liberal moral reasoner is impartial, if it is able, by a process of paring away the particular and concrete aspects of existence, to speak in universal abstractions, why would we need to challenge the legitimacy or effectiveness of the guarantee offered by the solitary reasoner? The very grounds on which such a challenge might be mounted are removed when, in order to make statements about what is just or right for all of us, the relevance to an assessment of rationality of the particular, concrete, and partial considerations that might have informed group understanding or practical experience is explicitly denied.

What Addelson's comments reveal is the assumption made by liberal moral philosophers that an ethical system properly places ethics in the service of reason.   This is the assumption to which I drew attention in my earlier discussion of Kant, Mill, and Rawls. It is also evident in Kohlberg's theory of moral development.   Here the nature of the link between being rational and being moral is discernible even in Kohlberg's methodological statement that the stage-assignment of answers to his hypothetical dilemmas is carried out "not on the basis of whether the action is judged right or wrong, but on the reasons given for the decision."[72]   Clearly, Kohlberg, like Kant, Mill, and Rawls, finds the glories of reason a more fitting crown for his ethical hero than any accolades acknowledging the contextual appropriateness or sensitivity of particular responses.

EPISTEMOLOGICAL PRIVILEGE AND MORAL UNDERSTANDINGS

In this chapter, my objective has been to clarify the way that the axioms that sustain the association of ethics with autonomous, impartial reasoners operate. I have shown how liberal moral philosophy constructs an ethics in the service of, or subservient to, reason. I have described the reasoning of the liberal moral agent as bound to and by the constraints of a rationality that privileges abstract, universal, and impartial thinking. I have argued that the confinement of ethics to the sphere of public, formal relations not only generates an inadequate account of these paradigmatic encounters but also promotes the conflation of the ethical and the rational stance.

What emerges from this consideration of the axiomatic assumptions sustaining liberal ethics is the suggestion that traditional deontological, utilitarian, and contract-based theories are both ethical and epistemological projects. What I mean is that the moral understandings that locate moral agents as agents of an abstract, universal, and impartial reason are understandings that are consistent with a particular set of epistemological concepts. In the case of duty, utility, and contract, these epistemological concepts are based on a series of assumptions that promote abstraction, universalisation, and the impartial application of rules and principles as the central tenets against which claims to know or to understand are measured. Care, by contrast, is said to value the particular, the concrete, and the partial, where partiality is understood in the sense of both incompleteness and interestedness. The charge that care is irrational or unreasoned is sustained in these question-begging terms: particularity, concreteness, and partiality are by definition not rational because rationality is defined in terms of universality, abstraction, and impartiality.

Three closely connected aspects of the epistemological privileging of the abstract, universal, and impartial are especially pertinent here. First, there is the notion of truth as a universal and unitary regulatory ideal. Here, knowledge-claims exist as universal viewpoints.[73] While knowers might be significantly differentiated in some (embodied) ways, as knowers they speak with one unified (and disembodied) voice, their knowledge a clear demonstration of the way reason operates to guarantee for knowledge an authority and certainty grounded in detached impartiality. Second, there is the radical separation both of the knowing individual from other knowers and of the subject and the object of knowledge. Knowers are autonomous in their knowing: what is known is a factor neither of who knows nor of how it is known.[74] Third, there is the assumption that if we are to be able to sustain shared belief systems, mutual understandings, and intersubjective agreements, we must, at least in the public sphere of formal relations, establish a common language in which to ensure the possibility that we might see the same things.

The crucial point to which I am leading is that these epistemological assumptions, which I develop in later chapters, undermine the very foundations of the ethic of care. As I will show in the second part of my discussion, the ethic of care, like ethics based on duty, utility, and contract, is also grounded in a set of epistemological assumptions. The epistemological assumptions grounding care, however, are not those connected with the epistemological privileging of the abstract, universal, and impartial. Rather than insisting on the notion of truth as a universal and unitary regulatory ideal, the moral understandings of care locate truth in the elaboration of the particular contexts in which we function as knowers. Rather than insisting on the autonomy of separate knowing individuals, the moral understandings of care identify knowers as selves-in-relation. Rather than insisting on the establishment of a common language, the moral understandings of care seek out particular shared interests as the basis of a commonality in which to see together. It seems to follow, then, that care can be sustained only if the philosophical axioms not only of liberal *ethics* but also of the foundationalist[75] *epistemology* that sustains liberal ethics are radically revised.

Conceived in these terms, the feminist ethical project might be conceived as a search for an epistemology consonant with an ethic of care. The problem, however, is that some versions of care either explicitly or implicitly set out to break the nexus between ethics and epistemology, while others fail to disrupt the axiomatic assumptions of liberal moral theory, which, as I have shown, confine ethics to the formal, public encounters of autonomous, impartial individuals. I subject these versions of care to critical scrutiny in the next chapter. Rather than searching for an epistemology consonant with an ethic of care, then, the first part of my constructive project involves developing a concept of care that sustains the nexus between ethics and reason *and* challenges the way that nexus is sustained in liberal moral theory.

This challenge, I suggest, starts from a consciousness alerted to the possibility that things philosophical may not be as they seem. Linking this consciousness with an understanding of how ethical and epistemological assumptions operate to privilege the abstract, the universal, and the impartial and to exclude the concrete, particular, and partial clearly confirms the endorsement I have made, in my Introduction, of Gatens' critical-interrogative approach. This is the approach that makes feminist theorists visible as women and as philosophers in a process where the objective is to undermine the exclusive authority of liberal moral philosophy to account for the human condition. Gatens' comments, as I will show, are particularly pertinent to questions about moral theory: "By *self-consciously* demonstrating that any philosophical paradigm is *not* neutral, these feminists make themselves, both as philosophers and as women, *visible*. By making themselves visible, they in turn throw into question the legitimacy of claims and assumptions in philosophy that have been taken as axiomatic."[76] My sense is that this approach probably cannot be articulated in the language of reconciliation recommended by some commentators.[77] The revision of liberal epistemological and ethical axioms is a project of rebellion, a project that challenges the methodological assumptions of traditional approaches by confronting their axiomatic claims in a way not open to those who would stress a synthesis or coincidence of interests.

It seems to me, however, that it is, at best, distracting and, at worst, destructive of the feminist enterprise to start this questioning by arguing the relative merits of universalisation, abstraction, and impartiality as opposed to particularity, concreteness, and partiality. Such argumentation fails to move outside the essentially dichotomous structure of Enlightenment thought. As Hekman points out, such a failure dogs many twentieth century attempts to disrupt the intellectual hegemony of Enlightenment epistemology, both in the social sciences and in feminist theory.[78]

A more interesting way of proceeding, I think, is suggested by the realisation that liberal ethics not only (by its own admission) fails to address relations that are not public and formal but also gives a less than adequate account of these public, formal encounters. I have, at least in part, accounted for this failure by pointing out that liberal ethics is less concerned with what particular people do or how concrete moral dilemmas are faced up to, than with exploring the ethical potentialities of a form of rationality that celebrates the human capacity to think in an abstract, universal, and impartial way. It seems to me that these ideas resonate with each other in a convincing way and form a solid basis of criticism from which to explore the possibility of transforming both care and reason.

NOTES

1. Gilligan, *In a Different Voice*, 29, talks of "seeing a world comprised of relationships rather than of people standing alone."

2. See, for example, Card, 'The Feistiness of Feminism,' and Cole and Coultrap-McQuin, 'Toward a Feminist Conception of Moral Life, and the collections of essays that these papers preface. I draw particular attention to these sources because both Card and Cole and Coultrap-McQuin note the emphases in feminist ethics on acknowledging the diversity of moral perspectives and revealing the range of oppressions that have removed those perspectives from mainstream accounts of moral philosophy. More generally, both Gilligan, *In a Different Voice*, and Noddings, *Caring*, take the exclusivity of traditional liberal moral theories as a starting point in their accounts of caring.

3. The collections of essays edited by Card, *Feminist Ethics*, and by Cole and Coultrap-McQuin, *Explorations in Feminist Ethics*, indicate the diversity of these approaches, as do the anthologies edited by Kittay and Meyers, *Women and Moral Theory*, and by Larrabee, *An Ethic of Care,* which are more specifically oriented around the ethic of care. See also Walker's summary, 'Moral Understandings,' 165, of the different strands in the conversation between those who believe that "feminist ethics clarifies the moral legitimacy and necessity of the kinds of social, political, and personal changes that feminism demands in order to end male domination" and those who hold that the objective of feminist ethics is to ensure that "the moral perceptions, self-images, and senses of moral value and responsibility of women have been represented or restored."

4. The problematisation of these associations is a common theme among feminist moral philosophers. In addition to the general sources cited in my Introduction (notes 16 and 22), see Addelson, *Impure Thoughts* and *Moral Passages*; Manning, *Speaking from the Heart*. For a specifically Aristotelian challenge to the assumptions about autonomy and impartiality made in the liberal moral tradition, see Nussbaum, *The Fragility of Goodness*.

5. The other ingredient is goodwill.

6. For an account of Kant's response to Constant, see Sullivan, *Immanuel Kant's Moral Theory,* 173–177. The question about how much of a problem Kant's "exceptionless rules" (Sullivan, 351, note 30) are is the subject of controversy among

commentators on Kant. Sullivan defends Kant from H. J. Paton's charge that Kant's response to Constant is merely "a temporary aberration of a cantankerous old philosopher" (Paton, 'An Alleged Right to Lie: A Problem in Kantian Ethics,' *Kant-Studien* 45 (1953–54): 190–203) by suggesting that Kant is arguing against a civil law or a "public juridical norm" mandating lying rather than about "the deliberation preceding a decision on how to act in a particular instance" (Sullivan, 176). Sullivan notes, however, Christine M. Korsgaard's comment that "one of the greatest difficulties with Kant's moral philosophy is that it seems to imply that our moral obligations leave us powerless in the face of evil" (Sullivan, 176). Sullivan cites Korsgaard, 'The Right to Lie: Kant on Dealing with Evil,' *Philosophy and Public Affairs* 15 (Fall 1986): 325.

7.   Kant says, "Some actions are so constituted that their maxim cannot even be conceived as a universal law of nature without contradiction, let alone willed as what ought to become one. In the case of others we do not find this inner impossibility, but it is still impossible to will that their maxim should be raised to the universality of a law of nature, because such a will would contradict itself." Kant, *Groundwork of the Metaphysic of Morals*, 91.

8.   In Chapter 5 I consider whether the distinction between moral epistemology and other fields of knowledge-making needs to be sustained by feminist philosophers and conclude that, at least in the context of my argument, it does not. I foreshadow that discussion here only to explain why I refer to the collapse of Kant's theory of knowledge rather than his theory of moral knowledge.

9.   Sherwin, 'Feminist Ethics and Medical Ethics', 43, makes a similar point about the requirement to calculate "the relevant utility values for all persons (or beings) affected by an action or practice and proceed according to a calculation of the relevant balances."

10.   Mill, 'Utilitarianism', 17.

11.   Poole, *Morality and Modernity*, Chapter 1, especially 8–17, argues that the extent to which utilitarianism does not operate according to rational principles is the extent to which it fails as a moral theory.

12.   Rawls, *A Theory of Justice*, 11. Although Rawls goes on to cite other characteristics (like being equal and mutually disinterested), I read these as being subsumed, explicitly or implicitly, under the headings of free and rational.

13.   Ibid., 12.

14.   Rawls says, ibid., 12: "I shall even assume that the parties do not know their conceptions of the good or their special psychological propensities."

15.   I think this holds as a basic Rawlsian premise even when modified by the difference principle.

16.   At this point, it may be objected that Rawls is elaborating a political framework for social justice or "political liberalism" rather than a moral conception of justice. Rawls himself puts forward this argument in the Introduction to the collection of his lectures in *Political Liberalism*, xiii–xxxiv and Lecture 1, 'Fundamental Ideas,' 10, 11. Bernstein, 'Rorty on Liberal Democracy and Philosophy,' in *The New Constellation*, 255, note 14, raises doubts about the possibility of a fruitful debate about whether Rawls' "political not metaphysical" argument represents a clarification of Rawls' original intentions, a change of mind, or a rewriting of Rawls' history. I recognise that my application of the example of lying follows the Rawlsian account of the derivation of the principles of justice in a speculative way. Nevertheless, I maintain that Rawls' notion of the political values and norms that regulate political, social, and economic institutions is not only continuous with, but dependent on, a conception of the moral norms that structure the relations between individuals. Although I accept Rawls' point that the idea of the original position is "a device of representation" (*Political Liberalism*, xxix), the

"political not metaphysical" argument does not seem convincing. Indeed, as I show later in note 66, Rawls specifically imagines individuals deliberating about what is "good," about what "ends" are rationally pursued. The quarantining of such deliberations as "political" as opposed to "moral" (see, e.g., Lecture 1, 'Fundamental Ideas,' 10, 11 in *Political Liberalism*) seems to beg significant questions both about how, or even whether, these realms are to be distinguished and about why the "main and enduring classical problems" with which Rawls wants to concern himself exclude certain "problems" (of gender and the family, e.g.) (*Political Liberalism*, xxix). What Rawls implies is that the distinction between a "conception of the good" (which is about "particular ends and interests," *A Theory of Justice*, 142) and the "theory of the good" (which is about what "in general" people must do "to protect their liberties, widen their opportunities, and enlarge their means for promoting their aims whatever these are," *A Theory of Justice*, 143) maps onto the distinction between moral and political norms. Rawls want his political norms to be "freestanding," specifically distancing his system, which he says involves "no wider commitment to any other doctrine," from utilitarianism, where "the principle of utility, however understood, is usually said to hold for all kinds of subjects ranging from the conduct of individuals and personal relations to the organisation of society as a whole as well as to the laws of peoples" (*Political Liberalism*, Lecture 1, 'Fundamental Ideas,' 13.) Rawls' assumption seems to be that there is a perspective in which his political norms stand apart from any particular doctrine. My point is that the political norms of his form of liberalism are "situated" just as firmly as any theoretical account of human practices in a wider picture of those practices than Rawls, at least as he modifies his account, is prepared to consider. I would also suggest that Rawls' social contractarian base means that lying might well be one of the aspects of justice discussed behind the veil of ignorance, which is where my speculative application of the derivation of the principles of justice to the example of lying takes place.

17. Rawls, *A Theory of Justice*, 47.

18. Ibid., 48.

19. This point is important. Defenders of Rawls might argue that his claims are based not necessarily on an intellectual elitism but on an understanding that we need a reflective equilibrium between our ordinary moral intuitions and the principles arrived at through a process of rational deliberation. My objection is not that commonsense considerations alone secure moral responses but that the capacity to respond ethically is equated by Rawls with the capacity to reason in a way that privileges abstract, universal, and impartial considerations.

20. Walker, 'Partial Consideration,' 763, calls Hare's archangels "celestial deliberators." In a subsequent paper, 'Feminism, Ethics, and the Question of Theory,' 31, she uses this notion and part of Rawls' reference to mathematics to illustrate her critique of "split-level" theorising. As a counterpoint to the Rawlsian approach, consider Murdoch's comment: "We are all artists and thinkers. We are all poets," *Metaphysics as a Guide to Morals*, 505.

21. Kant, *Groundwork*, 120.

22. Ibid., 121.

23. Ibid., 131.

24. Ibid., 56.

25. Ibid., 102.

26. In ibid., 138, note 66.1.

27. Kant says, 81, that for the divine or holy will "there are no imperatives: *'I ought'* is here out of place, because *'I will'* is already of itself in harmony with the law. Imperatives are in consequence only formulae for expressing the relation of objective

laws of willing to the subjective imperfection of the will of this or that rational being—
for example, of the human will."

28. "fidelity to promises and kindness based on principle (not on instinct)," ibid., 102.

29. Ibid., 130.

30. Ibid., 103, 106.

31. For Rawls, though, these resolutions are a matter of individual choice. It is Jürgen
Habermas' view, of course, that the repression of practical (as opposed to instrumental)
reason is a means of political control and manipulation. Ends, for Habermas, are taken as
given or already resolved by the naive consciousness, which does not perceive this
restriction of its capacity to reason about ends as well as means. See 'Technology and
Science as "Ideology",' 81–122.

32. Rawls, *A Theory of Justice*, 14.

33. Poole, *Morality and Modernity*, 9.

34. Singer draws the line between sentient and nonsentient, nonhuman animals
somewhere around mollusks and crustaceans, suggesting that the former deserve equal
consideration with sentient humans. See *Animal Liberation*, 178–179.

35. What Australians call economic rationalism is, I understand, known in North
America as a mixture of free market economics and "trickle-down" theory, sometimes
known popularly as "Reaganomics."

36. Rawls, *A Theory of Justice*, 13.

37. Ibid., 15.

38. Although Rawls is not unambiguous on the question of whether the reasoning of
the original position deliberators is ideal, he says (*A Theory of Justice*, 252–253) that
when people accept the principles that emerge from behind the veil of ignorance, they
"express their nature as free and equal rational beings subject to the general conditions of
human life. For to express one's nature as a being of a particular kind is to act on the
principles that would be chosen if this nature were the decisive determining element."
This does suggest that the reasoning in the original position is not just one form of
reasoning but is, in some sense, an ideal way of reasoning that realises the human
potential to be free and rational.

39. "[In the public sphere] individuals are treated as exchangeable means to
independent ends or as instances of general principles. Where there are relations in
which individuals figure as the objects of non-transferable emotions, these relations are
located in the realm of private life." Poole, 49.

40. For feminist critiques of the public-private, reason-emotion dichotomy, see
Elshtain, *Public Man, Private Woman*; Okin, *Women in Western Political Thought*;
Pateman, *The Sexual Contract*, and the essays collected in *The Disorder of Women*. For
nonfeminist approaches that insist on maintaining some form of distinction between the
ethical and the personal, see Kohlberg, *The Philosophy of Moral Development*; Kohlberg
et al. *Moral Stages*; Nagel, *The View from Nowhere*, and *Equality and Partiality*; Walzer,
Spheres of Justice; Williams, *Ethics and the Limits of Philosophy*. For the view that the
distinction between the public and the private, the rational and the emotional, the
impartial and the partial, can, in some sense, be mapped onto the distinction between
different parts of morality, see Blustein, *Care and Commitment*; Nunner-Winkler, 'Two
Moralities?'; see also my bibliographical references in note 18, Introduction.

41. Kant, *Groundwork*, 118.

42. Kant says, ibid., 119, that it "can vary a great deal according to differences of
sensibility in sundry observers."

43. Mill also cites benevolence as an appropriate attitude ('Utilitarianism,' 17). It
seems to me that, although we might not rule out benevolence as being appropriate in the
private sphere, it remains essentially a public attitude. We might be partial, interested,

and benevolent, but there is no contradiction in linking impartiality, disinterest, and benevolence.

44. This point is more relevant to act utilitarianism than to rule utilitarianism, although both forms distance the moral reasoner from personal and partial perspectives. Blustein, *Care and Commitment*, 8–9, notes that "utilitarianism . . . fares worse than Kantianism with respect to meeting the challenge of the personal point of view. Utilitarianism, and consequentialism generally, recommends the adoption of a viewpoint from which we regard our own personal concerns with indifference as means to the end of achieving some overall good."

45. Rawls, *A Theory of Justice*, 5.

46. Ibid., 8.

47. On this particular point, see Card, 'Gender and Moral Luck'; Okin, *Justice, Gender, and the Family*.

48. Rawls, in particular, may argue that this claim should be modified on the grounds that he eliminates the personal only to ensure that the principles of social justice are applied impartially. Even if this is so, it does not weaken my point, which is that, for liberal theorists, the concrete particularity that marks the partial perspective lies beyond the bounds of both ethics and reason.

49. See, for example, Pateman, "'The Disorder of Women'"; Lloyd, *The Man of Reason*; and the comments of Kant in *Observations on the Feeling of the Beautiful and Sublime* as quoted by Gould and Wartofsky, *Women and Philosophy*, 18, and Freud in 'Some Psychical Consequences of the Anatomical Distinction between the Sexes,' as quoted by Gilligan, *In a Different Voice*, 7.

50. I consider this and other problematic versions of care in Chapter 2. For an analysis of several different ways in which care and justice have been philosophically connected or distinguished, see Blum, 'Gilligan and Kohlberg.'

51. See, for example, Habermas, *Moral Consciousness and Communicative Action*; Lindgren, 'Beyond Revolt: A Horizon for Feminist Ethics'; Sher, 'Other Voices, Other Rooms?

52. I take this phrasing from Code, 'Is the Sex of the Knower Epistemologically Significant?'

53. Cf. the classic double-bind situation described by Bateson et al.: "a situation in which no matter what a person does, [s/]he can't win." 'Toward a Theory of Schizophrenia,' 173.

54. The point here, of course, is that, for liberal moral philosophers, moral codes exclude considerations of care. Blum, 'Gilligan and Kohlberg,' 62, describes this restriction of the moral realm: "Suppose it were replied...that the capacities of care, sensitivity to particular persons, and the like, may be good, and perhaps even necessary for the application of moral principle, but—precisely because they are not themselves a reflection of universal principle, impartiality, rationality, and the like—they are not themselves moral. Naturally if 'moral' is defined in terms of impartiality, then anything outside of impartiality—even what is a necessary condition of it—is excluded."

55. This is not to imply that all dilemmas in the public sphere are, for the liberal moral philosopher, moral dilemmas.

56. Sullivan, *Immanuel Kant's Moral Theory*, 174–175, notes that Kant might have objected to Constant's equation of the rule "I may not lie" with the rule "I must tell the truth." As well, Sullivan reminds critics of Kant that maintaining that lying is wrong does not commit Kant to insisting that we supply potential murderers with information about their quarries. However, Kant is quite specific: "Truthfulness in statements which cannot be avoided is the formal duty of an individual to everyone, however great may be the disadvantage accruing to himself or to another." (*Immanuel Kant: Critique of*

Practical Reason and Other Writings in Moral Philosophy, ed. and tr. Lewis White Beck, [New York: Garland, 1976], 347, quoted by Sullivan, 175.) Sullivan concedes that "Kant always—not just [in his reply to Constant]—held that we have a strict, negative duty not to lie. If there are no other alternatives available, then truthfulness is an unconditional duty, holding in all circumstances in the sense that it does not discriminate between persons having a right or not having a right to the truth." (Sullivan, *Immanuel Kant's Moral Theory*, 175.) Arguing against this view, Christine Korsgaard conceives of a two-tiered moral theory so that, for example, "the maxim of lying to deceivers is universalizable...in order to counteract the intended results of their deceptions." ('The Right to Lie: Kant on Dealing with Evil,' *Philosophy and Public Affairs* 15 (Fall 1986): 330, quoted by Sullivan, *Immanuel Kant's Moral Theory*, 351, note 30.)

57. Cf. Friedman, 'Beyond Caring,' 270: "The rational nature which Kant, for example, takes to give each person dignity and to make each of absolute value and, therefore, irreplaceable, is no more than an abstract rational nature in view of which we are all alike. But if we are all alike in this respect, it is hard to understand why we would be irreplaceable." Dillon (acknowledging Friedman) makes the same point ('Care and Respect,' 74): "There is a sense in which Kantian respect does in fact view persons as intersubstitutable, for it is blind to everything about an individual except her rational nature, which is what makes each of us indistinguishable from every other. Thus, in Kantian-respecting someone, there is a real sense in which we are not paying attention to her—it makes no difference to how we treat her that she is who she is and not some other individual. Kantian respect is thus not a respecter of persons, in the sense that it does not discriminate or distinguish among persons." For more sympathetic treatments of the Kantian concept of duty, see Baron, 'The Alleged Moral Repugnance of Acting from Duty'; Herman, 'Integrity and Impartiality'; O'Neill, *Acting on Principle*, and 'Kant after Virtue.'

58. Although communitarian moral philosophers like Sandel (*Liberalism and the Limits of Justice*) and MacIntyre (*After Virtue*) have formulated a similar critique of the self who is "unencumbered" by particular attachments, I argue in Chapter 7 that their analysis perpetuates the abstraction from the lived experience of relation.

59. I can, of course, talk about sons and fathers in an abstract way, but not about my son or father.

60. What I am pointing to here are the slippage between the identification of formalisability as morally significant in relations and the assumption that what is significant in relations in general is their formalisability. The liberal interest in accounting for the moral significance of relation where the particularity of "the other" is not relevant leads to the equation of "what can be formalised" with "what is essential in relation."

61. Anticipating the charge of anthropocentrism, I at this point acknowledge that an adequate moral theory will extend beyond human interaction. Several care theorists have recognised this necessity. See, for example, Noddings, *Caring*, Chapter 7, and Manning, *Speaking from the Heart*, Chapter 6. While I do not address this point directly, it seems to me that the decontextualisation insisted on by impartial rationality promotes a philosophical atmosphere in which anthropocentrism might flourish. By contrast, the concept of partial reason that I am developing is inherently contextual. It remains to be seen whether this concept might help us understand our relations with the nonhuman world in a way that is more satisfactory than either the emphasis on reciprocity (Noddings) or the extension of the paradigmatic case of care between persons (Manning).

62. Walker, 'Feminism, Ethics, and the Question of Theory,' 24. See Baier, 'The Need for More than Justice,' for an elaboration of the idea that justice is one virtue among many. See Flanagan and Jackson, 'Justice, Care, and Gender,' for the suggestion

of a contrast between seeing others "thickly" and "thinly." See Jaggar, 'Caring as a Feminist Practice of Moral Reason,' 184-187, for a survey of different responses to the question of whether care and justice thinking are compatible. Friedman's integrationist approach canvasses different ways of understanding the connection between "a primary commitment to abstract principles and values" and "a primary commitment to particular persons." *What Are Friends For?*, 138.

63. I discuss the nature of Gilligan's critique of Kohlberg in more detail in Chapter 5.

64. Burgess-Jackson, 'The Problem with Contemporary Moral Theory,' 163.

65. Kant, *Groundwork*, 96. See Paton's commentary (in Kant, *Groundwork*, 138–139, note 66) for confirmation that, for Kant, it is rational nature, rather than humanity per se, that is to be treated as an end in itself.

66. Rawls, *A Theory of Justice*, 11–12, emphasis added.

67. See Mill, *'Utilitarianism,'* 12. Here Mill explains that the principles of utility form the "standard of morality" as well as the "ultimate end" of human action.

68. For a useful summary of his work and responses to his critics, see Kohlberg, 'A Current Statement on Some Theoretical Issues.'

69. Defenders of Kohlberg might argue that his focus is on moral reason rather than on rationality per se. I am not persuaded by this argument. Kohlberg explicitly equates the morally mature perspective with the perspective of "any rational individual." The insight that is available to the mature moral reasoner is that the universal, abstract, and impartial principles of morality apply to me "as a rational person." (See 'The Six Moral Stages,' in Kohlberg, 'A Current Statement,' 488–489.) By necessary implication, then, Kohlberg's references to moral reason can be read as references to reason in a more general sense.

70. Addelson, 'What Do Women Do?,' 209.

71. Gilligan, *In a Different Voice*, 26. Although Jake, who said this, is only eleven years old, Gilligan notes that Jake's conception and appreciation of things that are "totally logical" capture a significant element of what Kohlberg defines as moral maturity.

72. Hilgard et al., 'Are There Universal Stages in the Development of Moral Values?,' in *Introduction to Psychology*, 80. Kohlberg distinguishes between the "content" and the "rationality" of a response, illustrating his "hermeneutic and reconstructive stance" by quoting Habermas: "Only to the extent that the interpreter grasps the reasons that allow the author's utterance to appear as rational does he understand what the author could have meant." (Kohlberg, 'A Current Statement,' 503). The reference is to Habermas, 'Interpretive Social Science vs Hermeneuticism,' in Norma Haan, ed., *Social Science as Moral Inquiry*, (New York: Columbia University Press, 1983.) See also Kohlberg, 'Stages of Moral Development as a Basis for Moral Education,' 55: "Like most philosophers from Kant to Hare…we define morality in terms of the formal character of a moral judgement or a moral point of view, rather than in terms of its content. Impersonality, ideality, universalizability and pre-emptiveness are among the formal characteristics of a moral judgement."

73. Even more strongly, a conventional epistemologist, distinguishing knowledge from belief, might deny that knowledge is a viewpoint, even if that viewpoint is universal.

74. I take this phrasing from Addelson, 'Knower/Doers and Their Moral Problems', in Feminist Epistemologies, eds, Linda Alcoff and Elizabeth Potter, (New York and London: Routledge, 1993), 267.

75. "Foundationalist" is not the only term which describes the epistemology sustaining liberal ethics. I explain my use of the term in more detail in chapter 5.

76. Gatens, 'Feminism, Philosophy and Riddles Without Answers', 25.

77. See, for example, Lindgren's plea for feminist moral philosophers to adopt a cooperative, non-confrontationist approach. Lindgren, 145, specifically criticises "the unfortunate way in which the discussion of feminist ethics is cast in the language of rebellion" by Walker in 'Moral Understandings'.

78. Hekman, *Gender and Knowledge*, Chapter 1.

Chapter 2

A Necessary Corrective?
Responses That Fill the Gaps

When eleven-year-old Amy failed to resolve the Heinz dilemma with a straightforward yes/no answer, feminist theorists were quick to recognise the significance and originality of talking about ethics in terms of context and caring connection rather than categorical rules for confrontation.[1] The refinement of a focus on the concrete, particular, contextual grounds for ethical response established the ethic of care as an effective way to hear many women speak of their moral experiences. Notions of care and responsibility have appeared to lend philosophical significance to empirical and anecdotal observations about the activities and expectations of women. The ethic of care has been used to illuminate and enrich diverse accounts of existence, ranging from the responses of Ceres[2] and Persephone[3] to the practices of the contemporary clinical nurse, citizen, friend, and parent.[4]

The ethic of care, at least as it has developed and expanded out of the work of Gilligan and Noddings, has taken the exclusions of liberal moral theory, to which I drew attention at the beginning of Chapter 1, as its first point of reference. Gilligan's original insight is that the apparent unsophistication of the responses of women[5] to Kohlberg's moral hypotheticals is evidence of a deficiency of *theory* rather than a deficiency of *women*. Kohlberg's stage theory of moral development might illuminate an aspect of human existence, but his claims to universality seem to be undermined when those who are excluded by his definition of moral maturity become theoretically visible. Revealing the theoretical deficiencies of Kohlberg's assumptions also problematises his explanation about why women seldom reach the (Kohlbergian) peak of moral maturity and challenges his conclusions that women have insufficient stamina for the moral haul and no head for moral heights.

While there might be a variety of ways to conceive of the project of feminist ethics,[6] it seems to me that the importance of imparting worth to women's experiences and significance to women's capacities and potential cannot be contended. Although the notion of "worth" is problematic when it emerges within frameworks of oppression and subordination, I use the term in Alison Jaggar's sense of taking the experiences of all women seriously, while agreeing with her that this is not necessarily the same as either "putting women's interests first; focussing exclusively on so-called women's issues; accepting women (or feminists) as moral experts or authorities; substituting 'female' (or 'feminine') for 'male' (or 'masculine') values; or extrapolating directly from women's experience."[7] This, I suggest, is the first of two parameters that establish a feminist framework for any project of moral philosophy. The second is that of calling into question the axiomatic assumptions that have excluded the possibility of taking the experiences of all women seriously. This is the critical and interrogative approach recommended by Gatens and endorsed in my Introduction. These two parameters are obviously not clearly separable, yet, as I believe my approach demonstrates, together they form a sound basis for both the critical and constructive phases of a feminist approach to ethics.

CARE AS COMPLEMENTARY

What I examine in this chapter is the way some versions of care fail to disrupt the axiomatic assumptions of liberal moral theory that confine ethics to the realm where autonomous, impartial reasoners engage in encounters that are formal and public. Fundamentally, these versions of care are constructed as supplementary or complementary to the models of liberal ethics that exclude the care perspective. They see care as what Tronto calls "a necessary corrective,"[8] an approach that fills the gaps conceded by liberal moral theory. Such versions of care, however, fail to acknowledge the significance of either of the parameters that guide my approach. As I will show, they neither challenge the moral essentialism that I associate with constructions of care as a supplement or complement nor interrogate the axioms that associate ethics with autonomous, impartial reasoners and care with the irrational, unreasoned, or purely instrumental response.

Paradoxically, these problematic versions of care may arise in the attempt to take the experiences of all women seriously when this attempt begins with a description of what women do. As a description of women's labour, care seems to fit neatly onto the agenda of feminist and nonfeminist promotions of essentialism. The ethic of care thus appears to describe what many women actually do in terms of the sexist division of labour. The empirical discovery that women seem to seek an expanded sense of context rather than the relevant principle "explains" why we function better in day-care nurseries than on the bench of a law court. Our tendency to be motivated by concrete considerations rather than abstract reference points "explains" our preference for shit and string beans[9] over Socrates and string theory. Constructing our ontological reality in terms of connection and relation "explains" why "Brian's Wife, Jenny's Mum"[10] prefers the particularised world of the family over the depersonalised public sphere.

The historical construction of women as purveyors of the virtues of caring practices is given philosophical substance by an ethic of care constructed out of a description of women's moral reality. Our association with the places where people go to be loved and nurtured is seen as a consequence of our natural *moral* rather than (or as well as) *biological* proclivities.[11] The gendered moral chauvinism of traditional liberal ethical theory (in which women are regarded as morally *incapable* or morally *inferior*[12]) is replaced by a moral essentialism (in which women's moral orientation is regarded as fundamentally *different* from men's). Biology becomes our moral destiny, a resource only to the extent that the "I must" of ethical caring reflects the effortless "I want" of the pre- or nonmoral response.[13]

Let me illustrate this point with three examples drawn from various points of the political spectrum. Consider the archconservatism of the verses printed as the frontispiece to the 1978 version of the *Country Women's Association of Australia Cookbook*:

> So long as there are homes to which men turn at close of day,
> So long as there are homes where children are, and women stay,
> If love and loyalty and faith be found across those sills,
> A stricken nation can recover from its greatest ills.
> So long as there are homes where fires burn, and there is bread,
> So long as there are homes where lamps are lit and prayers are said,
> Although a people falter through the dark, and nations grope,
> With God Himself back of these little homes we sure have hope.[14]

Does the ethic of care, as a description of women's moral reality, contest the stereotypical image of women as proficient homemakers on whose lamp lighting, bread baking, and praying the health and hope of nations depend? My suggestion is that, even given the good, strong light of feminist intentions, it is not clear whether the ethical carer and the women identified by the CWA poem are different people. If the possibility that they are not different has (at least) to remain open, so, too, must the question about whether the ethic of care sustains a notion of gendered moral essentialism. Thus, care might sanction a division of moral labour where men's (daytime) involvement in the promotion of justice, integrity, and rights is rewarded by the return to a home in which women care, love, and shoulder responsibility. Indeed, these sentiments clearly illustrate how the political and social construction of women as carers works to maintain the separation of the public and private as two distinct realms in which it is never appropriate to be both loving and fair, caring and just.

Liberal feminism provides a second example of how care might be used to corroborate assumptions of moral essentialism. The claim that women are as capable of running multinational companies as they are of running homes seems to be an appropriate peg on which to hang arguments equating women's oppression with lack of choice. But does a consideration of the ethic of care in the context of this argument necessarily enhance women's options, or does it merely sanction the notion that they have particular skills to bring to the corporate world? The magazine *Working Woman* shows some excitement about the newly discovered utility of caring values. "Something big is up, a revolution of sorts," it advises:

The age of the hierarchy is over....[Managers] have to see their roles as a combination of teacher, cheerleader and liberator, not controller....Kinder and gentler are the buzzwords on the management front these days [as companies] move away from fear and inhouse competition as management tools and toward cooperation and teamwork.[15]

Caring, then, becomes a business management tool aimed at increasing efficiency and productivity. Women, because of their essential propensity to care, are portrayed as the purveyors of humanitarian values in the corporate sector. Just as an ethical theory linking women and care is seen to justify the association of women with homemaking, so it might substantiate the argument about the inclusion of women in the public realm on the grounds that caring moderates the harshness of depersonalised institutional structures.

The third example of the essentialising tendencies of care as a description of what women do is the radical feminist incorporation of caring into a separatist agenda. Here the ethic of care is seen to promote the notion that women are essentially morally *better* than, as well as essentially morally *different* from, men. Supposedly, men's moral responses are limited by the abstract problem solving emphasised by an ethic of principles or rights. Women's propensity to care and relate elevates them to the high moral ground, on the basis of which they make ethically superior decisions. Thus, we have, to quote Judy Auerbach et al., "insensitive, instrumental men, and nurturing, moral women [cast] as paradigms of evil and good in our deeply gendered world."[16]

These three uses of the ethic of care, which I call conservative, liberal, and separatist, have led some feminist philosophers to suggest that there is a sinister aspect to the articulation of caring as a feminist ethic.[17] It appears that the establishment of the moral credentials of women might actually help to shore up, rather than to unravel, the ethical hegemony of the models of liberal moral thought that I considered in Chapter 1. If the celebration of care as a moral response leads to an endorsement of a gendered moral essentialism, then we will still be left with the washing up when the party is over. After all, whose worlds appear changed by the insights of the ethic of care? Surely, neither the world of the patriarchal conservative, who has always known that women's ontology is relational rather than atomistic, nor the world of the liberal chauvinist, who has structured reality to reflect women's and men's strengths and weaknesses, will require much (if any) revision to incorporate an ethic of care as the legitimation of an essentialist base for the division of moral labour.

Now these three examples of care are all grounded in an initial premise that the ethic of care is a complementary or supplementary moral system. Versions of care based on this premise portray care as a way of redressing the imbalance of a system that draws all its explanatory models from notions of autonomy and talks only of justice, rights, and obligation. As a complement or supplement to deontological, utilitarian, and contract-based ethics, the ethic of care restores balance to moral discourse, providing "a necessary corrective" to prevailing moral systems. This is the model of caring beyond which I am suggesting we need to move.

The idea of care as a complement or a supplement to liberal ethical models is implicit (if not explicit) in the conservative construction of women as carers in the private world. It is also used by liberal feminists to legitimate women's role in the public world. While the separatist agenda might be couched in more antagonistic and less congruent terms, it nevertheless retains the essential symmetry of male-female, justice-care and rational-irrational, the sense that what is present in women's experience is defined by what is lacking in men's.[18] However starkly the *contrasts* between justice and care are depicted in the examples I have drawn on, there remains a sense in which the ethic of care for women is *equivalent* to the ethic of justice for men.

As a description of a way of responding, a mode of existence, these versions of care might help attune inattentive philosophical ears to women's voices. But it is when the second parameter of a feminist approach to ethics is considered that we start to see accounts of care as complementing or supplementing justice as concealing an insidious slippage between description and prescription. An account of how women act morally is never *only* an account. The three examples I have given to show how a moral theory can be seen to justify a range of (suspect) political stances illustrate this point. The implications of this point are, I think, quite sinister: if women are the exemplars of caring practices, then caring is what women should do if they are acting morally *and if they are acting as women.*

The possibility I want to examine is that this slippage is a result of a failure to challenge the axiomatic assumptions of liberal moral theory rather than an intrinsic element of a feminist ethic of care. An ethic of care that apparently contains its own built-in definition of what it is to be a woman can be held at arm's length by traditional moral theorists with their (vested) interests in impartiality, universality, and abstraction. Carers can be cast as some kind of special or minority interest group, set apart, *by their own definition*, from mainstream moral theorising. Caring can be "place[d]...firmly outside a tightly defended barricade within which is claimed to lie all there is of reason, rationality, scientific method, truth, and guides to social policy that avoid privileging special interests."[19] This is not to suggest that caring will necessarily be *rejected* by defenders of the ethical status quo.[20] But it will be *condoned* only to the extent that it is seen to be an effective complement or supplement to the mainstream agenda. The conservative and corporate annexation of care described earlier provides concrete illustration of this point.

CARE AS IRRATIONAL

This brings me to what I see as a basic source of the problem caused by the failure to challenge the axiomatic assumptions that confine ethics to the realm of formal, public encounters between autonomous, impartial reasoners. The problem arises when care is construed in opposition to reason or, at least in some

significant ways, as irrational or unreasoned. A misreading of some of the
original literature on the ethic of care may, indeed, provide grounds for this
assumption. Gilligan notes that in the equation of masculine with adult
normality, women's knowledge is relegated to the sphere of expressive
capacities and labeled "intuitive" or "instinctive": "a function of anatomy
coupled with destiny." Women's ways of knowing thus contrast with men's
capacity for "autonomous thinking, clear decision-making, and responsible
action," which is then seen as being synonymous with the human capacity to
reason.[21] Gilligan offers these observations to elaborate the findings of research
into sex-role stereotyping and is explicitly critical of the failure of psychologists
to problematise these distinctions and to theorise the development of knowledge
in a way that does not exclude women.

Noddings, however, makes a much more problematic proposal when she talks
about an oppositional relationship between reason and care. She refers to the
essentially *non*rational nature of caring and the "feeling" mode of the caring
relation. She specifically wants to preserve "the ability to move back and forth"
between a "receptive" mode compatible with the concreteness of the ethic of
care and an "objective" mode appropriate to an abstract justice orientation.[22]

I perceive such an approach to be, at best, fraught with difficulties and, at
worst, counterproductive. Traditional Western philosophical thought is
legitimated by basic oppositional premises. The dualistic construction of
reason–emotion, thought–feeling, mind–matter, fact–value, culture–nature,
detachment–attachment, autonomy–dependency, object–subject, public–private
and male–female sanctions not only the intellectual hegemony of male
philosophers but also the political and social arrangements that invigorate Man
and enervate Woman. The obvious point (at least to feminist philosophers) is
that dualism is not a neutral methodological device. Dichotomies do not only
impart heuristic order. They also impart value and imply certain groupings and
associations of traits, qualities, and concepts. So we have the equation of
reason–thought–mind–and so on with the male and emotion–feeling–matter– and
so on with the female. Dichotomies presuppose not only the *opposition* of
reason–emotion, thought–feeling, mind–matter but the *superiority* of reason,
thought, and mind over emotion, feeling, and matter. The attributes clustered
around the female side of these dichotomies are devalued and dehumanised and
confined to the private sphere as the place where such emphases are
appropriate.[23] Thus, not just intellectual respectability but also full humanity
have traditionally been accorded to men living a life of the mind in the public
domain of the academy while producing detached, objective accounts of reality.
Women's association with the material, private realm where attachment is
nurtured and subjectivity endorsed has written us out of history, made us
philosophically and psychologically invisible, and removed us from the
mainstream of intellectual productivity.

So where does feminist theory go from the realisation that, in our philosophical
tradition, to be separately ordered is to be differently valued or, in Marilyn
Friedman's words, that separation is inherently unequal?[24] There are, I think,

three ways of responding that reflect the different approaches of women to philosophy identified by Gatens. The first two are illustrated by the versions of care that I have called separatist and liberal.[25] First, in separatist approaches, we might try to rebalance the weighted scale of the traditional system by privileging, for instance, emotion over reason, feeling over thought, and matter over mind. We might celebrate the traditional association of women with the material, with nature, as a way of acquiring special insights into human reality, elevating it over men's apparently dehumanising concentration on the cerebral.

Second, we might consider the possibility that, while thought and feeling, mind and matter, reason and emotion are constructed dualistically, their association with any particular end of the male–female polarity reflects (nothing more than) historical or sociological contingencies. These extensionist or liberal approaches would insist that there is no philosophical a priori in the identification of women with the material, emotional realm. Locating oppression in the exclusion of women from the rational rather than in the construction of rationality itself, this approach concentrates on the "add women and stir"[26] method of dealing with the basic oppositional premises of Western philosophy.

It seems to me that in important ways both the separatist and the extensionist approaches leave unchallenged the basic premises of the philosophical (as well as the patriarchal) status quo with its grounding in oppositional thought processes and the rational privileging of abstraction, universality, and impartiality. Neither insists on questioning the face value of traditional, liberal ethical and epistemological axioms.

A third approach involves the critical interrogation both of traditional ways of philosophising that silence women and of feminist philosophical responses that, while taking the experiences of all women seriously, accept traditional philosophical axioms at face value. In the terms of the argument I developed in Chapter 1, this approach involves problematising the axiomatic association of ethics with autonomous, impartial reasoners and of care with the irrational, unreasoned, or purely instrumental response. There I showed that these axioms operate to sustain certain assumptions, legitimate certain privileges, and disallow certain claims. I described liberal moral philosophy as constructing ethics in the service of, or subservient to, reason and advanced the claim that the reasoning of the liberal moral agent is bound to and by the constraints of a rationality that privileges abstract, universal, and impartial thinking. My suggestion there was that liberal moral theory not only begs the question about how the nexus between reason and ethics is sustained but also fails both to problematise its exclusion of the private realm and to provide an adequate account of formal, public encounters. What I want to do now is to show that accounts of care as supplementing or complementing liberal moral theory reinforce the ethical and epistemological axioms of liberalism. My objective is to give substance to the claim that an adequate feminist ethic of care will not leave these axioms in place.

LEAVING AXIOMS IN PLACE

The claim that care is an alternative moral theory is clearly not endorsed unanimously by either feminist or nonfeminist contributors to the care literature. Indeed, when the question of where care stands in relation to more established moral theory and moral capacities is not ambiguous,[27] several theorists explicitly endorse a concept of care ethics as a supplement or complement to the orientations of deontological, utilitarian, or contract-based ethics[28] or as a previously neglected moral component with which other orientations might be integrated.[29] While I see these understandings of care as contrary to mine, I want to locate this contrariety not so much in the substance of care's exegesis[30] but in the motives that such conclusions apparently satisfy.

Sandra Lee Bartky identifies two sources of motivation in theoretical approaches to caregiving. "Conservatives," she says, "extol traditional female virtues in the context of a larger defense of the sexual *status quo*." On the other hand, feminist exponents of an ethic of care "want to raise women's status by properly valuing...[women's] emotional work and to see this quality of caring extended to the formal domains of commerce and politics."[31] Now I want explicitly to distinguish my motives for theorising about care from both of these approaches. The first, by definition, venerates the hierarchical opposition according to which moral weight is given to the abstract, the universal, and the impartial. Here care is seen not as a corrective counterbalance (because it is not argued that moral weight is incorrectly distributed[32]) but as a source of moral fortification. It is care that helps to sweeten the often bitter pill of justice, where the possibility of questioning the prescription of the latter is not available.[33] This approach is illustrated by the verses I quoted earlier in this chapter, which describe care as being provided by women in private to children and to men returning from an uncaring public world.

The second approach, like the appropriation of care as a management tool, which I cited earlier, certainly attempts a redistribution of moral weight but fails, in my opinion, to resolve an extremely significant problem. The problem arises because of the extent to which nonprivate activities like commerce and politics (the formal domains cited by Bartky) are constituted not only in the *absence* of, but also in *opposition* to, the particular, the concrete, and the partial. Proponents of this second approach to care risk propagating the assumption that the absence of care in the public realm is like a vacuum, a lacuna that care might fill to the benefit of both the public realm (which is made more humane) and the private realm (where the status of caring values is increased). But what this second approach misses is the immensity of the formal and informal constraints that confine the values of care to the private realm and militate against their extension into the public realm. Neither cultural feminism nor liberal feminism, with their respective emphases on *revaluing* women's activities and attributes and *extending* women's access to public practices, sustains realistic strategies for the transformation of the private and public realms. As Bowden points out, an intrinsic part of the devaluation of care by nonfeminist moral philosophers is the definition of carers as dependent, subordinate, and lacking collective decision-making power. So defined, Bowden notes, carers are also subject to "constraints due to inequalities in material resources, education, language use, protection against violence, concepts of merit, as well as those due to deeply internalized experiences of self, one's potentials and inadequacies."[34] It may be that there are ways—for example, through consciousness-raising and the legitimation of marginalised standpoints—of at least identifying, if not overcoming, these constraints, of making explicit the social and political factors that sustain the dependency, subordinate status, and lack of collective decision-making power of carers. My suggestion is, however, that the assumption that women's status might be raised by properly valuing their emotional work misses the fact that the degrading of this emotional work is not *accidental* but *necessary* to the construction of both the formal, public and the informal, private spheres. The process of making the reasons for this devaluation explicit cannot, I submit, be one in which caring values are simply reshuffled so that they are divided more equally between the public and the private spheres. What I mean is that only on the most superficial level can the addition of caring values to the public realm be said to alter the "uncaring" nature of that realm.[35] Attempts to reshuffle are based on the understanding that the binary thinking that opposes the public to the private can be considered apart from the socially and politically oppressive institutional structures that distribute privilege unevenly between the two realms.

The distinction between binary thinking and social and political oppression cannot, I believe, be sustained. I have said that politics and commerce (the examples cited by Bartky) are constituted not only in the absence of, but also in opposition to, the particular, the concrete, and the partial. My point is that they are constituted in this way because of the axiomatic assumptions that ground the normative conceptual framework of the public realm. These are the axioms that privilege certain beliefs and claims about abstraction, universalisation, and impartiality. These oppositional axioms can be shown to be far more intransigent (and imperiling for feminist philosophers) than they might be if they were constructed only in contrast to the axiomatic assumptions that associate care with the particular, the concrete, and the partial. In other words, the conceptual framework of the public realm is constituted in such a way that abstract, universal, and impartial perspectives are not only different from, but also better than, the concrete particularity of partial perspectives. The relation between impartial and partial perspectives is not one of contrast or of complementarity but of privilege and disprivilege, superiority and inferiority, valuing and devaluing.

Let me illustrate this point, first by way of negation. An example of an attempt to dismantle the privilegings conferred by the axiomatic assumptions of traditional philosophy that does *not* recognise the link between binary thinking and social and political oppression is Elisabeth Porter's idea of a philosophy of synthesis. Her recommendation is that dualisms be reconceptualised as pairs that are not opposed and antagonistic but "complementarily coexistent."[36] She applies this idea to a list of some thirty "major tensions," which include "culture–nature," "reason–passion," "mind–body," and "justice–love," noting that "[m]ale–female opposition is at the heart of these contrasts."[37] The difficulty I have with this proposal is that the idea of synthesis seems to imply that some complete account of both sides of a duality might be given, that each aspect of a duality is essentially balanced against the other. To me, the notion of balance underplays the existence of the implicit debt that the "male" end of each duality owes to the "female". Porter's list could, I suggest, be reconstituted as "x–not x": "culture–not culture," "reason–not reason," "mind–not mind," "justice–not justice," and "male–not male." Her footnote excepting the "dark–light" opposition from the possibility of synthesis acknowledges that blind people experience the contrast to light not as dark but as nothingness. Attributing to this point more significance than Porter does, I want to suggest that, where privilege accrues to the "male" aspect of each duality, where "female" is defined in terms of what "male" lacks,[38] we cannot effectively alter the devalued status of the "female" aspect of a duality because it is dualistically construed as nonexistent.

My point about the privilegings of dichotomous philosophical thought is also illustrated with reference to historical context. The legacy of Cartesian dualism is a way of thinking premised on the identification of essential difference. Mind is essentially different from matter, masculine from feminine, culture from nature, public from private, detachment from attachment, autonomy from dependency, and objectivity from subjectivity. In the initial presentation of such differences as self-evident, polar opposites might appear to be regarded as superior or inferior only in relation to their context. So, for example, the feminine, the private, and the subjective might be privileged in the context of parenting, where attachment and dependency are appropriately cultivated and expressed. Similarly, the masculine, the public, and the objective might be privileged in the context of cultural institutions, which foster detachment and autonomy.

THE LOGIC OF DOMINATION

The question is whether such privilegings *are* confined to particular contexts or whether, at least in some manifestations, they necessarily result in oppression.[39] Oversimplifying the correlation between dichotomous thought and oppression might be misleading. It may be that, devoid of the capacity for either–or, superior–inferior dualistic thinking, I could neither park a car nor boil a kettle of water, let alone split the atom or theorise about primate behaviour. In one sense, the ability to make distinctions, to discriminate, to see one thing as essentially different from another, bears no necessary connection with the mode of thinking that establishes the beliefs and assumptions illustrated in the devaluation of care.

However, I suggest that it is disingenuous to present hierarchical and oppositional thinking as a neutral heuristic device, as simply a method of distinguishing the human capacity for clear reasoning from the gobbledygook of extraterrestrials.[40] The point is that where hierarchical and oppositional thinking operates within the framework of a "logic of domination," privilege and power implicitly attach to certain activities and characteristics. What particularly interests feminist philosophers is that these privileged activities and characteristics are precisely those that are not appropriate in the informal domains of women's emotional work.

The crucial aspect of the concept of the logic of domination for my argument is that it reveals a connection between hierarchical, oppositional thinking (which says that some attributes are privileged over others in particular contexts) and the justification for the unconditional ethical and epistemological privileging of abstract, universal, and impartial thinking. It is the logic of domination that operates to change *separation* into *inequality*, *difference* into *inferiority*. It sanctions the move from *contrasting*, say, the abstract with the concrete, the universal with the particular, and the impartial with the partial to an *opposing* of abstract to concrete, universal to particular, and impartial to partial. Where abstraction, universality, and impartiality establish the framework for rationality, what is *not* abstract, universal, and impartial is regarded as irrational and then devalued, oppressed, or subordinated on that basis. What is lost here—a loss that is justified by the logic of domination—is the context-specificity or the conditionality that might, in the absence of the logic of domination, yield understandings of difference that do not, necessarily, devalue, oppress, or subordinate even what is inferior or lacking desirable qualities.[41] A parent, for example, might use her superior knowledge, insight, and maturity to protect, nurture, and guide her child without dominating or subordinating that child.[42] The logic of domination, however, simply asserts that "for any X and Y, if X is superior to Y, then X is justified in subordinating Y."[43] This premise functions in conjunction with other premises about the superiority of Xs to Ys in particular contexts to decontextualise superiority or to make superiority unconditional. Where heirarchical, oppositional thinking says that Xs are superior to Ys in particular conditions, the logic of domination operates to elide the context in which that superiority *may* have been legitimate.[44] As superiority is decontextualised or made unconditional, so is the privilege that superiority entails. The logic of domination, though, is not about superiority and privilege, which might be conferred by hierarchical, oppositional thinking without subordination. What the logic of domination effects[45] is a movement that turns superiority and privilege into a justification of subordination. The result, as Warren notes, is to explain, justify, and maintain subordination where, in the absence of the logic of domination, there might have existed diversity.[46]

It seems, then, that hierarchical, oppositional thinking functioning in conjunction with the logic of domination effectively distributes privilege so that caring is devalued. The important point for my argument is that this devaluation of care is secured by two kinds of premises: premises about superiority and premises about subordination. The motives of those who try to promote care through a reshuffling of public and private values are, I suggest, to overturn premises of only one kind. Demonstrations of the value of care to the public realm are supposed to challenge a premise about superiority: justice, rights, duty, or utility is superior to care. Such demonstrations, however, implicitly leave in place premises about subordination. As a consequence, the level playing field on which the complementarity of justice, rights, duty, or utility to care might have been asserted does not exist. The challenge to premises about the *inferiority* of the private realm is not the challenge to premises about the *subordination* of the private realm. The former retains the dichotomous categories in which both sets of premises are framed. It is an approach that promotes certain values without recognising that these values are themselves constituted in a framework of subordination. Where premises of subordination are unchallenged, as they are by approaches that challenge only premises of inferiority, the concepts of, for example, the private realm, the feminine, partiality, and care are always and already secondary to the concepts of the public realm, the masculine, impartial reason and justice, rights, duty, or utility. Where premises of subordination are unchallenged, this secondary status is regarded as axiomatic rather than contingent, neutral rather than contentious. The logic of domination justifies subordination as the reflection of a natural or categorical order, so that the subordination of what is secondary appears as neutral or axiomatic. It thereby orients the norms of human existence in such a way that women, whose activities and characteristics are privileged in the private realm, are politically, socially, economically, and psychologically disadvantaged or oppressed. By showing that the logic of domination is not neutral as to gender (or race or class) and that it operates to stabilise an oppressive status quo, feminist philosophers throw into question the legitimacy of the claims and assumptions about the neutrality of either–or, superior–inferior thinking.[47]

The move from a theoretical understanding of the logic of domination, to a practical consideration of the sexual politics that subordinate care to justice, rights, duty, and utility reveals the degree of mutual reinforcement, or perhaps circularity, that links premises about superiority and premises about subordination. What I mean is that the logic of domination operates to secure some concepts as privileged, while at the same time the logic of domination is secured by this privileging. This is the point captured by Warren with the notion of "oppressive conceptual frameworks," where a conceptual framework is "a set of *basic* beliefs, values, attitudes, and assumptions which shape and reflect how one views oneself and one's world," and an oppressive conceptual framework is "one that explains, justifies, and maintains relationships of domination and subordination."[48] For the purposes of my argument, what I want to emphasise is the reflexive nature of these frameworks, which not only *shape* but are *shaped by*, not only *reflect* but are *reflected in*, the way we see the world. The failure to recognise this reflexivity focuses the attempt to revalue the attributes associated with the feminine on proving the illegitimacy of superior–inferior premises while leaving in place premises that secure the subordination or domination of what is not equal. What my argument draws attention to is the need to shift this focus away from demonstrating the illegitimacy of superior–inferior premises toward a critique of the premises that secure the privileging of the superior and the oppression of the inferior.

As Donna Haraway has pointed out, "Some differences are playful; some are poles of world historical systems of domination."[49] My contention is that the logic of domination can be revealed as oppressive only when a position of extreme scepticism is taken about claims to complementarity between, for instance, the private and the public realm. This scepticism is, I think, what is missing in the attempt to revalue care and transplant its values and practices into politics and commerce. Such attempts work on the basis that the differences between the formal domains of the public realm and the informal domains of the private are of the "equal but different" kind found in superior–inferior distinctions, which, as I have noted, are not necessarily oppressive.[50]

Two particular effects of the logic of domination on binary thinking indicate why such "equal but different" constructions disguise distinctions that are far from playful and are to be distrusted as explanatory models. The first effect of the logic of domination is the subtle, but complex, reordering of binary thinking so that it highlights differences not between "A" and "B" but between "A" and "not A."[51] This point elaborates my earlier critique of Porter's philosophy of synthesis. The association of women and caring furnishes graphic examples of how the reordering of binary thinking proceeds. Both women and care fall on the side of the dichotomy that is built on the idea of a lack or absence of qualities. Women are defined as what men are not.[52] In Gatens' words:

From Ancient Greece to our own time women have been defined not so much in terms of any positive qualities that they possess but rather in terms of the male qualities that they lack. For the Greeks it was lesser reason; for others it was lesser strength; for Freud women lack (or have only an atrophied) penis. The important feature to note is that there is a history of women being defined only in terms relative to men, who are taken as the norm, the standard or the primary term.[53]

Similarly, according to the thinking informed by the logic of domination, care is constituted by an absence of the reasoning identified with justice, rights, utility, and duty. As I show in Chapter 1, the latter, with its privileging of abstraction, universalisation, and impartiality, is regarded as a manifestation of the prevailing paradigm of rationality. By contrast, care is seen as irrational (because it is not accounted for in terms of impartial reason) and irredeemably personal (because the focus of concern in caring actions is whether they are *appropriate* in a particular context rather than whether they are *right* in a sense that is independent of any particular context[54]). Where the norm, the standard, the primary term of morality is an abstracting, universalising, and impartialist reason, care is philosophically invisible.

What I am suggesting is that once the thinking informed by the logic of domination is understood as transforming "A–B" distinctions into "A–not A" differences, the notion of complementarity between "A" and "B" (i.e., e.g., between the masculine and the feminine and between the public and the private realms) is revealed as illusory. "B" cannot be described as complementing "A" when "B" is defined only as the absence of "A." The notion of complementarity (of "equal but different") cannot survive the transposition, by the logic of domination, of privilege and superiority into a justification of subordination. Yet it is surely the assumption of complementarity that sustains the attempt to extend care into the public realm.

The second effect of the logic of domination follows from this conceptual privileging and furnishes a concrete example of how the attempt to extend care into the public realm fails. Defining women in terms of the masculine qualities they lack is not a "straightforward repudiation" of the feminine.[55] Take, for instance, the capacity for abstract thought, where this means the ability to reason in a way that can be detached from the concrete and particular context of the reasoner. The association of this capacity with the masculine confines the feminine within a narrowly defined stereotype, adherence to which confirms not only female but also male existence. This is a crucial point. The lack or absence of the capacity for abstraction is not simply attributed to the feminine in the sense of being discarded as worthless. Its attribution to the feminine is integral to the construction both of the masculine and of reason. It is, therefore, *devalued* as a feminine trait but *invaluable* in the maintenance of a form of rationality that is synonymous with the masculine. A concept of the feminine as immersed in personal and emotional particularity confirms a concept of the masculine as transcending the confines of the local and contingent.

This way of understanding what it means for the feminine to be constituted through exclusion[56] brings us closer to being able to articulate the problem inherent in the attempt to extend care into the public realm. What this way of understanding makes visible is the paradox at the heart of care, when care is assumed to originate in the emotional work carried out by women in the private realm. On one hand, the devaluation of care is apparent in the inferior status accorded to carers and caring work. On the other, a private realm characterised by care and caring values confirms the values of a public realm where attachment and emotion are shed. The clearer the definition of the private realm as the place for nurturing feminine connection, the clearer the definition of the public realm as the place for cultivating masculine detachment and autonomy. The simple proscription of the feminine would leave the masculine having constantly to reestablish itself. This concept of the feminine as proscribed, that is, as without worth or value in the construction of the masculine, is not, it seems to me, valid. My point is that the feminine is constituted by traits and attributes that are excluded by the masculine as being not male but that are *essential* to the maintenance of the masculine. The concept of the proscription of the feminine, by contrast, has the feminine constituted by what is *not essential* to the maintenance of masculinity. The constitution of the feminine through what is essential to the masculine, however, secures an identity for both the masculine and the feminine and confirms these identities as constitutive of male and female experience.

When women enter the public realm, according to the versions of care that I have problematised in this chapter, they are expected to do so as bearers of the values of the private realm. As a result, the movement between the public and the private realms *reinforces,* rather than *weakens,* the logic of domination that opposes the public and the private and distributes power and privilege in favour of the former. The qualities of being helpful, loving, sweet, nurturing, and supportive[57] that women bring to their work in the private realm are precisely the qualities that women are supposed to bring to their work in the public realm. Women who do *not* bring these qualities to their work in the public realm are seen not only as unfeminine but also as incapable, as lacking the skills to operate in the public realm. So, as Eva Cox has expressed it, the ultimate sin for women moving into the male world of power and influence is being a "poor people manager."[58]

ATTEMPTS AT RELATION

I have gone some way toward demonstrating that the language of caring may yet leave intact the axiomatic assumptions of liberal moral theory. The versions of care that I have problematised operate, I have suggested, in the spaces conceded by liberal moral theory. Such approaches, as I have shown, are not consistent with the motives of the critical-interrogative feminist philosopher, who is motivated to take the experiences of all women seriously while refusing to take the claims of liberal moral philosophy at face value. The version of care that I will develop, on the other hand, neither maintains the sexual status quo nor attempts to extend care into the public realm.

To conclude this chapter I want to consider another way in which approaches that appear to disrupt established philosophical axioms may serve to reinforce those axioms. What I will show is that some attempts to counter the emphasis placed by liberal moral philosophers on autonomy and impartiality by imparting philosophical importance to the capacity for caring relation and empathy[59] may not represent a significant departure from the claims that establish autonomy and impartiality as philosophical ideals. These attempts, like those that try to extend care into the public realm, do not go far enough in challenging the hegemony of the axiomatic assumptions of liberalism. Up to this point, I have been concerned to problematise versions of the ethic of care that tend to construct care as a complement or supplement to liberal moral theory. Now I focus specifically on the question of relation. My suggestion is that the language of caring relation and empathy, although it appears to describe a sense in which selves are constituted in relation, may not, in fact, loosen the stranglehold of autonomous, impartial constructions of the self. On the contrary, I argue that some forms of empathetic connection may effectively reinforce the concepts of abstract, universal, and impartial moral reasoning on which deontological, utilitarian, and contract-based theories are founded.

For the purpose of this discussion, I distinguish two different notions of how the empathetic response might be constituted. The first I call empathy as passive accommodation; the second, empathy as projection. I draw the first notion from feminist critiques of the way empathy is naturalised as a feminine characteristic and develop the second from what Noddings rejects as "a peculiarly rational, western, masculine way"[60] of establishing connection.

   The capacity to be empathetic in the sense of passive accommodation is one of the traits that Western philosophers have ascribed to women, along with the capacity to nurture and the capacity for emotional response. When it is seen as part of the spectrum of feminine qualities, empathy is not the active seeking out of another's perspective but the passive receptivity that accommodates the perspectives of the powerful.[61] This is not to say that such passivity does not require an active cultivation of empathetic skills. Empathy here involves reflecting back to the powerful an endorsement of that power. It is a survival technique based on the need to predict and therefore contain the responses of the oppressor. Here the empathetic woman works to anticipate the demands of a person of whom there seems to be no reciprocal requirement for accommodation.[62] As an example of this version of empathy, consider the following passage from the *Ladies' Handbook of Home Treatment*, published in 1945:

Home is the kingdom over which the wife should seek to reign as queen. So wholesome and attractive may the home be made by a contented, cheerful woman that the husband will leave it with reluctance, and will return to it at night, after the day's toil is ended, with naught but thoughts of quietness and peace. The possession of a sunny disposition is indeed a wife's most valuable asset, for it makes herself and all around her happy.[63]

Here empathy is synonymous with the "sunny disposition" that is sustained by the assumption that anticipating and meeting needs are a way of averting trouble. Drunken or sullen husbands return to homes that are not sufficiently wholesome and attractive; unquiet and unpeaceful thoughts plague the minds of men whose wives' sunny dispositions waver.

   On this account, then, the capacity for empathy is firmly locked into the grid of oppositional hierarchical thought that establishes and maintains women's silences. According to this argument, the valuing of empathy is actually the valuing of women's empathetic attitudes to men, where empathy is a manifestation of the "misplaced gratitude"[64] women feel toward their male protectors. As such, empathy is part of the oppressive machinery that subordinates the interests of women to those of men. Attempts to salvage elements of empathy for feminist theory represent part of the extensionist project identified and criticised by Gatens.[65]

   On this reading, the account of empathy as part of the spectrum of feminine qualities clearly disappoints the feminist expectation that theory will take the experiences of all women seriously. As I understand them, though, the objections by some feminist theorists to the use of the term "empathy" is not based on a perceived endorsement of a stance that derogates the experiences of women but on the fear that empathy is not a strong enough concept to provide the resources to ensure that empathisers can resist becoming exploited. Alternatively and not necessarily contradictorily, perhaps the fear is that the concept of empathy is *too* strong in that it remains as an imperative even in the face of exploitation.[66]

The passive accommodation version of empathy is based on a particular view of the moral self. This is the self who is, in Claudia Card's terms, "in danger of dissolving into a variety of personalities, changing [its] colors (or values) like a chameleon in changing environments."[67] Although at first sight this self appears to contrast with the autonomous self of liberal moral theory, it is actually more like a pathological version of the liberal individual. Empathy as passive accommodation is a defence mechanism or a survival technique devised by a self for whom relation is problematic.

I draw attention to two aspects of this version of empathy. The first involves imputing an essential difference to the individuals engaged in empathetic relation; the second, an imputation of essential sameness. First, this version of empathy promotes an understanding of the self–other relation as dichotomous. Even though the objective of the empathising self is to accommodate the other, self and other remain conceptually *distinct*. Adapting Haraway's mirror metaphor,[68] this dichotomous construction might be captured in the double images of reflector and reflected.

However, a second aspect of empathy as passive accommodation involves the disappearance of the self as different from the other. The self that passively accommodates the other is conceptually *indistinct* from the other who is accommodated. This is the self that Winnie Tomm calls the "soluble" self,[69] the self whose subjectivity is obliterated.[70] Here is the assertion or endorsement of essential sameness, which also finds expression in mirror images. Rather than the double image of reflector and reflected, what is captured here is the sense in which the empathiser becomes the mirror in which accommodated others see themselves reflected. Understood as passive accommodation, empathy does not describe *relation* at all. With the disappearance of the empathetic self, the relational aspect of empathy is empty.[71] In adapting to the perspectives of the powerful, other perspectives become indistinguishable from the perspectives of the powerful. There is only one subject position in such encounters: the subject-position of identity.[72]

There is no challenge here to either the ethical or the epistemological propositions of liberalism that construct impartial autonomy as an ideal and construe both people and situations as exchangeable. Indeed, as a pathological manifestation of those ethical and epistemological propositions, the self for whom empathy entails passive accommodation may confirm those propositions. Passive accommodation may signal either a failure of impartial autonomy or the inappropriateness of impartial autonomy in the private sphere. What is significant for my argument is that this version of empathy is compatible with the concept of autonomous, impartial reasoners who are radically separate from other reasoners and from the objects of reason.

Let me turn now to what I am calling the projection version of empathy, which involves a projection of the self into or onto the other rather than an accommodation of the perspectives of the other. To the extent that it involves the idea that an understanding of others' perspectives can be obtained by projecting the self into or onto the other, empathy establishes precisely the kind of connection endorsed by philosophers promoting autonomy and impartiality as philosophical ideals. Even the Rawlsian association of the moral stance with disinterest seems, as Okin notes,[73] to presuppose a capacity to empathise: how else would the deliberators in the original position have a sense of what it might be like to be among the "least advantaged members of society"?[74] I think that Kohlberg, too, draws on this projection notion of empathy. His highest level of moral development is marked, to quote Tronto, by "a complete commitment to understanding moral dilemmas from the standpoint of all concerned."[75] Kohlberg says: "At higher stages, prescriptive role-taking stems from the realization that one must (a) take into account the perspectives of others and (b) imaginatively change positions with others in such a way that one is satisfied with the outcome of the dilemma regardless of who one is."[76] Indeed, one of the ways in which Kohlberg has defended his account of moral development from charges of race, class, and gender bias is to explain that people who are not white, affluent, and male have fewer opportunities to practise the role-playing at which stage 6 attainers exhibit particular skills.[77] Supposedly, what is un- or underdeveloped in those who are less morally competent is the ability to see other points of view. This limits their moral responses to rule-following and punishment-avoiding, since, according to Kohlberg, anything more sophisticated requires the ability to perceive morality not only as a system of laws and deterrents but also as a delicate balance between individual rights and social constraints. The most morally developed, then, are those whose empathetic skills are so refined that, by viewing the situation from many perspectives, they can coalesce individual notions of justice into a universal moral law.

As projection, empathy comes in two forms.[78] Both of these forms, I suggest, are problematic. On one hand, empathy as projection may involve putting myself in your shoes in order to *account for* your feelings. In this form, we might talk about empathy in terms of the recognition of a common experience, as when we say something like, "I know how my grieving friend feels because I, too, have experienced grief" or "I understand how anxious you are about your thesis because I, too, have experienced this anxiety."[79] It is important that, in saying these things, I do not mean that I am actually grieving or anxious about the same thing that is causing you grief or anxiety (i.e., about *your* loss or *your* thesis). In other words, empathy is a recognition or assessment of *another person's* affective state. The degree of my empathy for you can be gauged according to how readily or how accurately I *recognise* your affective state or assess what is affecting you.

On the other hand, empathy as projection may imply that, in putting myself in your shoes, I myself am affected as you are. If empathy is gauged by how well I *recognise* your affective state, the degree of empathy might be judged by considering my answer to the question, "How does x feel?" If, however, empathy is gauged by how *affected* I am by your affective state, the degree of empathy might be judged by asking me instead, "How do you feel?"[80] If you are manifestly in pain or are weeping, and I report a feeling of pleasure, then my affect is not to be classed as an empathetic response. The crucial point is that, for our relation to be one of empathy, I myself must be affected *as you are*, which implies that there needs to be at least a degree of correspondence between your affective response and mine.

I have said that the passive accommodation version of empathy, far from establishing a basis for describing caring relation, leaves the relational aspect of empathy empty, thereby actively maintaining the ideals of autonomous impartial reasoners as selves who are radically separated from other selves. So, too, I believe, do both forms of empathy as projection (i.e., empathy as recognition of affective response and empathy as experience of affective response). This active maintenance works in two ways. First and most apparently, both forms of empathy as projection maintain the distinction between your response and mine, between what is happening for you in a situation and what is happening for me. If empathy as projection establishes relation between us, it is relation between a dichotomised self and other where this dichotomy separates your experience from mine, your perspective from mine, your affective response from mine. In other words, empathy as projection contrives relation between two people who are not otherwise related. Empathy is a bridge, or at least one of the bridges, across which I have access to you. This kind of relatedness implies nothing about whether the traffic over the bridge is two-way or whether the access provided by the bridge to the affective response of my son differs either qualitatively or quantitatively from the access it might provide to the affective response of a fictional character or of a stranger. My point is that empathy as projection, like empathy as passive accommodation, treats individuals as essentially separate from, or different from, each other.

Empathy as projection, then, like empathy as passive accommodation, promotes an understanding of the self–other relation as dichotomised. But, as I have suggested is the case with empathy as passive accommodation, empathy as projection moves from the assumption of self and other as different toward a premise about essential sameness or identity. This is the second way in which empathy as projection actively maintains the ideals of autonomous impartial reason. Whether I am recognising or experiencing your affective response, empathy as projection assumes a homogeneity of affective expression. The range of possible affective responses may be extensive, reflecting the entire gamut of human emotional reaction, but the expression of any particular affective response is circumscribed. So, for example, your affective responses may range from bliss to boredom, from delight to disappointment, from satisfaction to sorrow. But, if I am to step into your shoes, to see things from your perspective, I have to be able to assume some coherence between your current and particular responses and how I respond in a similar context. For me to be empathetic toward you, your affective response to, say, the death of your child has to be essentially the same as my (real or imagined) response. If my (real or imagined) affective response in this situation is that I am distraught, and you present to me as smiling and relaxed, it cannot be said that our affective responses correspond. In other words, my relation with you is not one of empathy unless there is at least a degree of sameness between my response and yours.[81] This is the case whether empathy is considered to be the capacity to *recognise* affective response ("How does x feel?") or to *experience* affective response ("How do you—the empathiser—feel?").[82]

The reason this insistence on affective homogeneity is significant is that it has the effect of grounding the concept of empathy as projection in the sense of being-like-me. As a result of this grounding, empathy does not exist between you and me if I cannot recognise or experience your affective response. In the case where I cannot recognise or experience your response, it would seem that I have two options. I can reclassify your affective response so that it fits with an affect that reconnects us in a relation of empathy. The intention here is to maintain a sense of you being-like-me. Or I can assume that your affective response is fundamentally incoherent and abandon the possibility of establishing a relation of empathy.[83] Here, my assumption that our affective responses are essentially not the same determines my sense of you as being-not-like-me.

Let me clarify the effect of grounding the concept of empathy as projection in the sense of being-like-me. My understanding is that, where empathy as passive accommodation involves revoking the perspective of the empathiser, at least to the extent that this perspective differs from the perspective of the other who is empathised with, empathy as projection involves a prior assumption that perspectives will coincide. In other words, what I assume when I approach you in this way is that there is a "fit" between your experience and mine, that I can "step into your shoes" or "see things from your perspective." My assumption that you are like me, that your experiences are like mine, seems to remove whatever might render you and your experiences opaque to me.

If this situation describes an approach of an empathiser, then it seems to me that empathy as projection is as devoid of relational content as empathy as passive accommodation. Rather than the disappearance of the self as different from the other, what we have here is the disappearance of the other as different from the self. Here it is the other who might be described as "soluble," the other whose subjectivity is obliterated. Empathy as projection is a process of self-reflection rather than an attempt to describe relation.[84]

So, neither empathy understood as passive accommodation nor empathy understood as projection describes selves as constituted in relation. Whether it is the empathetic self or the empathised-with other that disappears, the relational aspect of empathy is empty. For both empathy as passive accommodation and empathy as projection, there is only one subject-position in empathetic encounters: the subject-position of identity.

As I have said, the disappearance of the self as different from the other (in passive empathy) and the disappearance of the other as different from the self (in projective empathy) can both be linked with the radical separation or separateness of individuals. In Chapter 1, I claim that liberal ethics and the ethic of care are grounded in sets of epistemological assumptions.[85] In the case of liberal ethics, I have associated the epistemological privileging of the abstract, universal, and impartial with the notion of truth as a universal and unitary regulatory ideal, with the radical separation both of the knowing individual from other knowers and of the subject and the object of knowledge and with the assumption that the establishment of a common language is an effective way to ensure the possibility of sustaining shared belief systems, mutual understandings, and intersubjective agreements. Both ethically and epistemologically, then, the emphasis is placed on the connections between the self and what is known or understood rather than on the connections between selves. To the extent that liberal ethics and epistemology *do* establish connections between selves, the basis of these connections is that individual selves find themselves seeing, knowing, or understanding the same things. The act of seeing, knowing, or understanding, however, remains a solitary act. This is the concept of connection endorsed by both the passive and the projective versions of empathy.

I have said that both empathy as projection and empathy as passive accommodation move to convert difference into sameness. Both versions of empathy are problematic in that neither ascribes a relational content to empathetic connection. What I mean is that both versions of empathy construct relation as involving a loss of self: either the loss of the empathising self or the loss of the self who is empathised with. My suggestions are that the accounts of relation that emerge from these versions of empathy do not entail any significant revision of the ideals of autonomy and impartiality and do not constitute the basis of an account of caring relation. My point is not that the empathetic response *necessarily* establishes such an impoverished account of relation. The concept of seeing together that I develop in this discussion involves a sense in which I *can* say that I know just how you feel, as well as a sense in which that saying is consistent with there being degrees of overlap or commensurabilities between your knowing and mine, your feeling and mine. However, seeing together, as I begin to show in Chapter 3, involves concepts of relation that cannot be sustained by either of the versions of empathy I have considered here. Neither version challenges the idea that selves are essentially constituted as separate, autonomous, and impartial. Both present concepts of relation that reflect or are consistent with an emphasis on autonomy, impartiality, and separation.

When relation is understood to be connecting selves who are essentially separate, relatedness is a state in which selves are lost rather than constituted. When care is seen as a supplement or complement to approaches that emphasise autonomy and impartiality, caring is always and already subordinate to those approaches. What I establish in the following chapters, however, is that questions about relation and about care can be placed in another framework of moral understandings. When this framework does not privilege separation, autonomy, and impartiality, the possibility arises of transforming both ethics and epistemology.

NOTES

1. Amy is one of Gilligan's subjects in *In a Different Voice*.
2. Noddings, *Caring*, 40, passim.
3. Gilligan, *In a Different Voice*, 22–23.

4.   Bowden, *Caring.*

5.   And other "minority" groups. See Gilligan, *In a Different Voice,* 18.

6.   Jaggar, 'Feminist Ethics: Projects, Problems, Prospects,' 78–104, surveys the development of American feminist ethics.

7.   Jaggar, 'Feminist Ethics: Some Issues for the Nineties,' 91.

8.   Tronto, 'Beyond Gender Difference to a Theory of Care,' 247.

9.   French, *The Women's Room,* 63.

10.   *Brian's Wife, Jenny's Mum.* The title is taken from a poem, 'Identity,' 26.

11.   For an account of the "division of moral labor" see Friedman, 'Beyond Caring,' 258–273.

12.   See my references in Chapter 1, note 49.

13.   Noddings, *Caring,* 81–86, discusses care in these terms.

14.   *C.W.A. Cookery Book and Household Hints,* frontispiece.

15.   Austin, 'The Death of Hierarchy,' 22–25; Feinberg, 'A Few Kind Words about Fear,' 20.

16.   Auerbach et al., 'Commentary on Gilligan's *In a Different Voice,*' 150.

17.   For examples of different expressions of feminist reservations about care, see Card, 'The Feistiness of Feminism'; Grimshaw, *Feminist Philosophers,* Chapters 7, 8; Hoagland, 'Some Thoughts about *Caring*' and *Lesbian Ethics*; Houston, 'Gilligan and the Politics of a Distinctive Women's Morality' and 'Prolegomena to Future Caring'; Shrage, *Moral Dilemmas of Feminism,* especially 18–22.

18.   Benhabib, 'The Generalized and the Concrete Other,' 162, says: "Women are simply what men are not....*She* is simply what *he* happens not to be. Her identity becomes defined by a lack—the lack of autonomy, the lack of independence, the lack of the phallus." Later in this chapter I develop the idea that one aspect of a dichotomy is constructed in terms of what the other lacks.

19.   Harding, 'Feminism, Science, and the Anti-Enlightenment Critiques,' 87. She relates her observations to women and feminists generally. I think they are particularly relevant to proponents of versions of the ethic of care that I am problematising.

20.   That is, by philosophers who either fail to see or fail to problematise the exclusions of liberal moral theory or moral essentialism and the division of moral labour.

21.   Gilligan, *In a Different Voice,* 17.

22.   Noddings, *Caring,* 25, 34, 35, 61.

23.   The converse of this does not apply. Men are not restricted to the public sphere in the same sense that women are to the private. Poole, *Morality and Modernity,* 50, makes this point: "Women [are] equipped with those capacities necessary for the sphere of private life, [while] men hav[e] the capacity both to function in public life and to mediate between the two spheres."

24.   Friedman, 'Care and Context in Moral Reasoning,' 193.

25.   Ironically, the conservative version of care makes essentialist assumptions that bear similarities to those made by radical feminists. The difference is that conservatives tend not to problematise philosophy or at least to assume that philosophy is neutral, whereas radical feminists tend not to problematise the concept of "woman." Gatens demonstrates the inadequacy of both approaches in *Feminism and Philosophy,* Chapter 4, 'Language, Facts and Values.'

26.   This phrase is used by Mason Mullett, 'Inclusive Philosophy,' 75.

27.   Some commentators have suggested that Gilligan is ambiguous on the question of care's relation to established moral theory. I suspect a degree of misreading here, mirroring the misreading that has Gilligan construing care in opposition to reason. See, for example, Romain's comment that Gilligan fails to relate her psychological theory to

any moral theory or theory of value ('Care and Confusion,' 28). Jaggar, 'Caring as a Feminist Practice of Moral Reason,' 184, says that Gilligan does not explain how care and justice might be married. In this paper, Jaggar has a helpful survey of the various permutations of care and justice (especially 184–187), while Blum, 'Gilligan and Kohlberg,' 49–68, compares different responses to Gilligan. Here, Blum rejects the notion that Gilligan sees the relation between care and justice as an integration (66, note 14). I understand Gilligan to say that these confusions about the relation between care and justice arise when theorists fail to clarify how care is "framed." She says ('Hearing the Difference,' 124–125):

When care is framed as an ethic of selflessness and self-sacrifice in relationships it enjoins...inner divisions in women and catches women in a psychological and political trap....Any discussion of a care ethic, then, has to begin with the issue of framing. What is the framework within which we will compare and contrast justice and care? When I hear care discussed as a matter of special obligations or as an ethic of interpersonal relationships, I hear the vestiges of patriarchy. When I listen to care versus justice debated as if there was no framework, I hear the implicit patriarchal framework silently slipping back into place.

28. See, for example, Noddings, *Caring*, and the "separate spheres" arguments advanced by, for example, Held, in *Rights and Goods*. In 'The Meshing of Care and Justice,' 128, Held admits that her earlier arguments "that we need different moral approaches for different domains" have "failed to say enough" about "how unsatisfactory it is to assign justice to public life and care to private."

29. See, for example, Friedman, *What Are Friends For?*; Okin, 'Reason and Feeling in Thinking about Justice' and *Justice, Gender, and the Family*; Tronto, *Moral Boundaries*.

30. Although differences may exist here, too.

31. Bartky, 'Feeding Egos and Tending Wounds,' 118.

32. I think that Tronto (in, e.g., 'Women and Caring,' 184) is being overoptimistic in identifying this conservative position with the idea of care as a corrective. At least this idea would indicate an awareness of a malfunction in some aspect of conventional moral thought. My suggestion is that the conservative appropriation of care sees caring as more like the icing on the cake: as the icing makes the cake even more palatable, so care eases the burden of justice, but the existence of care (icing) does nothing to problematise justice (cake).

33. Or, as Gilligan says, "care becomes the mercy that tempers justice" ('Moral Orientation and Moral Development,' 36).

34. Bowden, *Caring*, 152, note 21, 153.

35. The futility of the attempt is conveyed in the quotations from the magazine *Working Woman* cited in this chapter at note 14.

36. Porter, *Women and Moral Identity*, 46. She acknowledges this phrase as Mary O'Brien's.

37. Ibid., 51–52.

38. As Benhabib suggests. See note 17.

39. Warren elaborates this concept in 'Feminism and Ecology,' developing it further in 'The Power and the Promise of Ecological Feminism.'

40. This sounds flippant, but it is precisely the way such "either–or" "A–not A" distinctions are presented to students encountering Aristotelian logic. See, for example, Ruby, *The Art of Making Sense*, 131: "If a creature should ever happen to come to us from outer space and tell us that he comes from a region called Betelgemania but that he does not come from Betelgemania, we could not proceed in conversation with him, for he

asserts something while simultaneously withdrawing it."

41. Although, as Warren notes ('The Power and the Promise of Ecological Feminism,' 129, note 6), in a society "so thoroughly structured by categories of gender, race, class, age, and affectional orientation...[there may be] no meaningful notion of 'value-hierarchical thinking' which does not function in an oppressive context."

42. This, I think, is the point missed by Kaufman, 'Warren on the Logic of Domination,' 333, who argues that "[w]ith appropriate qualifications, in certain contexts, it seems that superiority does justify subordination." He uses the example of parenting to illustrate his point. I take the notions of what a parent might do *without* subordinating her child from Ruddick, *Maternal Thinking*.

43. Warren, 'The Power and the Promise of Ecological Feminism,' 130.

44. As Warren points out in ibid., 130, many "superiority" premises are not beyond contention.

45. As is evident in the premise: for any X and Y, if X is superior to Y, then X is justified in subordinating Y.

46. Warren, 'Feminism and Ecology,' 6. Warren attributes this insight to Elizabeth Dodson Gray, *Green Paradise Lost* (Wellesley, MA: Roundtable Press, 1981), 20.

47. Cf. Gatens, 'Feminism, Philosophy and Riddles without Answers,' 25.

48. Warren, 'The Power and the Promise of Ecological Feminism,' 127.

49. Haraway, 'A Manifesto for Cyborgs,' 202–203.

50. I have, however, noted that the possibility of such nonoppressive distinctions existing in an oppressive conceptual framework might be qualified: see note 40.

51. This aspect of the critique of dichotomy has been fully articulated by Jay, 'Gender and Dichotomy.' Jay's analysis is endorsed by both Grimshaw, *Feminist Philosophers,* and Gatens, *Feminism and Philosophy.*

52. Cf. Benhabib at note 17.

53. Gatens, *Feminism and Philosophy,* 94.

54. Cf. Blum's sixth distinction between Kohlberg and Gilligan, 'Gilligan and Kohlberg,' 52.

55. As Lloyd points out, *The Man of Reason,* 105.

56. Ibid., 106.

57. Grimshaw, *Feminist Philosophers,* 189. Grimshaw cites *The Hite Report on Male Sexuality* (London: MacDonald, 1981) as the source of this male definition of femininity.

58. Eva Cox, *Leading Women,* 124, says: "Claims that women are naturally more warm and caring managers than men create different barriers to deny them entry to senior positions. Managerial women who are seen as not sufficiently caring are again in trouble for a flaw in what is nebulously called their style." I read Cox as implying neither that being a poor people manager or insufficiently caring is the only sin for which women in the public sphere are punished nor that being a good carer or people manager is an infallible way for a woman to succeed in the public sphere. The point is that the equation of women and care operates to disadvantage women in that, as I have said, if women are the exemplars of caring practices, then caring is what women should do if they are acting morally *and if they are acting as women.*

59. Code, 'I Know Just How You Feel,' 124, notes that "empathy often figures as a taken-for-granted component of care."

60. Noddings, *Caring,* 30.

61. See, for example, Baier, 'Trust and Antitrust'; Card, 'Gender and Moral Luck'; Hoagland, 'Some Thoughts about *Caring,'* although Hoagland notes (249) that Noddings distinguishes the "other-directedness" of which Hoagland is critical from empathy; Houston, 'Prolegomena to Future Caring.'

62. Cf. Bartky, 'Feeding Egos and Tending Wounds.'

63. Richards, *Ladies' Handbook of Home Treatment*, 33. The sentiments here are the same as those that inspire the CWA poet, quoted at note 13.

64. Card, 'Gender and Moral Luck,' 216.

65. Gatens, 'Feminism, Philosophy and Riddles without Answers,' 18.

66. In addition to the references cited in note 60, see Andolsen, 'Agape in Feminist Ethics'; Calhoun, 'Justice, Care, Gender Bias'; Frye, 'In and Out of Harm's Way.'

67. Card, 'Caring and Evil,' 107.

68. Haraway, 'Situated Knowledges,' 586: "The Western eye has fundamentally been a wandering eye, a traveling lens. These peregrinations have often been violent and insistent on having mirrors for a conquering self."

69. Tomm, 'Ethics and Self-knowing,' 102.

70. Code, 'I Know Just How You Feel,' 139: "the obliteration of subjectivity that bureaucratic institutions require for their efficient operation."

71. Cf. Hoagland, 'Some Thoughts about *Caring,*' 255: "[T]here must be at least two beings to relate. Moving away from oneself is one aspect of the dynamic of caring, but it cannot be the only defining element. Otherwise *relationship* is not ontologically basic...there is, as yet, no real relation."

72. Haraway, 'Situated Knowledges,' 586: "Only those occupying the positions of the dominators are self-identical."

73. Okin, 'Reason and Feeling in Thinking about Justice,' 245 passim. See also Friedman, 'The Impracticality of Impartiality,' especially Section 3.

74. Rawls, *A Theory of Justice,* 15.

75. Tronto, *Moral Boundaries,* 65.

76. For an account of the Kohlbergian stages of moral development see Kohlberg, 'The Six Stages of Justice Judgement,' reprinted in Kohlberg, 'A Current Statement,' 490–498. The passage quoted here is on page 490. This section of Kohlberg's paper was originally published as Appendix A in Kohlberg, *The Psychology of Moral Development,* vol. 2.

77. Kohlberg, 'A Reply to Owen Flanagan and Some Comments on the Puka-Goodpastor Exchange,' 518.

78. I draw these terms from Hoffman, 'Sex Differences in Empathy and Related Behaviours.'

79. The fact that empathy seems to be more readily associated with suffering or pain or at least with some unpleasant or undesirable feeling is perhaps a reflection of the preoccupation of traditional liberal ethics with dilemmas and crises rather than with the moral understanding of the uneventful—that is, with everyday or normal situations.

80. Hoffman, 'Sex Differences,' 712, calls these two forms of empathy "recognition of affect" and "vicarious response to another." I do not agree with him that the latter, rather than the former, explains what Smith and Rousseau mean by emphasising empathy as a basis for liberal society. Certainly, later proponents of liberal moral philosophy (e.g., Rawls and Kohlberg) seem more likely to emphasise the dispassionate assessment of other perspectives and interests as being of relevance in cultivating moral sophistication.

81. I might, of course, learn to recognise a range of responses as responses to loss, even though these responses do not initially appear to be like mine. This does not undermine my point, which is that, if I am to empathise with you, our *affective* responses must correspond: I will, in other words, empathise with you once I recognise your smiles and relaxed demeanour as evidence of your distraught state because I understand that you are affected as I am. If your smiles and relaxed demeanour indicate that you are not affected as I am, I cannot, according to this version of empathy, establish an empathetic

relation with you.

82. I have drawn these questions indirectly from Hoffman's account of how empathetic responses have been tested experimentally. "How does x feel?" requires me to assess the feelings of the other. "How do you feel?" requires me to assess my own feelings.

83. It seems to me that a third option, that of accepting your affective response as different and remaining empathetic, is specifically ruled out by both senses of empathy as projection.

84. In note 70, I used Hoagland's comments about relation to illustrate the emptiness of the relational content of empathy as passive accommodation. The same insight can be applied to the notion of relation here: there must be at least two beings to relate.

85. I do not mean to imply that *only* liberal moral philosophy and the ethic of care are grounded in epistemological assumptions. It would, however, be a different project to the one I have undertaken here to demonstrate how this nexus is established in other philosophical approaches.

Chapter 3

Theorising Connection as Primary: Understandings of Selves-in-Relation

In this chapter I consider some ethical and epistemological possibilities that arise when philosophical emphasis is shifted from individuals who are autonomous and impartial toward individuals constituted as selves-in-relation.[1] As I indicated at the end of Chapter 2, my belief is that when concepts of relation are placed in a framework of moral understandings where autonomy, impartiality, and separation are not privileged, the possibility arises of challenging liberal ethics and the set of epistemological assumptions in which liberal moral philosophy is grounded.

Importantly, this challenge to liberal thinking does not only contest the spaces left vacant by liberal accounts. Neither does it simply reverse the priorities and privilegings of liberal moral theory. Rather, it contests that theory on its own ground, starting with the assertion that a more adequate account of formal, public encounters becomes available when deep background assumptions constitute individuals as selves-in-relation rather than as autonomous, impartial, and separate.[2]

This redescription of encounters in the public sphere is one of several closely connected, but distinct, ways in which challenging the axioms of liberal moral theory is linked with presumptions about selves-in-relation. Other aspects of this challenge involve transforming the moral sphere and elaborating the concept of selves-in-relation. This interrogative approach also questions the requirement for either ethics or reason to function as the "glue" that connects individuals who are not otherwise connected and establishes care as an ethic rather than a nonmoral response that only complements or supplements liberal moral responses. These are the themes around which I have woven the ideas in the second half of this book. Various concepts of relation are deeply embedded in these themes. Here I am concerned less with the direct explication of relation in the realm of metaphysics and more with the way ethics and epistemology might be transformed by the presumption that individuals can be understood as selves-in-relation.[3]

While in no sense underestimating the complexity of the attempt to challenge the axiomatic assumptions of liberal moral theory, in this chapter I show how shifting the emphasis from autonomous, impartial selves toward selves-in-relation weakens or severs several different and important strands in the fabric of liberal philosophy.   The crucial point, however, is that my objective in emphasising relation is not to establish another hierarchical, oppositional dichotomy.   The setting up of a realm of relation *alongside* a realm of autonomy does not, I suggest, challenge the philosophical status quo in a convincing way. For me, what is compelling about the presumption that individuals can be understood as selves-in-relation is not that the presumption opens up another realm of explanation that supplements or complements the explanatory emphases of liberal moral theory but that it provides a more adequate explanation of experiences that liberal moral theory assigns to individuals who are ontologically autonomous.

In Chapter 1, I argued that, even in formal, public encounters between nonintimate equals or peers, the particularity of the other cannot be factored out of consideration. I add substance to that argument now by considering in more detail than I did in Chapter 1 what is supposed to be involved in the reasoning of autonomous impartial individuals.   This discussion is a central element in establishing that a challenge to liberal moral theory can be mounted on that theory's own ground rather than in the gaps conceded by that theory.

REDESCRIBING MORAL ENCOUNTERS

In the previous chapter I concluded that the kind of connection established by certain versions of the empathetic response assumes that human beings are not otherwise connected.   I link that conclusion with my argument about the inadequacy of liberal moral theory's account of public, formal encounters by looking at the assumption that, for autonomous, impartial individuals, the basis for connection is sameness. This focus on sameness, to which my discussion of empathy drew attention, is secured by premising connection on the possibility of eliminating or at least disregarding those aspects of the other that mark the other as different from the self.   In developing my argument, I am drawing on, and examining, Seyla Benhabib's distinction between the "generalised" and the "concrete" other.[4] Here, as well as associating these concepts with identity and difference, I also assume a broad link between the generalised other and the autonomy and impartiality that is supposed to characterise public and formal encounters.[5]

The assumption that the basis for connection is sameness clearly implies that what is particular or unique to you is not sharable by, or accessible to, me in a way that connects us morally. The point here, as Benhabib notes, is not so much that concrete and particular differences are denied but that they are deemed irrelevant.[6] What *is* relevant in establishing moral connection, then, is confined to what is not particular about individual existence.   These particularities, according to philosophers who draw their moral insights from "the perspective of the disembedded and disembodied generalized other,"[7] might include a person's race, gender, class, abilities, beliefs, and expectations.[8] What is left after these particularities are abstracted from the existential inventory are individuals resembling Rawlsian deliberators, who speak for other human beings because nothing remains to distinguish one perspective from another.[9]

The assumption that impels this process of abstraction is that the perspectives of concrete others, whose actual lived experiences take place in the context of their race, gender, class, abilities, beliefs, and expectations, do not establish the basis for moral connection. On the other hand, abstracting these particularities, classing them as not morally relevant, clears the way for me to take your moral viewpoint. In Benhabib's terms, moral perspectives that are sharable or accessible are perspectives of generalised rather than of concrete others. Thus, abstracted, generalised others can be "conceived as subjects."[10] The process of abstraction factors out any clear distinction between individual perspectives. It does so not necessarily by ignoring differences of race, gender, class, abilities, beliefs, and expectations but by insisting that these are not relevant to the constitution of your moral viewpoint, which exists independently of your race, gender, class, abilities, beliefs, and expectations. This process, it seems to me, is what Benhabib is illustrating when she says that total abstraction results in the disappearance of the other as different from the self.[11]

I suggest that there are two ways to read Benhabib's critique of generalised and concrete others. One way, for which there is strong textual support, is that the problem with confining an understanding of relation to the moral connections that might be established between generalised others is that the account of the generalised other is incomplete or limited. On this reading, Benhabib's dispute with philosophers who promote individual autonomy is that, by confining the concrete other to the realm of the private and personal, they leave the opposition between the generalised and the concrete other unexamined.[12] The constructive part of her project, on this reading, is the suggestion that the concrete other needs to be considered not as supplementing the generalised other but as a way of demonstrating the limits of moral theories that consider only the viewpoint of the generalised other. Insisting on the relevance of concrete particularity to the understanding of individual selves and their moral connection with other selves rectifies the imbalance created by focusing solely on the generalised other. The context of concrete particularity restores to individuals the individuating characteristics that turn out to be the prerequisites of the generalised moral reasoning that takes place behind the veil of ignorance. What I understand this to mean, in this version of Benhabib's argument, is that in order to take another's viewpoint, to see from another's point of view, I have to know something about the concrete circumstances in which that viewpoint has been fashioned. As Benhabib argues:

While every procedure of universalizability presupposes that "like cases ought to be treated alike" or that I should act in such a way that I should also be willing that all others in a like situation act like me, the most difficult aspect of any such procedure is to know what constitutes a "like" situation or what it would mean for another to be exactly in a situation like mine.[13]

For Benhabib this suggests that focusing solely on the generalised other is an epistemologically incoherent way of articulating the viewpoint of the other because it results in everything that distinguishes one viewpoint from another being excluded from consideration.   Overlooking the concrete other impoverishes the concept of the moral agent by limiting moral identity to abstract and universal attributes.   Introducing the concrete and particular other into consideration enriches the concept of the moral agent with the recognition that "every generalized other is also a concrete other."[14]

There is, however, a stronger reading of Benhabib.   The epistemological incoherence can, I believe, be taken to show not only that the universalistic discourse of the generalised other is *limited* but also that it is *fundamentally flawed*. One of the ways in which proponents of abstract individualism illustrate the effectiveness of attributing significance to the generalised other as the basis of moral theory is by considering the moral reasoning of generalised others in the abstract context of hypothetical situations. Now it seems to me that, if the concept of the generalised other is going to work effectively anywhere (in other words, if it is merely limited, as the weaker reading of Benhabib suggests, rather than flawed), we might expect that it would be convincing in moral reasoning about hypothetical cases where there are, by definition, no concrete others involved. In other words, if reasoning effectively is reasoning that concerns not particular people in particular situations but people and situations as instances of general rules, this reasoning would surely be manifest when the reasoner is presented with abstractions and expected to make universal moral pronouncements.

But, as Friedman has shown, this is not the case.[15] By retelling the story of Heinz, Friedman demonstrates that even in the processes of what is supposed to be archetypal abstract moral reasoning, the reasoner takes concrete and particular considerations into account. Her achievement, as I interpret it, is the problematisation of two distinctions: the distinction between the universal and the particular in the context of human relationships and the distinction between abstract principles and concrete responsibilities in the context of how, on the basis of lived experience, we sort out what to do.

Friedman recasts the Heinz dilemma in three stages.   First, by way of a transition, she reverses the genders in Kohlberg's story. This reversal not only effects the politically desirable end of portraying women as active but also serves to raise questions about the apparent gender neutrality of Kohlberg's original presentation. When it is Heidi who is tempted to steal the drug from Hilda in order to save her husband, it seems far less clear that the principle "life is worth more than property"[16] can be applied without reservation.   Theft and imprisonment seem to carry different and perhaps more severe risks and impacts for a woman than for a man. It might also seem somewhat harder to take at face value the suggestion that two women could have failed to negotiate a workable alternative in such a dramatic situation. As Friedman notes, "[w]ith women as the protagonists, the very plausibility of the 'Heinz' dilemma as an exercise in forced choice diminishes dramatically."[17]

The second stage of Friedman's reformulation retains the gender reversal but casts Heidi as a perfect stranger rather than as the sick man's wife. What begins to emerge in this formulation of the dilemma is the contingent nature of the principle "life is worth more than property." Where the gender reversal made the application of the principle subject to some hesitation, the removal of the "particularistic" relation, with its "affectively-tinged ideas and attitudes of *caring, love, loyalty, and responsibility,*"[18] seems to alter radically the presumption that the principle should be enforced. What this reworking shows is that even the minimalist sketches presented by Kohlberg's formulation of the dilemma allow us to glean sufficient detail about the concrete particularities of Heinz's situation to make a reasoned response that is specific to the context in which Heinz finds himself and is not necessarily relevant to Heidi or, indeed, to Heinz in a different context. Friedman's insight is that altering the concrete particularities of the hypothetical situation alters the outcome of moral deliberation. So, she argues, "our judgements about the right thing to do under the circumstances of the Heinz dilemma . . are strongly affected by who the players are and how they are interrelated."[19]

Friedman reinforces this point with a final revision that shows that the conclusion that we should not steal to save the life of a stranger does not simply denote a failure of reasoning.[20] In this third formulation of the dilemma, *I* am the person with the opportunity to save the life of a stranger by stealing a drug. The conclusion that I might not take this risk for the sake of someone unknown seems to undermine the universalisability of the principle that Heinz's dilemma was designed to test. The question, however, is whether this indicates that I am wrong not to enforce the principle and take the risk of stealing for a stranger. If this is so, Friedman points out, then we all act wrongly by not acting illegally to secure better treatment for the many people who, even in relatively affluent societies, do not receive optimum levels of health care. Perhaps, however, the problem of enforcing the apparently universalisable principle "life is worth more than property" lies not with our lack of moral resolve but with the confinement of effective moral reasoning to reasoning that concerns people and situations as instances of general rules: perhaps the problem lies with the concept of universalisability itself. This is the way I interpret the doubts that Friedman's revisions of the Heinz dilemma cast on the applicability of Kohlberg's universal principle. In this case, Friedman's alterations to Heinz's story can be seen to show that deliberations about her three formulations as well as about Kohlberg's original account of the Heinz dilemma manifest reasoning that concerns particular people in particular situations rather than reasoning about people and situations as instances of general rules. It seems that even where the particularity of relationships is at its most attenuated, we nevertheless reason on the basis of concrete assumptions, with these assumptions going far beyond what is given in the minimalist sketches usually provided in hypothetical scenarios.

The three forms of the Heinz dilemma developed by Friedman suggest that at least two contingencies imply exceptions to the principle that "life is worth more than property": the gender of the person taking personal risks to comply with that principle and the nature of the relationship between that person and whoever benefits from the theft. The conclusion I draw from Friedman's imaginative exploration of these and other contingencies is that Kohlberg misunderstands the responses to the Heinz dilemma when he construes them as the confirmation of general rules or universal principles determined by a reasoning process devoid of partial, concrete, and particular considerations. What better describes these responses, even when they are expressed in the language of universal principles, is that they are contingent on the particular set of contextual considerations read by the respondent as a subtext of the given hypothetical. To his most mature moral reasoners, Kohlberg attributes the capacity to see past particularity to the universal. In fact, what these reasoners might be doing is hearing Kohlberg's abstract formulation of Heinz's dilemma as an account of a specific set of circumstances, where the conclusion is liable to change as aspects of the circumstances change. So, the conclusion that Heinz should steal the drug because "life is worth more than property" might be contingent not only on assumptions about gender and relation but also on the assumptions that Heinz's wife wants to live, that the drug will restore quality to her life, that the pharmacist will not suffer significant hardship as a result of the theft, and that Heinz will either escape apprehension or encounter a judiciary that shares his value system. What is significant to the coherence of the conclusion, then, is the way that it is informed by the particular and concrete contextual details that are assumed in the fashioning of a response even when they are omitted from the explicit formulation of the dilemma.

The significance of this point for my argument is that it exposes the inadequacy of the concept of the generalised other right in the heart of the philosophical territory where it is assumed to be at its strongest. As I have said, if the concept of the generalised other provides a sound account of a way of reasoning that abstracts what is particular and concrete to form a universal viewpoint, where universality is understood to rule out the contingent, then this reasoning would surely be manifest when the reasoner is presented with abstractions and expected to make universal pronouncements. Instead, what Friedman makes apparent is that Noddings' observation that "the hypothetical is filled with real persons"[21] applies as much to reasoning associated with the supposedly abstract, universal standpoint of generalised others as it does to reasoning where the orientation is more overtly concrete.

This point is directly relevant to my earlier question about whether Benhabib's argument reveals liberal moral thinking as radically flawed or merely as limited. The crucial issue is whether revealing the contextual sensitivity of the standpoint associated with the "disembedded" and "disembodied" generalised other[22] implies only that that standpoint is incomplete or limited. This, it seems, is the implication drawn by Benhabib, which leads her to argue that the viewpoint of the generalised other is incoherent because it is totally abstract.[23] I think that a stronger and quite different conclusion is warranted.   By linking Benhabib's argument with Friedman's, what I have shown is that, *even on its own terms,* theorising from the viewpoint of the generalised other involves an ascription of concrete identity and a recognition that this concrete identity entails responsibilities and sympathies that are not captured in an abstract moral calculation. What makes the viewpoint of the generalised other incoherent, then, is not that it is totally abstract but that, even as it uses the language of the abstract, universal, and impartial, it is immersed in the concrete.

It is important, I think, to clarify precisely the point on which I disagree with Benhabib. My argument is that it does not significantly move the critique of liberal philosophical thinking along merely to stress that the liberal account of ethics is limited (in that it accounts only for the generalised other in public and formal settings). Rather, what I want to do is establish that the liberal account of ethics does not do what it professes to do. It claims to operate from a viewpoint that is universal and impartial.   It claims that this viewpoint is abstract, decontextualised, and disembodied, that the perspective of the generalised other is not locatable, not situated. What counters these claims is an analysis not only of *moral practice* but also of *moral reasoning* that shows that the moral beholder cannot be detached from what is beheld. What is a plausible or appropriate outcome depends on whose outcome it is. Whether "life is worth more than property" depends on whose life and whose property we are talking about. Principles are tied to a specific range of contingencies and contexts, even though the details of these particular contingencies and contexts are omitted from liberal accounts of principled reasoning.[24]

My argument, then, is that if the viewpoint of the generalised other is epistemologically incoherent, this is not only because the constitution of "moral dignity" cannot be confined to what selves and others have in common, as Benhabib argues.[25] Rather, it is because we misunderstand what is going on in moral reasoning and in moral practice if we accept the Heinz dilemma as illustrative of the process of moral deliberation. If, as Friedman suggests, even hypothetical moral reasoning can never be completely abstracted from the concrete particularity of moral subjects, then clearly the paradigmatic status of abstract thought in moral deliberation is highly questionable, and an important element of the distinction between the reasoning of the generalised and the concrete other is broken down.

Once we realise this, we can see that the problem with basing moral relation on sameness is not that commonality or mutuality is itself a false basis for establishing connection. Rather, the problem is that where sameness is a result of abstracting from the particularity of the other, the result of this abstraction— sameness—is a delusion. Both the generalised other as abstract reasoner and the generalised other as the product of abstract reasoning carry concrete entailments, even at the level of hypothetical constructs.[26] One of the insights to be drawn from Friedman's discussion of contextual sensitivity is that it always matters who is encountering whom, that the acknowledgment of rights, obligations, and entitlements is always contingent on who is claiming them, on how they are being claimed, and on the ends to which they may be put. If Benhabib is right, and I think she is, when she says that moral deliberation should be something we do in actual dialogue with others rather than on our own, then it may be that she, too, suspects that the generalised other, the other besides whom all others disappear, is a flawed illusion. It does not even exist, as Friedman shows, in what is proclaimed as the most abstract hypothetical reasoning.

Let me clarify exactly what I am claiming here. In arguing that there is a radical flaw in thinking that equates the stance that is moral with the stance of the generalised other, I do not mean to endorse a moral stance that equates solely with the stance of the concrete other. I am not disputing that there may be universal moral ideals or principles that all moral deliberation needs to heed. I do not want to deny moral significance to the common interests that seem to transcend particular contexts or to the useful nature of an account of generalised others in distinguishing between competing or conflicting moral claims. There may be occasions where the abstract, universal and impartial moral point of view is precisely the one that can be called upon to protect interests that would otherwise be discounted. There may be occasions where the equivalence of, for example, black to white, poor to rich, and female to male interests is ensured by the "blindness" of moral judgment to particularity. There may be occasions where the threat to autonomy establishes both the necessary and the sufficient grounds for intervention on ethical grounds.

What is at stake here, though, is the question of how relation is to be conceptualised within the framework of moral existence.[27] The relation of concrete selves, of selves marked by their partiality and particularity, is confined by liberal moral philosophers to the nonmoral or premoral private realm, *where it is denied moral significance*. Within the framework of moral existence, those adhering to the liberal tradition are concerned to ensure that moral interaction is not contingent on who is interacting. In pursuing this objective, liberal moral philosophers end up confining moral significance to those aspects of relations between persons that are public and formal. That there exists relation that is grounded in concrete particularity is, of course, not denied by liberal moral philosophers. What is denied is that such relation is morally significant. This is an important, if obvious, point. Liberal moral theorists have not been taken to task because they fail to attribute *any* significance to relation that is concrete, informal, and given rather than freely contracted. They have, however, been criticised for failing to attribute *moral* significance to that relation.[28]

What I have shown by drawing a stronger conclusion than does Benhabib about the inadequacy of the concept of the generalised other is that, although the account of the generalised other may serve certain purposes in clarifying and expanding the range of moral thinking, the categorical distinction that liberal moral philosophers make between generalised and concrete others cannot be sustained even in paradigmatic accounts of moral reasoning. Generalised others, let me repeat, are supposed to reason effectively by factoring out the concrete and particular distinctions between one point of view and another. They are supposed to secure and reinforce their moral autonomy and impartiality in the process of connecting with others who are regarded as similarly morally autonomous and impartial. They are supposed to be able to reason morally under the demand for universality.

These suppositions ground the approach of liberal moral philosophers to theorising relation. The validity of these suppositions is challenged by the revelation of fundamental flaws in the concept of the generalised other as categorically distinct from the concrete other. In Chapter 6, I explore another way to interpret responses to the Heinz dilemma. There I suggest that Kohlberg's account of the Jake and Amy interviews can be used to illustrate the epistemological and ethical imperatives that apply to selves-in-relation. For now, though, I want to link the breakdown of the distinction between the generalised and the concrete other (which I have shown to emerge from a reading of Benhabib and Friedman) with the question of how relation is to be conceptualised within the framework of moral existence.

It may seem that if, when we examine the reasoning of generalised others, we find a reliance on concrete and particular considerations to make fine distinctions between points of view, a search for an outcome that is relevant to a specific context, and a receptivity to the full range of relational nuances, then we are left without a workable concept of relation in the realm of formal, public encounters. But what I have shown in my argument about how the distinction between the generalised and the concrete other can be broken down is that the realm of public, formal encounters is not accounted for primarily in terms of autonomy and impartiality, as liberal moral theorists suggest. Understood in the terms I have drawn from Friedman's recasting of the Heinz dilemma, what better describes even our public, formal encounters is the language that liberal moral theorists reserve for what they claim is the nonmoral or premoral world of private relatedness. This is the language of care and partiality.

TRANSFORMING THE MORAL SPHERE

I have suggested that even in the realm of public, formal encounters, it is not adequate to account for relation in terms of the connection of autonomous impartial individuals. For liberal moral theorists, the realm of public, formal encounters represents the moral sphere, the sphere in which freely contracting individuals assert rights and fulfill obligations that transcend the particularity of the concrete individual. Outside this realm is the nonmoral or premoral sphere, the private realm where relation is "given" rather than freely contracted, where responsibilities arise in specific contexts and attach to particular people.

Now the distinction between the moral and the non- or premoral sphere is central to liberal moral theory and is clearly constructed and maintained by the whole fabric of liberal philosophy rather than by a single strand of argument. It does seem, however, that if axiomatic assumptions about the elimination of concrete particularity from the moral sphere can be called into question, as I have suggested they can be, then the establishment of this sphere as distinct from the sphere of concrete particularity can no longer be regarded as necessarily valid. Behind the veil of ignorance, there are supposed to be clear "epistemic restrictions" operating to privilege the universal over the particular and the abstract over the concrete.[29] These restrictions, however, appear not to result in any such privileging, since even the paradigmatic universalising reason associated with the attenuated sketches presented by Kohlberg can be shown to depend on an acknowledgment of concrete and particular assumptions about identity.

To countenance the possibility that the concrete and the particular are not eliminated from the moral sphere (i.e., that the concrete and the particular cannot be eliminated from moral thought) is, as I have said, not to establish an alternative realm of explanation but to venture onto ground that has been claimed by liberal moral theory. Pushing further into this territory, I suggest that a moral sphere in which the concrete and the particular are acknowledged is not a moral sphere that is necessarily peopled by individuals who are autonomous and impartial.

The key to explaining this problematisation of autonomy and impartiality is to link it with the account of relation as the impartial connection of autonomous individuals, where this relation is premised on sameness. Sameness, as I have said, is the result of peeling away the concrete particularities that distinguish one point of view from another. Relation here is contrived: it is the freely contracted association of essentially separate and essentially identical individuals. But, I repeat, this is not the only account of relation given by liberal moral theorists. Outside the moral sphere, relation is not contrived but given. Rather than attempting to peel away what distinguishes different points of view, such "given" relations are immersed in the concrete particularity that makes individuals and situations unique.

Where the moral sphere exclusively privileges reasoning that is premised in terms of the abstract and universal, it would seem that there is a necessary connection between that mode of reasoning and autonomous, impartial reasoners. Abstract and universal reasoning is supposed to reflect the perspective not of the individual reasoner but of the "moral point of view."[30] Indeed, this moral point of view *is* the abstract and universal point of view, where this is understood as "a point of view which ideally all human beings should take toward one another as free and equal autonomous persons."[31] To reason from this moral point of view is to apply universal principles with an impartiality secured in the understanding that all reasoners reason morally in the same way.

My suggestion is that if concrete particularity cannot be eliminated from the moral sphere, then the need to define moral reasoners as autonomous and impartial, even in an ideal sense, loses some of its cogency. Furthermore, if the mode of reasoning we understand as moral is substantively concrete and particular rather than abstract and universal, then the definition of moral reasoners as autonomous and impartial may not only lose some of its cogency but actually be flawed and misleading, describing as it does individuals who are essentially separate when these individuals are more appropriately described as constituted in relation. Let me link this point directly to the insights I have drawn from Friedman's revision of hypothetical thought.

On the basis of Friedman's amendments of the Heinz dilemma, concrete particularity is revealed as being of fundamental significance in moral reasoning. The coherence of the stories about Heinz, Heidi, and Hilda and the moral relevance of what we conclude about their actions, are established by our understanding of, and our sensitivity to, the specific relational contexts in which each player is situated.[32] Now the point is that consideration of specific relational context is precisely what is ruled out in autonomous, impartial reasoning. The universality of the knowledge-claims of autonomous knowing individuals is supposed to be secured by being decontextualised: removed from particular contexts and unmediated by the contexts of either knowers or what is known. The philosophical endorsement of autonomous, impartial reasoning, then, may signify what Gilligan calls "a blindness to relationships,"[33] not so much at the practical level (where, in spite of claims by liberal moral theorists to the contrary, relational contexts are relevant) but at the level of moral epistemology, where it is manifest as a blindness to the link between moral meaning and the relational realities by which moral meaning is informed.

This point is illustrated by the different ways of understanding responses to the Heinz dilemma. If we understand these responses as establishing the credentials of autonomous impartial knowers, we may attribute Heinz's dilemma to the failure of the individuals concerned to keep out of each other's way. What we are blind to, in that case, is the possibility that the dilemma arises from a failure of relation rather than a failure to remain separate. While the specific relational contexts or relational realities of the players in Heinz's dilemma may implicitly inform the moral meaning conveyed by the responses to the Heinz dilemma, this is precisely what is omitted in the account of these responses as emanating from autonomous, impartial reasoners, the clarity of whose reasoning is supposed to depend on their being oblivious to the discourse of relation. On the other hand, we might understand these responses as illustrating not the capacity to abstract relation in the search for an essential autonomy but the capacity to imbue even the most abstract relational realities with moral meaning. In this case, we not only acknowledge the relational reality that informs the moral meaning conveyed in the responses, thereby devising the kind of nuanced understanding of the responses to which Friedman's discussion points, but also make it possible to discern the ways in which the discourse of relation might be subverted when moral meaning is detached from relational reality.

I have said that it is my intention to focus on the way ethics and epistemology might be transformed by the presumption that individuals can be understood as selves-in-relation rather than on the direct explication of relation in the realm of metaphysics. In keeping with this focus, I acknowledge that the propositions that moral reasoners are autonomous and impartial, that relation is contrived only by abstracting an essential sameness from concrete particularity, and that there is a necessary connection between abstract, universal reasoning and autonomous, impartial reasoners may not be conclusively refuted by demonstrating that moral reasoners are immersed in concrete particularity and that specific relational contexts generate moral meaning. What this demonstration achieves, however, particularly when it is linked to a critique of the supposedly abstract and universal reasoning of autonomous and impartial individuals, is a problematisation of assumptions about the insignificance of concrete and particular relation to moral reasoning. If relation *is* significant to moral reasoning, and especially if the kind of relation that is significant is concrete and particular relation rather than abstract relation (i.e., what Heinz-Heidi should do in this particular situation involving these particular people rather than what husbands-wives should do in general), then the link between moral reasoning and impartial autonomy has not been established. Furthermore, where moral reasoning is seen to proceed not by abstracting from the particularity of the other, not by eliminating from consideration those aspects of the other that mark the other as different from the self, but by supplying contextual specificity even where it is withheld (as Kohlberg withholds contextual specificity from the respondents to his hypotheticals), then moral reasoning might more appropriately be seen as contiguous with the private realm where the dependency of relation on the concrete particularity of the other is not denied.

Again I stress that establishing this link between moral reasoning and the private realm necessarily entails neither the assertion of the ethical priority of the private realm nor the confinement of an ethic that recognises concrete particularity to an ethic of intimate relations. Instead, what I take the establishment of this link to show is that the definition of the moral sphere as distinct from the private sphere is faulty, at least in the sense that this distinction is not confirmed by a clear difference between abstract and concrete reasoning, universal and particular concerns, generalised and concrete others. The reinterpretation of moral thinking prompted by Friedman complicates the difference between the abstract and universal and the concrete and particular, showing that even classic examples of abstraction are infused with concrete particularity. This infusion cannot leave the distinction between the public, formal realm of autonomous and impartial moral deliberation and the private, informal realm of relation and partiality intact. The result is a transformation of the moral sphere. No longer to be accounted for solely as the province of autonomous, impartial individuals, the moral sphere is informed by understandings of relation not only as formal and public but also as concrete and particular, by understandings of individuals not only as standing alone but also as selves-in-relation. Premised on relation, moral deliberation is about the *quality* of relatedness. Theorising connection as primary establishes the ethical project as relevant to broad aspects of human existence, ending the circumscription that operates, in liberal ethics, to keep moral theory and relational reality apart.

SUSTAINING THE CONCEPT OF SELVES-IN-RELATION

I have said that the separation of the moral from the non- or premoral sphere, which is central to liberal moral theory, is not secured by a single strand of argument but by the whole fabric of liberal philosophy. So far in this chapter I have considered two distinctions that form part of this fabric: the distinction between abstract universalisation and concrete particularity and the distinction between the public, formal realm of autonomous and impartial moral deliberation and the private, informal realm of relation and partiality. I have shown that, contrary to the premises of liberal moral philosophy, moral encounters, moral reasoning, and the moral sphere itself are suffused with the kind of partial considerations that liberal moral theory specifically excludes.

In the course of my arguments, I have contrasted the autonomous, impartial individuals of liberal moral theory with individuals constituted as selves-in-relation. I have introduced the concept of a discourse of relation and of a relational reality that is established when moral meaning is located in a relational context. In all these references to relation, the emphasis is on concrete, particular, and partial considerations rather than on the abstract and impartial deliberations that characterise the formal, public relation with which liberal moral theorists are concerned.

Up to this point, I have focused my critical comments on the version of relation that depends on sameness, where this sameness is secured by the operations of impartial reason and a process of abstraction that has the effect of eliminating from consideration those aspects of the other that mark the other as different from the self. This is the concept of relation as it applies to the connection of so-called generalised others: it is relation between individuals who are not otherwise related. What I think is implicit in this concept of relation is a sense that the dependence on sameness coexists with a dichotomous construction of self and other, where this dichotomous construction establishes self and other as not connected. Selves who are constituted as not connected with others *contrive* relation. The concept of selves-in-relation, however, starts with a premise that selves are always and already in relation.

There are three central aspects of the "relatedness" of selves-in-relation. Clarifying these three aspects will help to substantiate the claims I have already made about the transformation of the moral sphere. This clarification also sets the scene for the chapters that follow and establishes some frames of reference within which my references to relational reality and a discourse of relation can be construed.

First, selves are always and already related to other selves. In this sense, it is relation that makes moral deliberation coherent. This is the sense of relation that is revealed in Friedman's accounts of Heinz and Heidi. Friedman focuses on the identification of Heinz and Heidi as selves-in-relation, that is, as selves whose deliberations and actions take place in the context of their relation to others. It seems to me, however, that as well as reasoning *about* selves-in-relation, we also reason, morally and epistemologically, *as* selves-in-relation. On this understanding I develop a reading of the responses of Jake and Amy to the Heinz dilemma in Chapter 6. I mean this relation of selves to other selves to be understood in concrete terms: actual encounters and relations with particular others enable the moral and the epistemological responses of selves-in-relation.

Second, the concept of selves-in-relation refers to the sense in which selves are always and already embedded or situated in contexts. This sense of relation is not necessarily clearly distinguishable from the first sense in which selves are related to other selves. It does, however, recognise the possibility that contextual relation may include relation that is not interpersonal. Like the relation of selves to other selves, contextual relation is to be understood in concrete terms. Selves-in-relation respond from particular locations, and the coordinates that identify particular locations recognise that selves live in connection with the physical world, with institutional and social structures, with worldviews that make accounts of particular contexts coherent (or incoherent). I am referring here to the sense in which, as selves-in-relation, we see Heinz not only as living in connection with particular others but as immersed in networks of social understandings about, for example, health and illness, crime and punishment, which are not totally accounted for in terms of his connection with particular others. In making this claim, I certainly do not mean to imply that these social understandings exist independently of the connection of selves to other selves. I am, however, pointing to a concept of contextual relation that includes the connection of selves to other selves *and* the location of selves in webs of understanding that are not entirely accounted for in terms of interpersonal relation.

Finally, the relatedness of selves-in-relation is to be understood not only as interpersonal and contextual but also as self-reflexive. Selves-in-relation reason with an awareness of their positioning in interpersonal and contextual relation. This aspect of the relatedness of selves-in-relation refers to a sense of connection that is "intrapersonal." Selves-in-relation know themselves in relation to other selves and in relation to contexts. In Chapter 6, I link this aspect of selves-in-relation to the concept of critical positioning, associating it with the possibility of assuming responsibility for relation. Here I want to identify this aspect of selves-in-relation as the missing element in selves whose relation is "selfless." Of the subjects in her abortion decision study, Gilligan notes, "Speaking of connection, of responsiveness and responsibility in relationships, women heard themselves sounding either selfish or selfless, because the opposition of self and other was so pervasive and so powerfully voiced in the public discourse."[34] Linking "the separate self" with "the selfless woman,"[35] Gilligan identifies the latter with:

[a form of] psychological dissociation: a process of inner division that makes it possible for a woman not to know what she knows, not to think what she thinks, not to feel what she feels. Dissociation cuts through experience and memory, and when these cuts become part of cultural history, women lose the grounds of their experience and with it, their sense of reality.[36]

As I understand it, the sense of relational dissociation or selflessness arises when what Gilligan calls "the paradigmatic human voice"[37] of the moral agent is predicated on separation and autonomy, impartiality and detachment. The paradigmatic human voice provides selves with relational identities only in public, formal relations.[38] Relations that are private and informal, relations that involve concrete, partial considerations rather than abstract, impartial deliberation, cannot be conceptualised in the terms on which the paradigmatic moral voice is predicated. The self that is involved in the concrete and partial considerations associated with private and informal relations is the self whose relation is morally insignificant.

It is not this lack of moral significance per se that accounts for the sense of relational dissociation or selflessness in relations that are not formal and public. However, where the moral sphere privileges separation, autonomy, impartiality, and detachment, the realms of moral significance and moral insignificance cannot be regarded as equivalent. This point is crucial: where the paradigmatic self is separate and autonomous, paradigmatic relation is impartial and detached. But an implicit part of the paradigmatic definition of separate selves and impartial relation is the assumption of a realm of selflessness and partiality. The paradigmatic voice premised on separation therefore gives the impression of accounting for all relation without remainder: formal, public relation is facilitated by separate, autonomous selves; informal, partial relation is facilitated by selflessness. Such distinctions, as Gilligan notes, tend to appear "natural and inevitable, necessary and good."[39] The assumption is promoted that relation that falls outside the province of liberal moral theory is premised on selflessness, while relation that falls inside the province of liberal moral theory is premised on separateness.

The selfless self cannot be said to be self-reflexive. Selves-in-relation, however, both sustain and are sustained by their positioning in relation to other selves and to contexts. These are selves whose subjectivity is neither obliterated[40] nor isolated by their connections with other selves, selves whose reasoning neither transcends nor is determined by the contextual specificity of concrete and particular considerations.

These three aspects of selves-in-relation—interpersonal, contextual, and self-reflexive relation—represent alternatives to the concepts of selves that are available in liberal moral philosophy. Selves-in-relation to other selves are not like selves who are separate and autonomous. Selves-in-relation to contexts are not like selves who are impartial and detached. Selves-in-relation to themselves are not like selves whose thinking is dissociated from relation.

I have said that my objective in shifting the philosophical emphasis away from individuals who are autonomous and impartial toward individuals constituted as selves-in-relation is neither to attempt a direct explication of relation in the realm of metaphysics nor to set up another realm of explanation alongside the realm of liberal moral philosophy. My point is not to eliminate the possibility that it might sometimes be useful to think of selves as autonomous and impartial. Rather, my objective is to problematise the assumption that such an understanding is *foundational* to accounts of moral reasoning. I do not, therefore, promote the concept of selves-in-relation as "natural and inevitable, necessary and good." The concepts of concrete particularity and partiality are not offered as replacements for the transcendental conditions of autonomy and impartiality in generating moral understandings. My claims about the three aspects of the relatedness of selves-in-relation that I have developed in this section are not claims about universal or universalising human experiences. If theorising selves as selves-in-relation seems to create viable conceptual alternatives to the autonomous, impartial selves of liberal moral theory, it is because the concept of selves-in-relation represents the attempt to avoid reductive approaches to understanding selves. As Michele Moody-Adams remarks: "A willingness to resist the reductive tendencies inherent in the idea that some single capacity makes a being distinctively human might prove to be one of the most beneficial contributions that feminist moral inquiry can make toward transforming moral thinking."[41] I want to resist propagating the belief that any one set of metaphysical conditions or assumptions constrains the moral understandings with which I associate the ethic of care and the concept of partial reason. At the same time, I do not want to suggest that selves-in-relation simply coexist, at the conceptual level, with the autonomous, impartial selves of liberal moral theory. In making autonomy and impartiality foundational to understandings of duty, utility, and contract, liberal moral theory makes the reductive move I want to avoid. The concept of selves-in-relation, on the other hand, links moral possibilities with a range of relational considerations that cannot be expressed in terms of sets of conditions or assumptions.

The point is that the relational selves who might be said to coexist with the autonomous, impartial selves of liberal moral theory are not the selves-in-relation associated with the ethic of care and the concept of partial reason. Neither are the autonomous selves who might be said to coexist with selves-in-relation the autonomous selves of liberal moral theory. I have conceded that it might sometimes be useful to think of selves as autonomous and impartial.[42] However, where this thinking is not divorced from the presumption that individuals can be understood as selves-in-relation, where this thinking is not premised on the primacy of autonomy and impartiality in accounting for moral responses, such thinking does not illustrate the coexistence of selves-in-relation and the autonomous, impartial selves of liberal moral theory. Because the theoretical moves I am associating with the concept of selves-in-relation directly challenge the capacity of liberal moral theory to provide an adequate account of the philosophical territory it claims as its own, the need to situate selves-in-relation alongside liberal autonomy is obviated. That I link these theoretical moves with a determination to avoid a categorical replacement of one set of foundational assumptions with another indicates the complexity of the challenge and the wide-ranging implications of shifting philosophical emphasis toward selves-in-relation.

QUESTIONING THE NEED FOR ETHICS AND REASON AS GLUE

In the remaining sections of this chapter I look at two more ways in which the presumption that selves can be understood as selves-in-relation challenges the axioms of liberal moral theory. The first involves the need for either ethics or reason to function as the glue that holds essentially unrelated individuals in relation. My suggestion is that, where the self is regarded as separate and autonomous, impartial reason is supposed to establish both the means for the separate self to connect morally with others and the end served by this connection. When the theoretical emphasis is on connection, on the other hand, both reason and ethics might be seen as the projects of selves-in-relation, for whom connection is not an abstract contrivance but the concrete context that enables understanding of relational reality.

I have referred several times in this and previous chapters to the assumption that, where the dichotomous construction of self and other keeps us apart, what remains after particular differences have been abstracted are individuals who are essentially the same. This sameness, I have said, is the basis for establishing relation between individuals who are ontologically autonomous. I have noted that one of the ways in which differences are subsumed or abstracted is in the privileging of the perspective of the "moral point of view."

The moral point of view, for liberal moral theorists, represents far more than a consensus position. As I show in Chapter 1, the concept of the moral point of view has normative implications for both ethics and epistemology. It is supposed to be the position reached by reasoning that is sound or correct, where soundness or correctness is defined in the terms that are central to liberal rationalism: abstraction, universalisation, and impartiality. It is therefore supposed to represent an ideal way of generating the most adequate moral insights by using the most sophisticated reasoning skills.

The crucial aspect of the moral point of view, at least for my argument here, is the assumption that it secures *rational agreement.* While this might be overtly the case only in the case of contractarian moral theories, I show in Chapter 1 that both deontological and utilitarian approaches implicitly equate moral principles with the principles of an impartial, formal reason. The moral point of view is the point of view that elicits agreement. I am not suggesting that agreement is the *grounds* of the moral point of view. Rather, I am pointing to the sense in which, for liberal moral theorists, agreement is a desired *outcome* of moral deliberation. What is assumed to secure this outcome is the impartial, formal thinking of rational moral agents. Liberal moral philosophers distinguish the moral point of view, which is, or would be, held by anyone reasoning in abstract, universal, and impartial terms, from points of view that reflect only personal, partial perspectives, which are inseparable from the concrete particularity of our individual existences.

The way the liberal moral point of view is constituted by, and distinguished from, perspectives that are not abstract, universal, and impartial is made clearer with an example, for which Heinz will once again suffice. When we consider the moral point of view by studying reasoning about the Heinz dilemma, we are, in fact, looking at the thought processes of several people. This is because the test of whether a resolution of the dilemma represents *the* moral point of view or just *a* point of view is assumed to lie in establishing whether it is a resolution that secures rational agreement.[43] As a respondent to the dilemma, I might conclude that Heinz should steal the drug because life is worth more than property. But the important thing is that I can claim that this represents the moral point of view only if I can say that Heinz, Heinz's wife, and the pharmacist are all rationally bound to the same conclusion.[44] To substantiate this *latter* claim, I have to be able to place myself in the position of each of these other reasoners and show that, whatever role each of us is in, the conclusion that Heinz should steal the drug because life is worth more than property remains valid. This complex process, which Kohlberg calls "moral musical chairs,"[45] involves me not only in a direct *reversal* of perspectives (where my reasoning is that if I were in that position, I should endorse this conclusion) but also in a *transcendence* of perspective (where my reasoning is that regardless of what position I were in, I should endorse this conclusion).[46]

Direct reversibility does not necessarily ensure the rational agreement secured by the moral point of view. Considering what I would do if I were you assumes that your conclusions will be informed by the same considerations that inform my conclusions. So, to suggest that I would endorse the conclusion that Heinz should steal the drug even if I were the pharmacist from whom the drug will be stolen is to assume that the pharmacist has the same experiences, expectations, and sense of value that I have. Similarly, by a process of direct reversal I might say that Heinz's wife would endorse the conclusion that Heinz should steal the drug even if *she* were the pharmacist from whom the drug will be stolen.[47] The conclusion that *cannot* be directly reversed, in the original account of the dilemma, is the pharmacist's: that Heinz should not steal the drug because we do not have a right to the property of others. Assuming that the pharmacist and I have the same experiences, expectations, and sense of value, he will have to concede that, if he were in the position of Heinz's wife, he would not want others to uphold his conclusion because his conclusion leads to the death of Heinz's wife.

The problem here for liberal moral theorists is that testing particular conclusions for direct reversibility may not necessarily ensure that *agreement* is *rational* where rationality is defined in terms of abstraction, universality, and impartiality. Indeed, the assumptions that ground direct reversibility, at least in the Kohlbergian account, seem explicitly contextual in their imputation of one reasoner's particular experiences, expectations, and values to another. Even in the case of direct reversibility (where I am completely satisfied that my conclusion applies equally to everyone) I might not be sure that my conclusion is universalisable in contexts where experiences, expectations, and values are different. The question, then, is how to ensure that a conclusion is not contingent on the existence of particular experiences, expectations, and values. The answer, for liberal moral theorists, is that as well as being directly reversible, a conclusion must transcend particular perspectives. In other words, in establishing the rational agreement that marks the moral point of view, we need to be able not only to *describe* the responses of others in terms of their reversibility but also to *evaluate* those responses in terms of their ability to transcend particular perspectives. The nonreversibility of the pharmacist's response to Heinz's dilemma, then, indicates that his view is not the moral point of view. The failure of his response to transcend his particular perspective indicates that his view is irrational.[48]

Clearly, there are several extremely troubling and problematic assumptions sustaining the concept of the moral point of view. Identifying one of the most obvious also, I think, explains why it is difficult to give a coherent account of how the moral point of view is established. It is that the central normative assumption—that the moral point of view is also the point of view that is morally sound or correct—begs the question of how reversibility or universality is connected with what is morally correct. On this point, I agree with Don Locke: "We need to distinguish the claim that a correct solution will be one on which rational people ought ideally to agree, from the claim that a solution on which rational people can agree must therefore be the correct one."[49] My discussion earlier in this chapter has raised other doubts about whether the transcendence of particularity and the confinement of morality to reasoning that is impartial are philosophically sound. The chapters that follow establish a constructive response to the critique of liberal moral theory, of which the moral point of view is one element. For now, though, I want only to draw attention to the central role accorded by liberal theorists to abstract, universal, and impartial reason in establishing human connection, where connection is the agreement of rational people who are ontologically autonomous. This is the most basic sense in which reason and the moral thinking that reason informs effectively act as the glue enabling disparate viewpoints to coincide.

The point is that even the paradigmatically autonomous reasoner is not assumed to reason alone, at least not in the sense that, for example, solipsism or relativism places reasoners in isolation. The autonomous reasoner may be able to deliberate on moral issues without engaging in dialogue, but what ensures this ability is the certainty that the moral point of view engages *all* reasoners *as* rational beings. Again I emphasise that, for liberal moral theorists, the connection established by reason is not the only form of human relation. When relation is *not* informed by reason, however, it is confined to the realm of the private and partial, where it lacks philosophical significance. In the formal, public realm, reason provides the *means* of establishing that we can sustain shared belief systems, mutual understandings, and intersubjective agreements. But it also provides the *end* of establishing these understandings and agreements.[50] Where, as reasoners, we proceed by abstracting from the concrete and universalising the particular, the end is rationality itself: a rationality grounded not on the partisanship and specificity that distinguish my perspective from yours but on our capacity to transcend our individual perspectives, a rationality that is "the relation of rational beings to one another."[51]

This is the sense, then, in which, for liberal moral theorists, reason both secures and is secured by the moral point of view. It secures the moral point of view by eliminating the concrete, particular, and partial considerations that might debase the universality on which the moral point of view depends. It is secured by the moral point of view in that the moral point of view apparently yields a sound or correct way of understanding the moral world. Without rationality, we remain morally separate insofar as we lack the cohesion required to sustain shared belief systems, mutual understandings, and intersubjective agreements. With rationality, we can connect morally with others in an accord that, because it cannot be subverted by concrete, particular, partial interests, affords a secure place from which to generate descriptions and evaluations about the moral world in a voice that is unanimous.

Shifting the emphasis from autonomous, impartial selves toward selves-in-relation has the immediate effect of raising doubts about the existence of the separate self whom reason and ethics are supposed to connect morally with others. This is an important point: as I have explained in the previous section, I do not mean relation to function ontologically as a replacement for the glue of impartial reason. Relation, in other words, does not connect separate selves. Rather, selves-in-relation are constituted in and by relation. The concept of selves-in-relation conveys a sense of selves whose relatedness is given. Selves-in-relation have no need of a glue whose purpose is to hold together what would otherwise be separate.[52] From the perspectives of selves-in-relation, the separate self, like the generalised other, appears to be a philosophical abstraction: an idealised fantasy rather than a reflection of lived experience.

In the chapters that follow, I develop the ethical and epistemological implications of the replacement of the separate self with selves-in-relation by distinguishing between "seeing the same thing" and "seeing together." Seeing the same thing is the objective associated with the connection of separate selves. Seeing together is a description of the epistemological and ethical activities of selves-in-relation.

One final point needs to be made about the effects of focusing philosophically on selves-in-relation. I have said that the moral point of view is distinguished from perspectives that are not abstract, universal, and impartial. The moral point of view is supposed to secure rational agreement, while concrete, particular, and partial perspectives are understood to lack the cohesion required to sustain shared belief systems, mutual understandings, and intersubjective agreements. However, what I want to dispense with by shifting the philosophical emphasis from autonomous, impartial selves to selves-in-relation is neither rational agreement per se nor the possibility of creating and sustaining shared belief systems, mutual understandings, and intersubjective agreements. Indeed, a substantial part of my critique in Chapter 2 involves questioning the assumption that an ethics and an epistemology that are not premised on autonomous selves must be cast in opposition to reason. But the confinement of moral relation to the rational agreement secured by an abstract, universal, and impartial reason makes moral relation an achievement of separate selves. Instead, what I am proposing is that moral relation *constitutes* selves, so that reasoners reason morally as selves-in-relation in a process of generating understanding that bears little resemblance to the impartial reason that informs the moral point of view.

In the next chapters, I develop the argument for an ethic of care and an epistemology grounded in partial reason. The point to be made here is that shifting the emphasis from autonomous, impartial selves toward selves-in-relation not only dispenses with the need for either ethics or reason to function as glue but also opens up the possibility of fundamentally altering the concepts of ethics and reason.

ESTABLISHING CARE AS AN ETHIC

Where the autonomous, impartial self assumes priority, care is inevitably confined to contexts in which impartiality is inappropriate. However, as I have begun to show in this chapter, shifting the emphasis from autonomy to relation reveals that moral judgment is not an impartial evaluative mechanism but a way of illuminating the contexts in which selves-in-relation make sense of relational realities. My suggestion is that emphasising relation rather than autonomy at the level of ontology problematises the liberal distinction between care and ethics, where care is context-dependent, and ethics is based on considerations that are abstract, universal, and impartial. This problematisation represents a challenge to the axioms at the heart of liberal moral theorising that promote the assumption that the distinction between care and ethics is "natural and inevitable, necessary and good." I want to show that the distinction between care and ethics, between a caring and a moral response, is not necessarily beyond contention and might be appropriately understood as a move to secure a form of ethics that is immune from the contingencies of the partial, the concrete, and the particular.

I illustrate this point by considering the accounts of moral reasoning and care given by Gilligan's subjects to see whether a distinction between care and ethics is detectable. It seems to me that two components of their accounts would alert us to such a distinction. The first would be reported as something like, "This is what was right but this is what I did." This, I submit, is not manifest. Indeed, what we can detect, at least in the views on which Gilligan bases her version of mature, postconventional moral thinking, is that there is something *distinctively moral* about expressions of care.[53] But here morality is not expressed as an abstract "prescription, a thing to follow"[54] to make life with each other livable. Captured in expressions of care is the idea that "[m]orality is doing what is appropriate and what is just within your circumstances," an emphasis on context or circumstances so that moral understandings are a way of defining responsibilities in a world that "is full of real and recognizable trouble."[55]

A second sense in which the accounts of Gilligan's subjects might alert us to a distinction between ethics and care would involve the reporting of a difference between what is done because it is demanded morally and what is done because we care. This, too, I believe, is not evident. In fact, this is precisely the distinction that leads to the conflicting images about the integrity of self and the integrity of relation that beset those in the process of developing an apprehension of self and others. From the perspective of Gilligan's mature, postconventional moral thinking, such distinctions are seen to be the result of "a faulty construction of reality"[56] that invariably generates irreconcilable and irresolvable demands.

Challenging the distinction between care and ethics raises a further question: whether the assertion of a clear distinction between the moral and the nonmoral can be taken at face value. Harry Frankfurt, whose theory of care I discuss in the next chapter, categorically asserts such a distinction, believing that "There is nothing distinctively moral...about such ideals as being steadfastly loyal to a family tradition, or selflessly pursuing mathematical truth, or devoting oneself to some type of connoisseurship."[57]   But it seems to me that there is nothing distinctively moral about such activities only if they are conceived as abstract or context-free, that is, as pertaining to selves who are constituted as not-in-relation. The idea expressed by Gilligan's subjects is that the concerns of care cannot be detached from the particular circumstances of deliberators, that caring deliberations are informed by the circumstances in which they arise. The point is that steadfast family loyalty does not exist in isolation from the real and recognisable troubles of the world. Neither caring nor ideals can be understood without reference to the context in which they are grounded, where this context is understood as concrete and particular, a living kaleidoscope of perspectives, interests, and values. Within this contextual framework, different ways of caring about family traditions, mathematical truth, or connoisseurship can be evaluated. Qualitative differences can be distinguished between the kind of steadfast loyalty to family traditions that promotes the destruction of both Montagues and Capulets and the kind that generates Romeo and Juliet's pledge to unite both families in love; between the selfless pursuit of mathematical truth that involves neglecting those for whom I am responsible and the same dedication that honours those responsibilities; between connoisseurship involving the expropriation of indigenous artefacts and the cultivation of an expert understanding and appreciation of the cultural significance of those artefacts.

The difference between responding morally and responding with care begins to evaporate once care is understood to have its basis in understandings of selves as selves-in-relation. The assumption that the distinction between ethics and care is beyond contention is not well founded, at least when we consider accounts of the relational reality of caring. As I proceed with my elaboration of care in the next chapter, I consider and reject other assumptions that operate to sustain the distinction between care and ethics. I address, for example, the assumption that, out of ethics and care, only the former has an evaluative dimension. I also look at the assumption that the distinction between ethics and care can be mapped onto the distinction between questions about how I should conduct my relations with others and questions about how I should live. The conclusion for which I argue is that what emerges when ethics and epistemology are redescribed around notions of relation rather than autonomy and impartiality are concepts of ethical care and partial reason, both of which accord significance to the possibility of creating and sustaining shared belief systems, mutual understandings, and intersubjective agreements.

This brings me to a final point that needs to be made in order to set the scene for the discussion about ethics and epistemology in the chapters that follow. In my critique of liberal moral philosophy in Chapter 1, I have shown how deontologists, utilitarians, and contract theorists construct an ethics in the service of, or subservient to, the epistemological ideals that are central to liberal rationalism: abstraction, universalisation, and impartiality. What I perceive in accounts of care constructed in opposition to reason are attempts to break this nexus between reason and ethics, to loosen the bonds between what is rational and what is morally right, what is irrational and what is morally wrong. The approach I am advocating, on the other hand, does not locate the problem with liberal moral philosophy primarily in its linking of the rational and the ethical and so does not construct care in opposition to reason. Rather than breaking the nexus between reason and ethics, the focus of my critique is on understanding the limitations imposed on the moral response when rationality is confined to the capacity for abstract, universal, and impartial thinking. It seems to me that retaining the nexus between ethics and reason provides the basis for developing alternative accounts of both ethics *and* reason, where neither moral responsiveness nor moral reasoning is separate from our concrete and particular responsibilities. In the development of this critique and the arguments that articulate the ways in which ethics and reason might be transformed, I mean to capture the sense in which ethics is as impoverished when it is restricted to a consideration of an abstract, universal, and impartial moral reason as it is when it is restricted to a consideration of moral practice. My criticism of the priority of epistemology over ethics in traditional moral philosophy need not imply that I endorse a reversal of this prioritising. The idea of a nexus, for me, suggests not that epistemology is included in ethics but that many of the philosophically interesting questions that arise in connection with ethics are epistemological questions, just as many of the philosophically interesting questions that arise in connection with epistemology are ethical questions. Both ethics and epistemology, then, generate the kinds of questions that Gilligan calls "questions about our perceptions of reality and truth; how we know, how we hear, how we see, how we speak."[58] So, while respecting the significance of the distinctions to be drawn between thinking, knowing, understanding, reasoning, and rationality in some philosophical argumentation, in the chapters that follow I link them as *epistemological* concepts[59] in order to reveal the consequences of retaining the nexus between epistemology and ethics, between partial reason and ethical care, while yet problematising the epistemological and ethical privileging of an abstract, universal, and impartial rationality.

NOTES

1. Gilligan, 'Hearing the Difference,' 122, says: "A feminist ethic of care begins with connection, theorized as primary and seen as fundamental in human life."

2. In Chapter 1 I show that liberal moral theory provides a less than adequate

account of public, formal encounters.

3.   For a more directly metaphysical approach to relation, see Whitbeck, 'A Different Reality.' For other ways of exploring the relatedness of selves, see, for example, Hoagland, *Lesbian Ethics,* and Mason Mullett, 'Inclusive Philosophy.' Hoagland's term "autokoenony" *(Lesbian Ethics,* 145) and Mason Mullett's concept of "relational thinking" (78–85) are both important contributions to a broader conception of selves than is available in liberal moral theory.

4.   Benhabib, 'The Generalized and the Concrete Other,' 163, refers to the standpoint or perspective of the generalised other as a concept of "self-other relations" that delineates "both moral perspectives and interactional structures." This suggests to me that it is both a standpoint we assume and a standpoint that governs our relation to the other. I take it, then, that the concept of the generalised other applies both to the self and to the other: I am supposed to be able to see as a generalised other myself and see others as generalised.

5.   I think this link is compatible with Benhabib's definitions. She says, ibid., 163, that the perspectives of the generalised and the concrete other "reflect the dichotomies and splits of early modern moral and political theory between autonomy and nurturance, independence and bonding, the public and the domestic, and more broadly, between justice and the good life. The content of the generalized as well as the concrete other is shaped by the dichotomous characterization, which we have inherited from the modern tradition."

6.   Ibid., 165.

7.   Ibid.

8.   See, for instance, Rawls, *A Theory of Justice,* 137.

9.   Benhabib, 'Generalized,' 166: "There is no real *plurality* of perspectives in the Rawlsian original position, but only *definitional identity.*"

10.   Ibid., 164, quoting Kohlberg, 'Justice as Reversibility: The Claim to Moral Adequacy of a Highest State of Moral Judgement,' in *The Philosophy of Moral Development,* 194: "Moral judgements involve role-taking, taking the viewpoint of others conceived as *subjects* and coordinating these viewpoints."

11.   Benhabib, 'Generalized,' 165. Expressed in other terms, rendering particularity irrelevant and even the elimination of the other as different from the self can be linked with Kant's objectives in establishing the Kingdom of Ends, where moral worth attaches "impersonally" to individuals. In Chapter 1, at note 57, I draw attention to the ambiguity of a notion of moral worth that, while it seems, on one hand, to make moral worth unconditional, seems, on the other, to make each individual indistinguishable from the next and perhaps, therefore, not irreplaceable.

12.   Ibid., 169: "The point is to think through the ideological limitations and biases that arise in the discourse of universalist morality through this unexamined opposition."

13.   Ibid., 167.

14.   Ibid., 168.

15.   References are to Friedman, 'Care and Context in Moral Reasoning.'

16.   For Kohlberg, morally mature responses to the Heinz dilemma assert the logical priority of life over property. See Locke, 'A Psychologist among the Philosophers, 22; Gilligan, *In a Different Voice,* 26. For a more sophisticated version of Jake's expression of this reasoning, see Kohlberg's account of Joan (Kohlberg, 'A Current Statement,' 528): "Her thinking . . . is centred on a single general principle, doing that which respects, preserves and enhances human dignity."

17.   Friedman, 'Care and Context in Moral Reasoning,' 198.

18.   Ibid., 193, quoting Kohlberg et al., *Moral Stages,* 20–21. See also Kohlberg, 'A

Current Statement,' 541, for a description of the care orientation as "a moral orientation to particularistic relationships of kinship and friendship."

19. Friedman, *What Are Friends For?*, 105, note 37. Chapter 4 (91–116) is a revised version of 'Care and Context in Moral Reasoning.'

20. Friedman draws additional conclusions about the gap between moral reasoning and moral practice. For reasons that will become clear in subsequent chapters, this is not a point I want to emphasise.

21. Noddings, *Caring*, 44.

22. Benhabib, 'Generalized,' 165.

23. Ibid.: "In this case the other is…constituted…as a consequence of total abstraction from his or her identity."

24. This is not necessarily an argument against principled reasoning per se (as Noddings, e.g., might insist). It is, however, an argument against approaches that quarantine principles from context. Kohlberg might respond by saying that this charge of inflexibility caricatures or parodies his position. His emphasis, however, in stage 6 deliberations is on "thinking . . . centred on a single general principle" (Kohlberg, 'A Current Statement,' 528). General principles, he says, "apply to all persons and situations" (497). Kant's response to Constant, to which I refer in Chapter 1, is indicative of similarly inflexible moral understandings. In anticipating how such stances might be defended, it is worth recalling that what is at issue are conceptions of *ethics*, of what constitutes *moral* responses, rather than whether responses are principled or whether principles are ethical. What I am criticising is the liberal insistence that only reasoning that is informed by considerations that are abstract, universal, and impartial is moral reasoning.

25. Benhabib, 'Generalized,' 163.

26. See my comments in note 4 about the application of the concept of the generalised other to both the self and the other.

27. I mean the term "relation" to refer to the connections between individuals. As will become clear later in this chapter, I draw moral implications from a range of relational considerations that are excluded from the moral frameworks established by liberal moral theory. In any particular situation, liberal moral theory is concerned to define as morally relevant only those aspects of the connections between individuals that are public and formal (as, e.g., the connection between contractor and contractee). I want to use the term "relation" to bring into moral consideration not only the aspects of public, formal situations that are *not* public and formal (e.g., for example, the concrete particularity of the contractor and contractee) but also those aspects of relation that are concrete, particular, and partial. What I am interested in is the sense in which individuals are always and already "selves-in-relation" and the implications for moral theory of this relatedness. I develop the concept of selves-in-relation later in this chapter.

28. See, for example, Baier's critique of individualism in ethics and epistemology and her concept of "second persons" in her essay 'Cartesian Persons.'

29. I agree with Benhabib, 'Generalized,' 165, when she says that the veil of ignorance governs, or places "epistemic restrictions" on, the reasoning of those presented with Kohlberg's hypothetical dilemmas as much as it does the Rawlsian deliberator.

30. Kohlberg, 'A Current Statement,' 489. 'The Six Moral Stages' table from which I draw this phrase was originally published in Kohlberg, 'Moral Stages and Moralization,' and in Kohlberg, *The Psychology of Moral Development*. Locke notes, 'Psychologist,' 36, that the philosophical concept on which Kohlberg bases his notion of the moral point of view is developed by Kurt Baier in *The Moral Point of View*.

31. Kohlberg, 'A Current Statement,' 496. For original publication details of 'The

Six Stages of Justice Judgement' table from which I draw this phrase, see Chapter 2, note 75.

32. I am not suggesting that all accounts of the Heinz dilemma will be the same but that they all, even socalled abstract ones, involve concrete relational considerations. That the specific relational contexts that influence moral reasoning include the relational contexts of reasoners or knowers as well as of players is a point I develop in Chapter 6.

33. Gilligan, 'Hearing the Difference,' 122.

34. Ibid., 121.

35. Gilligan, ibid., 120, is talking about bringing women's voices into theoretical frameworks: "Men's disconnection from women, formerly construed as the separation of the self from relationships, and women's dissociation from parts of themselves, formerly interpreted as women's selflessness in relationships, now appeared problematic."

36. Ibid., 123–124.

37. Ibid., 121.

38. One of the ways of demonstrating this point, as I indicate in Chapter 1, is to show that where the paradigmatic human voice considers relation that is not formal and public, it does so in the terms established by that voice. So, as Gilligan notes ('Moral Orientation and Moral Development,' 35), framed in these terms, the abortion dilemma is expressed as a conflict of rights or as a question of respect for human life.

39. Gilligan, 'Hearing the Difference,' 122.

40. See my reference to Code at note 69 in Chapter 2.

41. Moody-Adams, 'Feminist Inquiry and the Transformation of the "Public" Sphere in Virginia Held's *Feminist Morality'*, 162.

42. This might be so, even when, as I have suggested, the definition of moral reasoners as (ideally) autonomous and impartial has lost some of its cogency.

43. This emphasis on rational agreement is found in deontological and utilitarian as well as contractarian approaches. Although deontology applies the test of consistent universality, and utilitarianism applies the test of maximal happiness, both stress that the application of the tests are carried out by rational agents. As well as my argument in Chapter 1, see, for example, Kohlberg, 'The Six Moral Stages,' reprinted in 'A Current Statement,' 489: "[The p]erspective of a moral point of view . . . is that of any rational individual recognizing the nature of morality."

44. See my discussion about lying in Chapter 1 for an account of the link between what is moral and what is rational. Making a different point from mine, Locke notes Kohlberg's assumption that it would be irrational for the pharmacist to reverse his decision that property is worth more than life. Kohlberg says (quoted in Locke, 'Psychologist,' 32): "Presumably...if it were his life at stake, the druggist would be rational enough to prefer his right to life over his property and would sacrifice his property."

45. Kohlberg, 'A Current Statement,' 497.

46. Locke, 'Psychologist,' 35, makes a distinction between simple and ideal reversibility, arguing that the latter, which Kohlberg fails to distinguish from simple reversibility, is "a requirement imposed on moral judgements in order to ensure a form of impartial, rational agreement."

47. Defenders of Kohlberg might object that I have misunderstood his notion of reversibility, which is intended to convey the sense that, in taking another's point of view, I relinquish my own viewpoint. What I am arguing here, though, is that in order to secure this relinquishment, Kohlberg (in an exemplification of liberal moral theorists' assumptions about the constitution of the moral point of view) implicitly introduces a transcendent aspect to reversibility. Direct reversibility allows a reasoner to apply the "if

I were you" test. Establishing agreement on this basis does not secure the moral point of view. The universality required by the moral point of view is secured only by moving beyond the "if I were you" test of direct reversibility to the "regardless of who you and I are" test, which depends on being able to transcend the particular contexts in which we deliberate.

48. It may be objected that I am overstating Kohlberg's case here by limiting "rationality" to "acting in accordance with reversible or universalisable maxims." I have already noted (this chapter, note 44) that Kohlberg considers it rational to prefer one's own life over property. In line with my argument in Chapter 1, then, it seems that the pharmacist who says that Heinz should not steal the drug is trying to maintain two propositions simultaneously: "life is worth more than property" (which, according to Kohlberg, is a universal rational proposition) and "property is worth more than life" (which is the premise implied in the pharmacist's response to Heinz's request for a discount—or threat to steal the drug). For Kohlberg, this surely constitutes an irrational as well as an immoral response. I cannot see that Kohlberg leaves himself room to say that if the pharmacist wants to assert only the second proposition ("property is worth more than life"), he might be being immoral and rational. Indeed, the commitment to certain universal moral principles about the value of life seems to be taken by Kohlberg as an a priori condition of reason. Kohlberg certainly cannot concede that there might be two moral points of view about the relative values of life and property. Friedman, 'Care and Context in Moral Reasoning,' 201, notes that the pharmacist might have good reason for refusing to give the drug away, but in Friedman's scenario this refusal can be construed as both rational and moral.

49. Locke, 'Psychologist,' 36. As I have noted, Locke distinguishes between simple reversibility and ideal reversibility and argues that neither helps Kohlberg show that the latter proposition quoted earlier, needed to sustain the Kohlbergian theory of moral reasoning, is true.

50. For a more detailed discussion of reason as an end in itself, see Chapter 1.

51. Kant, *Groundwork*, 102.

52. This does not mean that selves-in-relation necessarily are aware of, or understand, their in-relatedness.

53. I realise that Gilligan's evidence is bound to support her conclusion that care is a moral response. Nevertheless, if care and ethics *are* to be distinguished, her evidence might be expected to yield to the different readings I explore here.

54. Gilligan, *In a Different Voice*, 98.

55. Ibid., 96, 99.

56. Ibid., 91.

57. Frankfurt, 'The Importance of What We Care About,' 258.

58. Gilligan, 'Letter to Readers, 1993'; Preface to 1993 edition of *In a Different Voice*, xiii.

59. Recognising that the same links are not necessarily made by the theorists I critique.

Chapter 4

Seeing Together: Care
as Disposition

The substance of my criticism of some feminist and nonfeminist approaches to care, which I discuss in Chapter 2, is that they may ultimately fail to disrupt the axioms that associate ethics with autonomous, impartial reasoners and care with the irrational or unreasoned response. These approaches are not consistent with a feminist project that is critical and interrogative rather than separatist or extensionist. For the critical, interrogative approach with which I have identified both the critical and the constructive aspects of my argument, the undermining of philosophical axioms—in this case the axioms that associate ethics with reason and care with the irrational—is critically important because these axiomatic assumptions not only silence women but also excise their capacity to speak. The task of disrupting or undermining axiomatic assumptions cannot be undertaken by the feminist philosopher who is not visible as a woman. To be visible as a woman involves self-consciously separating the experience of being a woman from the traditional philosophical account of the feminine by showing that the latter is derived not from a neutral philosophical viewpoint but from a viewpoint that judges all human experience against an implicitly male standard.

GILLIGAN'S "VISIBLE" VOICE

It seems clear to me that the task of separating the actual lived experience of women from stereotypical accounts of the feminine is precisely what Gilligan undertakes in *In a Different Voice*.[1] Her motive, according to her *Reply to Critics*[2] (but also evident in the original Introduction to *In a Different Voice*), is to explore the possibility of articulating a "different way of constituting the self and morality."[3] She specifically distances her approach from those approaches founded on the "equal but different" assumptions of complementarity by revealing the male bias in the (unasked) question "equal to what?" Rejecting such approaches because they can inquire only about women's adherence to, or deviation from, an implicitly male standard, Gilligan looks for a moral viewpoint that is not acknowledged within the traditional philosophical account of human moral experience. Like the traditional philosophical account of the feminine, this latter derives from a perspective that judges all human experience against an implicitly male standard.

Gilligan restates her motive in a defence of her methodology. She says: "To claim that there is a voice different from those which psychologists have represented, I need only one example—one voice whose coherence is not recognised within existing interpretive schemes."[4] As my argument in Chapter 2 about the logic of domination shows, it is important to note that existing, mainstream interpretive schemes do not necessarily exclude a consideration of caring. If my understanding about the way the logic of domination operates is sound, we certainly find a version of care in deontological stage theory that stresses justice, rights, and the morality of contract. As a step on the way to justice, care represents a form of moral reasoning that is both immature and inadequate yet is an intrinsic aspect of justice or contract-based moral theory. Care is constituted by what is excluded by rights and justice reasoning. As such, it is bound by a standard that endorses rights and justice reasoning. Care, then, is not discounted by this interpretive scheme as morally worthless. But its identification as an inferior form of moral response assures it that paradoxical status that is conferred by the logic of domination. In paradigmatic justice reasoning, care is *devalued* as a moral response but *invaluable* in the construction and maintenance of a noncaring (i.e., abstract, universal, and impartial) moral rationality. Justice is care transcended, where care represents the viewpoint bounded by concrete particularity, and justice represents "a perspective outside of that of . . . society."[5]

Interestingly, if Gilligan had been looking for either a *woman's* voice or a *caring* voice, she need have gone no further than what she calls the existing interpretive schemes. But what Gilligan sees is that to limit the understanding of care to the way it is portrayed in Kohlberg's third and fourth stages is to service only the stereotypical images that define women solely in terms of what they lack. For Kohlberg, women are invisible[6] yet fully accounted for in terms of the male norms established in his interpretive scheme. He is able not only to locate woman's place on man's moral map but also to explain why (most) women are morally inferior to (most) men. Following an intellectual trail blazed by Kant and Freud, Kohlberg knows where to look for women: not in the public realm of abstract, universal principles but in the sphere of the private, the affective, and the relational, where what matters to women resides. What I am saying is that the voice that Kohlberg associates with women and with care is a voice whose coherence is readily recognised within the philosophical paradigm of justice and contract.[7] Gilligan's exposure of the extent to which this paradigm relies on normative standards that are not neutral but male enables her to hear moral voices that are not constituted only by what they lack or by their exclusion from mature moral discourse.[8] To the extent that these are the voices of women and of caring *where women and care are not subordinate to justice,* they lack coherence for Kohlberg. Gilligan's insight is that Kohlberg finds the voices of women and care coherent only when what they say is morally insignificant.[9] Her attribution of moral significance establishes a framework in which both the form and the content of prevailing notions of morality are opened up to question.

In her most recent writing, Gilligan acknowledges that her early work leaves unresolved the question of whether care and justice coexist as accounts of human connection and separation or whether, by beginning with a premise about the centrality of relational realities, it is possible to explore new ways of doing ethics and other ways of reasoning where care does more than complement or supplement justice. Her thinking on this issue remains guarded, although when she refers to the account that links detachment and separation with psychological development and well-being as "a seedbed for lies," and when she talks about "the ongoing historical process of changing the voice of the world,"[10] it seems to me that she is willing to entertain the possibility that new conversations may herald new ways of thinking.[11]

What I want to do, having identified Gilligan's motives as reflecting the priorities I am endorsing as part of an approach that is critical and interrogative, is to see what happens when the concept of care is developed not only through an empirical examination of female experience but also through a process of philosophical analysis. My objective in this and the three subsequent chapters is to show that an ethics and an epistemology that are not constituted around the priorities, privilegings, and exclusions of liberal moral theory are conceptually distinct from the ethics and epistemology endorsed by that theory and, indeed, from the ethics and epistemology endorsed by philosophers who leave those priorities, privilegings, and exclusions intact.[12]   This objective involves developing the philosophical significance of Gilligan's finding about the coherence and significance of care into a statement about the coherence and significance of ethics and epistemology.

In moving toward this objective, I am not seeking to develop the concept of care as philosophically foundational, thereby appropriating for care the place preserved for justice by Kohlberg (et al.).[13] Philosophically, it seems to me, foundationalism can never avoid hardening into the autocratic stance that is blind to its own limitations. As Iris Murdoch notes, "[a]n idea which sheds much light may also effectively obliterate other ideas."[14]   Rather, I would expect the metaphysical notion of care to identify both foundationalism and relativism as examples of the bifurcating effects of the logic of domination. Similarly, I would expect care to emerge from philosophical scrutiny not necessarily rejecting abstraction, universalisation, and impartiality in favour of concrete, particular, and partial thinking but as complicating these distinctions, thereby offering the terms in which to give a more adequate account of human existence than is provided by existing explanatory frameworks, which operate through systems of privilege and exclusion.

"WE ARE CREATURES TO WHOM THINGS MATTER"[15]

In this chapter, I present a concept of care that not only avoids the pitfalls encountered by some feminist and nonfeminist versions of care but also has sufficient philosophical substance to be able to contribute toward the objective I have set myself: developing a conceptually distinct statement about the coherence and significance of ethics and epistemology. My starting point is to distinguish two different aspects of care, only one of which has been the focus of most accounts of ethical care. I argue that although we cannot talk about care coherently without talking about caring *action*, care is given more philosophical substance when it is also elaborated in the notion of care as *disposition*.[16] The inclusion of care as disposition, it seems to me, opens up the possibility of talking about the *inherent* value of care as well as its *instrumental* value and of bringing into consideration the *qualitative* as well as the *quantitative* aspects of the caring response.

I have found the work of Frankfurt to be a helpful catalyst in clarifying the distinction between care as action and care as disposition. Although I disagree not only with Frankfurt's conclusions but also with many of his basic premises and his mode of reasoning, I have nevertheless found that some of his observations about what it means to care contribute to my argument.

Frankfurt's innovation, I suggest, is to deem philosophically interesting the idea that human beings are "creatures to whom things matter." Philosophical inquiry, for Frankfurt, can be divided into three areas, each reflecting a "thematic and fundamental preoccupation of human existence."[17] Two of these— epistemology (derived from a concern with what to believe) and ethics (derived from a concern with how to behave)—are clearly delineated in the philosophical canon. The third area of philosophical inquiry, which derives from a concern with what to care about, explores the notion of importance, of mattering in the sense that there are things that matter to me or that are important to me.[18]

Frankfurt's contention is that, although questions about how to behave and what to care about are intimately connected,[19] ethics and caring originate from two distinct lines of questioning. On one hand, there are the questions that arise from a perception of *relation*. This involves the understanding that human life cannot be lived without encountering others and that that encounter takes different forms. This perception generates the desire to cultivate a sense of what is right and to express this sense in terms that define the grounds and limits of relational obligations. This is how Frankfurt delineates the concerns of ethics. On the other hand, there are questions that Frankfurt traces to the interest in "deciding what to do with *ourselves*."[20] These are questions concerning what matters to us, what is important to us, what we care about. If ethical concerns arise from a perception of *relation*, these care concerns arise from *self*-perception. They are, according to Frankfurt, addressed in terms of identifying not relational obligations but obligations to the self, the fulfillment of which ensures a sense of personal integrity.

This form of Frankfurt's argument—that there is a distinction between what is (impersonally) right and what is (personally) important—is the softer version of a much more radical statement that Frankfurt goes on to develop. In this stronger form, his assertion is that there is *always* and *necessarily* a distinction between what is cared about and the moral ideals that determine ethical considerations. This is not, of course, the same as asserting that there cannot be a coincidence between what is cared about and a moral ideal. It is, however, to say that, even when they coincide, each is distinguishable from the other.[21]

This point and its implications for Frankfurt's concepts of care and ethics are made clearer by looking at Frankfurt's two examples of how questions about importance (about what is cared about) and questions about moral rightness are distinguishable. In the first situation, Frankfurt considers someone faced with alternatives and no knowledge about which alternative is morally best. This person, Frankfurt says, might consider that the amount of time and effort needed to devote to working out the moral implications of each alternative cannot be justified. What I understand Frankfurt to be saying is that something more important than determining moral correctness claims this person's time and energy. In the second situation, Frankfurt finds someone who *does* know which alternative is morally best but who nevertheless chooses another option, where the latter reflects something of importance to that person. Frankfurt's insistence is that both these people take morality seriously but that both are capable of justifying their decision; that is, neither is moved by any consideration that they have to attribute to anything other than their capacity to reason.[22] So, in both situations we have someone who says that what is morally right is only one of the things to which he or she may accord importance and, therefore, that what is morally right may be overridden by other considerations of importance.

These illustrations help to clarify the stronger form of Frankfurt's argument because they elaborate his concepts of ethics and of care. It is important that caring, for Frankfurt, is something people *do* (the carer is "active in a certain way"[23]), rather than a way of reasoning or deciding. Caring ideals are captured in the activities associated with, for instance, love (in its several varieties),[24] steadfast family loyalty, the selfless pursuit of mathematical truth, connoisseurship,[25] and even avoiding pavement cracks.[26] Ethics, in contrast, is the search for principles under which to subsume action. What Frankfurt means, I think, is that the link between ethics and action, unlike the link between care and action, is indirect. Ethical ideals are supposed to guide action by testing, rather than by dictating, action. Thus, for Frankfurt, the categorical imperative per se does not stipulate specific actions (which would thereby render moral *judgment* unnecessary). Its force takes the form of a demand that an action must satisfy if it is to be considered a moral action.[27] So, an ethical principle (the categorical imperative, e.g.) tells me not how to act (i.e., whether to protect or abandon my child) but how to reason (i.e., what demand my action needs to satisfy for it to be morally right).[28] On the other hand, care *necessarily* entails certain behaviour or action. To abandon that for which I care would be internally inconsistent, a violation of my self-identity as someone who cares, of my self-reflexive sense of agency.[29]   The link between care and action, for Frankfurt, is direct, then, when my action is the action of one who cares. Protecting the child about whom I care is not the result of a decision to care but of an actual state of affairs[30]: it is brought about by my sense of who I am, a sense that is constituted by that with whom or with which I am identified. So, for Frankfurt, to abandon the child about whom I care is to violate not an ethical ideal but myself.

Frankfurt secures the distinction between ethics and caring in two other respects. First, despite the fact that they are contingent on both personality and personal circumstances, judgments based on moral reasoning, he argues, are *impersonal*.   According to Frankfurt: "What renders these judgements impersonal is that the claims they make are not limited to the person who makes them; rather, it is implicit that anyone who disagrees with the claims must be mistaken."[31]   On the other hand, judgments based on care are *personal* in the sense that they are not logically binding on anyone but the carer.[32]   What they lack, in Frankfurt's terms, is "logical and causal necessity."[33]   But this, Frankfurt claims, does not mean that judgments based on care are arbitrary or otherwise not compelling or unconstrained. Frankfurt's second distinction is between the *ethical* necessity[34] involved in following the dictates of moral maxims (even if these maxims test, rather than generate, principles of action) and what he calls the *volitional* necessity that governs action associated with what we care about. Responding to ethical necessity requires competence in exercising the sort of (intellectual) skills that can translate the categorical imperative or the principle of utility into notions of right and wrong actions.[35]   My understanding of Frankfurt is that ethical necessity ushers in a moral "I must," where the compulsion or constraint originates not in an act of self-definition but in the impersonal demands of rational consistency. As I go on to explain, Frankfurt's conception of ethics is such that ethics is not constitutive of my sense of self, while caring (acting in a way that is consistent with my cares) is self-defining. The "I must," then, places the moral subject (the "I") under the rubric of the universal, so that what the "I must" reflects is the notion of obligation per se rather than what is important in making individual lives coherent. I should note at this stage that Frankfurt's notion of ethics has to be gleaned by inference and has, in consequence, a slightly slippery feel to it. However, it seems to me that if the recognition of *volitional* necessity binds together "the moments in the life of a person who cares about something,"[36] giving that life a sense of purpose, (or, as Alasdair MacIntyre might say, a sense of narrative unity[37]), it seems reasonable to infer that *ethical* necessity fails to provide such existential coherence. In contrast with ethical necessity, volitional necessity describes the "I must," where the sense of compulsion or constraint arises not from the impersonal demands of rational consistency but from a sense of the responsibilities I shoulder as a result of my caring. Frankfurt's point is that when I act as a person who cares, it is the care itself that generates action. Although the locus for action is different, this move reminds me of the connection made by some communitarian ethicists.[38]   The communitarian might find a locus for action in relational characteristics or social identity, so that when I reason or make judgments about what to do, I do so as the bearer of some social identity. Frankfurt locates the agent primarily as a person with cares, so that, when I reason or make judgments about what to do, I do so as someone who cares. Frankfurt does not mean that every action can be accounted for in this way: he distinguishes caring activity from actions generated by habits, "involuntary regularities," desires, beliefs, and impulses.[39] These actions may be bound by some kind of necessity,[40] but not the volitional necessity that distinguishes caring activity from activity generated by, say, habit.[41]

Frankfurt intends the notion of volitional necessity, which he admits is a "somewhat obscure kind of necessity,"[42] to capture a number of paradoxical aspects of the caring response. There is the sense, for example, in which the carer is *not* bound by necessity at all. The more philosophically common definitions of necessity—causal and logical necessity—are commonly associated with the demands of logic or with ability or capacity. In these more common senses, to say "I can do no other" either means, "There are no good reasons for doing other" or "I am not strong enough to do other" or "I am incapable of doing other." This is not what is meant by volitional necessity. Thus constrained, I might say, "I can do no other," even though there are good reasons for doing something else, and I am sufficiently strong and capable of doing something else (i.e., I am not logically or causally restrained from doing something else). I am, in other words, *able* to do other than I do, except for the constraint that is generated by care itself.

Frankfurt's meaning can be drawn out of an example he provides of how volitional necessity operates:

If a mother who is tempted to abandon her child finds that she simply cannot do that, it is probably not because she knows (or even because she cares about) her duty. It is more likely because of how she cares about the child, and about herself as its mother, than because of any recognition on her part that abandoning the child would be morally wrong.[43]

His point is that this person is constrained to do what she does only by the "I must" associated with her caring. While it may coincide with the ethically necessary "I must," the volitionally necessary "I must" keeps us faithful to a personal ideal by making alternative courses of action "unthinkable."[44] Abandoning (or otherwise violating) what I care about undermines my personal integrity in a way that abandoning an ethical ideal does not. An ethical ideal, with its emphasis on universality and formal consistency, is not constitutive of my sense of self. What I care about, which reflects my personal ideals, my personal passions, confers a sense of coherence on my own existence and is therefore integral to my sense of self. This insight enables Frankfurt to draw out the sense in which what is of most philosophical interest about care is the importance of caring itself. What matters to me when I care are not only what I care about but also my caring. We are creatures to whom things matter, and one of the things that matter is caring. We are, that is, creatures who care about care.[45]

On this point Frankfurt himself concedes the possibility that the notion of care might evaporate in the circularity of an argument about whether more philosophical interest resides in caring itself or in caring about caring. This circularity reveals another paradoxical aspect of the caring response. Frankfurt's concept of volitional necessity is supposed to capture the sense in which the carer is passive and determined in the face of constraints generated by care itself and yet active and autonomous in taking responsibility for those cares. Volitional necessity is both self-imposed and imposed involuntarily. These are points of salience in the critique of orthodox deontological theory. In the example of the mother and child, Frankfurt would say that the fact that a parent cares about a child tells us something about that person's will. That is, we can account for a person responding with a protective act rather than with abuse or indifference in terms of what the person chose to do. But Frankfurt's point is that to couch this account *solely* in terms of duty is to misunderstand the nature of will or at least to understand it too narrowly as relating only to what we can directly control.[46] Such an account applied to Frankfurt's example would either discount or fail to register the consequences of care for action. For Frankfurt, care is both a fact about will (in that the choice to care is a voluntary choice) and a fact about something that is *not* willed (in that the choice to care is not necessarily wholly under the carer's voluntary control).[47]

This is a complex and enigmatic point, and I want to make clear what I understand Frankfurt to be saying. It seems to me that the critical point of tension in Frankfurt's account of volitional necessity is sustained by the paradox that caring is both a matter of will and a matter of necessity. That is, the sense that care is done "at will" is not weakened by the sense that I "cannot but care."[48] Frankfurt points out that this is not as singular a problem as it might seem, with similar apparent contradictions occurring elsewhere in philosophy. He cites as example the concept of logical necessity, where constraint by logical tenets is not experienced as a loss of autonomy or will.[49]

Frankfurt's doubts about the adequacy of the post-Kantian concept of will are similar to those articulated by Murdoch. What he conveys with the concept of volitional necessity is a sense of volition not expressed by the notion of what Murdoch calls the "empty choosing will," which wanders unconstrained in a world that is not in any way connected or tied to the chooser.[50] This empty choosing will is isolated[51] from the "contamination" that connection and ties represent.[52] In this sense, "I choose to do this" is assumed to mean the opposite of "I submit to a rule" or "I obey." But for Frankfurt, as for Murdoch, will cannot be other than situated, constrained by the necessities that are generated by the realities of human existence.

My proposition is that Frankfurt's concept of volitional necessity reshapes the understanding of will so that decisions and choices can be seen to be the concrete expression of the "structures of value round about us,"[53] rather than, or as well as, the abstract expression of impersonal preference. What follows from this, as I now proceed to argue, is that two distinct aspects of care, which have not been clearly distinguishable in most attempts to construct or critique care as a feminist ethic,[54] emerge for consideration. By clarifying the nature of these two aspects of care and determining how each contributes to caring, a clearer picture of the ethic of care emerges.

CARE AS ACTION

My discussion of these two aspects of care grows out of Frankfurt's insight that caring is both a matter of will and a matter of necessity. Frankfurt summarises the paradox in three propositions: "(a) the fact that a person cares about something is a fact about his will, (b) a person's will need not be under his own voluntary control, and (c) his will may be no less truly his own when it is not by his own voluntary doing that he cares as he does."[55] The first aspect of care, which is already well canvassed in feminist theorising about care, is caring action. Caring action is action that shows that I care: the protection of a child, the phone call to a friend, the visit to a parent. Caring actions are, I want to say, done *at will* in the sense that they are associated with a decision to act in a certain way. I am talking about the sense, clearly conceded by Frankfurt, in which the mother *does* have a choice about whether to abandon or protect her child, in which it is open to me either to tend or to neglect my friends and parents. Indeed, that such (caring) actions are carried out with a sense of agency, with a sense that they are deliberate, is an intrinsic part of what makes them *caring* actions rather than actions associated with, for example, habit.[56] Ruddick's work on maternal thinking shows, among other things, that the activities of care are necessarily neither automatic nor instinctive nor spontaneous[57] but are associated with a process of rational deliberation and reflection on the demands that inform the practices of care, which, in her analysis, are the practices of mothering.[58] There will doubtless continue to be philosophical argument and disagreement about how these demands and practices are constituted and how they relate to the ethic of care. In this discussion, I leave these questions aside and underline the fundamental point that we cannot talk about care coherently without talking about caring action and that caring action involves the decision to act in a caring way. Caring involves making choices and decisions that may be so obvious and mundane that we hardly register them as decisions or so agonising and complex that no choice seems to be the right one. Importantly, though, whether the care that my action honours is for intimates or nonintimates, its expression is properly seen as an act of volition, as something that I decide rather than something that is determined by the toss of a coin, a habitual reflex, or some other process over which I have no control.

I have said that we cannot talk about care coherently without talking about caring action and that caring action involves my decision to act in a caring way. But neither can we talk about care coherently by considering caring action *only* in terms of a decision to act caringly. To limit our understanding of care in this way would be to overlook or underrate the significance of three considerations about caring.

The first consideration is that the sense in which I *do* have a choice about whether to abandon or protect my child, to tend or neglect my friends and parents seems to be overridden by the sense in which I cannot choose other than to protect or tend *while I care*. In other words, part of the decision to abandon and neglect would be the decision to cast myself as not-caring. A familiar (though seldom admitted) aspect of the frustrations of care is captured in the feeling that "if only I did not care, I could act differently." What this "if only" expresses is the sense in which, while I care, I make decisions as one-who-cares, despite the fact that these decisions may involve heartache and anxiety. I might decide to neglect my child and others for whom I might have cared in order to spare myself various miseries,[59] but I cannot do so under the rubric of care. I cannot decide to neglect while I am one-who-cares. We might say, then, that the decision to act caringly does not arise in a neutral context but in a relational context where the decision maker acts, in relation to what is cared about, as one-who-cares. This does not imply that the fact that I care necessarily determines what I should do. Heartache and anxiety arise precisely because the fact that I care does not mean that I necessarily know what to do or that I necessarily act in a way that shows I care.

A second consideration, which provides an important refinement to the first, is that the kind of choices I have associated with caring action and the decision to act in a caring way seem not to be experienced as "to care or not to care" choices but as decisions premised on "given that I care." The choice about whether to abandon or protect, neglect or tend, is *not* necessarily a choice about whether (or not) to care. For example, it does not follow that a mother who is tempted to abandon her child is necessarily tempted to stop caring for her child. In other words, there is no necessary correlation between care and particular caring actions. In a world full of "real and recognizable trouble,"[60] mothers do abandon their children while still caring for them: they abandon them in order to protect them. What I am pointing to is the difference between decisions premised on caring and decisions premised on an absence of care or on indifference. This distinction is not noticed, or not regarded as important, by Frankfurt. His distinction is between caring and neglecting or caring and abandoning. I am suggesting that a more telling distinction is drawn between caring and indifference or not caring. To conflate the choice between caring and indifference into the choice between caring and neglecting is to acknowledge care only in a quantitative sense, so that deciding whether to neglect or care becomes an exercise in allocating the resources of care. What I want to draw out here is the sense in which the choice about how to act, about how to express my care (about whether or not to abandon a child, whether or not to visit my parents, whether or not to phone a friend), is not necessarily a choice about whether or not to care. My suggestion is that the premise "given that I care" is indicative of a qualitative relation by which caring decisions are informed. Again, this points to the fact that caring decisions are not made in a vacuum but in a relational context of caring.

The final consideration involves the sense that, for selves-who-care, the situation itself is active in the process of choosing. In other words, the situation itself makes demands. Whatever we choose, however we act, we do not choose or act as individual agents exercising autonomous wills but as selves-in-relation. In the traditions criticised by Frankfurt and Murdoch, the "empty choosing will" operates in, or on, an essentially passive world. As selves-who-care, however, we have the sense that our wills are constantly subject to the contingencies that inhere in the context of our caring. As selves-who-care we cannot, therefore, consider our wills to be free from determination. Indeed, that caring actions are not carried out in isolation from the reality of "how things are," that they are always provisional and subject to modification according to circumstances, is an intrinsic part of what makes caring actions relational rather than actions associated with autonomous individuals.

CARE AS DISPOSITION

These three considerations or insights, which arise from the carer's experience of care as action, reveal a second dimension of care that I call care as *disposition*. I suggest that care as disposition establishes the philosophical substance of care as a feminist ethic. What care as disposition opens up is the possibility of illuminating care in philosophical terms in a way that may not be apparent when the concept of care is developed mainly through an empirical examination of female experience[61] or when care is seen as the vehicle for either enforcing an oppressive sexual status quo[62] or extending women's emotional work into the formal, public domain.[63]

If care as action captures the sense in which caring is done "at will," care as disposition refers to the sense in which I "cannot but" care. This is the moment to distance my argument from the conclusion reached by Frankfurt about the paradox that caring is both a matter of will and a matter of necessity. It is important that Frankfurt considers the paradox to be resolved once we understand that the notions of "at will" and "involuntarily" can be sustained simultaneously.[64] Clearly, for him, this resolution lies in extending the concept of "at will" to include situations in which I cannot completely determine what I will, where the notion of "deciding" what to do is in tension with the sense that I could not but act in a certain way.

I am wary of such a resolution. Partly, my wariness is due to the possibility that resolving difficulties in this way leads to an oversimplification of the complex links between care as action and the disposition to care. In this case, what is "rescued" from the paradox are the concept of my will as my own and the validity of talking about decisions, choices, and actions as properties of individuals. Mainly, however, my wariness is due to the tendency for such a resolution to keep the focus firmly on care as action, on care as a function of what my will "truly *is*."[65] Such a focus, I think, risks sharpening an image of human individuality in which autonomy and choice are far more salient than Frankfurt might have intended them to be.[66]

To talk about care as disposition, however, I need to be able to talk about an aspect of care in which the paradox—whereby caring is both done "at will" and yet entails the sense that I "cannot but" care—is not *resolved* but *sustained*. Without a concept of care as involving something more than, or other than, action, it is hard to account philosophically for the three considerations or insights that arise from the experience of care as action: that decisions to act caringly arise in a relational context, that caring decisions are informed by qualitative relation, and that caring actions are undertaken by selves-in-relation.[67] What these insights reveal is that if we limit our concept of care to care as action, we, at best, restrict and, at worst, prevent consideration of care as anything more than the capacity to act in a caring way toward others.

What I am seeking here is a way of explaining how conceiving care as both a matter of will *and* a matter of necessity, as both action and disposition, opens up the possibility of talking about the relational context of caring and the inherent *qualitative* value of the caring relation. It is my contention that neither the relational context of caring nor the inherent value of the caring relation can be talked about coherently when the concept of care is limited to care as action. Neither, I submit, does care as action generate discussion about the self as carer. I want to show how care as disposition fills out these three philosophical dimensions of care by looking again at care as action. My interest is in how practical acts of caring might be reconceived if the paradox between will and necessity is sustained. What I want to capture is the idea that care is a rational response to an appreciation or awareness of the reality of selves-in-relation, where this reality involves more than the meeting of needs. If caring reality is confined to neediness, we are left with an instrumental version of care that can be understood in terms of an instrumental rationality. What I want to develop are concepts of care and of reason that sustain ethical and epistemological imperatives premised on the inherent *value* and the inherent *rationality* of care for selves-in-relation. What I will show is that the liberal assumption that care is irrational or unreasoned or accounted for solely in terms of an instrumental rationality reflects a failure to understand that care is subject to the constraints of reason, even though the reason by which care is constrained is not the impartial reason of liberal moral thought.

There is, obviously, a sense in which care as action *is* an instrumental response to the demands of others. I want to take this "demand-meeting" aspect of care as a starting point for an elaboration of care as disposition. When I talked earlier of the protection of a child, the phone call to a friend, the visit to a parent, I was offering examples of actions that respond to the needs or the demands of others with care. These examples, however, encompass only a narrow sense in which care is a response to the demands of others. To assume that this narrow sense of responding to demands provides an adequate account of care as a response to another is, I think, to impute only instrumental value to care, to see care as a means to an end or as a substitute for other "assets" of which a person may be deprived. Such a version of care might be illustrated with examples of the needs of, and responses to, people with AIDS or people who are homeless, where care clearly emerges as a way of compensating for a deficit: in these cases, the loss of health or shelter. Care in this instrumental sense arises only in response to needs; we cease to care once there are no needs to be met.[68]

I do not find this instrumental version of care helpful, because it fails to establish the relational context of caring. In other words, in celebrating only the instrumental value of care, what is missed is the notion of the inherent value of the caring relation itself. The mistake its proponents make, I think, is to assume that establishing the instrumental value of care is a *sufficient*, rather than a *necessary*, condition of establishing an ethic of care. For the latter proposition— that instrumental caring is a necessary component of an ethic of care—there may be a cautious case to be made.[69] However, to presume that instrumental care establishes sufficient grounds for an ethic of care is to risk perpetuating stereotypical assumptions about those who give and those who receive care.[70]

The sense in which care is more than a response to the demands of others emerges from the observation made by Frankfurt that we are creatures to whom things matter. What I suggest is that, where meeting needs in the instrumental sense *quantifies* care, the notion of "mattering" reveals care as a *quality*. What care describes, then, is not (or not only) my *action* but my *disposition*. Care describes my action when I protect, phone, or visit you. But it also describes me, by revealing me as a person to whom something—that is, you—matters. What I establish when I care for you is not (or not only) that you have needs that I can meet but that you matter to me. The failure of care is experienced not only as the failure to meet needs but as the failure to be disposed as one-who-cares. This latter failure, which seems to be the more significant, conveys the sense that caring involves "mattering" and that "mattering" is not necessarily equivalent to the meeting of needs.

This link between caring and "mattering" points to a serious difficulty for the assumption that the meeting of needs constitutes a sufficient condition for establishing an ethic of care. Confining care in this way means that what matters is conceivable only in terms of things to which needs can be imputed, effectively eliminating all nonliving and most nonhuman things.[71] But what matters may have needs that are not relevant to my caring, or my caring may be unrelated to its needs, or, indeed, it may not make sense to talk about its having needs.[72] In any case, what I mean to clarify by linking caring and mattering is that care is the qualitative expression of your mattering to me, that to care is to be disposed to you because you are one-who-matters to me. What I do when I care, then, is sustain particular kinds of relation, ones that are not adequately portrayed as instrumental, needs-engendered relations.

I have established that the philosophical interest in care is not confined to care as action but extends to care as disposition. What I want to do now is show that care as disposition is not arbitrary, not instinctive, and not to be understood as "just another response." I suggest that the concept of care as disposition is another crucial element in establishing not only that care is an *ethical* response, as I argued in Chapter 3, but that care can also be understood as a *rational* response, as an expression of the realities of selves-in-relation that generate particular ethical imperatives and constraints.

It is important to draw a distinction between my concept of care as disposition and the way the concept of care as disposition has been understood by others. For me, care as disposition does not imply that care is defined only as an emotional response. Neither does it entail understanding care as just one response among many possible responses. Tronto is one theorist for whom care as disposition is subject to such limitations. Although she introduces the idea that "[c]are is both a practice and a disposition,"[73] she focuses her account on care as a practice, fearing that the emphasis on care as a disposition leads to a version of care in which "any individual's ideals of care fit into the world view that the individual already possesses."[74] As I interpret her concerns, they relate to the commodification of care, the warm fuzziness (Tronto uses terms like sentimental and romantic[75]) engendered by corporate sloganising of the caring theme, where the theme is completely detached from, and unsupported by, caring acts. As will become clear, my use of the term "disposition" does not entail defining care as an emotional response or as the project of "an autonomous individual who is motivated to care and for whom care is analogous to just any other project."[76] For me, the value of the idea of care as disposition is precisely that it clarifies the sense in which care is a moral stance in which practical acts of caring, the self as carer, and the relational context of care are evaluated by selves identified as selves-in-relation. As well, I find that, if consideration of care as disposition along with practical acts of caring can be shown to sustain the paradox between will and necessity, the ethic of care emerges as the expression of reality for selves-in-relation, a concept far removed philosophically from Tronto's attitudinal care, which she associates with care as disposition.

The establishment of the concept of care as disposition is, as I have said, a crucial step in arguing that the ethic of care is a rational response. Now I want to show how care as disposition is subject to the strong ethical imperatives implied in my concept of "seeing together." Seeing together invokes the notion of a reality that is constrained by, or dependent on, the particular kinds of relation sustained by care.

SEEING TOGETHER

The concept of seeing together is one of the key ideas on which my argument is based, and its full elaboration in both ethical and epistemological terms forms a substantial component of the remaining chapters. For me, however, the concept of seeing together first arises in the attempt to account philosophically for the particular kinds of relation that are sustained by care. Specifically, it strengthens the account of the strong ethical imperative that I want to associate with the idea of care as disposition and clarifies the sense in which ethical care can be said to be the expression of reality for selves-in-relation.

My concept of seeing together germinates in the idea of attention as it is developed by Murdoch. For Murdoch, attention is "a just and loving gaze directed upon an individual reality."[77] It is "a patient, loving regard, directed upon a person, a thing, a situation."[78] Attending "properly" means seeing the demands of a situation, accurately discerning "how things are" in a world where we are concerned and engaged participants rather than disinterested and detached spectators. The "patient eye of love"[79] does not look *at*, like the "heartless long-distanced look"[80] of traditional metaphorisations of vision. It looks *into*, it establishes the intimacy of eye contact, it is contemplative, meditative, continuous and reveals a reality in which the self, the see-er, is a "smaller and less interesting object"[81] than it has traditionally appeared to be.

What can be inferred from the account of attention is the inappropriateness of equating moral agency with detachment and autonomy, of portraying moral agents as essentially indifferent to anything other than themselves. As I show in Chapter 1, the liberal moral agent is, above all, a rational being, and the demands of liberal morality are ultimately identical with the demands of reason. Reason requires the separation of the knowing subject (the self) from the object of knowledge (the other). Attention, by contrast, involves a transformation of the subject–object distinction. This does not imply a loss of identity on the part of the subject or the object,[82] but a shift of emphasis, a relaxing of the need to assert an autonomous, independent identity. Neither does attention necessarily preclude the ability to control, at least in the sense that a "just and loving gaze" may help us anticipate or predict the demands of particular situations. What is relinquished is the objective of control that is informed by the desire to dominate and contain the other.

Attention involves the idea of meeting the other as subject, so that neither the other nor the self is objectified by the encounter.[83] This is a process that relinquishes the objectives of control and domination of the other. Control and attention are antonymic. The controlling self, for Murdoch, is detached and objective, possessed of "anxious avaricious tentacles."[84] The attentive self, perceiving the objectives of control and domination to be a fantasy, stills or relaxes its egocentricity. As Murdoch says: "In intellectual disciplines and in the enjoyment of art and nature we discover value in our ability to forget self, to be realistic, to perceive justly. We use our imagination not to escape the world but to join it."[85] This forgetting of self is nothing like the chronic self-denial that results in a loss of identity. Neither does it describe the "peculiar habit of self-effacement" that is "like having an inaudible voice."[86] In another paradoxical move, the forgetting of self describes a stronger notion of self, stronger, that is, not only compared with the effaced or denied self but also compared with the self who is supposed to be detached and objective. If attention is conceptually linked with humility,[87] what is implied is not submission but modesty. Partly, the modesty of attention is accounted for by the fact that what attention reveals is always partisan or biased. In another, crucial, sense, however, what attention reveals is also perspectival or fragmentary. The self who is forgotten in attention is the autonomous self, the self who is whole (rather than fragmentary), self-contained (rather than perspectival), the self who acts on the world as a bearer of rights, the self who deliberates as a detached, neutral observer. When I attend, however, I have a sense of my receptivity, my connectedness, a sense that I am constituted in the relation established by attention. The solitary self gives way to the relational self, the self who sees itself not as acting *on* the world but as acting *in* the world where its own relatedness is constituted, the self whose reflexive consciousness knows itself through an awareness of its own attentive practices.

I said that my concept of seeing together germinates in Murdoch's notion of attention. The significance of Murdoch's insight into the attentive response is that it sheds light on an aspect of caring that is not instrumental, where care is an end in itself. Murdoch draws out the crucial distinction between attention and indifference, where attention establishes what I am calling the realities of selves-in-relation.

As I have noted in my comments about Frankfurt, the key to articulating the notion of care as disposition and to opening up the dimensions of care that involve consideration of the relational context of caring, the inherent value of the caring relation and the self as carer, is to find a concept that unambiguously sustains the tension between will and necessity. Caring, I have said, involves both will (because caring actions are chosen rather than automatic responses) and necessity (because we "cannot but" respond with care). The term endorsed by Murdoch as sustaining this tension is "obedience." She talks of a "notion of the will as obedience to reality, an obedience which ideally reaches a position where there is no choice."[88]

The term "obedience" does not find great resonance in the conceptual scheme I associate with an ethic of care. Neither does the notion of reality as revealing "how things are" or as set apart from human volitions or social constructs have a place in philosophical discourse that is informed by the embedded and embodied insights of contemporary feminisms.[89] My suggestion, however, is that such considerations do not necessarily require that we must abandon attempts to link care with a concept of reason and reality, to describe care as subject to the constraints and imperatives entailed by rationality, and to argue that the ethic of care provides a more adequate account of our moral potential than other ethics. It seems to me that the sense of constraint or imperative conveyed by obedience can be retained while yet moving away from foundationalist constructions of reason and reality by developing the concept of *seeing together*.

The concept of seeing together takes the central insights of attention but transforms them by placing them in the context of *relation* and *partiality*. Selves who attend are relational selves, or selves-in-relation. Crucially, attention goes on *in relation;* it is something we do as selves-in-relation. What is revealed by me attending to you is revealed *to us,* not to me and to you individually. What guides attention lies within our relation: I attend because you matter to me, because our particular relation matters to me. That relation is marked by its partiality in a double sense: our connection is not complete or direct, and our connection is marked by our personal preferences or biases. But as selves-in-relation we are relational not only in the interpersonal sense but also in that we are embedded or situated in particular contexts and in that we are self-reflexively aware of our positioning in interpersonal and contextual relation. When we attend as selves-in-relation, then, what attention reveals are partial insights about relation rather than direct connections with things as they really are.

Introducing relation and partiality into the concept of attention transforms Murdoch's insights. For her, attention is a way of *ridding* the self of partiality and of relation in order to see things as they really are. This is apparent in Murdoch's example of the mother (M) and her daughter-in-law (D). In order to see the "truth" about D, to see D as she "really" is, M need not attend to the concrete particularity of her relation with D. Indeed, in Murdoch's example, M imagines that D has died or migrated. In other words, M's "ceaseless work"[90] need not involve the concrete and particular D.[91] M's objective is to see D's "independent reality." In contrast with the concept of *seeing together,* this kind of connection establishes that we (for any particular "we") are *seeing the same thing.* This is the sense, noted by Bowden, in which, for Murdoch, "just and loving attention simply will progressively reach towards the perfection of a direct connection with the world."[92]

My concept of seeing together draws a seemingly disparate source into the elaboration of attention. Although attention is not a term used by Haraway, her work on critical positioning establishes a crucial dimension that is missing from Murdoch's account. For Haraway, to be critically positioned is to understand that our accounts of reality are partial, in the senses of being both partisan and fragmentary,[93] and that this partiality carries with it an obligation to seek out, rather than to deny, other perspectives and to take responsibility for how we see. To be "attentive," on these terms, is to see the relation between the self and the other in all its complexity, to "join with another, to see together without claiming to be another."[94] Attention is attuned to resonances, to the sense of affinity that yet honours otherness, difference, and specificity.[95] Murdoch's notion of attention portrays M as engaged in a search for the real D and ultimately, in a foundational sense, for the real world. Haraway's "attentiveness," on the other hand, locates reality in the partial relations that give both M and D their senses of self, of each other, and of the contexts in which mothers and daughters-in-law interact. What Haraway points to, I think, is the sense in which we can retain concepts of reason and reality as constraints on our practices of caring and knowing without resorting to foundationalist constructions of reason and reality if we understand the establishment of reality as a process of seeing together rather than as something that exists independently of our seeing. If establishing a sense of reality is primarily a question of seeing the same thing, then what is integral to our understanding of reality is the connection between the individual's attention and reality itself. If establishing a sense of reality is primarily a question of seeing together, then what is integral to our understanding of reality is the relation between us.

As I have said, the concept of seeing together first arises for me in the attempt to account philosophically for the particular kinds of relation that are sustained by care. Its significance, which I continue to develop in the next chapters, is that it reveals selves not as a freely contracting, autonomous moral agents but as selves-in-relation: selves who are both relational and partial. The autonomous moral self encounters others in a sequence of moves choreographed by abstract principles: principles that discount what is unique in the encounter and that distance deliberators from their deliberations.[96] The autonomous moral self is isolated from the neediness of others by the principles that govern its action[97]; it defines its existence in terms of its detachment. But the relational self is constituted ethically by the encounter with another. In the very process of attending to the other, where attention is not separable from our concrete relations or our partiality, the relational and partial self comes into being.

It is important to note that arguing for a concept of the relational and partial self does not necessarily present a challenge to the liberal moral views of relation. Those who consider the relational and partial account of the self to provide a more adequate picture of moral life might simply be considered to be morally deficient by proponents of other views. As I have said, these other views easily accommodate the idea that relation might be other than freely contracted, on condition that these other forms of relation are confined to the realm of the private and personal. Similarly confined, the concept of the relational and partial self actually affirms the moral insignificance of the private realm. The relational self is the self who relinquishes the objectives of control; it is the self who is constituted in the attentive process. While moral agency is confined to selves who are autonomous, selves who are relational and partial will not interest those exploring the moral, public realm.

What I want to do, however, is redescribe the concept of the relational self so that it does not simply maintain the complementarity between the givenness of relation in the private realm and the freely contracted relations in the public realm of the autonomous self. This redescription sustains the tension between autonomy and relation. It seems to me that where this tension is not sustained, dichotomous thinking about relation and autonomy, private and public, is propagated. The confinement of autonomy to the public realm and relation to the private realm reinforces the philosophical grounds for devaluing the private realm and the relational and partial self, thereby serving to retain the framework in which the logic of domination operates. A redescription of the self that sustains the tension between autonomy and relation will disrupt many of the dichotomous assumptions that have confined care to the realm of the irrational, the unreasoned, or the strictly instrumental.

My suggestion is that this redescription might be based on Frankfurt's account of the self who cares, the self as a creature to whom things matter. Frankfurt's account of the caring self and the volitional necessity that constrains the activity of this caring self opens up the possibility of understanding the self as both autonomous and relational.[98] The extent to which the self is autonomous is captured in the experience of care as action. At the same time, however, this action takes place under the necessity of the self disposed to care, the relational and partial self to whom caring itself is important.

CARE AND EVALUATION

Having linked these possibilities with Frankfurt's argument, an immediate qualification is required. What I find lacking in Frankfurt's account of the caring self is any acknowledgment that, as selves-who-care, we do not exist in a state of isolation from what is cared about and the relational context of caring. This renders aspects of Frankfurt's account fundamentally problematic, for what Frankfurt's account of the caring self omits is an exploration of the *relational* and *evaluative* aspects of caring. These are precisely the dimensions I have added to caring with the concept of seeing together, where seeing together involves not a direct connection with the world but the partial connections of selves-in-relation. In the process of seeing together, we are constantly checking, judging, and assessing not only the appropriateness of our practical acts of caring but also our own worth as carers about care. What seeing together reveals is "how things are," not as a remote metaphysical construct but as a consideration of what concrete reality prevails in this particular context.

Part of caring, then, is the evaluation of caring action as an expression of care. When we attend to children, parents, or friends, one aspect of the realities revealed to us as selves-in-relation is the effect of our caring. If we attend well, we will be able to protect without overprotecting, to show concern without manipulating or harassing.[99] The point is that as selves-in-relation we cannot judge these things without attending: we can assess only whether actions are caring actions, whether they have worth as caring actions, by attending.

But there is another kind of evaluation going on when we care that is expressed in terms of the value of caring itself. As selves-in-relation, what we have to evaluate here is not whether caring actions are appropriate but whether what we care about is "worth" caring about.[100] In talking about care as disposition, I need to retain a sense in which being disposed to care does not commit selves-in-relation to responding blindly with care, a sense in which selves-in-relation are able to discriminate between what is worth caring about and what is not.[101] It is important to understand that the concept of worth as I use it here refers to something other than an abstract, quantitative calculation of the value of another. I mean it primarily to refer to the testing of particular claims to care. The idea that as selves-in-relation we test the worth of what we care about by deliberating about the worth of this child or this friend clearly implies a calculative approach to caring relation that is alien to the ethic of care. With the notion of care as disposition, however, I have introduced the idea that part of what selves-in-relation care about is caring itself, that when as selves-in-relation we care for this child or this friend, what matters are that child or friend *and* our caring for that child or friend. I am therefore distinguishing between evaluating the worth of this child or this friend, which is not an intrinsic part of the ethic of care, and evaluating the worth of our caring. Without the possibility of evaluating our caring, of deciding that our caring is not "worthy," we are denied the possibility of removing ourselves from situations where our caring is rejected or abused.[102] Even more important for my argument, the idea that care does not have a discriminative or evaluative component, that care is arbitrary, instinctive, or "just another response," contributes to the divorce of care from reason.

Although problematic in other senses, Murdoch's example of the mother (M) attending to her daughter-in-law (D) clarifies how the processes of discrimination and evaluation might be understood in the context of care. As M attends to D, she not only begins to see *D* as worthy but also comes to value *herself* as a perceiver of D's worth. The "let me look again" follows M's dissatisfaction with the possibility that, in not valuing D, M is identifying herself as old-fashioned and narrow-minded, as snobbish and jealous. Were *these* attributes valued by M, she presumably would not be impelled to look again. What M does when she attends to D is not adequately captured by saying that she evaluates D or evaluates her behaviour toward D. In the process of attending, M tests whether what she cares about, which is identifying herself as someone who cares about not being narrow, snobbish, and jealous, is worth caring about, whether attending to D, seeing D justly and lovingly,[103] is important.

Intriguingly, two threads in Frankfurt's discussion indicate that something like the concept of attention is implicitly involved in his account of the caring process. First, there is the reference by Frankfurt to the narrative order that care imposes, the coherence that caring imparts to the existence of the self who cares.[104] Second and perhaps more significantly, Frankfurt's concept of volitional necessity, like the concept of attention, entails the sense in which establishing the caring self involves a forgetting of self.

Yet, I repeat, Frankfurt's notion of care has no evaluative dimension. Although Frankfurt concedes that we *need* a way of testing both our practical acts of caring and our disposition to care, he does not indicate what such a test might be like or, crucially, whether such a test might be a component part of care itself. My suggestion is that Frankfurt has effectively barred himself from developing this aspect of care, thereby depriving his account of care of a vital dimension, because his conceptual scheme admits of no evaluative process other than the impersonal mechanisms of rationality and moral judgment. For Frankfurt, the volitional necessities that constrain care do not generate the consistency that these formal mechanisms of evaluation require. If volitional necessity is personal, if it is binding only on the carer, no sense can be made of saying that what I care about is worth caring about or not worth caring about. Such observations, for Frankfurt, would be mere tautologies, since the concept of worth in these contexts could mean only "important to me," not right or good, wrong or bad. For Frankfurt, questions of right and wrong, good and bad cannot be framed in terms of care.

I certainly do not want to argue that care can be understood in a framework of right and wrong, good and bad. But what the concept of attention, which I have associated with seeing together, contributes to the conceptual scheme of care is an understanding that our practical acts of caring *and* our caring about care can be evaluated, can be understood, in terms of the imperatives and constraints of the realities of selves-in-relation. Here, of course, reality is not a remote metaphysical construct but a living kaleidoscope of perspectives, interests, and values. On the basis of this understanding of the realities of selves-in-relation, attention is the quest for *appropriate* responses, that is, responses that are in accord with the demands of the situation. Attention, then, is what relates care to the realities of selves-in-relation. Care recognises the constraints that inhere in these realities. Caring can be judged according to whether it honours the imperatives, perspectives, interests, and values of which the realities of selves-in-relation consist.

What this evaluative dimension of care illustrates is that the distinction between ethics and care, on which philosophers in the liberal tradition insist, not only is unnecessary but also has the effect of obstructing the attempt to develop the concept of care through a process of philosophical analysis. To explain why this is so, I want to look more closely at what is entailed by the assumption that care and moral judgment are qualitatively different undertakings. What interests me is that Frankfurt explicitly draws this distinction on the grounds that ethics is about the integrity of *relations with others* and that care is about the integrity of the *self*. As I have noted, Frankfurt's assertion is that there is always and necessarily a distinction between ethics and caring and that this distinction remains in place even when they coincide. Ethics, then, is concerned with what is not incorporated under the rubric of care. Its claims are therefore set apart from the claims of care. Where the latter are limited and personal, the former are impersonal, operating as rules that are beyond my control and indifferent to my personal desires.

Clearly, Frankfurt's assumption is that there is nothing problematic in characterising ethics as being confined to this impersonal realm. But what is taken for granted in making this assumption and generating a concept of care that sustains this conclusion about ethics is precisely the premise that feminist moral philosophy, as I construe it, criticises: that questions about the personal and the particular, questions about my existence, about what is important to me, what honours or violates my sense of integrity are not ethical questions *because they are personal.* Frankfurt, of course, reverses the priority that traditional liberal moral theorising accords the personal. What he retains, however, is the central tenet of that style of moral reasoning: that moral relevance is confined to relation that is not caring relation and that caring relation is not rational.

One way of expressing what it is about this version of the ethical project that is so troubling to feminist moral philosophers (and others) is that, in defining the exclusive focus of moral philosophy as questions about the integrity of relations with others, it precludes the development of a moral framework for questions like "How should I live?"[105] or "What sort of person am I to become?"[106] Relational ethical activity, here, operates in the narrowed moral field bounded by questions about rules: "What rules ought I to follow?" and "Why ought I to obey these rules?"[107] It seems clear to me that Frankfurt's awareness of the conceptual distinction between these two sets of questions generates his efforts to articulate what is excluded from philosophical consideration by this narrowing of the moral field. Although it might seem that his elaboration of care represents an *expansion* of the range of human experiences open to philosophical scrutiny, I suggest that constructing care as conceptually distinct from ethics and epistemology has the effect of *reinforcing* the philosophical status quo. As such, an approach to care that denies it an ethical and a rational foundation is open to the same charges as I have laid against the theoretical approaches to caregiving that I examined in Chapter 2.

The difference between responding morally and responding with care begins to evaporate once care is understood to have its basis in the realities of selves-in-relation that are revealed, in a process of seeing together, by attention. What is evident in Frankfurt's example of the protective mother is the implicit assumption that, out of ethics and care, only the former has an evaluative dimension. Rationality and moral judgment, which focus on the integrity of relations with others, supposedly afford the impersonal evaluative mechanisms that disentangle the abstract and universal (in this example, motherhood) from the concrete and particular (in this example, me as the mother of this child), privileging the former as providing the basis of moral understanding. Moral action is therefore assumed to be based on impersonal, generalisable criteria that become personally relevant to me only to the extent that I construe myself as acting under the rubric of the universal and abstract.[108] Care, which focuses on the integrity of the self, is assumed to afford no such evaluative dimension. Caring action is supposed not to be distinctively moral because what it yields is not impersonal, generalisable criteria but insight into a self that is as context-dependent as its signature or fingerprints.

At this point the key to problematising the conception of ethics as distinct from care is revealed. This distinction is, as I have said, dependent on the validity of another philosophical distinction: that between questions about how I should conduct my relations with others and questions about how I should live. Frankfurt, in keeping with the tradition of liberal philosophy, clearly takes this distinction as axiomatic.[109] Taking it as his starting point, he is able to remove questions about the integrity of relations with others from the realm of caring into the realm of ethics. This bracketing confirms the self-understanding of liberal moral theorists in the deontological, utilitarian, and contractarian traditions. In these traditions, the relevance of "How should I live?" questions is strictly limited, not extending beyond the rules and principles governing the conduct of relation. So Rawls, for example, frames his response to "How should I live?" questions in terms of these rules and principles, conceiving "fundamental moral virtues" in terms of "strong and normally effective desires to act on the basic principles of right."[110] What distinguishes care from ethics, then, for Frankfurt, is that care addresses "How should I live?" questions because care moves beyond the parameters established by ethical rules and principles. In developing this notion of care, Frankfurt opens up the possibility of articulating questions about the integrity of the self that cannot be subsumed into the narrowed field of ethics. What is not challenged, however, is the adequacy of the account of relation within this narrowed moral field. Neither is the validity of setting consideration about the integrity of relation apart from consideration about the integrity of the self called into question. The way to articulate this challenge, I believe, is to point toward a richer way of understanding both ethics and care. This understanding recognises that ethics is impoverished unless it involves a notion of the integrity of self and a contextual framework, while care is impoverished unless it involves a notion of the integrity of relation and an evaluative framework. Once care is placed in an evaluative framework, it can be seen as subject to the constraints and imperatives that link care with reason and sustain concepts of caring reality.

In this chapter I have shown that care can be understood as entailing both practical acts of care and the disposition to care about care. Central to the notion of care as disposition is the evaluative dimension of care. This dimension of care confirms the caring response as subject to the constraints of the strong ethical imperative to see together, which I have linked with the concept of attention. In order to show how this ethical imperative is associated with a transformed sense of the rational, I need to develop a concept of reason that is not premised on impartiality. It is to this task that I now turn.

NOTES

1.   Others disagree about Gilligan's motives. See, for instance, Davis, 'Toward a Feminist Rhetoric,' for a summary of the range of reproaches and commendations Gilligan has elicited.

2.   This originally appeared in *Signs: Journal of Women in Culture and Society* 11 (1986): 324–333. It is reprinted in Larrabee, ed., *An Ethic of Care*, 207–214. My references are to this reprint.

3.   Gilligan, 'Reply to Critics,' 207.

4.   Ibid., 210.

5.   Gilligan, *In a Different Voice*, 20, quoting Kohlberg.

6.   Ibid., 18, says that in Kohlberg's research "females simply do not exist."

7.   Gilligan, 'Letter to Readers, 1993,' xvii, distinguishes "the created or socially constructed feminine voice" from "a voice which [women] hear as their own."

8.   Ibid., xiv, says that it was when she made relational realities explicit and central to moral concerns that "[w]omen's voices suddenly made new sense."

9.   Ibid., x, refers to "women's need to silence false feminine voices in order to speak for themselves."

10.   Ibid., xxvii.

11.   Gilligan has recently said: "I have theorized both justice and care in relational terms," and she refers to "a growing body of evidence which cannot be incorporated within the old paradigm." 'Hearing the Difference,' 125, 123. The remarks lend weight to my suggestion that she is willing to entertain radical possibilities for care.

12.   I take seriously Witt's comment, 'Feminist Metaphysics,' 279: "In order to show [that traditional categories need to be thought through again] . . . it is necessary to show not only that women have been excluded in the tradition but also that their inclusion makes a conceptual difference."

13.   See Flanagan and Jackson, 'Justice, Care, and Gender,' 70: "[Kohlberg] proposed that virtue is one and 'the name of this ideal form is justice'. For Kohlberg the morally good person is simply one who reasons with, and acts on the basis of, principles of justice as fairness." The Kohlberg quotation is from Kohlberg, *The Philosophy of Moral Development*, 30–31.

14. Murdoch, *Metaphysics as a Guide to Morals,* 186. She is commenting on Kierkegaard's proposition that "philosophy is like sewing, you must knot the thread."

15. Frankfurt, 'The Importance of What We Care About,' 257.

16. Although most accounts of ethical care have focused on care as action, I think Noddings, *Women and Evil,* 237, is articulating a similar distinction to mine when she talks about two kinds of relational virtue. This distinction is noted by Brennan, 'Review of *Women and Evil* by Nel Noddings,' 144.

17. Frankfurt, 'The Importance of What We Care About,' 257.

18. These delineations are clearly not uncontroversial. Not only does Frankfurt omit any reference to ontology or metaphysics in his philosophical scheme, but he also defines epistemology and ethics in ways that appear to beg important questions. My intention in this section of this chapter, however, is not to present a detailed critique of Frankfurt's argument but to outline his theory of care. In subsequent sections of this chapter, I use his theory as a springboard to develop a concept of care that could not be entertained in Frankfurt's philosophical scheme.

19. Frankfurt, 'Importance,' 257.

20. Ibid.

21. In Chapter 3 I show, with reference to Gilligan's subjects, how this distinction might be overturned.

22. They "plausibly judge" (Frankfurt, 'Importance,' 258).

23. Ibid., 260.

24. Ibid., 263.

25. Ibid., 258.

26. Ibid., 271. This last, Frankfurt admits, 259, is an error of caring, although he is unsure, assuming that what is cared about is something that is really important to the carer, how this can be demonstrated without succumbing to a circular argument about the importance of something being important.

27. This is a mark of Frankfurt's neo-Kantian stance. A more orthodox understanding of Kant insists that the categorical imperative *generates* maxims rather than tests them. As Blum notes, 'Gilligan and Kohlberg,' 55, the orthodox understanding of Kant traces moral maxims to "pure reason alone," whereas for neo-Kantians "the original source of maxims is allowed to lie in desires." This is an important point because for Frankfurt's distinctions to hold there has to be a sense in which what is required by duty may *not* be "categorically preemptive" (Frankfurt, 'Importance,' 258), while what we do because we care involves a sense that we could not act otherwise. In critiquing Frankfurt's position, I am not endorsing Kant's. Both conceive ethics as impersonal in a sense that precludes care.

28. As I understand Frankfurt, the same argument applies to the principle of utility or contract.

29. I understand this notion of consistency to be akin to the idea that a smoker has not given up smoking until she identifies herself as a nonsmoker. A smoker who is not smoking at this moment is not a nonsmoker. A nonsmoker, on the other hand, is not only not smoking at this moment but also committed to act in a certain (nonsmoking) way in the future. She "guid[es her]self along a distinctive course or in a particular manner" (Frankfurt, 'Importance,' 260) in a way that makes her action inseparable from her sense of agency. (Frankfurt uses the case of the reformed smoker to illustrate a different point from mine.) In the case of contradictory cares, I might be prompted to choose one action rather than another because one, more than another, maintains this sense of internal consistency. Frankfurt, 262, refers to being "moved irresistibly to pursue . . . [a] course of action" and to "powerful and persistent natural inclinations" to act in a certain way.

Only when I do not know which of my cares I care about more, or when I care equally about both cares, do I have a difficulty (262).

30. Frankfurt, 'Importance,' 261.

31. Ibid., 267.

32. In her response to Frankfurt, Baier argues that this point needs to be qualified. Frankfurt, ibid., says, 267: "A declaration of love is a personal matter . . . because the person who makes it does not thereby commit himself to supposing that anyone who fails to love what he does has somehow gone wrong." Baier's response ('Caring about Caring,' 281) is that "typically the lover *does* want others to find the loved one lovable, wants to sing his praises, repeat his name." I do not think that Baier's qualifications undermine Frankfurt's point, at least as I develop and criticise that point.

33. Frankfurt, 'Importance,' 264.

34. Which, for Frankfurt, is a *logical* necessity.

35. This recalls Walker's description ('Moral Understandings,' 23) of ethical propositions as "philosophical brain-teasers, data begging for the maximally elegant theoretical construction."

36. Frankfurt, 'Importance,' 261.

37. MacIntyre, *After Virtue,* 218.

38. For example, MacIntyre, *After Virtue,* and Sandel, *Liberalism and the Limits of Justice.*

39. Frankfurt, 'Importance,' 260–261.

40. By, for example, biological, psychological, spiritual, logical, or causal necessity.

41. It should be noted that Frankfurt also leaves open the possibility that the direction and intensity of care may *not* involve an encounter with necessity. He admits, 'Importance,' 263, that "[w]hen a person cares about something, it may be entirely up to him both that he cares about it and that he cares about it as much as he does." Such caring does not generate the sense that I "cannot but" (Baier, 'Caring about Caring,' 275) act in a certain way. Frankfurt is clear that the difference between caring which is and is not subject to volitional necessity is not a difference in *degree* but a difference in *kind.* What Frankfurt says he is trying to distinguish are different ways of caring, so that caring that is subject to volitional necessity is only one of several ways in which caring might be manifest. It seems to me that this distinction is very ambiguous. Certainly, there is a sense in which we might say "she cares about x differently from the way I care about x," where what we mean is not "she cares about x more (or less) than I do." I suspect, however, that Frankfurt wants the distinction to capture some sense in which I can care without being compelled to act in a certain way as well as under the compulsion of volitional necessity. As will become clear as I develop my argument, I do not find this distinction valid or useful. My suspicion is that it is relevant only to a version of care that eschews any relational context, but I do not want to preempt a discussion of this point here.

42. Frankfurt, 'Importance,' 263.

43. Ibid., 268.

44. Ibid., 263.

45. Frankfurt's emphasis is on "the worthiness of the activity of caring" (ibid., 272). He does not develop the concept of "caring about care," focusing instead on the question of "worth." The idea that we can distinguish abstractly between what is worth caring about and what is not worth caring about is troubling from my perspective (and undoubtedly from many others). By contrast, caring about care, which seems to focus on the worth of my caring rather than the worth of what I care about, opens up some productive areas for discussion, as I show in the final section of this chapter.

46. "or do *'at will'"* (Baier, 'Caring about Caring,' 275).

47. Although, as I have noted in note 41, Frankfurt leaves open the possibility that my cares and caring may be "up to me." I have expressed reservations about this possibility.

48. Baier's terminology, 'Caring about Caring', 275.

49. Frankfurt, 'Importance,' 266–267.

50. Murdoch, 'The Idea of Perfection,' 35.

51. Ibid., 8, 23. Murdoch also uses the word "lonely," 36.

52. Cf. Naomi Scheman's comments about "contamination by connection" in respect of the products and producers of the epistemology of modernity ('Commentary,' *APA Feminism and Philosophy Newsletter* 88, no. 3, [1989]: 42, as quoted by Code, 'Taking Subjectivity into Account, 30).

53. Murdoch, 'The Idea of Perfection,' 37.

54. I have noted two exceptions: see note 16.

55. Frankfurt, 'Importance,' 266.

56. This is not to overemphasise the deliberative process: such overemphasis runs the risk of endorsing the kind of overdeliberation that Williams refers to as "one thought too many" ('Persons, Character and Morality,' in *Moral Luck*, 18).

57. Although, of course, they may be all three.

58. Ruddick's emphasis in *Maternal Thinking* on the rationality of the maternal will marks her place in the post-Kantian tradition. Her elaboration of the Weil-Murdoch notion of loving attention, in which the fact-value distinction between *is* and *ought* is replaced by the idea that we can come to see things as they really are through patience and honesty, signals her radical departure from that tradition. Cf. Grimshaw, *Feminist Philosophers,* Chapter 5, especially 229–235.

59. Both Frankfurt ('Importance') and MacIntyre ('Comments on Frankfurt') are content to deliberate on the highly abstract example of the mother and child without asking what miseries "tempt" a mother to abandon her child or, more significantly, whether such a dilemma (to protect or abandon?) might itself be a product of care.

60. Gilligan, In a Different Voice, 99.

61. As Gilligan does, for example.

62. This is the concern, for example, of Hoagland, 'Some Thoughts about *Caring';* Romain, 'Care and Confusion'; and Card, 'Caring and Evil.'

63. As I think both Tronto and Held tend to do. See Bartky, 'Feeding Egos and Tending Wounds,' for a discussion of different approaches to care. The problem with linking particular theorists with different approaches to care is that it tends to de-emphasise their common interests and to gloss over the riders and caveats with which many of their arguments, particularly the arguments that are critical of the approaches taken by Gilligan and Noddings, are prefaced. Hoagland, for example, says "my concern is not to challenge caring as a pivotal point for ethical theory but rather to question a particular portrayal of caring." ('Some Thoughts about *Caring,'* 249). Neither should my comments and references in this paragraph be taken as implying that these different approaches are *un*philosophical or that there are not other ways of developing care philosophically. Other approaches have been taken by, for example, Manning, *Speaking from the Heart,* and Hekman, *Moral Voices, Moral Selves,* both of whom show how care might be illuminated in philosophical terms that are very different from those I use.

64. Frankfurt, 'Importance,' 266.

65. Ibid., 261.

66. I take it that Frankfurt, like Murdoch, rejects the "image of man as a highly conscious self-contained being" who "freely chooses his reasons in terms of, and after surveying, the ordinary facts which lie open to everyone: and he acts." (Murdoch, 'The

Idea of Perfection,' 35).

67. In Chapter 3 I begin to elaborate in a concrete way the senses in which selves-in-relation are selves related to other selves, selves embedded in contexts and self-reflexive selves.

68. This is the position defended by Tronto: "Care is the response to a need; if people didn't have needs that they needed others to help them meet, there would be no care" (*Moral Boundaries*, 170). Jaggar ('Caring as a Feminist Practice of Moral Reason,' 189), tends similarly to confine care, criticising the care tradition "for failing to explain how care thinking may be properly critical of the moral validity of felt, perceived, or expressed needs, so that it can avoid permitting or even legitimating morally inadequate responses to them."

69. Such a case might note the difficulty of endorsing a version of care that did *not* meet instrumental needs.

70. This risk is cogently articulated by Tronto, who presumably does not associate it with limiting care to the meeting of needs. See *Moral Boundaries*, especially 'Marginalizing Care,' 111–122, and 'Moral Dilemmas in the Practice of Care,' 137–147.

71. This is particularly so if we understand needs in Tronto's highly specific sense of arising "out of the fact that not all humans or others or objects in the world are equally able, at all times, to take care of themselves" (*Moral Boundaries*, 145). See also her reference to "needs that they needed others to help them meet," 170. It seems that, here, caring becomes the meeting of needs *that cannot otherwise be met*. It is worth noting that, despite her reference to "others and objects in the world," only *human* needs are indexed in Tronto's book. My comment about the elimination of most nonhuman things from the lexicon of needs-based caring is not supposed to imply that nonhumans cannot have clear and recognisable needs. My reservation is rather that, as countless examples attest, the capacity of humans to correctly assess, let alone meet, the needs of nonhumans is minimal.

72. These are other reasons that the case for establishing instrumental caring as a necessary component of the ethic of care has to be very cautiously phrased.

73. Tronto, Moral Boundaries, 104.

74. Ibid., 118.

75. Ibid.

76. Ibid., 207, n. 34.

77. Murdoch, 'The Idea of Perfection,' 34.

78. Ibid., 40.

79. Ibid.

80. Two important critiques of the way the metaphor of vision operates in traditional philosophy are Fox Keller and Grontkowski, 'The Mind's Eye' and Mortimer, 'What If I Talked like a Woman Right Here in Public?' This quote is from Mortimer, 45.

81. Murdoch, 'The Idea of Perfection', 67–68.

82. That care might be premised on a loss of identity is a concern expressed by many feminist philosophers. For a discussion of some arguments that seem to reject not only *individualism* but also *individuality*, see Grimshaw, *Feminist Philosophers*, Chapter 6, especially 176–186.

83. There is a comparison to be made here with Kant's notion of respect, which entails seeing others as ends in themselves. As I note in Chapter 1, however, if encountering the other morally involves abstracting from the particularity of the other, then we risk losing a sense of precisely what might have constituted those concrete others and their particular ends. Such abstraction is not a feature of Murdoch's concept of attention.

84. Murdoch, 'The Idea of Perfection,' 103. See also Murdoch's references to "the greedy organism of the self" (65) and "the fat relentless ego" (52).

85. Ibid., 90. McClintock speaks in similar terms: "As you look at [the chromosomes], they become part of you. And you forget yourself" (quoted in Fox Keller, *Reflections on Gender and Science*, 165).

86. Murdoch, 'The Idea of Perfection,' 95.

87. The endorsement of humility is rightly regarded by feminist philosophers as a risky move. See, for example, Houston, 'Rescuing Womanly Virtues.' That humility need entail neither self-denial nor self-effacement is therefore a crucial point to emphasise.

88. Murdoch, 'The Idea of Perfection,' 41. Nothing in Frankfurt's account of volitional necessity contradicts the idea of will as obedience, although it seems to me that will as obedience might sustain, rather than resolve, the paradox that care is both self-imposed and imposed involuntarily. Although sustaining the paradox is my objective, I cannot endorse the concept of will as obedience without expressing major reservations, for reasons that will become clear.

89. Although her emphasis on these notions is thoroughly consistent with Murdoch's Platonic allegiances.

90. Murdoch, 'The Idea of Perfection,' 37.

91. I do not mean to imply that we cannot use imagination to generate understandings of concrete and particular others. My point is only that M's understanding of D seems to involve a sense in which it makes no difference to M's ceaseless work of attention whether D is a concrete and particular other or an abstraction. This assumption, of course, is crucial to Murdoch's objective which is to show that "behaviourist, existentialist, and utilitarian" versions of the moral self that discount "what goes on inwardly" are mistaken and misleading ('The Idea of Perfection,' 8, 9). So, M *could* have attended to D as a concrete and particular other, but the fact that attention can be divorced from the concrete and particular other indicates that attention for Murdoch is not the relational concept that I am describing.

92. Bowden, 'Ethical Attention,' 11.

93. Which are the terms in which I have explained Murdoch's notion of humility, or modesty.

94. Haraway, 'Situated Knowledges,' 586.

95. Haraway, 'A Manifesto for Cyborgs,' 196–199.

96. See Grimshaw's account of abstraction, *Feminist Philosophers*, 204–205.

97. See, for example, Noddings' story about Manilus, *Caring*, 44.

98. This possibility is not explored by Frankfurt.

99. It is MacIntyre's (Aristotelian) insight that for every virtue there are two vices (*After Virtue*, 154).

100. See my reservations about the concept of worth in note 45. Note also that in this discussion of care, I am not making a distinction between caring for and caring about. Although Noddings finds it useful to do so, I remain unconvinced of the wisdom of drawing lines so definitely.

101. For a very different way of answering these questions about evaluation, see Baier's response to Frankfurt: 'Caring about Caring.' For Baier, 274, "to care about caring commits one to evaluation of one's loves and loyalties." Her somewhat tentatively expressed conclusion, 277, is that "the traditions which have evolved the concepts of the perverse or unnatural love, and of false consciousness, and of displaced and disguised objects of love, are what we must turn to. . . . The Aristotelian-Christian concept of the unnatural love, the Hegelian-Marxist concept of the fetishistic loves of those with false

consciousness, and the Freudian concept of the unrecognized oedipal fixation, all offer us ways of seeing loves critically."

102. Noddings, *Caring,* 19: "If I care and you do not, then I may put my presence at a distance. . . . To be treated as though one does not exist is a threatening experience, and one has to gather up one's self, one's presence, and place it in a safer, more welcome environment."

103. Murdoch, 'The Idea of Perfection,' 23.

104. Frankfurt, 'Importance,' 260–261.

105. See, for example, the articulation of this question in Taylor's 'Leading a Life.'

106. MacIntyre, *After Virtue,* 118.

107. Ibid., 118–9.

108. Rich, *Of Woman Born,* would say that most mothering is so construed.

109. Frankfurt's three philosophical questions involve what to believe, how to behave in relation with other persons, and what to care about (see text at note 18). My argument does not involve replacing questions of what to care about with questions about "How should I live?" Rather, I am saying that understanding questions of what to care about as *excluding* questions about how to behave in relation means that "How should I live?" questions cannot encompass a response that is both caring and ethical.

110. Rawls, *A Theory of Justice,* 436, as quoted by MacIntyre, *After Virtue,* 119.

Chapter 5

Understanding Partiality:
Problematising Conceptions
of Knowledge and Knowing

With the description of care in terms of both action and disposition, it begins to be apparent that the philosophical elaboration of the ethic of care consists less in describing the *content* of care and more in describing the *reason* by which care might be informed and constrained. Where care is confined to the meeting of needs for care or, more generally, to care as action, it may be that the sufficient conditions of care can be determined. However, where care is understood to involve not only practical acts of care but also the disposition to care, the sufficient conditions of care are not quantifiable. Here, the evaluation of care involves not a quantitative assessment of needs-meeting but a qualitative assessment of the appropriateness of caring responses in particular relational contexts of caring.

Caring action, I have said, involves choice and deliberation, while care as disposition is understood in terms of an ethical imperative: the "I must" associated with the awareness that I "cannot but" act as one-who-cares. Now, where the concept of reason is inseparable from the stance of the impartial, autonomous self, the claim that the "I must" of care is informed and constrained by reason seems to undermine the association of care with partiality and relation. The presumption of ontological relation, however, suggests the possibility of transforming the concept of impartial reason by which liberal moral thought is informed. In this chapter, I lay the groundwork for developing the concept of *partial reason*. In Chapters 6 and 7, I show that the implications for both ethics and epistemology of associating rationality with partiality are profound.

As I have said, the focus of my critique of liberal moral philosophy is not primarily on its linking of the moral with the rational. Rather than breaking the nexus between reason and ethics, the objective of my critique is to reveal the limitations imposed on the moral response when reason is restricted to abstract, universal, and impartial thinking. By retaining the nexus between reason and ethics, I think it is possible to elaborate transformed senses of reason and of ethics, presenting neither as immutable and both as shedding light on how we make sense of our cares and responsibilities. Countenancing the mutability of reason and of ethics draws attention to the sense in which liberal moral philosophy presents reason as *im*mutable and ethical responses as *accountable only to reason*. In part, my criticism of the idea that care is irrational or unreasoned is that this version of care risks enshrining, rather than challenging, the immutability of reason, while my criticism of approaches that make ethics subservient to reason is based on the observation that such ordering may divorce the reasoned moral response from the concrete activity of sorting out responsibilities.

Drawing attention to the nexus between ethics and reason has the effect of giving substance to my rejection of accounts of care as irrational or unreasoned. As I interpret them, these accounts assume that the revelation of the reliance of liberal moral philosophy on the detached, impartial neutrality of traditional knowledge claims entails accepting that the ethic of care, with its emphasis on partiality and concrete particularity, is, in some sense, established contrary to reason. In Chapter 2, I point to some of the feminist sources of the idea that care is irrational or unreasoned.[1] What troubles me about construing care as irrational or unreasoned is that such construals promote the assumption that both epistemology and ethics can be read in dichotomous terms that map onto the distinction between feminist and nonfeminist approaches. Here, a dichotomous reading of ethics (in terms of justice–care, fairness–responsibility) seems to entail a dichotomous reading of epistemology (in terms of abstraction–concretisation, universality–particularity), so that problematising the privileging of an abstract, universal, and impartial rationality is assumed to entail an endorsement of what is concrete, particular, and partial and an association of the concrete, particular, and partial with an ethic of care and responsibility. The conclusion is that an epistemology consonant with a feminist ethic can be read as the antithesis of traditional epistemologies.

Examples of this assumption abound. Ruddick makes it explicit:

In one [kind of moral reasoning], the mode of reasoning is abstract and hypothetical, the subject of reason is rights and duties. One's duty is to accord people their rights, which are themselves determined according to fair, principled procedure. The primary virtue of individuals and institutions is fairness; the primary defects are isolated egoism and aggrandizing aggression; the primary conflicts are between competing rights. One can call this, in short, the morality of justice. This morality is connected to a conception of mature or "developed" selves as autonomous individuals related through hierarchical connections which, though threatened by egoism and aggression, are stabilized by the restraints of justice. In the second moral voice, the mode of reasoning is contextual and narrative, its subject is responsibility and response. One's moral aim is to respond to people's real needs. The primary virtues of individuals and institutions are caring and the realistic perception of needs; the primary defects are misperception of needs, failure to respond, and sacrifice of one's self; the primary conflict is between incompatible responsibilities. One can call this the morality of love. It is connected to a conception of "developed" selves as individuals related through overlapping networks of mutual dependencies which, though threatened by parochialism and self-sacrifice, are stabilized by the responsibilities of care.[2]

This kind of approach is summarised by Walker:

From an epistemological angle, one might gloss (one) view as: adequacy of moral understanding increases as this understanding approaches systematic generality. The alternative moral epistemology . . . holds, to the contrary, that: adequacy of moral understanding decreases as its form approaches generality through abstraction.[3]

On one hand, then, the epistemological emphasis is on a mode of reasoning that is contextual and narrative. On the other, the relevant epistemic mode is abstract and formal.[4]   The result of such antithetical approaches, according to some observers, is that moral philosophy has reached an impasse.[5] At least in terms of the moral orientations they underwrite, these two modes of reasoning I have described are supposed not to be commensurable, in the sense that the Gestalt images of the faces and the vase are not commensurable: we see the faces only by not seeing the vase, and vice versa.

My suggestion is that whether we accept the notion of an impasse, to say nothing of how we deal with it, depends on whether we accept that it is helpful to understand an epistemology consonant with a feminist ethic as the antithesis of traditional epistemologies. It seems to me that, although the strategy of doing so has been useful in the process of critiquing woman's place in man's life cycle,[6] such dichotomising is not so effective when it comes to the task of constructing epistemological and ethical frameworks in which to develop the philosophical potential of this critique. This is because the opposition of abstraction and formalism to contextuality and narrative sets up the philosophical debate in terms that are too readily condensed into the language of foundationalism versus relativism, of objective reality versus boundless difference.[7] Such condensations issue dire warnings to feminists about the danger of allowing one's feminist theorising to slip into oblivion between two philosophical stools. So Miranda Fricker cautions that "either we retain the 'totality' of a unitary truth as a regulatory ideal, or we suffer the dire consequences of the strong postmodernist position." Louise Antony warns that we can't "steer some kind of middle course between absolutism and relativism" without "eschew[ing] the notion of *truth*."[8]

Such debates seem to me to be problematic for feminist theorists for two reasons. First, they beg important questions because the establishment of the available alternatives depends on prior assumptions about the framework of dichotomous thinking. So, for instance, the claim that a dichotomous choice is restricted to either x or y depends on a prior assumption that x is accurately defined as being not-y.[9] The understanding is, then, that the move to reject the legitimacy of abstract, universal, and impartial modes of thought as epistemologically privileged is identical with the move to endorse concrete, particular, and partial thinking as privileged.   This, I argue, is a misunderstanding.

Second, establishing the debates in these terms means that they tend to remain stuck to the terms of modern-postmodern epistemological arguments.   The bifurcation of reason and emotion, public and private, male and female is mapped onto opposing notions of truth as either universal and unitary or multiple and unassessable. Declaring war on totality[10] is assumed to involve localising truth to the extent that no truth transcends the individual viewpoint. Feminist argument that enters the debate on these terms is caught by the paradox captured by the warnings of Fricker and Antony: either we retain the possibility of intersubjective agreement, a "common language" in which to name oppression and exploitation, or we celebrate the irreducibility of human experience, which cannot be captured by universal common themes in either theory or practice.[11]

My intention is not to oversimplify the way these dichotomous themes arise but to show how intricately woven are the assumptions on which the presentation of the debate in these dichotomous terms is grounded. What my argument shows is that debates about care versus justice, partiality versus impartiality, may be conducted in the absence of a consideration of one of the significant insights arising from the version of care in which I am interested. The insight is that the ethic of care establishes alternative possibilities to those canvassed in the dichotomous terms of the debate. So, a philosopher concerned with, say, abuses of international human rights might argue that "justice" sustains her intuitions more fruitfully than "care." To the extent that these intuitions probably cannot be sustained in the absence of a fairly robust notion of truth, she may reject an ethical approach to which is ascribed the privileging of concrete, particular, and partial thinking. My argument reveals that basing care on these latter ascriptions amounts to a parody of caring. My version of the ethic of care shows that care sustains a robust notion of truth while yet problematising accounts that dichotomise truth as either unitary and universal or multiple and unassessable.

Constructing an epistemology consonant with a feminist ethic as the antithesis of traditional epistemologies and being drawn into debates conducted in the terms I have elaborated lead feminist theory to a dilemma that, indeed, seems to represent an impasse. My assertion, however, is that the impasse dilemma is a false one. What is more, I would argue that to be caught up in addressing this dilemma in the terms in which it is presented sidetracks, rather than strengthens, feminist philosophy because what gives rise to the dilemma is a misunderstanding of a central feminist concept. The impasse therefore fails to arise if the alternatives in the dilemma are re-presented. The concept that is central to these re-presentations is *partiality,* and it is to a re-presentation of the alternatives in terms of their understanding of partiality that I now turn.

THE CRITIQUE OF IMPARTIALITY: PART I

In developing my argument, I follow a similar course to the one I adopted in the previous chapter. There I showed that the insight that "we are creatures to whom things matter" can be developed in such a way that care is placed in an evaluative framework and seen as subject to the constraints and imperatives that link care with reason and sustain a concept of the reality of selves-in-relation that is revealed in the process of seeing together. Such a development represents a transformation of care, opening up for consideration the possibility of transforming the understanding of reason by which the impartial stance of the liberal moral reasoner is informed. Now I want to show how feminist insights about the inappropriateness of impartiality can be developed in such a way that the nexus between care and reason becomes sustainable. The challenge here is to show that the claim that the "I must" of care is informed and constrained by reason sustains, rather than undermines, the association of care with partiality and relation.

For the purposes of setting up my argument, I start by outlining, in a way that is necessarily highly condensed, *foundationalist* accounts of epistemology, in opposition to which many contemporary feminist and nonfeminist epistemologies are generated. In foundationalist epistemology, epistemic authority is established and maintained by calling upon what Lorraine Code calls "the ideals of the autonomous reasoner,"[12] in which the variables pertaining to the knower are assumed to be as controllable as the other variables in the epistemic equation. The open mind for the autonomous reasoner is the mind cleared of preconception and perspective, the mind that operates both "from nowhere" (i.e., in a social, historical, political, and cultural vacuum) and "from everywhere" (its product is universalisable knowledge).[13] The link between open mindedness, knowledge and truth lies in the aperspectival nature of truth. So, in the terms of one exemplary account: "Truth is *what is so* about something, the reality of the matter, as distinguished from what people wish were so, believe to be so, or assert to be so. . . . [P]eople do not *create* truth. . . . They reach out to apprehend it and construct expressions that they hope represent it faithfully."[14] Foundationalism is explicitly couched in terms of impartiality and the belief that it is both desirable and possible for the knower to be impartial: to be open-minded and unbiased.

Feminist critics of traditional philosophy, particularly of analytic philosophy, are often accused of erecting straw men as their targets.[15] Certainly, establishing the objectionable proclivities of particular philosophers by a process of exegesis seems bound to invite counterclaims by their defenders.[16] One way of avoiding this accusation, it seems to me, is to illustrate the position being criticised not only with reference to particular philosophers and their critics but also by showing how assumptions propagated by the position being criticised "trickle down" as accepted wisdom. The preceding quotation about truth, which illustrates the position I am calling foundationalist, is from a textbook published in 1995 introducing students to critical and creative thinking. This definition of truth is provided to students as part of the process of "sorting out helpful from harmful notions, and establishing a firm conceptual foundation."[17] It is neither argued for (except by some dismissive comments about the crude relativism endorsed by "otherwise intelligent people"[18]) nor presented as problematic (except for the caution that students should "reserve the word *truth* for the final answer to an issue"[19]). I use it to illustrate the aperspectivity of foundationalist thought in order to show that, while there might be disagreement as to whether an individual philosopher might be labeled foundationalist, foundationalism represents a set of assumptions that create an atmosphere that is unreceptive (if not actually hostile) to challenges to aperspectivity.

There are, of course, adjectives other than foundationalist that describe the account I have summarised here, although both Addelson and Lynn Hankinson Nelson find foundationalism a workable term, describing as it does the belief in an epistemological end point or "the provision of some sort of foundation for knowledge."[20]   Code talks about the "positive-empiricist orientation" of "the epistemologies of the mainstream" whose pursuit of "universally necessary and sufficient conditions" for knowledge leads to a privileging of scientific knowledge.[21]   Code also uses the adjective "malestream,"[22] contrasting the approaches that she criticises with an "epistemology of everyday lives."[23] Richard Bernstein describes what, for me, is central to foundationalism as the belief that "there is or must be some permanent, ahistorical matrix or framework to which we can ultimately appeal in determining the nature of rationality, knowledge, truth, reality, goodness, or rightness."[24]   Charles Taylor uses the term "theories of unity" to convey similar theoretical assumptions. He says that "the appeal of [theories of unity] is readily understandable. They seem to introduce both clarity and decidability into ethical life. . . . They show a very diverse array of moral intuitions and felt obligations to be the realizations of a single purpose."[25]   Jean Grimshaw uses the term "positivism" to refer to an epistemological stance committed to the ideals of value-freedom, the detached, objective stance, and the discovery of the truth.[26]

The important aspect of foundationalist epistemology for my argument is that it sustains a form of rationality that celebrates and privileges the capacity to think in an abstract, universal, and impartial way. My concept of partial reason involves an account of epistemology that entails quite a different notion of rationality. The account of epistemology with which I want to associate partial reason explicitly dissents from foundationalist epistemological premises in several ways. First, rather than privileging some beliefs or concepts as prior to, or as grounding, others, the dissenting epistemology asserts that all knowing presumes other knowing, that all theorising takes some knowledge for granted. Second, rather than constructing knowers as passive or neutral observers of data or facts, the epistemological assumption is that we are active in the construction of knowledge, that theory is not completely determined by the data or facts supporting it, so that what we know is not reducible to the evidence cited for that knowledge.[27]   Third, with the recognition of the theory-dependence of observation comes the breakdown of the fact-value distinction. Who knows, what they know, and how they know it[28] are crucial elements in epistemological analysis. The relatively transparent process of theory generation identified by foundationalist epistemologists gives way to an understanding that epistemological practices are, at least to some degree, opaque. The relation between empirical evidence and knowledge or theory may not be obvious; indeed, knowledge may not be reducible to empirical evidence, and theories may derive from sources other than the data on which they are based. Finally, from the understanding that the location of the knower, the situatedness of knowledge, and the context of discovery are significant follows the insight that it is not possible for knowers to be *im*partial. Partiality in the sense of being partisan or biased is an epistemic resource without which we know less.

FIELDS OF KNOWLEDGE-MAKING

My next task is to show how the acknowledgment of partiality can be developed in two directions, only one of which sustains the concept of partial reason. Before I go on to that task, however, I must clarify my understanding of the distinctions between fields of knowledge-making. This clarification anticipates the objection that my account of foundationalism and, indeed, my major premises about the epistemological assumptions sustaining the concept of partial reason make a mistake in failing to distinguish moral from scientific knowledge.

I preface my remarks by acknowledging two significant points. The first is that "anti-foundationalism" is not a catchall term. Clearly, many significant antifoundationalist accounts do not reduce to the four points I have cited at the end of the previous section. So, for example, Kuhn's understanding that all observation is theory-laden leads him not to an endorsement of partiality but to a new account of *im*partiality.[29] While, for Kuhn, knowledge production itself can be contextualised at the level of the paradigm, what this contextualisation problematises is the taken-for-grantedness of theory choice rather than the ability of knowers to operate impartially within the terms established by the paradigm. Kuhn's interest, then, is in the perspectives (which may, e.g., be social, political, metaphysical, and economic[30]) that determine paradigmatic thinking at the level of standards of evidence, modes of discourse, criteria of relevance, and types of explanation rather than in the perspectives of knowers.

The second point is that some philosophers have found it useful to distinguish between scientific and moral epistemologies, or between the refutation of foundationalist ethical assumptions and the problematisation of scientific foundationalism. The "naturalising" of epistemology may entail a commitment to notions of truth as a universal and unitary regulatory ideal and to forms of epistemological individualism while yet eschewing the moral absolutes of traditional ethical theory. This kind of distinction between science and ethics is, I think, apparent in the tradition of American pragmatism and is evident even in some of the contemporary critiques of traditional epistemological premises that, as Code notes, "are continually disturbing the smoothness of the mainstream."[31]

Having made these two acknowledgments, however, my suggestion is that the distinction between moral epistemology and other fields of knowledge-making is not a distinction that feminist philosophers need to sustain.[32] It seems to me that the received notion of moral epistemology can be linked with the restriction of the moral realm that I have identified with approaches emphasising duty, utility, and justice. Where ethics is confined to relationships that are formal and public (i.e., to Walker's "relations of nonintimate equals and transactions or contracts among peers"[33]), morality and moral knowledge become synonymous; in other words, ethics is defined as duty, utility, or justice, while what is good or bad, right or wrong, is interpreted as the categorical imperative, the utilitarian calculus, or the principle of justice as fairness.[34] The confinement of ethics and the province of moral epistemology have implications, of course, for other fields of knowledge-making. Thus, S-knows-that-p claims come to symbolise the epistemological realm, where that realm is not assumed to generate ethical propositions.

The purpose of a feminist critique of these received notions of ethics and epistemology is, I suggest, to question whether S-knows-that-p claims and universal moral formulas can account adequately for more than a limited range of epistemological and ethical possibilities. An integral part of this questioning is directed toward problematising the implicit assumptions on which the realms of epistemology and ethics are established. One of these assumptions is that the context of "S" is less significant in the epistemic equation than the content of "p."[35] In ethics, this same assumption confers more significance on elaborating the content of a moral formula than on elaborating the context in which a formula might be applied. Broadening the scope of epistemology and ethics to include consideration of who knows, what they know, and how they know it is one way to start the process of problematising the exclusion from epistemology of ways of knowing other than those captured in "knowing-that" claims and the exclusion from ethics of ways of relating other than those characterised as formal and public.

Another way of problematising these exclusions is to re-moralise epistemology. This process involves questioning the nature of the distinction to be made between knowledge-claims that are obviously heavily constrained empirically and those that are not so obviously constrained. A failure to question the nature of this distinction leads to the epistemological privileging of S-knows-that-p claims, where knowledge is supposedly heavily constrained.[36] This empirical constraint seems to make knowledge-claims unambiguously either right or wrong. I know that this material is not flammable, I know that objects fall down when dropped, and it would seem that what is epistemologically significant about this knowledge is exhausted in its propositional content.

Questioning this assumption about empirical constraint does not necessarily issue in the absurd proposition that empirical constraints are epistemologically irrelevant. What such questioning does is insist that no knowledge-claim, no matter how firmly it appears to be empirically constrained, no matter how remote it seems to be from ethical propositions about good or bad, right or wrong, can be *assumed* to be morally neutral. The point is not that theories of combustion or gravity necessarily have direct ethical significance but that what *is* ethically significant may not be isolatable from such theorising. This is what I mean by questioning the nature of the distinction between seemingly straightforward empirical knowledge-claims and other claims to know. With a sharp distinction in place, the bombing of Hiroshima is not linked with the splitting of the atom, any more than the action of suicides who leap off cliffs is linked with the theory of gravity. Questioning the nature of the distinction opens up the possibility that what is ethically significant may implicate straightforward empirical knowledge-claims, so that our confidence in declaring any particular theory ethically *in*significant is not necessarily well placed. I emphasise again, however, that problematising the assertion that any theory is ethically insignificant is not the same as endorsing the assertion that all theories necessarily have direct ethical significance. Rather, the idea is to show that *all* knowledge-claims can be pressed on the question of whether their ethical interest is confined to, or exhausted in, its propositional content or whether we increase our understanding, our epistemological and ethical understanding, of a knowledge-claim by placing its propositional content in the context of who knows, what they know, and how they know it.

My thinking about whether the distinction between moral epistemology and other fields of knowledge-making needs to be sustained by feminist philosophers and my conclusion that it does not have been, in part, shaped by Code's comments about Ursula Franklin's "impact studies":

During their summer jobs, however menial, however "non-scientific," engineering students were to record the impact of their work on the immediate environment—an exercise designed to teach them that whatever they did, from house painting, to child minding, to table serving, would produce effects they would not have thought to notice. At issue were not simple empirical claims of the S-knows-that-p variety: Sara knows that paint is messy, that children need good food, that coffee needs to be served hot. Hence the point is not that such claims take on direct ecological significance. But only by discerning their impact, which extends well beyond one's first imaginings, can evaluations within a larger ecological network be conducted. Franklin's purpose was to show that there is no knowledge, and no knowledge-informed practice, that is without consequence, and hence none that escapes critical scrutiny.[37]

My argument is based on the understanding that, like the ecological impact, the *ethical* impact of simple empirical claims may extend well beyond our first imaginings.

TWO KINDS OF PARTIALITY

I have said that my argument asserts that the dichotomous distinctions between foundationalism and relativism, between truth as unitary and universal and "truth" as multiple and unassessible, between objective reality and boundless difference, do not exhaust all the possibilities open to feminist philosophers. The assumption around which I want to frame my discussion of the concept of partiality that informs partial reason is that arguments against foundationalism erode, or at least place at risk, the possibility of creating and sustaining shared belief systems, mutual understandings, and intersubjective agreements. That we need to create and sustain shared belief systems, mutual understandings, and intersubjective agreements is a proposition with which I agree. However, I argue that in order to fulfill this need, we do not have to retain a notion of truth as universal and unitary.

The distinction I make is between the concept of partiality as *bias* and partiality as *perspectivity*. Understood simply as bias, partiality entails only a *political* or *methodological* imperative not to eclipse the points of view of others.   Understood as perspectivity, partiality becomes a specifically *epistemological* concept, which I call strong epistemological partiality.   Strong epistemological partiality envisages knowers as always and already existing as selves-in-relation.   Importantly, this strong epistemological sense of selves-in-relation does not refer to relations between individual knowers who know prior to their relatedness.   But neither does it contrive relation between knowers who are otherwise not related, as separate entities needing to be brought together (in shared belief systems, mutual understandings, and intersubjective agreements). The strong epistemic aspect of selves-in-relation expresses the sense, noted by Nelson, in which "you or I *can* only know what *we know* (or could know), for some 'we.'"[38]   Strong epistemological partiality reflects the idea that knowledge is enabled by partiality.   I argue that strong epistemological partiality enables an understanding of truth that is neither universal and unitary nor multiple and unassessible.

As I have made obvious, I consider Gatens' account of the different possible relationships between feminism and philosophy to generate extremely productive criteria by which to distinguish different theoretical approaches.   It is within Gatens' framework that I want to situate the accounts of partiality developed in this chapter.   Specifically, I argue that the understanding of partiality as limited to bias is identified with the approaches of *extensionist* feminist philosophers, while the concept of strong epistemological partiality is consistent with the challenging of axioms that distinguishes *critical-interrogative* approaches.

I elaborate the extensionist position with specific reference to the work of Antony and Fricker.   It seems to me that not only do their arguments illustrate the approach described as extensionist by Gatens but also that it is a description that would be welcomed by these theorists, both of whom tend to promote the view that philosophy occupies a relatively neutral position vis-a-vis the oppression and exploitation of women.   The reason I choose to refer to their work is that, as my earlier quotations indicate, both explicitly situate their arguments in terms of the either-or choice between foundationalism and relativism, objective reality and boundless difference.   As well, I see their ideas as contiguous with an influential nonfeminist, antifoundationalist current of thought, in critical relation to which I situate my work.[39]

PARTIALITY AS BIAS

I present the extensionist version of partiality as bias, not as a straightforward exposition but as emerging in the responses to three epistemological propositions expressed as alternatives.   Later I present very different responses in the terms of strong epistemological partiality.   These three alternatives are, for me, implicit in the warnings issued by Antony and Fricker about absolutism and relativism.[40] The first alternative is that either we retain the notion of truth as a regulatory ideal, or we restrict knowledge-claims to statements about personal perspectives. The second is that either we endorse the separate, autonomous individual as the epistemic agent, or we concede the possibility of making authoritative knowledge-claims.   The third is that either we insist on a common or universal language, or we sanction the lapse into an incoherent babble. The possibilities for which I argue with the concept of strong epistemological partiality are, first, that we might undermine the notion of truth as a regulatory ideal by securing the notions of truth and knowledge in the universally operative requirement for the elaboration of the context in which we function as knowers; second, that we might replace the insistence on the individual agent's epistemic authority with a concept of the authority of selves-in-relation; finally, that we might replace the notion of a common language (which is totalising) with commonality (which is a source of understanding).

The key to explaining how extensionist feminist philosophers come to frame the set of alternatives that structures their account of epistemology lies in their critique of impartiality. Now, importantly, this critique starts off on the same track as the one I have endorsed, with the claim that partiality is not only impossible to eliminate but actually integral to the process of knowing: that partiality is both unavoidable *and* useful. Minds that know cannot literally be open, because all knowing is grounded in the preconceptions and prejudgments of knowers who can see only in terms of their partial perspectives. What can be exposed in foundationalist epistemology, then, are the preconceptions, prejudices, and perspectives of knowers whose knowledge-claims cannot evade the contingent, from which impartiality was assumed to secure exemption.

But, having uncovered the partiality of foundationalist accounts of knowledge, the extensionist argument begins to develop in a direction that I see as problematic. If partiality is integral to knowing, extensionists argue, then the critique of foundationalism cannot be expressed in terms of the *partiality* of foundationalist accounts. Such an expression leads to what Antony calls the bias paradox. Feminists cannot, she maintains, espouse partiality while at the same time criticising foundationalism for its bias: "If we don't think it's good to be *im*partial, then how can we object to men's being *partial?*," she asks.[41]

I want to look very closely at the nature of this paradox and particularly at the understanding of partiality that informs the statement of the paradox. Given that the paradox depends on there being some significant sense in which there *is* something objectionable about foundationalist theorising, it seems that the only way of avoiding the paradox is to relocate the criticism so that it focuses on some aspect of foundationalism other than partiality. For Antony, such a relocation is readily effected:

The real problem with the ruling class worldview is not that it is biased; it's that it is false. The epistemic problem with ruling-class people is not that they are closed-minded; it's that they hold too much power. The recipe for radical epistemological action then becomes simple: Tell the truth and get enough power so that people have to listen.[42]

This relocation of the foundationalist problematic brings the issue back onto established philosophical territory, which is, of course, what would be expected of extensionist approaches. The question now is not what is wrong with men's partiality (to use Antony's terms) but whether foundationalist theories are true or false. If bias per se does not lead to false theories, then we can stop worrying about whether a particular bias is "good" or "bad" (because "the 'biasedness' of biases drops out as a parameter of epistemic evaluation"[43]) and focus our energies on establishing whether theories are true or false. Biases are "good," according to Antony, "when and to the extent that they facilitate the gathering of *knowledge*—that is, when they lead us to the truth. Biases are bad when they lead us *away* from the truth."[44] Antony's recommendation is that we "evaluate the overall theories in which the biases figure . . . identify[ing] the particular empirical presuppositions that lie behind a particular program of research so that we can subject them, if necessary, to empirical critique."[45] What this approach vindicates, for Antony, is the conviction that a sound challenge to pernicious theories that rely on foundationalist assumptions must establish that they are false, not that they are sexist, racist, or classist. In other words, if all knowing is biased, and if bias includes sexism, racism, and classism, knowledge cannot be false *because* it is biased, that is, *because* it is sexist, racist, or classist.[46]

For Antony, the key to determining whether or not a theory is true is empirical evaluation. At the level of theory formation, the focus is on determining whether the "empirical presuppositions"[47] on which a theory is built are empirically valid and on whether the selection of the theoretical parameters of inquiry is empirically grounded. Antony illustrates how such empirical evaluation works, using the example of theories that compare race and "innate" levels of intelligence.[48] Importantly, to be consistent with her claims about bias, what Antony must look for is evidence that such theories or the empirical presuppositions on which they are grounded are false, not evidence that either the theories or presuppositions are racist. At the level of theory formation, she finds evidence that the empirical presuppositions on which these theories are built are not empirically valid. Race and "innate" intelligence are not categories or classifications that can be correlated, because, while "innate" intelligence is biologically determined, "there's no biologically defensible definition of 'race.'"[49]

For Antony, theories can also be empirically evaluated at the point at which conclusions are generated. I understand this evaluation to involve the same kind of analysis or reanalysis of empirical presuppositions in which Antony recommends we engage at the level of theory formation. Antony is clear that, if theories comparing race and "innate" intelligence are false, they are false not because of their "bad" bias (racism) but because they "lead us away from the truth." It follows that the epistemological grounds on which racist theories can be condemned cannot be articulated in terms of the racist nature of their conclusions; on epistemological grounds, they can be condemned only because their conclusions are false.

The problem I perceive with the assumption that empirical presuppositions can be assessed with reference to empirically available evidence, both at the level of theory formation and at the point at which conclusions are generated, is that it depends on the further assumption that empirically available evidence will not confirm theories or presuppositions that are false. So, theorists comparing race and "innate" intelligence, for example, can be forced to reanalyse their conclusions and empirical presuppositions because the empirically available evidence contradicts those presuppositions, thereby rendering their conclusions invalid. My suggestion is that this statement is far too categorical. Although I concede that theories comparing race and "innate" intelligence *might* be invalidated if the empirically available evidence contradicts their presuppositions or conclusions, my concern with the unqualified statement is that it does not leave open the possibility of saying that a theory is wrong or false, even though it is *not* contradicted by the empirically available evidence. In other words, I am suggesting that we need to be able to critique theories comparing race and "innate" intelligence even when the established empirical evidence suggests that blacks score lower on intelligence tests than whites, just as we need to be able to critique theories comparing gender and moral maturity even when the empirical evidence shows that women score lower on ratings of moral maturity than men. If we cannot do this, we risk leaving intact the circularity whereby the racist argument collapses the categorical differences between race, "innate" intelligence, and IQ scores (just as the sexist argument collapses the categorical differences between gender, moral maturity, and impartial reason). Defenders of the race–"innate" intelligence correlation draw the social and the biological together, so that their claims about biological parameters (e.g., lesser intelligence) are then used to establish precisely what was not empirically available prior to their research: a "biologically defensible definition of 'race.'"[50]

Antony is clear that the empirical evaluation of theoretical conclusions and presuppositions is not only a process of *describing* biases (which would assess theories in terms of their acceptability, asserting, e.g., that a theory comparing race and "innate" intelligence is unacceptable because it is racist) but also a process of making *normative* statements about biases (which would assess theories in terms of their truth, asserting, e.g., that racist theories are wrong).[51] The basis of my critique of Antony is that both in the description and in the normative assessment of biases, she too readily presumes that the empirical and the theoretical can be distinguished. So, in the case of a theory comparing race and "innate" intelligence, I am supposed to be able to make an empirical assessment of the concepts of race and intelligence to decide whether the theory's presuppositions and conclusions are empirically confirmed. Where correlations are being made between uncorrelatable categories, the theory is necessarily mistaken.

My difficulty with the proposition that the empirical can be dissociated from the theoretical or the conceptual in this way is not that empirical evidence is too limited a basis for understanding concepts like race and intelligence or that Antony's emphasis on the empirical evades the question of whether there might be stronger objections to the methodological assumptions that make race and "innate" intelligence comparable (although there may be grounds for both such objections). Rather, my point is that the concepts of race and "innate" intelligence and, indeed, the concept of racism are themselves the products of theories or of ways of knowing about the world. The facts about race and "innate" intelligence are not clearly separable from the values that inform our understanding of those concepts. Antony argues that correlations can be made only between similar categories. Defenders of race–"innate" intelligence correlations say that the categories they select *are* similar. Antony's faith in empirical critique, her insistence that *"[w]e must treat the goodness or badness of particular biases as an empirical question,"*[52] ensures that the discussion focuses on methodological questions about the selection of analytical categories: on the facts about race and "innate" intelligence. What I question, however, is not only the assumption that what is "innate" can be equated with the biological or that racial characteristics are the product of social convention but also the assumption that the biological and the social are categorically distinct. Antony seems to assume that the biological and the social,[53] being categorically distinct, are each tightly constrained in terms of the conceptual discourses they employ. I think that even if these categorical distinctions exist at some level of abstraction, they cannot be relied on to generate empirical evidence separating the concept of race from the concept of intelligence.

My problem, then, is not that I disagree with Antony's conclusion that theories comparing race and "innate" intelligence are pernicious because they are false. It is, rather, that, because of the way she links the pernicious with the false, I fear for our ability to sustain the argument that racist, sexist, and classist assumptions are themselves pernicious even when they seem to be confirmed by what is empirically the case. Antony might argue that this "seeming confirmation" is illusory: that confirmation of racist, sexist, and classist assumptions depends on the acceptance of the terms established by theories that are grounded on those assumptions. My point is that for us to be able to make the empirical assessments that would enable us to distinguish between what *is* confirmed and what *seems to be* confirmed, theory would have to be transparent. In other words, the nature of the relation between theory and data, between facts and values, between knowledge and empirical evidence, would have to be plain, with each readily distinguishable from the other. I understand Antony to be arguing, however, that the relation between theory and data, between facts and values is such that neither is necessarily clearly distinguishable from the other. If this is so, then I simply cannot determine with the certainty presumed by Antony which correlations are reliable and which are not in the process of undertaking an empirical critique of theoretical presuppositions and conclusions.

This is an important, but complex, point, and an example will clarify what I understand it to mean. What I want to do is to see how Antony's method of determining whether theories are true or false works when it is applied to Kohlberg's stage theory of moral development.[54] Kohlberg set out to study the development of moral reasoning.[55] There are a number of different claims in Kohlberg's work, and I do not mean to imply that all of them resist Antony's approach.[56] What I am interested in here are Kohlberg's claim about the universality of his stage sequence and his conception of moral maturity that effectively marks as morally deficient those who are not male, white, and affluent.

My suggestion is that Antony's exhortation that we critique empirical presuppositions and conclusions when assessing the truth or falsity of claims assumes a level of clarity and precision in theory generation that might once have been imputed to the scientific laboratory. At least in Kohlberg's case, however, teasing out the empirical presuppositions on which the claim to the universality of the stage sequence of moral development rests is far from straightforward. That Kohlberg did not control his original studies for gender or race and class seems, using Antony's parameters, to indicate one of two things. On one hand, he may have worked on the empirical presupposition that the categories and parameters of gender, race, and class are *not* connected in any significant way with the development of moral reasoning. On the other, he may have worked on the empirical presupposition that the categories and parameters of gender, race, and class *do* affect the development of moral reasoning and must therefore be controlled by excluding them in the development of the initial hypothesis. Remember that Antony has said that the biasedness of biases drops out as a parameter of epistemic evaluation. This means that no judgment can be made at this stage about what biases Kohlberg's methodology might betray. Remember also that Kohlberg claims that his stage theory is universal. Only if he did not claim universality could his methodological exclusions be interpreted at face value, as evidence of an intention to restrict his theory to the moral development of white, affluent males.

My observation is that in defending the universality of his stage sequence, Kohlberg slips between these two, radically different and contradictory empirical presuppositions. The possibility that boys and girls are essentially different is borne out in his studies showing the precise stage at which their cognitive abilities diverge. As I say in Chapter 2, women *do* exist in Kohlbergian stage theory.[57] In this case, Kohlberg's exclusion of those who diverge from the "norm" in the development of his stage sequence is, from his point of view, vindicated. The universality of the stage sequence is confirmed rather than undermined by the identification of those who diverge from the "norm." Although he might have to broaden his sample to avoid further accusations of sampling errors, in doing so he broadens, rather than narrows, the explanatory framework of his theory.[58]

On the other hand, this same evidence of divergent male and female development has been taken by Kohlberg as confirming the hypothesis that the sequence of the development of moral maturity is universal, even though this sequence is not independent of social environment. Should people's social environment not provide them with the opportunity to undertake the sort of cognitive reorganisation that signals the move from one stage up to another, they will not progress to moral maturity. In the case of women, then, the lack of appropriate moral stimulation keeps them confined to lower levels of moral maturity, rather than any essential gender difference.[59]

Now the point is that both these contradictory presuppositions both relate to empirical data that *do* show women and men reaching different degrees of moral maturity in terms of Kohlberg's measurements. What I cannot determine empirically, then, is that the bias that leads Kohlberg to say that women (and others) are morally immature is "bad bias" in Antony's sense that it is a bias that leads us away from the truth. In other words, I cannot show empirically that the stage sequence theory is false. This is simply because the theory that says that moral development progresses through a series of stages, the highest of which women (and others who are not white, affluent, and male) seldom reach is *not* empirically false. So, while not denying that Antony's empirical critique might be effective in some relatively straightforward cases, it does not seem to me to adequately acknowledge the possibility that the relation between empirical evidence and theory is opaque, that conclusions may slip between contradictory presuppositions, that theoretical conclusions "infect" observation, and that theories may not be derived solely from empirical evidence.[60]

Antony might retort that Kohlberg's mistake occurs at the level of theory formation rather than at the level of empirical validation. Perhaps, like race and "innate" intelligence, gender and moral reasoning or moral development are not categories that can be correlated. The problem with this line of argument is that it avoids the question of how such categorical differences are to be sustained. I have shown how Kohlberg avoids this question as he slips between two contradictory empirical presuppositions: that gender and the development of moral reasoning *are* linked and that gender and the development of moral reasoning are *not* linked. In Kohlberg's case, the possibility of critiquing the universality claimed for his stage sequence by referring to his empirical presuppositions is doubly complex. If Kohlberg's argument about the universality of the stage sequence theory begs the question about whether gender (or race or class) and moral maturity can be correlated, it does so because it assumes that *whether gender (or race or class) and moral maturity are linked or not*, the stage sequence is universally valid.

Another way of expressing my point about the problems of applying Antony's empirical critique to Kohlberg's claim about the universality of his stage sequence is in terms of the "invisibility" of Kohlberg's major premise. Perhaps the slipperiness of the presuppositions grounding his claim about how moral reasoning develops can be accounted for, critically, by revealing the way this claim conceals what turns out to be his major premise. Where this major premise is expressed in terms of the equation of mature moral reasoning with impartiality, universalisability, reversibility, and prescriptivity,[61] and where these terms resonate with the prevailing philosophical metanarrative, Kohlberg's stage sequence theory can be seen to be about the *definition,* rather than the *development,* of moral reasoning. That even "submerged"[62] major premises can be made visible is obvious—my point is that the process of making them visible involves something other than an evaluation of the level of empirical support for a premise or conclusion. Indeed, it is not apparent to me that there could be an empirical test for this premise about the *definition* of moral reasoning that did not beg the question about the equation of impartial principled reasoning and moral maturity.

Antony does point to one slightly different parameter for detecting the truth and falsity of theories. Her suggestion is that a "theory that purports to say what human beings are like essentially must apply to all human beings; if it does not, it is wrong, whatever its origins."[63] My suggestion is that it is as problematic to tackle Kohlberg in terms of this assessment of theoretical truth and falsity as it is to try to assess his empirical presuppositions and conclusion about the universality of his stage sequence. It seems to me that there can be little doubt about how Kohlberg would respond to a question about whether his theory applies to, or accounts for, all human beings. Kohlberg cannot admit that his theory does not apply to all human beings without losing his theoretical innocence. This is because foundational accounts of knowledge elide the issue of contextuality: "*whose* moral reasoning?" is not a question that can be asked in Kohlberg's framework, precisely because that framework purports to be able to say what *all* human beings are like essentially. In other words, Antony's question (does this theory that purports to say what human beings are like essentially apply to all human beings?) presumes a subtext of other questions. These have, indeed, been asked by other feminist philosophers. Code, for example, urges us to "ask for whom this epistemology exists; whose interests it serves; and whose it neglects or suppresses in the process."[64] My point is that Kohlberg (and other foundationalists) cannot hear these questions, let alone respond to them, while working in a paradigm where the criteria of impartiality, universalisability, reversibility, and prescriptivity account for all epistemic possibilities without remainder.

The obvious rejoinder to my argument at this point is that it is not open to *foundationalists* to judge the truth or falsity of foundationalist premises and conclusions but to *critics* of foundationalism. I want to suggest that even such critics cannot show Kohlberg to be wrong on the basis of Antony's method without contradicting their own epistemological premises. Let me explain why this is so.

As I have said, women are *not* missing in foundationalist moral theory. But the position from which Kohlberg has looked at them, at "all human beings," is the unmarked position of theoretical privilege and authority. Thus, as Antony admits: "Members of the dominant group are given no reason to question their own assumptions: Their worldview acquires, in their minds, the status of established fact. Their opinions are transformed into what 'everybody' knows."[65] What this describes, it seems to me, is a situation in which foundationalists shift the onus of proof while yet predetermining the only legitimate terms in which dissent can be expressed. If this is so, it follows that the falsity of the "ruling-class worldview" could not be established empirically, even by critics like Antony, because the only empirical "facts" available to critics are those established by the theory being criticised.

It may be argued that, given the underdetermination of theory by data, all theorising has some degree of immunity when it comes to confirming or refuting theoretical conclusions. One of the insights that I think is contained in Quine's observation that "[t]he edge of the system must be kept squared with experience"[66] is that confirmation or refutation may not be an all-or-nothing process. The closer knowledge lies to the edge, the more empirical evidence may constrain it, and the more certainty it may impart. Knowledge lying closer to the centre may be less constrained by evidence and consequently expressed with less certainty. The spatial metaphor accounts for the obvious point that some theories are more problematic than others when it comes to an empirical evaluation of their truth or falseness.

My point is, however, that the question of where any particular theory lies and therefore of how data and theory are connected in that particular theory is precisely what is at issue. In other words, part of what I understand to be contestable about Kohlberg's stage sequence theory is whether it lies closer to the centre than to the edge of the system, whether there is a high level of agreement about the values that inform the inferences from his data to his theory or whether these values might be contested. It may be, to pursue Quine's metaphor, that Kohlberg disguises his stage sequence theory as one that lies close to the edge, thereby putting his correlation of theory to data in the same category as, say, the correlation of data about falling apples and planetary movements to the theory of gravity.[67] The squaring with experience, then, would be "confirmed" by the empirical support Kohlberg himself generates for his conclusions. Because of this link with what is empirically true, it would become as eccentric and perverse to dissent from Kohlberg's theory as it is to dissent from the theory of gravity.

Obviously, I am not suggesting that the premise of underdetermination makes all criticism problematic (in the sense that I am saying that a criticism of Kohlberg in the terms laid down by Antony is problematic). As Helen Longino points out, the argument about the complexity of the relation between theory, data and empirical presuppositions is not that "all science is value-laden" but that "not all science is value-free."[68] In Antony's terms, the argument is not that all biases affecting the movement between premises and conclusions are objectionable but that some premises and conclusions are more tightly constrained by data or empirical evidence than others. As I have said, how tightly particular premises and conclusions are constrained by data or empirical evidence and how sharply the distinction can be drawn between tightly and loosely constrained premises and conclusions are precisely what is at issue. Antony's reluctance to examine biases themselves for an answer to this question means that she has to trust that theories that comprise premises and conclusions that are not "legitimately" constrained by data or empirical evidence will generate false conclusions. My argument is that, in some cases, empirical support for premises and conclusions does not indicate that the premises and conclusions are generally agreed upon or generally acceptable—that is, not contested or contestable. This is not to say that in many or even in most cases empirical support for premises and conclusions indicates that the theory is not contested or contestable. Neither does it follow that a conclusion cannot be shown to be false by pointing to the contested nature of the values reflected in the way the moves between premises and conclusions are made. My point is only that an empirical evaluation of a theory like Kohlberg's stage sequence, which Kohlberg claims *is* tightly constrained by the data, is extremely problematic because what is objectionable about that theory occurs not at the point of moving between empirical evidence and premises and conclusions but at the point of taking highly contested values and assumptions[69] as proven.

It seems to me that it is precisely the point about the opacity of the relation between universal claims and empirical evidence that Gilligan implicitly acknowledges by not attempting an empirical evaluation of Kohlberg's stage sequence theory and focusing instead on problematising Kohlberg's "hidden" premise defining moral reasoning.[70] If Gilligan had focused on an empirical critique, we might expect to see three elements in her refutation of Kohlberg's claim about the universality of the stage sequence theory. First, she might argue that women *can* reach stage 6 on Kohlberg's scale. This would involve showing that the data placing women in general lower down the scale than men are aberrant in some way. Second, she might argue that principled reasoning and moral maturity are not confined to stage 6. This would involve redefining the reasoning manifest at stages 3 and 4 to show that mature moral reasoning extends to the stages where women's development seems to peak. Third, she might argue that the methodology of extrapolating conclusions about moral maturity from hypothetical reasoning does not produce reliable moral theory. This would involve demonstrating that there is something about moral reasoning that cannot be assessed from reasoning about hypothetical, as opposed to actual, experience.

None of these elements appear in Gilligan's argument. First, her concern about Kohlberg's method is aroused by the observation that women do not reach stage 6 on Kohlberg's scale. At no point does she argue that they can. Second, far from arguing that principled reasoning is not confined to stage 6, or that stages 3 and 4 represent mature moral reasoning, Gilligan retains Kohlberg's three levels of preconventional, conventional, and postconventional morality. She detects no difference in the way that the reasoning of women and men moves from egocentricity to universality, claiming, "This shift in perspective [identified in Kohlberg's three levels] toward increasingly differentiated, comprehensive, and reflective forms of thought appears in women's responses to both actual and hypothetical dilemmas."[71] For Gilligan, as for Kohlberg, reasoning at the conventional level is comparatively immature. That Gilligan is led to redefine the content of the levels and stages is beside the point, which is that she does not refute Kohlberg's claim about the universality of the stage sequence theory by relocating moral maturity. Third, although Gilligan is mainly interested in finding out how people think about their actual experience in moral terms rather than how they deal with problems that are given to them for resolution,[72] she does not argue that hypothetical reasoning is *necessarily* flawed. Indeed, her account of care germinates in the hypothetical reasoning of Amy and the reasoning of girls and women in response to the Heinz dilemma.

The point is that none of these three claims—that women can reach stage 6, that principled thinking appears at stages 3 and 4, that a methodological reliance on hypotheticals is unsound—would have enhanced Gilligan's fundamental criticism, because that criticism questions not adherence to the rules but the rules themselves.   The force of *Gilligan's* argument depends not on determining whether Kohlberg has correctly applied the criteria of impartiality, universalisability, reversibility, and prescriptivity to the development of moral reasoning (which would entail questioning Kohlberg's adherence to, or application of, the rules) but on showing that Kohlberg has misidentified these criteria as the main elements in the definition of moral reasoning (which involves questioning the rules themselves). The force of *Antony's* argument depends on the possibility of showing that there is an empirical discrepancy between a theory that is wrong and the reality it purports to describe. Antony's ultimate line of defence against "bad" biases, then, is that the theories they inform will not match how the world is. In other words, to evaluate a theory empirically in Antony's sense means checking to see that the empirical presuppositions on which a theory is built are empirically valid. As I have noted, Antony specifies the need to make normative as well as descriptive statements about biases. What the example of Kohlberg's stage theory shows, though, is that the content of these normative statements is confined to a judgment about the distance between what the theory tells us about the world and how the world is, which is a judgment about a theory's proximity to truth.

This seems to me to be an immensely problematic way of describing a feminist critique of knowledge-production. The idea that "how the world is" might be taken as a gauge of the "truth" of a theory or the "goodness" of a bias appears, at the very least, to assume that there is some way of gaining access to the world other than in terms of what we know about it. In other words, it is an idea that radically contradicts the premises of the critique of foundationalism. As I have summarised these premises, they entail the propositions that all knowing presumes other knowing, that our epistemic practices are not transparent, that as knowers we are active in the construction of knowledge, that all observation is theory-dependent, and that it is both undesirable and impossible for the knower to be impartial. What I want to show is that this contradiction is generated by the understanding of partiality that informs the statement of Antony's bias paradox: "If we don't think it's good to be impartial, then how can we object to men's being *partial?*"[73]

THE CRITIQUE OF IMPARTIALITY: PART II

What Antony has missed is that there is another way of formulating the critique of the impartiality of foundationalism. My argument is that the feminist critique of foundationalism is *not* grounded in an objection to men's partiality per se (or not limited to an objection to men's partiality). Rather, this critique consists of three quite different arguments.   The first involves problematising any assumption that there is a world against which theories can be checked. The second is the explicit renunciation of the premise of unpremisedness. The third involves an objection to the pejorative use of the notion of partiality. Framing the feminist critique of foundationalism in these terms shows the inadequacy of accounting for the critique solely in terms of the revelation of bias. My strong belief is that the notion of partiality cannot be reduced to the political or methodological imperative not to eclipse other perspectives or condensed into the realisation that there are social preconditions of knowledge, which are the reductions Antony and Fricker imply. As might be expected in the critical-interrogative approach with which I have identified my work, working out the implications of the critique involves questioning the rules themselves rather than adherence to the rules, that is, questioning the philosophical axioms that define moral reasoning in terms of impartiality, universalisability, reversibility, and prescriptivity rather than questioning how these criteria apply to the development of moral reasoning. The three points around which my discussion is based bring to the fore important elements of the foundationalist approach that are overlooked or avoided by extensionist analyses that endeavour to remain within the confines of traditional philosophical approaches. Let me take each of the points in turn to show that this is, indeed, the case.

Checking Knowledge against Reality

Despite the attempt by theorists like Antony and Fricker to distance themselves from the strong realism of foundationalism by drawing attention to the underdetermination of theory, the active nature of the knowing subject, and the inappropriateness of privileging epistemological neutrality, there remains a sense in which their notions of truth and reality require the postulation of a world against which theories can be checked. This may not be the same world against which the knowledge-claims of foundationalist theories of representation or correspondence are checkable—a world where physical nature is isolated from human practices. Nevertheless, in Fricker's argument, the failure to "pick out real states of affairs in the world" reduces knowledge to nothing more than the meanderings of historical accident.[74] For Antony, as I have noted, the critic of foundationalism is required to evaluate theories empirically in order to determine whether the biases they inevitably incorporate are objectionable.

It seems to me that the assumption that there is some standard against which knowledge or theories can be assessed is extremely problematic, even when that standard incorporates the understanding that both knowledge and experience are socially and politically mediated. Both Antony and Fricker agree that "there are no 'facts' in the requisite sense."[75] Just as fact is permeated by value, so, too, is value permeated by fact. What Antony and Fricker want to resist, however, is giving too strong a role to value. If facts are not clearly distinguishable from values, then it seems that the connection between knowledge and reality may dissolve into the preconceptions and preferences and value judgments of individual knowers. No longer willing to accept the radical separation of fact and value that was supposedly ensured in foundationalism's impartial stance, extensionists fear that knowledge might be left unconstrained, because what constrained knowledge for foundationalism—the separation of fact from value—has been lost. Yet some form of normative constraint is required if we are to be able to say that the claim that women are not morally immature is no more arbitrary than the claim that the sun is shining. Fricker and Antony locate this normative constraint in the empirical evidence of sunshine and female maturity. Up to a point, the reliance on what is empirically the case seems unproblematic. But, as I have said, it is one of the roles of feminist theory to question whether what applies in the straightforward case applies generally. In the straightforward case it may be that the norms involved in determining what is empirically the case are not contestable. As Fricker explains:

We might say that reality anchors our belief-system, for it provides substantial empirical constraints on what we may believe. These constraints, however, become weaker the further towards the centre of the belief-system we go. That is to say, empirical constraints obviously restrict empirical beliefs *more*, and more directly, than they restrict, say, political beliefs.[76]

What this assumes is that knowledge-claims are locatable at points on a fact-value spectrum marked at one end by knowledge that is strongly constrained by fact and at the other by knowledge that is not strongly constrained by fact.[77] Fricker adds, however, that at no point do "values . . . have *carte blanche* in constructing knowledge."[78]

I think that such a scheme is problematic not because I want to pursue different ends (as I explain in the next chapter, I share the commitment to a minimal realism) but because I do not think that it represents a sufficient departure from foundationalist ways. In those ways, there is supposed to be no link between facts and values. The fear of extensionists like Fricker and Antony is that once this link is established (as it is in the four basic premises of antifoundationalism I have outlined in this chapter), we risk having to concede that facts may be nothing more than expressions of value, that the results of our inquiries are nothing more than the inevitable results of our presuppositions. What Fricker and Antony do is sift our conclusions, in which facts and values, biases and empirical considerations, are mixed, through a filter of normative constraint. Now, like Fricker and Antony, I want to be able to say that some conclusions (e.g., that women are mature moral reasoners) are better than others (e.g., that women are immature moral reasoners). I am, however, not convinced that this possibility is secured by relying on norms that are generated empirically. Perhaps there *are* knowledge-claims that can be secured in this way, but it seems to me that the question of how fact and value, what is and what ought to be, are connected in any particular knowledge-claim is precisely what is at issue in the cases that are most philosophically interesting, that is, in cases that are not straightforward. As I have said, part of what I understand to be contestable in Kohlberg's theory is its proximity to the edge of the system. If making the inference from data to theory is *always* a matter of mixing facts with values, mixing empirical considerations with biases, how can we determine how strongly the "facts" suggest that we "ought" to take any particular conclusion to be true?

What is at issue here, of course, is what sort of match we might expect between knowledge and reality, what sort of checks or assessments might help us work out the extent to which what we know matches what actually is. Like many others, I want to situate feminist theorising in a framework of minimal realism in which there are constraints on what is known. In the next chapter I develop the argument that, epistemologically speaking, not anything goes. Here I want to note that, given this commitment to minimal realism, it nevertheless seems to me that there is a circularity in the argument that I can check knowledge by ascertaining whether it is normatively constrained, particularly when the normative constraint is provided by "the truth," as it is for Antony and Fricker.[79] Three aspects of this argument concern me. First, it assumes that is possible to match knowledge-claims to real states of affairs in the world. Second, it implies that the judgments I have already made are sound. Third, it separates what is real from the ways in which what is real is known. Let me show how each of these three aspects of the argument about the match between knowledge and reality contributes to the problematising of the assumption that there is a world against which theories can be checked.

First, it seems to me that no feminist theorist has cause to be too sanguine about the possibility of confidently assuming that any particular knowledge-claim picks out a real state of affairs in the world. This caution denotes not the radical scepticism on which Enlightenment epistemology was grounded but a wariness about where "the edge of the system" lies. For example, claims about the oxymoronic status of marital rape and claims linking the education of girls with womb-withering have been confidently matched with reality, squared with the edge of a system of beliefs about women and marriage. Foundationalism teaches us that we *can* make knowledge-claims with certainty (and confidence), providing we observe a few basic rules.[80] While anti-foundationalism challenges this certainty with notions of the underdetermination of theory, the active knowing subject, and the partiality of perspective, it opens, rather than closes, the question of how we might yet make confident knowledge-claims. Extensionist feminist philosophers want to establish the grounds for confidence by making the bias of knowers a necessary condition of knowledge. But if bias affects both knowledge and reality, then, extensionists claim, we must look *outside* knowledge and reality for the measure of how they match.

This brings me to my second point. In the cases of falling apples and flammable materials, it may be that knowledge and reality are tightly constrained empirically (by the facts) and that normative considerations are relatively insignificant. Part of my assessment about the match between combustion or gravity and reality will assume that what I already know about combustion or gravity is substantially correct. The problem here is the one I have already discussed in this chapter: how accurately any particular knowledge-claim matches reality is precisely what is at issue. S-knows-that-p claims apparently take us through life dealing competently and effectively with falling apples and fire lighting. But to make straightforward cases (in which theory choice appears not to reduce to norm choice), the model for other cases is to risk obscuring important differences in the way that facts and values connect in different knowledge-claims. If the theory says all swans are white, and I have seen or can find a black swan, I can confidently judge that the theory does not pick out a real state of affairs in the world. But the crucial assumption here that introduces at least a degree of circular reasoning is that I already know what swans are like before I make the judgment about whether the theory is a good theory.[81] The problem, of course, is the one eloquently articulated by Code in her critique of S-knows-that-p models of knowledge. What works reasonably well for swans proves far more problematic when it comes to dealing with things other than medium-sized physical objects.[82]

It would, of course, be as misleading to say that theory choice is always reducible to norm choice as it is to say that theory choice is always independent of norms. Nevertheless, the circularity I detected in matching knowledge and reality in the case of swan colouring risks becomes vicious in the case of an epistemology that is prepared to concede that theory is underdetermined, that the knowing subject is active, and that the privileging of epistemological neutrality is inappropriate. The point is that I cannot, for example, assess whether the designation of women as immature moral reasoners picks out a real state of affairs in the world when my epistemological premises tell me that what is real is a function of the ways in which what is real is known.

Here is my final reservation about the assumption that there is a world against which theories can be checked. Certainly, Fricker and Antony want to rule out the possibility that there is necessarily a sharp distinction between knowledge that is more constrained and knowledge that is less constrained. Certainly, they heavily qualify the certainty with which we can discern the match between knowledge and reality. Nevertheless, the safety net they erect to prevent the descent into a postmodern relativism is the ideal of truth, where this ideal generates normative constraints in cases where the fit between theory and norm choice is tight. The descent into relativism is not, as I have said, one that I want to make. But dissension from the conclusion that what is real and the ways in which what is real is known are separable does not necessarily commit me to a deterministic version of the relation between what is real and the ways in which what is real is known. The other factors, apart from what is real and the ways in which what is real is known, that might shape understandings of reality are as numerous and diverse as the needs and expectations of knowers. However, it does seem to me that, in their concern to be able to secure the match between knowledge and reality, Antony and Fricker construe truth in a way that leaves what is true standing apart from the human practices that constitute knowledge and reality. That knowledge and reality involve normative constraints is crucial to my position as well as to the positions of Fricker and Antony. That normative constraints are grounded in, or generated by, what is true seems to me to be moving perilously close to the privileging of empirical knowledge-claims, which is a mark of some brands of foundationalism.

What I am questioning, then, is not so much the idea that we might be able, with varying degrees of confidence, to assess the match between knowledge and reality but the suggestion that the measure of this match stands outside the practices in which knowledge and reality are formed. The idea that there is a world that generates the criteria against which the match between knowledge and reality can be checked leaves open the possibility that the measure of how knowledge matches reality is independent of the processes of constructing knowledge and reality. That we might cultivate understandings of knowledge and reality as human practices is a possibility welcomed by feminist theorists. The infusion of these understandings with accounts of human needs and aspirations is an important part of feminist theorising. Where I distinguish a crucial difference between the way extensionist and critical feminists develop their argument from this point, however, is that extensionists locate the normative constraints on which knowledge and reality depend *outside* the epistemic practices of knowers. Where truth is a regulatory ideal, it stands apart from the processes of constructing knowledge and reality. What I am arguing for, on the other hand, are notions of knowledge, reality, and truth that are secured in the universally operative requirement for the elaboration of the context in which we function as knowers.

The Premise of Unpremisedness

This is the second important element of the foundationalist approach that extensionist feminist philosophers overlook. My suggestion is that advocating an assessment procedure on the bases Antony and Fricker outline indicates a serious underestimation of the effect of the premise of unpremisedness, where to be unpremised is to be without perspective. What I argue is that knowledge built on the foundationalist assumption of aperspectivity actually corrupts the process of understanding. Far from its being an empirical question whether theories based on foundationalist assumptions are true or false, determining their truth empirically is not possible. The history of ideas shows that knowledge-creation based on the premise of unpremisedness is built to withstand precisely the kind of empirical evaluation advocated by Antony and Fricker. For example, if, as in Kohlberg's case, a theory privileges the experience of white, affluent males, this is taken to show that there is something "wrong" with women and with nonwhite, nonaffluent males. Only by questioning the rules themselves can it be shown that such exclusions indicate that there is something wrong with that theory or that way of theorising. Working within the framework of empirical evaluation[83] assumes what the premises of antifoundationalism explicitly deny: that evaluators can remain unaffected by the theory they are evaluating. What is more, where this evaluation proceeds on the understanding that a theory acknowledges its own heritage in a way that makes this heritage transparent, this contradicts the premises by which the epistemology explicitly endorsed as antifoundationalist by Antony and Fricker is supposedly informed. These premises, as I have elaborated them, say that evaluators are not only located but are a product of their location and that what they evaluate is the product of a heritage that is not transparent.

What I am saying is that, if we admit that knowledge-claims may have consequences, then we cannot be confident of judging knowledge-claims from a position that is not shaped by those knowledge-claims.[84] I cannot judge, in any absolute sense, whether a theory coheres with experience when that experience is itself shaped by theory. Given the underdetermination of theory, I cannot separate myself from the preconditions of theory, since those preconditions have also shaped me. As I have said, the notion of a position's being shaped by knowledge or of an experience's being shaped by theory does not have to entail either that *only* knowledge and theory shape our situations and experiences or that the relation between knowledge and speaking position, between theory and experience, is deterministic. Nevertheless, the ultimate line of defence for an epistemology that involves correlating "the world as we see it" with "the world as it is" is that, even if there are no other features distinguishing them from theories that are right, theories that are wrong will not truthfully account for the way the world is. This is so even when realism is modified to insert the "conceptual gap" of underdetermination between the world as we see it and the world as it is.[85]

It is important to emphasise that I am *not* suggesting that all the judgments we make about theories, truth-claims, and experience are unsound. My point is that the kind of evaluation that involves correlating the world as we see it with the world as it is runs the risk of propagating the assumption that what is true (and therefore what counts as knowledge) can be established or determined *prior to,* or *apart from,* the practices of selves-in-relation, in which notions of knowledge and truth are worked out. In other words, the assumption is that what is true, what counts as knowledge, is not part of theorising itself but is the frame within which our theorising takes place. What is overlooked in making this assumption is the possibility that where reality is socially constructed, where it is the product, rather than the goal, of theory, there needs to be room to say that "empirically this might be the case *but . . . ,*" to say that a knowledge-claim is wrong or false even when it seems to be confirmed by the empirically available evidence.[86] For philosophers like Antony and Fricker, this would count as charging that the rules of epistemology are themselves suspect. If the project of philosophy is sustained in the tension between what we know about the world and how the world is, as it is for Fricker and Antony, then questioning the rules, rather than questioning *adherence* to the rules, runs the risk of breaking this tension. In breaking this tension, we supposedly relinquish the capacity to make normative statements about good and bad biases.

My argument, however, is that the rules are, indeed, suspect when they result in a notion of truth whose content it is theory's role to elaborate. The elaboration of the content of truth is not an epistemological aspiration consonant with feminist theory. When feminist theory does not distance itself from this aspiration, it is limited in the kinds of ways elaborated in my critique of extensionism. Having shown that the feminist critique of foundationalism is misrepresented if it is interpreted solely as revealing bias (as it is by Antony and Fricker), I want to proceed to establish a different understanding of partiality. What emerges from this different understanding is that feminist theory, rather than elaborating the content of truth and confirming the authority of separate, autonomous knowers, moves always toward an elaboration of the contextual reality of selves-in-relation.

The Pejorative Use of Partiality

I conclude this chapter by looking at the third significant aspect of foundationalism that extensionist feminist philosophers overlook. What I find in both Antony's and Fricker's account of what constitutes a usable notion of partiality is an assumption that the foundationalist claim to neutrality simply arises because foundationalists think that neutrality is "a good thing."[87] This being the case, what we have to do is replace one norm with another: the obligation on the knower to remain neutral gives way to the obligation "to place herself within the critical field, opening her mind to how her own 'situation' may influence her beliefs."[88] What this interpretation ignores is the extent to which the foundationalist endorsement of impartiality is based on the view that *partiality* is a *very bad* thing. Impartiality, for the foundationalist, is not just an efficient and effective way of establishing reliable claims to knowledge. It is the *only* basis on which knowledge can be claimed. Partiality, then, is antithetical to the foundationalist epistemological project. Partiality *tarnishes* reason.[89] Biases are "obvious sources of error."[90] Where partiality carries this pejorative tag, it makes no sense to use the notion of partiality as in any sense *interchangeable* with neutrality in an epistemological framework. Either one is neutral, or one cannot make epistemological claims. What I am saying is that situating the knower *radically* affects the notions of truth and knowledge. To say that feminists object to men's being partial[91] is to seriously misread this aspect of the feminist critique, which is more appropriately understood as an objection to the complete devaluation of partiality as an epistemological resource.[92]

What begins to be apparent here is the difference between the partiality that is linked by extensionist feminist philosophers like Antony and Fricker with the acknowledgment of bias and the partiality that is excluded from epistemology by foundationalists. For the extensionist, as I have said, knowers are partial in that all knowledge-claims are affected by the bias of the knower. These biases reflect the personal preferences and theoretical preconceptions of knowers. Preferences reflect personal tastes, what we like and dislike. My liking for sweet things and my dislike of tobacco make me partial to chocolate and air that is free of cigarette smoke. For the extensionist, preconceptions are associated with the possibility of knowledge itself. These preconceptions provide the theoretical underpinning of knowledge, where the assumption is that all knowing takes some premises as given.[93] Both personal preference and theoretical preconception, for the extensionist, must be accommodated in an adequate account of epistemology. This is because both personal preference and theoretical preconception have the potential to affect knowledge adversely, to lead the knower to conclusions that are false. The epistemological project, then, includes a consideration of partiality and the imperatives that are associated with the need to ensure that the adverse effects of partiality are eliminated. Importantly, though, these imperatives are methodological and political rather than epistemological. Methodologically, knowers are required to check empirically their claims and presuppositions on the understanding that, where bias is of the kind that affects knowledge adversely, these claims and presuppositions will not be empirically sustained. Politically, knowers are required to be aware of their own personal preferences and theoretical preconceptions and sensitive to the personal preferences and theoretical preconceptions of others.

It is vital to note the precise nature of the disparity between this account of partiality and what is rejected as partial in foundationalist accounts of epistemology. In an important sense, the concept of partiality that is accepted by Fricker and Antony is *not* the concept of partiality that is rejected by foundationalism. If the concepts of partiality were the same, we might expect the foundationalist to say that what tarnishes reason, what constitutes the obvious sources of error, is the bias that describes situated knowers, where this bias is reflected in personal preferences and theoretical preconceptions. But what the foundationalist wants to avoid is not *bias* but *irrationality*.

Certainly, foundationalism insists that the personal preferences and theoretical preconceptions of knowers should be ruled out of consideration as epistemological resources. But this ruling out does not adequately account for the foundationalist ideal of the knower. Foundationalist knowing individuals have done more than rule out their personal preferences and theoretical preconceptions; they have *transcended* them: they are *without* personal preferences and theoretical preconceptions. As knowers, they are without context. Knowledge is value-free, not made or generated but *found* by a knower who is neutral. The neutrality claimed for knowers and knowledge by foundationalism is not achieved simply by ruling out personal preferences and theoretical preconceptions as epistemological resources. Rather, this neutrality is secured by reducing all bias to personal idiosyncrasy and eliminating it, by a process of rational evaluation that eliminates all that is concrete and particular, on this basis. The concept of partiality that extensionist feminist philosophers like Antony and Fricker embrace involves tempering neutrality with an acknowledgment of bias. The partial perspective that foundationalist philosophers reject, however, is the perspective that is irredeemably irrational. The danger, it seems to me, for a feminist critique of impartiality is that it is easy to slip between the impartial perspective understood as unbiased and the impartial perspective understood as rational. I suggest that slippage leads to a focus on developing the partial perspective as biased. Distinguishing between these different understandings, however, enables a philosophical challenge to the notion of rationality that foundationalists secure in the impartial perspective. Assuming that both foundationalism and antifoundationalism *share* an understanding of partiality as bias, we can proceed along the path that Antony and Fricker take, where all that is objectionable in foundationalism is the invisibility of the foundationalist knower. However, where partiality denotes irrationality, my suggestion is that we need to problematise not only the invisibility of the foundationalist knower but the very conception of knowledge and knowing presumed by the foundationalist account.

What I am suggesting is that ideal foundationalist knowing individuals are not knowers who check their knowledge against their personal preferences and theoretical preconceptions but knowers who are purged of such idiosyncrasies. As I have shown with reference to Kohlberg, there is a sense in which it is no part of foundationalism to distinguish facts from biases.[94] What counts as fact, what counts as bias, is not established in particular contexts but in the mien of the rational, autonomous knower. In other words, we cannot superimpose questions about the effects of particular preferences and preconceptions on an approach that admits to neither.[95] Where knowers are presumed to be without personal preferences and theoretical preconceptions, questions about what constitutes fact and bias, the rational and the irrational, cannot be answered without tautology: "facts" are what reason shows to be true; "biases" are what reason guards against.

Of course, for many critics of foundationalism the proposition that knowers are without biases is as problematic (and as puzzling) as the proposition that philosophers are without bodies. Feminist philosophers taking the critical-interrogative approach claim that the solution to the "disembodied philosophers" problem is not simply to "embody" philosophy. Such a move would be effective only if what disembodiment sanctioned was the removal of the body from philosophy. This is not the case. Disembodiment does not remove the body from philosophy but conceals an ideal body, which, in the history of Western philosophy, is male. The focus, then, has to be on disentangling or unpacking the concept of disembodiment to reveal the way philosophy itself is embodied as male.[96]

It transpires that the disembodied philosopher may be the philosopher with a certain kind of body. Similarly, once we start looking more closely at the concepts of bias and irrationality, it seems that the unbiased knower may be the knower with certain kinds of biases. The way to understand the philosophical significance of these biases, however, is not (or not only) to reveal them and demand that they be accounted for but (also) to reveal the way epistemology itself has been made to accommodate the partiality of the impartial knower.

I have drawn attention to three highly questionable and problematic assumptions made by foundationalism and not specifically addressed in the restriction of partiality to bias. In the next chapter, I show that problematising the assumption that knowledge can be checked against reality as well as the premise of unpremisedness and the pejorative use of partiality opens up the possibility of arguing for the set of alternatives that I set out at the beginning of my discussion of partiality as bias. The alternatives for which I argue involve redescribing knowledge and truth in terms of an elaboration of the context rather than the content of truth claims, redescribing knowers as selves-in-relation rather than separate, autonomous knowing individuals and redescribing the cultivation of a sense of commonality rather than a common language.

NOTES

1.   In 'Caring as a Feminist Practice of Moral Reason,' 181, Jaggar says: "Care and justice thinking have sometimes been portrayed by contrasting allegedly dispassionate justice with supposedly nonrational care, but in fact such portrayals caricature both care

and justice." While not disagreeing with Jaggar, the point I am developing is that recognising the cognitive elements of care and the emotional elements of justice may still leave care subservient to approaches which endorse abstract, universal, and impartial moral reasoning. So even an approach like Held's, which contrasts the "different epistemic role" of emotion in care and justice perspectives (Jaggar, ibid.), does not necessarily challenge the perception that care operates in the gaps left by impartial moral reason. I argue that this perception tends to be fostered wherever care is established on the assumptions that "many women—perhaps most women—do not approach moral problems as problems of principles, reasoning, and judgement" (Noddings, *Caring,* 28), that carers, in contrast to impartial moral reasoners, eschew theoretical responses (see, e.g., Walker's remarks about Baier, 'Moral Understandings,' 15) or that carers, in contrast to impartial moral reasoners, "speak from the heart" (as Manning's title suggests).

2. Ruddick, 'Remarks on the Sexual Politics of Reason,' 240. Ruddick's footnote at the point where she refers to the morality of love says: "In my parlance, care is the primary virtue of the morality of love."

3. Walker, 'Moral Understandings,' 20.

4. Gilligan uses these terms in *In a Different Voice,* Chapter 2.

5. See, for example, Deveaux, 'Shifting Paradigms,' 117.

6. Which Gilligan says is to protect the "recognition of the continuing importance of attachment in the human life cycle . . . while the developmental litany intones the celebration of separation, autonomy, individuation, and natural rights" *(In a Different Voice,* 23).

7. This is not to say that the terms on each side of the oppositions are necessarily synonymous.

8. Fricker, 'Knowledge as Construct,' 103; Antony, 'Quine as Feminist,' 190. The argument that follows Antony's warning makes it clear that, for her, truth is confined to absolutist accounts. Later in this chapter I focus on Antony's and Fricker's arguments in order to develop a critical framework in which to locate my concept of partial reason.

9. This is only a restatement of the feminist insight that dichotomous terms reflect negative relations when they are classified as x, not-x rather than as a, b. So, for example, reason and emotion are negatively related when the emotion is classified as irrational.

10. Jean-François Lyotard's phrase is quoted by Lovibond, 'Feminism and Postmodernism,' 8; Fricker counterattacks in these terms ('Knowledge as Construct,' 102–103).

11. Neither Fricker nor Antony, as I will show, sees this as a paradox. Both are committed to a position that rejects the second option as philosophically untenable. A similar argument is found in nonfeminist antifoundationalist accounts. Malpas, for example, says: "To reject the notion of truth as consistent and unitary is to reject the notion of truth as such" ('Speaking the Truth,' 161).

12. Code, 'Taking Subjectivity into Account,' 21.

13. Bordo uses these terms ('Feminism, Postmodernism, and Gender-Scepticism,' 136.

14. Ruggiero, *The Art of Thinking.*

15. See, for example, Nussbaum, 'Feminists and Philosophy,' and several of the papers in *Hypatia* 10, no. 3 (Summer 1995), the Special Issue on Analytic Feminism.

16. See, for example, Antony's reading of Descartes, 96, passim.

17. Ruggiero, *Art of Thinking,* 18.

18. Ibid., 19.

19. Ibid., 21.

20. Addelson, 'Knower/Doers and Their Moral Problems,' 271; see Nelson, 'Epistemological Communities,' 121 and note 3, 152.

21. Code, 'Taking Subjectivity into Account,' 16.

22. Code, 'Experience, Knowledge, and Responsibility,' 188.

23. Code, 'Taking Subjectivity into Account,' 16; see also Code, *Rhetorical Spaces,* xi.

24. Bernstein, *Beyond Objectivism and Relativism,* 8.

25. Taylor, 'Leading a Life,' 2.

26. Grimshaw, *Feminist Philosophers,* 90.

27. Quine expresses the underdetermination thesis in terms of "the relation between the meagre input and the torrential output . . . that we are prompted to study . . . in order to see how evidence relates to theory, and in what ways one's theory of nature transcends any available evidence" ('Epistemology Naturalized,' 25).

28. I take this phrasing from Addelson. See my reference in Chapter 1, note 74.

29. Kuhn, *The Structure of Scientific Revolutions.*

30. These are not terms used by Kuhn.

31. Code, *'What Can She Know?,'* 124. I have in mind here the approaches taken by, for example, Malpas, 'Speaking the Truth,' and Taylor, *Sources of the Self.* Code critiques some of the implicit assumptions of Quine-derived epistemological naturalism in 'What is Natural about Epistemology Naturalized?' Harding sets up an interesting debate between epistemologists and philosophers of science, sociologists of knowledge, and postmodernists that illuminates some of the issues raised in contemporary critiques of foundationalist epistemology in *Whose Science? Whose Knowledge?,* Chapter 7, especially 165–173. I have found the work of Nelson to be particularly helpful in understanding how a relation might be established between pragmatism and/or naturalism, on one hand, and feminist ethics and epistemology, on the other, even though this relation is not one I have explored here. As well as her 'Epistemological Communities,' see 'A Question of Evidence' and *Who Knows? From Quine to a Feminist Empiricism.*

32. I base this suggestion on my reading of feminist epistemologists like Code and Haraway. This is not to suggest that either Code or Haraway would agree either with my reading or with the conclusions to which that reading leads me.

33. Walker, 'Feminism, Ethics, and the Question of Theory,' 24. See my discussion in Chapter 1, text at note 62.

34. Cf. Walker, 'Moral Understandings,' 15: "Current philosophical practice still largely views ethics as the search for moral knowledge, and moral knowledge as comprising universal moral formulae and the theoretical justification of these"; Addelson, 'Knower/Doers and Their Moral Problems,' 271: "within the traditional epistemology, science was defined as *the knowledge* made in science ."

35. Cf. Code, 'Taking Subjectivity into Account,' 20: "My thesis . . . requires epistemologists to pay as much attention to the nature and situation—the location—of S as they commonly pay to the content of p."

36. Or, in the case of relativism, to the devaluing of S-knows-that-p claims.

37. Code, 'What Is Natural about Epistemology Naturalized?,' 14.

38. Nelson, 'Epistemological Communities,' 124.

39. I introduced one problematic version of antifoundationalism in the text at note 30. For a summary of the variety of attitudes to the relationship between feminist philosophers and the traditions of philosophy, see the Introduction by Antony and Witt to *A Mind of One's Own.*

40. See text at note 8.

41. Antony, 'Quine as Feminist,' 189. See also Nelson, 'Epistemological Communities,' 146, on "the potential paradox of arguing (or implying) that science influenced by politics and gender is, by virtue of the fact, bad science."

42. Antony, 'Quine as Feminist,' 214.

43. Ibid., 215.

44. Ibid. Antony's language here is reminiscent of Harding's description of "strong objectivity" in *Whose Science? Whose Knowledge?*, Chapter 6, especially 149. Harding's association of objectivity with socially situated knowledge, and particularly with feminist standpoint theory, distinguishes her account of specifically feminist epistemologies from Antony's analysis of truth and knowledge. The criticisms I level at Antony cannot, I suggest, be applied to Harding.

45. Antony, 'Quine as Feminist,' 215, 216.

46. So Antony says, ibid., 214: "The Dragnet theory is not false because it's pernicious; it's pernicious because it is false." "Dragnet theory" is Antony's caricatured version of foundationalist epistemology (see 205).

47. Ibid., 216: "We can identify the particular empirical presuppositions that lie behind a particular program of research so that we can subject them, if necessary, to empirical critique."

48. Ibid., 217, considers claims that "blacks are 'innately' less intelligent than whites."

49. Ibid., It does not seem to me that this is a particularly strong argument: Antony's account of sociobiological determinists' definitions of race and "innate" intelligence begs obvious and important questions about social and biological construction. Presumably, sociobiological determinists would defend their position by removing Antony's scare quotes and citing their own evidence for the biological construction of race. Rather than enter into this infinite regression by critiquing the arguments that Antony employs as examples, however, what I want to do here is illustrate her notion of empirical evaluation.

50. So that intelligence becomes one of the parameters in a biological definition of race. Compare the point I make in Chapter 2, where I suggested that if women are the exemplars of caring practices, then caring is what women should do if they are acting morally *and if they are acting as women.*

51. Antony, 'Quine as Feminist,' 190.

52. Ibid., 215.

53. Presumably, other categories like the ethical, the political, and the psychological.

54. In my earlier comments about removing the distinction between moral epistemology and other fields of knowledge-making, I have anticipated both the possibility that Antony may object to this use of Kohlberg on the grounds that moral epistemology is not amenable to the same methodology as "our collective understanding of knowledge" ('Quine as Feminist,' 218) and my response to that objection.

55. For a summary of Kohlberg's changing definitions of his project, see Kohlberg, 'A Current Statement,' 485–486.

56. For a summarised account of the wide range of conclusions and claims that can be read into Kohlberg's account and defence of his theory, see Blum, 'Gilligan and Kohlberg.'

57. Although I appreciate Gilligan's reasons for saying that they do not, *(In a Different Voice,* 18). I think her strategic use of the idea of women's exclusion is in creative tension with (rather than opposition to) my point.

58. It is Gilligan's point *(In a Different Voice,* 18) that, where males represent the norm, females represent "a curiosity."

59. See Kohlberg and Kramer, 'Continuities and Discontinuities in Childhood and Adult Moral Development.'

60. Some of these possibilities are conceded by Antony. My point is that we cannot allow for these possibilities while recommending the kind of empirical critique Antony endorses.

61. Kohlberg, 'A Reply to Owen Flanagan and Some Comments on the Puka-Goodpaster Exchange,' 524, says that "truly moral reasoning involves features such as impartiality, universalizability, reversibility and prescriptivity."

62. Addelson, 'Knower/Doers and Their Moral Problems,' 272, discusses the possibility that some units of epistemology—meanings, propositions, theories, conceptual schemes, and the person or individual—are "so deeply presupposed" that they are "submerged."

63. Antony, 'Quine as Feminist,' 216. If normative assessments of bias are to be made only in terms of the truth or falsity of the theories, Antony presumably means to use the term "false" rather than "wrong" here.

64. Code, 'Taking Subjectivity into Account,' 23.

65. Antony, 'Quine as Feminist,' 213.

66. Quine, 'Two Dogmas of Empiricism,' 45.

67. It may be, for example, that he acknowledges the empirical presupposition about gender, race, and class differences being (potentially) irrelevant to moral maturity to the extent that this presupposition seems to place his stage sequence theory closer to the edge of the system. What I am suggesting may be his major premise—that morally mature reasoning is principled reasoning—seems to place his stage sequence theory further from the edge of the system.

68. Longino, 'Can There Be a Feminist Science?,' 208.

69. In this case, these assumptions premise theorising on the privileging of impartiality, universalisability, reversibility, and prescriptivity.

70. In suggesting that Gilligan's argument does not attempt an empirical evaluation of Kohlberg's stage sequence theory, I am not denying that there are empirical aspects to her refutation of Kohlberg's various conclusions. However, Gilligan's central achievement is to problematise Kohlberg's premise that moral maturity is measured in terms of principled reasoning. I maintain that no amount of empirical data about moral reasoning could effectively problematise that premise.

71. Gilligan, In a Different Voice, 75.

72. Ibid., 3.

73. Antony, 'Quine as Feminist,' 189.

74. Fricker, 'Knowledge as Construct,' 95, 99.

75. Antony, 'Quine as Feminist,' 215; Fricker, 'Knowledge as Construct,' 100, proposes a dialectic of fact and value, so that reality and thought, the empirical and the political, fact and value are mutually constraining.

76. Fricker, 'Knowledge as Construct,' 106.

77. Cf. Code, What Can She Know?, 30: "Specific instances of knowledge fall along a continuum, where some are more purely objective; others manifest a greater interplay of subjectivity and objectivity; others again are more purely subjective." Code's employment of the continuum metaphor is not introduced in order to safeguard objectivity, as I am suggesting it might be for Fricker.

78. Fricker, 'Knowledge as Construct,' 106.

79. Antony, 'Quine as Feminist,' 215: "Biases are good when and to the extent that they facilitate the gathering of *knowledge*—that is, when they lead us to the truth. Biases are bad when they lead us *away* from the truth"; Fricker, 'Knowledge as Construct,' 103:

"While all belief is inevitably permeated by social, historical and linguistic influences, our practices of belief-justification must nevertheless be oriented to an ideal of truth . . . a unitary—i.e. self-consistent—truth."

80. Rules about, for example, impartiality, autonomy, and the separation of fact and value.

81. And that the social construction of what is visible "allows" me to see black swans.

82. Code, 'Taking Subjectivity into Account,' 19.

83. This is not to suggest that the empiricism of extensionist feminist philosophers is not to be distinguished from foundationalist empiricism is significant ways. My point is that a better case can be made of anti-foundationalism, and this is the case for which I am preparing to argue.

84. Of course, not all knowledge-claims have the same kind of consequences. The point, reflecting Longino's (cited in note 68), is not that all knowledge-claims have consequences affecting the judgment of knowers but that not all knowledge-claims are, for knowers, consequence-free.

85. As Antony does, 'Quine as Feminist,' 190.

86. I do not want to limit this to cases where we might want to say that "your interpretation or assessment of the empirical evidence is mistaken." I am not talking only about different interpretations or assessments of the same "facts." What I have in mind is the process of showing that facts and empirical evidence may themselves be interpretations or assessments: they may not be neutral pieces of data anteceding the interpretations or assessments that assign them to knowledge-claims.   That the epistemological methodology endorsed by Antony seems to lead in the direction of this latter proposition is perhaps a mark of her Quine-derived assumption that epistemology is better consigned to natural scientists than to metaphysicians.

87. See for example Antony, 'Quine as Feminist,' 217: "the empirical inadequacy of the theory of mind and knowledge that makes perfect neutrality seem like a good thing."

88. Fricker, 'Knowledge as Construct,' 101.

89. See, for example, Hampton, 'Feminist Contractarianism,' 235: "Rawls, in particular, concentrates on defining the hypothetical people who are supposed to make this agreement to ensure that their reasoning will not be tarnished by immorality, injustice, or prejudice."

90. According to Sidgewick. See Walker, 'Moral Understandings,' 20.

91. Antony's terminology, 'Quine as Feminist,' 189.

92. Although Harding's concept of strong objectivity is, as I have said in note 44, not open to many of the criticisms I make in this chapter, it is worth noting here how she conceives of the partial. Gorham, 'The Concept of Truth in Feminist Sciences,' 112, note 7, says: "Though it is never given a detailed explication, the concept of partial truth is ubiquitous in Harding's work." Where Harding's use of the notion of partiality differs markedly from mine, though, is that she seems to envisage a link between *more partial* and *distorted* beliefs, so that the move toward strong objectivity and the "less false" is a move *away* from partial and distorted claims. See, for example, *Whose Science? Whose Knowledge?*, 159, 185.

93. Or as Antony puts it, 'Quine as Feminist,' 210: "We must take some knowledge for granted."

94. In another sense, of course, the distinction between facts or knowledge and values, opinion or bias is crucial to foundationalism.   What I mean is that, for the foundationalist, the discourse that establishes the foundationalist reasoner is only about the *elimination* of bias, so that the reasoner reasons not in a process that distinguishes knowledge from bias but in a process that is bias-free.

95. It would, I suggest, be regarded by Kohlberg as complex questioning to ask him whether his conclusions are adversely affected by his preferences and preconceptions (i.e., questioning of the "have you stopped beating your dog?" variety). He cannot answer yes *or* no without admitting a link that he denies.

96. These ideas, to which I can make only passing reference here, are elaborated in Braidotti, *Patterns of Dissonance* and 'Embodiment, Sexual Difference, and the Nomadic Subject'; Diprose, *The Bodies of Women;* Gatens, 'Corporeal Representation in/and the Body Politic'; Lloyd, 'Maleness, Metaphor, and the "Crisis" of Reason'; Pateman, *The Sexual Contract.* See also many of the papers in addition to those I have cited in Alcoff and Potter, *Feminist Epistemologies;* Diprose and Ferrell, *Cartographies;* Lennon and Whitford, *Knowing the Difference;* Nicholson, *Feminism/Postmodernism.*

Chapter 6

Partial Reason: The Epistemological Imperatives of Partiality

I set out my critique of the extensionist concept of partiality as bias in terms of the elaboration of three alternatives. The first refers to the choice between retaining the notion of truth as a regulatory ideal and restricting knowledge-claims to statements about personal perspectives. The second asserts that either we endorse the separate, autonomous individual as the epistemic agent or we concede the possibility of making authoritative knowledge-claims. The third contrasts the insistence on a common language with the lapse into an incoherent babble. The alternatives that I have introduced with the concept of strong epistemological partiality are, first, that we might replace the notion of truth as a regulatory ideal by securing the notions of truth and knowledge in the universally operative requirement for the elaboration of the context in which we function as knowers; second, that we might replace the insistence on the individual agent's epistemic authority with a concept of the authority of selves-in-relation; third, that we might replace the notion of a totalising common language with a commonality of mutual understanding.

These alternatives are linked with the critique of impartiality that focuses not on the biased nature of foundationalist theory but on problematising any assumption that there is a world against which theories can be checked, on explicitly renouncing the premise of unpremisedness, and on objecting to the pejorative use of the notion of partiality. Where these objections lead to the questioning of traditional assumptions that privilege the abstract and the universal and locate epistemological constraints outside epistemological practice, the result is the establishment of the link between epistemology and context that is central to my notion of partial reason.

MINIMAL REALISM

For me, partial reason can be understood as being consistent with a version of minimal realism. That it is possible to sustain a challenge to foundationalism while yet holding the line at a defence of at least a minimal realism is not a novel suggestion. I agree with other feminist philosophers that, in order to argue *philosophically* that sexism is wrong,[1] we must be able to make knowledge-claims that have validity outside the context of this time, this place, and this person. Minimal realism, in the sense that it is defended by feminist theorists, is the recognition that "not anything goes" when it comes to describing and evaluating the world and our place in it. It is the understanding that there is a constraint on what is known, that all knowledge-claims are not equally acceptable. It is implied in comments like those of Evelyn Fox Keller: "The constraints imposed by the recalcitrance of nature are reminders . . . that, despite its ultimate unrepresentability, nature does exist."[2] In a similar vein, Longino says: "Obviously model choice is also constrained by (what we know of) reality, that is, by the data."[3] Sandra Harding talks of more plausible, less distorted claims and theories that are "more likely to be confirmed by evidence,"[4] while Code identifies the "need to be able to assume [the world's] 'reality' in some minimal sense" that gives rise to the necessity "to achieve some match between knowledge and 'reality.'"[5]

While the maximal realism of correspondence and representational theories of truth satisfy this requirement for a sense of epistemological constraint, they do so only at the expense of acknowledging the social and political aspects of our knowledge of reality. Minimal realism, on the other hand, eschews the language of truth as revelation, where what knowledge reveals is an objective realm that exists independently of that knowledge, while yet retaining the possibility that what is true is not necessarily solely a function of who says what, when, and where. As Anne Seller says: "It is false to say that a woman's womb withers if she uses her brain, irrational to use sexual characteristics rather than economic position as the deciding factor in granting a mortgage, and patently unjust to pay less to a woman than a man for completing identical tasks."[6] It is, I suggest, the capacity to make this kind of judgment and articulate this kind of argument that may be lost in the antirealism of postmodern epistemology or, indeed, any position that forecloses on the possibility of saying with Seller that there are certain truths to which we all now agree.

What is important for my argument is that these claims to a minimal realism need to sustain the recognition that "not anything goes," that some knowledge-claims are sounder than others, *without* endorsing a regulatory notion of truth, a concept of truth as universal and unitary, or an epistemological emphasis on elaborating the content of truth. My requirement of a minimal realism is that it should secure the possibility of creating and sustaining shared belief systems, mutual understandings, and intersubjective agreements. I argue that the notion of partial reason, entailing as it does an emphasis on elaborating the contextual realities of selves-in-relation, might secure these possibilities, where other notions of truth-seeking place them at risk.

ELABORATING THE CONTEXT OF TRUTH

The first epistemological possibility I want to associate with the concept of partial reason is that the notion of truth as a regulatory ideal might be replaced by a notion of truth as the elaboration of the context in which we function as knowers.[7] As I have said, my intention is to secure a version of minimal realism with a robust notion of truth while, at the same time, problematising accounts that dichotomise truth as either unitary and universal or multiple and unassessible.

It seems to me that no matter how heavily we qualify the notion of universal and unitary truth, it remains wedded to the idea that speaking, thinking, believing, acting, and feeling all reflect reality, or the way the world is. This remains so, I think, even when the reality that universal and unitary truth reflects is understood as a social construction. To the extent that speech, thought, belief, actions, and feelings are meaningful, then, they are supposed to express our sense of "how things are." As speakers, thinkers, believers, actors, and feelers, we are assumed to be "enmeshed in a speaking that implicitly makes some claim to be truthful."[8] This enmeshing relies on our sense of the constraints imposed by the requirement of consistency when we make claims or assertions about the world. Too much inconsistency empties our claims and assertions of content.[9] For Quine, as I have noted, "[t]he edge of the system must be kept squared with experience."[10]

In the previous chapter, I draw attention to the contested nature of claims about where the edge of the system lies. I press the point further now by connecting this contestation with an additional point about the implications of "the requirement of consistency." Proponents of a universal and unitary notion of truth assert that our claims and assertions are "conditional on our prior involvement with the world," so that inconsistency marks not just the failure of belief but the failure of our relation to the world.[11] This is the failure identified by Fricker: "How can I genuinely *believe* it is raining if I simultaneously hold that I might equally well believe it is dry and sunny?"[12] This failure can be avoided, according to Fricker, by making genuine beliefs "answerable to empirical matters,"[13] in other words, by checking our speaking about the world against the world that is spoken about.[14]

I suggest that no matter how provisional we make the notion of "the world that is spoken about," an epistemology that uses such a notion to constrain knowledge remains focused on one particular kind of knowledge and truth and one particular kind of world. This is the kind of knowledge that reads the world under the demand for truth, that looks to its prior involvement in the world for evidence of consistency and finds in that evidence confirmation both that the world is knowable and that we can give an account of the world that is reliable, consistent, and coherent. This reliability, consistency, and coherence are a product of our successful mapping of the way we speak about the world onto the world that is spoken about.

My suggestion is that Gilligan's account of the way we actually talk about the world and about what we know and what is true shows that knowledge and truth are not a *product* but an ongoing *process* of trying to understand the world and ourselves. This process is not necessarily one of resolving inconsistencies but of sustaining and tolerating an awareness of irreconcilable clashes, oppositions, and tensions that leaves us suspended between ideals and needs. We are caught between desires—"the wish not to hurt others and the wish to be true to [ourselves]"; the "wish to be both honest and caring, '[. . .] committed to certain ideas but . . . able to relate to other people and to respect other people's ideas and yet not compromise and not be just submissive and accommodate to other people'"[15]; the wish to be both selfless and self-asserting, to avoid both selfishness and self-sacrifice—so that to assert one priority seems to deny another. Knowledge or understanding in the terms described by the participants in Gilligan's studies is less a matter of establishing a unified truth than of elaborating the context in which claims to know or understand might be made. For Gilligan, unified truth is like "a poem as round and hard as a stone," which, by eliminating the "variegated edges" of irreconcilable tensions, ends up saying nothing.[16]

Of course, one of the difficulties in elaborating a critique of the concept of truth as a regulatory ideal, of truth as unitary and universal, is that that concept does not literally say nothing. In fact, it purports to deal effectively with what has been claimed to be by far the most philosophically significant aspect of our understanding of the world, where knowledge involves reading the world under the demand for truth. What I am suggesting, however, is that this is one particular construction of knowledge and one particular way of perceiving the world. According to this perception, individual selves, as knowers, are not positioned in relation. Individual selves know to the extent that they can map their claims and assertions about the world onto the world as it really is. These individual selves are able to come to shared understandings to the extent that their claims and assertions about the world are self-consistent and consistent with the claims and assertions of others. When individual selves share understandings, then, they "see the same thing."

The perception that I think provides a more adequate account of shared understandings, however, is of selves-in-relation, where this positioning in relation enables knowing.[17] Here, shared understandings arise out of knowers' relations to each other rather than out of the relation between their claims and assertions. What regulates knowing is the ability of knowers to articulate knowledge as what *we* understand, the ability of knowers to locate knowledge-claims in the meaning-generating "life context"[18] where we know what we know because we can connect across our differences. The shared understandings of selves-in-relation are reflections not of what individuals know as individuals but of the situation of individuals in epistemic relation. This perception distinguishes "seeing the same thing," which is the product of the shared understandings of individual selves, from "seeing together," which describes the process whereby the knowledge-claims of selves-in-relation are secured.

I first drew this distinction between individual selves "seeing the same thing" and a relational "seeing together" when I refined the concept of attention in Chapter 4. Responses to the Heinz dilemma provide further evidence of the difference between knowledge-claims that involve seeing the same thing and knowledge-claims that involve seeing together. For Amy, to whom Heinz's problems appear not as "a conflict between life and property that can be resolved by logical deduction" but as "a fracture of human relationship that must be mended with its own thread,"[19] the solution is not contained in Kohlberg's posing of the dilemma. Her responses show her worrying over the material presented to her, unable to move with a sense of certainty because she simply cannot discern what would constitute knowledge or understanding in that situation. None of the available alternatives are acceptable to her because what makes the world knowable or understandable has been omitted. What Kohlberg describes, to Amy's ears, is a world without human connection, a world devoid of the context that enables knowledge and understanding. Amy's responses represent the attempt to refashion the one-dimensional hypothetical into a three-dimensional narrative of relatedness, from which she hopes to see how the contradictions she senses in Kohlberg's story are sustained.

The substance of Jake's responses are usually taken as demonstrating a different approach from Amy's. What I suggest, however, is that a quite different construction might be placed on his interview if, instead of taking the responses of both interviewees as indications of what they know as individuals, we consider their responses as also reflecting an epistemic relation, that is, as being the epistemic responses of selves-in-relation.[20] Straightaway, it seems to me, we see that Jake is talking to someone with whom he feels he has something in common. His responses are confirmed by the interviewer; there is a sense of dialogue, of a confident exchange.[21] However, Jake's dealing with the content of the Heinz story is similar in crucial ways to Amy's. Both of them set about trying to establish the "life context" in which the actions of Heinz, his wife, and the pharmacist have meaning. That Jake does so is far less obvious than in Amy's case, because of the common understandings shared by Jake and the interviewer. As I show in Chapter 3, Friedman[22] has demonstrated that Jake's responses are based on assumptions that go far beyond the abstract contextual backdrop provided by Kohlberg. (It is noteworthy, e.g., that in Kohlberg's hypothetical example neither the wife nor the pharmacist has a name). She does this by showing that Jake's responses are specifically tied to his understanding of the precise nature of the relationships between Heinz, his wife, and the pharmacist and that these responses change as those relationships are altered. So, Jake, like Amy, seeks to supplement Kohlberg's abstract contextual backdrop with an understanding of the meaning-generating "life context" in which Heinz is situated. That Jake is able to do so where Amy is not is, I suggest, because Jake's understanding is what "*we* understand," for the "we" constituted by Jake and the interviewer.

This is the place at which the notions of epistemic relatedness of selves-in-relation and of knowledge as the elaboration of context connect. For what we can now see is that, to respond adequately, both Jake and Amy must themselves be engaged as knower/doers,[23] must themselves be identified as selves-in-relation. It is easy to imagine how differently Amy's responses might have read if she had been interviewed by someone prepared to engage her in dialogue. The difference between the two interviews, then, is not only that they illustrate different ways of constructing knowledge or truth but that one interview reflects shared understandings, and the other, a failure of epistemic relation. In both cases, the factors determining the outcome of the interview include not only the authoritative pronouncements of individual knowers but also the relation between the interviewer and interviewee. What Friedman shows is that Kohlberg's conclusions, which focus only on what individuals are assumed to know, are mistaken. For Kohlberg, truth lies in the elaboration of the content of truth. The kinds of answers given by Jake, which Kohlberg processes as universal and unitary, seem to supply this content, where Amy's do not. However, to rate the interviews in this way is to discount the significance of the context of each interview. The players here are the interviewer and interviewee. Their encounters, as much as Heinz's, take place in a "life context." Elaborating this "life context" means asking who talks to whom about what, or who knows, what they know, and how they know it. Seen in this light, both Jake's and Amy's responses appear to be contingent, to a significant extent, on the interview encounters and the way that those encounters facilitate, or fail to facilitate, an account of Heinz's options. Such encounters do not generate the kind of data that advance Kohlberg's case. Rather, they show that there is an account of truth that is better sought in the elaboration of the context in which knowledge and understanding might be constituted.

I suggest that elaborating the content and the context of truth are not two sides of the same epistemological coin. Rather, they are aspects of two radically different approaches to the philosophical understanding of knower/doers, two radically contrasting views about what is philosophically interesting and significant about human thought and action. Let me be specific about where I locate some of these points of difference by considering three particular distinctions.

First, the concern with *content* leads toward closure, to a point of resolution at which I can say that I know with some certainty. This concern starts by defining what is at issue, what is causing uncertainty. Once we have "a math problem with humans,"[24] a conflict-of-meaning problem, or a life-is-worth-more-than-property problem, we can draw on the resources appropriate to dealing with that problem. The concern with *context*, on the other hand, is the concern to keep relational possibilities open or to repair connections where they have been fractured. It is the concern with seeing what is unique about a situation, with retrieving what might be lost in subsuming the particular case under the general rule.

Second, the concern with *content* locates particular individuals as abstract, interchangeable role-players. So, the Heinz dilemma is presented in terms of the husband, the wife (who is also the victim or the patient), and the pharmacist. My resolution of the dilemma is not supposed to apply to this particular husband, wife, or pharmacist but to all cases manifesting this problem (however this problem is defined). The concern with *context* is less interested in the role of husbands (victims, pharmacists) than in the way this person's relation with this particular other is sustained. The approach concerned with context locates people in concrete relations, where they are not interchangeable.[25]

Third, the approach that emphasises the elaboration of the *content* of truth establishes the success or failure of a knowledge-claim according to an ideal standing outside particular practices of knowing. Whether the ideal insists on the self-consistency of propositions or on the conformity of propositions to empirical reality (or on a mixture of both), it imposes a direction on discourse by dictating what can and what cannot be taken as knowledge. The approach that emphasises the elaboration of the *context* of truth, on the other hand, establishes the success or failure of a knowledge-claim according to whether it maintains and enhances the capacity to see together. This approach, as I have said, views knowledge less as a *product* of our engagement with the world and more as a *process* of engaging, where this process depends on the possibility of being self-reflexively aware of ourselves as selves positioned in relation. This awareness, however, does not function as a regulatory ideal standing outside particular claims to know but is brought into existence in particular knowledge-claims where these claims are claims to see together. Another way of expressing this point is to say that where the approach concerned with content asks of a particular knowledge-claim, "Is it true?," the approach concerned with context asks, "For whom is it true?" Here the concept of truth, of what it would mean for a claim to be true, is not separable from the concepts of knowledge as what is seen together and of knowers as selves-in-relation. These "for whom" questions augment the interest in what is known with an interest in who knows and how they know it.

These points illustrate that to endorse a concept of truth as an elaboration of context is not necessarily to endorse forms of thinking that are unprincipled or forms of thinking that are immersed in the concrete and particular. Such a concept, as I have shown, does include criteria for evaluating knowledge-claims and does support the notions of truth rather than truths and of knowledge rather than knowledges. In contesting the concept of truth as unitary and universal, the concept of truth as an elaboration of context is not, therefore, to be equated with accounts that portray truth as multiple and unassessible.

I have said that elaborating the content and elaborating the context of truth are not two sides of the same epistemological coin. I have also said that the elaboration of the context of truth is not the endorsement of a concept of truth as multiple and unassessible. Taken together, these statements imply that truth understood as the elaboration of context is to be recommended over other understandings of truth. This, it seems to me, is indeed the case, yet what the substantiation of the case depends on is a *redescription* of the thoughts and actions of knower/doers rather than the replacement of one set of norms with another. This is because the question of what criteria are relevant to guiding the elaboration of context is not open to predetermination. To suggest that the criteria of relevance for the elaboration of context can be predetermined would be to suggest a return to a framework of elaborating the content of truth.[26] But that the criteria of relevance cannot be predetermined does not necessarily mean that no such criteria exist. Take, for example, the experience described by Seller in her paper 'Should the Feminist Philosopher Stay at Home?'[27] Faced with an apparently unbridgeable gulf between her understandings of the world and those of the Indian women with whom she was working, Seller explains how she initially understood her role. "Primarily," she says:

I saw myself in the attitude of a listener; I would listen, listen, listen, and together we would develop a dialogue across our two different cultures, maybe creating a space from which we could think together about each of them. . . . I was so eager to create an atmosphere in which talk could flow freely, so anxious about the power relations between others, that it was a long time before I realized how I was inhibiting the dialogue. . . . In short, I refused to allow them to tell me the things that they thought I believed, or to express their own discontents within the vocabulary of the western feminist movement. Note that "I wanted . . ." "I refused . . .", and ask, as I did not: "But whose seminar is this?" . . . In short, in the interests of an open and equal dialogue which was to be both critical and creative, I effectively closed off all of the means available to them for expressing a view. And I did not notice what I was doing. Looking back, it is a testimony to their wit and pride that we broke through the resounding silences I was busy building.[28]

Breaking through these multifaceted silences resulted in Seller and the Indian women sustaining a capacity to see together. Later in this chapter I draw on this example to illustrate several other points in relation to my argument. Here, however, I suggest that, at least in part, such seeing together is premised on the establishment of criteria of relevance. These criteria are certainly not the ones that Seller initially deemed to be relevant, but, had she refused or been unable to revise her understanding of how complex the selection and establishment of criteria can be, she and the women may have been left without any context in which they could see together. There are criteria of relevance operating in my reading of the Jake and Amy interviews, too. The failure of relation discernible in Amy's interview suggests the inadequacy of the criteria of relevance that structured the interviewer's encounter with Amy. But I can imagine the different outcome that might have ensued had Amy been engaged in dialogue without my being able to say precisely why the encounter failed or what relevant criteria were omitted.

The crucial point about this redescription of the actions and thinking of knower/doers is that it follows the understanding that the versions of knowledge and truth that explicitly rule out the elaboration of context are actually concealing an implicit reliance on context in order to impart sense to their knowledge-claims. So, the axiomatic status of autonomous, knowing subjects conceals knowing subjects positioned in relation, just as the axiomatic status of autonomous, moral subjects conceals moral subjects positioned in relation. These autonomous individuals have been sustained in their autonomy by ethical and epistemological practices that rule out the elaboration of context. With different understandings of ethical and epistemological practices in place, these autonomous subjects are revealed as subjects positioned in relation. These different understandings redescribe encounters, as I have redescribed the encounters between Amy and Jake and their interviewers. My redescription does not supplement or complement Kohlberg's description of the responses of autonomous subjects. Rather, it reveals his description as being dependent on concealing a significant range of human responses, as severing the connections that link both children with their interviewer and both their accounts with Heinz's "life context," as equating philosophical maturity with an autonomy that is imposed by philosophical construct rather than by the nature of human responses. In short, if truth understood as the elaboration of context is to be recommended over other versions of truth, it is because it provides a more adequate account of the way knower/doers think and act by making explicit what other versions of truth obscure.[29]

It is important to note that when I talk about redescription, I am not promoting the straightforward privileging of one independent entity (context) over another (content). I have said that truth understood as the elaboration of context is to be recommended over other understandings of truth. But I have qualified this assertion by saying that the elaboration of context entails a process of redescription rather than of replacement: that we need to redescribe separate, autonomous selves as selves-in-relation rather than replace one set of guiding norms with another. The crucial point is that the concern with context is not a disregard for content but a concern not to obscure the extent to which context imparts sense to knowledge-claims.

ELABORATING THE CONCEPT OF SELVES-IN-RELATION

In Chapter 5 I say that feminist proponents of truth as a universal and unitary regulatory ideal regard the attack on totality as equivalent (in effect) to the destruction of the possibility of creating and sustaining intersubjective agreements and shared belief systems. They distinguish only two possibilities: either truth is universal and unitary, or it is multiple and unassessible; either truth transcends the individual viewpoint and is valid outside the context of this time, this place, and this person, or truth is irredeemably personal, local, and historical.

The suggestion I am exploring with the concept of partial reason is that this contrast does not utilise every epistemological resource available to feminist philosophers. What I am arguing is that we might reject the notion of truth as a universal and unitary regulatory ideal, *without* rejecting the possibility that there is a standard or gauge for deeming some knowledge more sound, more true than another. In other words, I am raising the possibility that we might reject unitary and universal concepts of truth *without* sacrificing the ability to create and sustain intersubjective agreements and shared belief systems. I am canvassing the idea that we might turn the epistemological emphasis away from elaborating the content of truth toward a recognition of the significance of the context in which truth-claims are made *while yet* preserving a robust notion of truth. The key to identifying such possibilities is the recognition that partiality entails not only methodological and political but also *epistemological* imperatives.

In this strong epistemological sense, partiality is not considered as a handicap or limitation but as the possibility that *enables* knowledge. By contrast, the arguments of those who endorse only a weaker political sense of partiality see partiality, at least potentially, as a threat to the authority of the individual knower. Both senses of partiality are consistent with the antifoundationalist critique I outline in Chapter 5. This critique replaces the idea of the knower as the passive processor of facts with an awareness of the self as active in the process of knowledge-construction; it attenuates the connection between knowledge and fact; it complicates the distinction between fact and value, description and evaluation, how things are and how knowers feel about them.[30] The introduction, by this antifoundational critique, of partiality into the epistemic equation challenges the authority of the autonomous, impartial, individual knower. But where partiality is seen to entail only *political* and *methodological* imperatives, it may be that the challenge to the authority of individual knowers can be resisted. What I detect in the understanding of partiality that I have discerned in the accounts of the antifoundationalist, extensionist feminist epistemologists examined in Chapter 5 is a move to show that epistemology can survive the discrediting of the impartial knower; that knowers who are biased politically and methodologically (as all knowers are) can still claim to know. Where partiality is seen to entail *epistemological* imperatives, on the other hand, a different and, I suggest, more radical move might be upheld. Rather than focusing on the possibility of resisting the challenge to the authority of individual knowers, the concept of strong epistemological partiality suggests the possibility of redescribing individual knowers as selves-in-relation.

As a starting point for this elaboration of the concept of selves-in-relation, I want to suggest that an important presumption made by those feminist antifoundationalists who resile from the notion of strong epistemological partiality is not well founded. The presumption is that the endorsement of strong epistemological partiality amounts to an endorsement of partiality for its own sake. Showing that this is not necessarily the case is a way of highlighting significant differences in the approaches taken by critical and extensionist feminists to questions about who knows, what they know, and how they know it.

The presumption that the endorsement of strong epistemological partiality amounts to an endorsement of partiality for its own sake is, as I will show, connected with the premise that knowledge and, indeed, bias belong to, or are a property of, individuals. My alternative proposition, the basis for which is that knowledge and bias are properties of selves-in-relation rather than of individuals, is that strong epistemological partiality does not entail reducing partiality to the bias of individuals. Far from endorsing partiality for its own sake, strong epistemological partiality suggests the possibility of relocating epistemological interest from biased individuals to the connections and relations that make knowledge possible.

I have referred to the need to defend at least a minimal realism in order to argue, for example, that sexism is wrong. This implies, I noted, the need be able to make knowledge-claims that have validity outside the context of this time, this place, and this person and to claim that knowledge as true. My argument now is that we can, indeed, make such knowledge and truth claims, while yet ruling out of order claims of truth as a universal and unitary regulatory ideal, once we break the nexus between truth and the knowing individual. That there *is* a constraint on what is known is accepted. A minimal realism can be accommodated without a notion of truth as a regulatory ideal once we realise that the removal of the individual agent's epistemic authority does not necessarily mean that none of us know. The more restricted alternative, based on the assumption that either we endorse the separate, autonomous individual as the epistemic agent, or we concede the possibility of making authoritative knowledge-claims, is one of the oppositions established when contrasting philosophical dichotomies are condensed into the language of formalism versus relativism or objective reality versus boundless difference, as I discuss in Chapter 5.[31]

My argument here and throughout my discussion of partial reason depends on being able to identify possibilities that are not contained in these oppositional assumptions. In this chapter I have argued already that the notion of truth as a regulatory ideal might be undermined by securing the notions of truth and knowledge in the universally operative requirement for the elaboration of the context in which we function as knowers. In the final section of this chapter I consider the possibility that we might displace the dream of a common language[32] with notions of commonality. Here I am focusing on the idea that we might replace the insistence on the individual agent's epistemic authority with a concept of the authority of selves-in-relation. This idea is closely linked with the connection of truth and context that I have discussed in the previous section of this chapter. One of the keys to breaking the nexus between truth and the knowing individual is to problematise the notion of truth as a universal and unitary regulatory ideal. I have begun this problematisation with the suggestion that truth can be understood in terms of context rather than in terms of establishing the necessary and sufficient content of truth-claims. I have illustrated the difference between understanding truth in terms of context rather than in terms of content by distinguishing seeing together from seeing the same thing. In this section I continue the development of these themes by considering what the seeing together of selves-in-relation might involve.

The conclusion that to attribute an epistemological imperative to partiality is to endorse partiality as an end in itself or for its own sake is reached by both Antony and Fricker. For Fricker, such an endorsement invokes partiality itself as the criterion of truth: "Crudely put," she says, "the more partial the perspective, the more reliable the beliefs which issue from it."[33]   Following such a train of thought has the "devastating consequence" of rendering any shared notion of truth "a pernicious act of coercion."[34]   Antony is equally explicit in her condemnation of arguments that promote the ubiquity and utility of partiality yet fail to address the need to make normative distinctions between different partial perspectives.   By only *describing* bias, she says, we effectively "give up *criticising* bias."[35]

As I have remarked, the fear that sustains the rejection of a strong notion of epistemological partiality is the fear of sacrificing the possibility of creating and sustaining intersubjective agreements and shared belief systems. I think that this fear would be warranted *if* the strong notion of epistemological partiality necessarily entailed endorsing partiality for its own sake.   My contention is that such an endorsement is not inevitable.   As I understand it, the concept of partiality does not convey the ways in which particular individual knowers fail to be impartial or the connections between particular individual knowers and what is known.   In fact, the possibility of its doing so arises only when the concept of partiality has been seriously misunderstood.   To assert such a possibility implies that the concept of partiality is primarily a way of bringing to the fore the differences between knowers.   What partiality is about to proponents of this position is the particular beliefs of *a subject* and the way these beliefs are influenced by the temporal and spatial location of this subject.   This position leads to the conclusion that partiality is a "splintering dynamic."[36]   Partiality fractures both the knower's self-identity (since individual identity seems to be not only influenced but determined by its location) and the knower's relational identity (since only I can know from this location).   On this view of partiality, neither internal plurality nor the positioning of knowers, which I discuss in more detail in Chapter 7, provides epistemological resources because partiality is translated as irredeemable difference, signaling the disconnection of individuals and their closure to each other.   I suggest that it is in order to avoid these consequences that some theorists have refused to embrace partiality as an epistemological imperative.

There is, however, an alternative reading of partiality that, while not disregarding the sense in which partiality does, indeed, carry the political imperative not to eclipse others' views, emphasises *relation* as a key epistemological concept.   Rather than being concerned with describing and evaluating the particular biases that affect knowledge, this alternative approach understands partiality as integral to the processes of knowing.   This understanding of partiality is a specifically epistemological proposition that, because it illuminates and is illuminated by the concept of selves-in-relation, can be seen as informing feminist notions of both knowledge and care.

I base this alternative reading, which I call strong epistemological partiality, on Haraway's account of critical positioning.   The first point I want to note is the resonance between the critical-interrogative stance that marks my approach to philosophy and Haraway's use of the term "critical positioning."   In both usages, what I understand "critical" to convey is the sense of self-reflexivity that is one of the aspects of the philosophical attitude distinguishing those who contest traditional philosophical axioms from those who accept or work around them. There is a sense, then, in which we might be *un*critically positioned. Indeed, if to be critical is to be self-reflexive, *un*critical positioning would describe the version of partiality that is restricted to bias, where bias is equated with a description and evaluation of the sociopolitical coordinates of individuals. Such individuals account only in a relatively abstract way for their location in the world. *Un*critically positioned philosophers might locate themselves as white, Western, and feminist, but there remains a sense, a sense that I claim is very significant, in which such locations might be acknowledged while yet retaining the assumption that knowledge can be controlled for the biases of knowers. Here partiality is understood as belonging to individuals. The knowing individual who is made visible by the acknowledgment of partiality understood as bias might be given a sociopolitical outline without necessarily being deprived of the autonomy on which the authority of knowledge-claims of *impartial* knowers is supposedly based.[37] Sociopolitical coordinates function like addresses and telephone numbers: while they are crucial for locating people, they provide no more than the most bland description of whom they locate and may actually obscure what is interesting or relevant.

I consider some arguments that confine the understanding of partiality to bias in the previous chapter. In summary, those arguments assert that if *all* knowledge-claims are affected by the bias of the knower, the extrication of knowledge from bias depends on distinguishing between knowledge-claims that are *adversely* affected by bias and knowledge-claims which are not. Knowledge-claims adversely affected by bias are false claims; bias is pernicious to the extent that it generates knowledge-claims that are wrong.[38] The acknowledgment of partiality, then, is the acknowledgment of an epistemic limitation whose disabling effects can be overcome by keeping the focus of epistemic interest firmly on the impartiality of the knowledge-claims generated by partial knowers whose biases do not affect their knowledge-claims adversely. This is the understanding of partiality that informs the arguments of the uncritically positioned philosopher.

To be *critically* positioned, on the other hand, involves locating myself in my particularity, understanding my perspective as not only partisan but also fragmentary. To be critically positioned is to be aware that it is my positioning that enables me to know myself, others, and the world. Here, acknowledging my position as partial is not only an acknowledgment of bias but also an acknowledgment that as a knower I am positioned in relation to other knowers.

Self-reflexivity plays a particularly significant part in the critical-interrogative approach of feminists to philosophy. At least in part, the failure to be critically positioned leads some feminist philosophers to talk about the exclusion of women from philosophy as something that might be rectified by extending the boundaries of philosophy to include them.[39] What such a move misses, I think, is the deep implication of concepts of women and the feminine in the axioms of traditional philosophy. Only by recognising ourselves in these axioms can we start to understand the intricate processes of a critical feminist approach. Only when we are critically positioned can we speak as women while yet dismantling the concept of "woman," can we make ourselves visible as women by showing how the feminine is rendered philosophically invisible.[40]

The sense in which to be critical is to be self-reflexive is, I think, linked to the possibility of taking responsibility not for some discrete aspect of ourselves but for our positioning as selves-in-relation. This sense of responsibility, a responsibility that is directly relevant to our practices as selves positioned in relation, makes Haraway's use of the term "critical" resonate with that of Gatens'.

Haraway starts with an observation that is similar to those made in the other antifoundationalist feminist accounts I have been considering. For her, bias is construed metaphorically as the conclusive establishment by modern technology, with its reliance on visual aids (e.g., cameras and microscopes), that it is impossible for vision to be passive or unmediated. Perception, then, is the active process of organising the world, of connecting and translating what she calls "highly specific visual possibilities."[41] By stressing the partiality of vision, the metaphor makes the point that all acts of seeing are *ways* of seeing; that eyes or cameras do not transcend what they see. They are temporally and spatially located, *situated*, not disembodied. Vision, both human and mechanical, is limited and particular, finite rather than boundless, specific rather than unrestricted. Vision cannot be abstracted from perspective and context; eyes, like cameras, peer from somewhere, not nowhere, and the perspective and context in which they operate are factors in determining what is seen.

What Haraway offers in her account of critical positioning are

partial, locatable, critical knowledges . . . [and a] doctrine and practice of objectivity that privileges contestation, deconstruction, passionate construction, webbed connections, and hope for transformation of systems of knowledge and ways of seeing.[42]

For Haraway, critical positioning requires a commitment to both "mobile positioning" and "passionate detachment."[43] These are important terms in her analysis, capturing as they do the paradoxical nature of acts of situated or critically positioned knowledge. I think that this sense of paradox or ambiguity links Haraway's argument with my problematisation of the notion of truth as a universal and unitary regulatory idea, which, I have suggested, is the key to displacing the link between knowledge and the individual knower. Mobile positioning and passionate detachment convey a sense in which the *relation* between knowers *affects* the concepts of the knower and the known and of knowledge itself. The knowing subject and the object of knowledge seem to dissolve as independent entities in a process of knowing characterised by the meeting of subjects, selfless perception,[44] or conversation. The concepts of passionate detachment and mobile positioning also, I think, establish a strong link between the notion of partiality as an epistemological imperative and the ethic of care. Situated or critically positioned knowers, like ethical carers, can tolerate paradox. Like Gilligan's subjects, they know that "[i]n life you never see it all, that things unseen undergo change through time, that there is more than one path to gratification, and that the boundaries between self and other are less clear than they sometimes seem."[45] Situated or critically positioned knowers do not rely on abstraction to simplify the concrete or on universals when faced with the particular. They avoid resorting to principle when this involves halting the process of reality-in-the-making. The point I want to underline is that for situated or critically positioned knowers, terms like passionate detachment or mobile positioning do not cease to be paradoxical. Rather, for situated or critically positioned knowers there can be no such thing as *dis*passionate detachment or *im*mobile positioning. The dispassion and immobility of the impartial stance are exposed by situated or critically positioned knowing as fallacious concepts reflecting the political agenda, the value system, the perspectives of a particular philosophical tradition with particular philosophical commitments to hierarchical structures and relations of domination. The important point is that knowers as selves-in-relation do not expose the investments and concerns of traditional philosophy in order to instate an ethics and an epistemology *without* investments and concerns. Rather, they aim to transform the very conceptions of ethics and epistemology so that knowing and caring might become a means of articulating our concerns and clarifying our investments. Such clarification is an essential precursor of the possibility of taking responsibility for our positioning in relation, a possibility that I have identified with the notion of being positioned *critically*.

The crucial point here is that when I associate critical positioning with stances that avoid resorting to abstractions, universals, and principles, this does not necessarily commit me to privileging the concrete, the particular, or the partial for their own sake. Neither does it mean that I read Haraway as endorsing such a privileging. There are, indeed, some fine distinctions to be made here. Sometimes universals sustain us as we puzzle over particulars. Sometimes abstractions provide reliable insight into the concrete. It seems to me that what critical positioning opens up is the possibility that, as selves-in-relation, we might discover resources in both abstract and concrete thinking, in orientations to both the universal and particular. I have already alluded to the possibility, in connection with both ethics and epistemology, that the rejection of abstraction, universalisation, and impartiality that is assumed to privilege the concrete, particular, and partial may, in fact, problematise both. What critical positioning suggests is that neither abstract nor concrete thinking, neither universal nor particular orientations guarantee that we can know well. But to be critically positioned is not only to be aware of the limits and contradictions[46] implicit in the practices of knowing but also to understand that these limits and contradictions might be tolerated rather than transcended at the level of epistemology.

This is an important and complex point that requires some development, not only so that its philosophical significance can be distinguished from its rhetoric but also in order to address the question that is implicit in the crude equation of partiality with an epistemic ideal (the more partial, the better). This question might take several forms. In the terms established by my argument, it involves understanding how to distinguish between seeing together and seeing the same thing at the concrete level of ordinary conversation. This is a question to which I return in the next chapter when I connect partial reason with the ethic of care. Now, though, I want to show how critical positioning illuminates the concept of seeing together for selves-in-relation. I also want to link the concept of selves-in-relation with the possibility that the toleration of limits and contradictions at the level of epistemology might increase the possibility of understanding.

It seems to me that the notion of strong epistemological partiality, when it is informed by Haraway's concept of critical positioning, supports an epistemological approach that accepts the complexity, ambiguity, and contradictory nature of human reality and avoids artificial and distorting simplifications of human experience. For approaches that limit the relevance of partiality to the weaker political imperative to avoid eclipsing others' views, contradictions are not sustainable epistemologically. As Fricker says, "The entertainment of contradictory beliefs is strictly provisional: contradiction remains intolerable at the level of epistemology."[47] There is a sense, however, in which the resolution of contradiction depends on the establishment of just that regulatory notion of truth that I am questioning. Once truth is established as a regulatory ideal, the suggestion that determining what is contradictory might not be straightforward is passed over, as is the possibility that the tensions sustained by contradiction might promote understanding. That we are aware of contradictions, for theorists of Fricker's persuasion, is a consequence of acknowledging the existence of other epistemological perspectives. That this awareness itself is as contingent as our epistemic location—that is, that contradictions are not self-evident, that what you see as a contradiction depends on where you are seeing from—is overlooked by approaches that insist that contradictions are resolved at the epistemological level.

There may certainly be some senses in which identifying and resolving contradictions are not problematic. In a strictly logical sense, I cannot believe that it is raining and that it is not raining.[48] What is more, this contradiction can be resolved with reference to what is true. Either you or I can find out what is true (whether it is raining) and resolve any contradictory beliefs. The straightforward or strictly logical case, however, does not seem to me to capture what is interesting about deciding what is contradictory. This is because there are two senses in which contradictions arise. The first, which I think Fricker may have in mind when she says that contradiction is not epistemologically tolerable, arises when "what I know" contradicts "what I know." This is the case with the rain example, where to say both that it is and that it is not raining is to assert something nonsensical. But the other sense of contradiction arises when I am standing in the rain asserting that it is not raining, when "what I know" seems to contradict "what is true." In the first case, the problem is that I do not seem to know anything. In the second, the problem is that what I say I know contradicts what seems to be happening. Now if we are obliged to tolerate contradictions at the *political* level, where this toleration represents the determination not to eclipse the views of others, it is surely in this second sense. But Fricker's implication is that, at the *epistemological* level, we can resolve contradiction (tolerated at the political level) by appealing to what is happening, what is true. This implication, though, involves the assumption that I have already problematised in talking about the exclusion from epistemology of ways of knowing other than those captured in "knowing-that" claims and the exclusion from ethics of ways of relating other than those characterised as formal and public. This is the assumption that a sharp distinction can be made between knowledge-claims that are obviously empirically constrained and those that are not so obviously constrained. This assumption depends on our ability to distinguish clearly where boundaries lie, where the edge of the system falls. Yet this assumption, I have said, is precisely what is contested in the stronger reading of partiality that I have presented.

Fricker's assertion that contradiction must be eliminated in the move from politics to epistemology implies that the boundaries between a political claim and an epistemological claim are clearly distinguishable. So, for example, in the case where I am standing in the rain asserting that it is not raining, Fricker might tolerate the contradiction politically with the concession that what is rain for me may not be rain for you. But when it comes to establishing a knowledge-claim, she will expect to be able to find out what is true (whether it is raining) and resolve the contradiction. Where such expectations falter, though, is in their insistence that it is truth as a regulatory ideal that flushes out contradictions in this second sense, which makes contradictions between "what I know" and "what is true" self-evident. As I have said, what the regulatory ideal supplies is the *content* of truth. It tells us of what truth consists, what we need to know in order to know what is true. Yet at the political level, we are able to tolerate contradiction because different accounts of the same thing might be true.[49] At the political level, what regulates truth and, therefore, what determines what we see as contradictory, is where we see from. In other words, what regulates truth at the political level is not an ideal but the context in which I assert something to be true. Fricker wants to be able to eliminate contradiction in the move from the political level, at which truth is regulated by the context of knowers, to the epistemological level, at which truth is regulated by the content of an ideal, by appealing to "what is true," to what is actually the case. It is this appeal that I am questioning. For Fricker to identify and resolve contradictions in the first kind of contradictory claim, where what I know contradicts what I know, the appeal to "what is true" does not have to be made. In an important sense, we move no closer to establishing what sort of claim is being made by producing either logical or empirical evidence relating to what is claimed. In the harder case represented by the second kind of contradictory claim, though, the caution Fricker shows at the political level about tolerating the views of others, presumably because we cannot necessarily assess "what is true," seems to be dispensed with at the epistemological level. At the political level, Fricker can identify a contradiction from her perspective but tolerate it on the grounds that others may see things differently. At the epistemological level, though, the perspectival nature of seeing, of knowing drops away. The determination that "that is a contradiction from my perspective" becomes the determination that "that is wrong."

This appeal, at the epistemological level, might be legitimate in cases of knowledge-claims that are tightly constrained in an empirical sense, as claims about rain might be said to be.[50] The crucial point is that for claims that are not constrained empirically or claims whose empirical content is contestable, the appeal to what is true may be just the kind of coercive move that Fricker presumably wants to avoid: a move that separates the political from the epistemological, separates the context of truth-claims from the content of truth-claims in order to secure a notion of philosophical truth.

It is important to emphasise at this point that my argument with Fricker is not only that determining what is contradictory might be more problematic than her position infers. Such an argument might complicate her position, but it would not necessarily undermine the claim that contradictions are intolerable at the level of epistemology. It is this latter claim that I refuting, at least in so far as it implies that the perspectival caution employed at the political level is not relevant in the assessment of epistemological claims.

Let me illustrate this elusive point with a concrete example of the way in which contradiction might be sustained epistemologically. In her interactions with Indian academic women, Seller learned that what she initially saw as contradictions attributable to the inadequacy of their theorising were better understood as conflicts of values or concerns. Her accounts of how she tried to establish dialogue (often unsuccessfully) show how the attempt to resolve contradictions by appealing to a unitary and universal notion of truth fails. Faced with the concurrent assertions that domestic violence and divorce are both wrong, that unmarried women and women with small dowries who are killed by dissatisfied husbands are both to be pitied, she gradually realised that these contradictory beliefs *could* be tolerated in the contexts in which they were asserted. Although initially confused "because I could see the appeal (value) of [their] position, while finding it unworkable in my own life," Seller came to the conclusion that "[w]hat we choose to see as contradictions . . . reveals our values."[51] What is important for my argument is that Seller did not *resolve* the contradictions but came to see them as mutually sustainable in the context in which they were asserted.

Seller's experience is, I think, not adequately captured by describing her as coming to appreciate the ideals of truth that enabled the Indian women to hold such contradictory beliefs. Her insight, it seems to me, is not into *their* ideals but into *her own*. What makes her account so moving are her initial reluctance to shift away from, or modify, her own ideals—which inform her understanding of the Indian women's beliefs as contradictory—and her dawning realisation that those ideals themselves are inseparably bound up with her own perspective. What is interesting is not so much how contradictory views (i.e., the views of the Indian women) can be held together (because to focus on this aspect of epistemology is to retain the focus on the content of truth-claims) but how contradictory perspectives (Seller's and the Indian women's) can be mutually informing (which is to shift epistemological interest to the context in which we know). Again I make the point that Seller's story does not conclude with the resolution of contradictions but with the opening up of the possibility of inhabiting those contradictions by increasing her understanding of the place from which contradictions are perceived, the context in which she herself is located.

For Haraway, Seller's insight is available to knowers who are critically positioned. The concept of critical positioning develops from Haraway's point about the impossibility of passive or unmediated knowledge construction. The visual allegory says that to see, we need instruments of vision. Whether we use our eyes or technologically sophisticated digital transmitters, vision is mediated by the instruments of vision. If direct vision is impossible, the positioning of the instruments of vision—the siting of the camera, for instance—becomes a decisive factor in determining what is seen. Thus, for Haraway, "an optics is a politics of positioning."[52]

This brings me back to the point I have made about the value, for feminist epistemology and for feminist ethics, of replacing the autonomous, knowing individual with notions of selves-in-relation. Only if we conceive the act of knowing as *unpositioned*, as *unmediated*, can we (pretend to) speak authoritatively of and from a position other than our own. Such authoritative speaking as Seller might once have thought possible is limited to analysing the position of other women in terms of my own experiences, to naming their oppression in terms that elucidate my own. In responding in this way, I am looking for the factors that make this situation *similar* to mine. To use Haraway's terms, I am seeking a subject position of *identity*.[53] In other words, I respond to the situation of other women to the extent that it is the same as my own. But the notion of critical positioning suggests another response. Critically positioned, I see that it is a fallacy to assume that I can either assimilate the experiences of other women into my own or speak with authority from their position. To be critically positioned is to be reflexively aware of my own acts of knowing, the "instruments of knowledge" that connect me and my experiences with, in Seller's case, those of the Indian academics. Critical positioning admits that it *is* relevant that I am white and affluent. If I am *not* critically positioned, my response might appear, particularly to the Indian women, to be disembodied or transcendent. Critical positioning, on the other hand, makes me able to "join with another, to see together without claiming to be another."[54]

What critical positioning reveals, then, is knowers as selves-in-relation. Now if this revelation remains located within the paradigm where a distinction between moral epistemology and other fields of knowledge-making is sustained, I might have to concede that, while critical positioning is important to knowers as selves-in-relation, that is, to moral epistemology, there are other domains of knowledge where critical positioning is not relevant. I have already argued, in Chapter 5, that the distinction between moral epistemology and other fields of knowledge-making does not need to be sustained by feminist philosophers. The revelation of knowers as selves-in-relation strengthens this argument by disrupting two assumptions held by those who would sustain distinctions between domains of knowledge on the basis of whether critical positioning is important. The first assumption is that we are not always positioned. This assumption does not survive even the relatively weak assertion of partiality that recognises that all knowing proceeds from a human point of reference. Where the critical-interrogative approach of feminism to philosophy differs from extensionist arguments, though, is in the insistence that we are not just positioned but *critically* positioned. That is, we are not only positioned in the political and methodological sense of being locatable according to our biases but also *critically* positioned in the sense that our thinking is reflexively bound up with our positioning: that the capacity to think is the capacity to think self-consciously as selves-in-relation.

Although this implies that S, in S-knows-that-p knowledge-claims, is always critically positioned, it does not entail the further implication that critical positioning is always especially relevant to S's understanding of p. There is, however, a second assumption required to sustain the suggestion that critical positioning is relevant in some domains of knowledge and not in others. This is the assumption that the question of where the edge of the system lies is open to conclusive resolution. This, I suggest in Chapter 5, is clearly not necessarily the case. Part of what knowledge-claims claim is where they are located in relation to the edge of the system, how they "square with experience." Certainly, some knowledge-claims appear not to be contestable, appear to be so tightly constrained empirically that understanding who knows, what they know, and how they know it seems to add nothing to our understanding of what is claimed. That we can identify these claims depends, however, on our being critically positioned.[55] The distinction I am drawing here is between being critically or uncritically positioned, rather than between being positioned or unpositioned. To be uncritically positioned is, I have suggested, to locate oneself in the world in a relatively abstract way, to equate what is partial with what is biased or partisan rather than with what is fragmentary. One of the problems I have identified in this equation of partiality with bias is that it does not provide an adequate basis for contesting how tightly a proposition is empirically constrained. Yet such contestation is vital if we are to be able to demonstrate *philosophically* that the inferences from data to theory that sustain propositions about withering wombs and morally immature women are qualitatively different from those that support propositions about falling apples and the movement of planets. To be critically positioned, however, is to be self-reflexively aware of our own knowing practices, where these practices are always processes of creating and sustaining shared understandings. Critically positioned, we can press *all* knowledge-claims on the question of how their propositional content is related to evidence and whether we increase our understanding of what is being asserted by asking who knows, what they know, and how they know it.

It is important to my argument about the *critical* aspect of positioning to emphasise Haraway's point that positioning is not *passive* or *innocent.* If positioning is allegorically linked with the siting of the camera (or other instrument of vision), then I have to take *responsibility* for how and where it is sited. In other words, I am responsible for my acts of knowing. To explain this point by drawing another contrast, if I am *not* critically positioned, I may evade this responsibility by disappearing behind disembodied knowledge claims. I will say that, for example, my whiteness and my affluence have no relevance to the validity of my responses to the situations and circumstances of Indian women. Critically positioned knowledge, however, names itself as white and affluent and admits that it establishes not direct, but *partial,* connections between subjectivities.

The notion of critical positioning further develops the crucial question about *how* to see. Here we find both the internal plurality of the knowing self *and* the positioning of knowing subjects used as resources in the critique of the knowing self as a unified point of knowledge seeking identity with an object. But the crucial realisation is that neither resource is effective unless we replace the autonomous, knowing individual with selves-in-relation who know and see only when they know and see together. In rejecting identity and endorsing critical positioning, Haraway is *not* abandoning the search for commonality or mutuality. The critically positioned knower recognises that knowledge involves not the expropriation of another subject position (which is exploitation) but the location and nourishment of particular points of shared or mutual interest (which is caring).

The reason I have developed Haraway's position in some detail is that it clearly indicates the consonance between the concept of strong epistemological partiality and the possibility of creating and sustaining intersubjective agreements and shared belief systems. That it does so is, I believe, because strong epistemological partiality is primarily a way of drawing attention to the *connections* between knowers. Rather than describing the particular beliefs of *a subject* and the way these beliefs are influenced by that subject's location, strong epistemological partiality establishes the ground for knowledge itself in the critically positioned—"constructed and stitched together imperfectly, and therefore able to join with another"[56]—knowing of selves-in-relation. Far from being a splintering dynamic, strong epistemological partiality sets up the possibility of engaging knowers in a "power-charged social relation of conversation"[57] in which mutuality and connection are both important epistemological resources. Haraway is specific on this point, endorsing "not partiality for its own sake but, rather, for the sake of the connections and unexpected openings situated knowledges make possible."[58]

In this chapter, I have developed two possibilities that are central to my understanding of partial reason. The first is that the notions of truth and of knowledge might involve emphasising considerations of the context rather than the content of truth. The second is that knowers might be located as selves-in-relation, where relation involves a self-reflexive awareness of our positioning as selves-in-relation.[59] Taken together, these two possibilities indicate that, at least in the strong epistemological sense in which I use the term, partiality establishes the terms in which to redescribe the preconditions of intersubjective agreements and shared belief systems. My final move in this chapter is to link these two possibilities with the proposition that the notion of commonality is more conducive to seeing together than the notion of a common language. I have said that where a common language is totalising, commonality is a source of understanding. An explanation of the distinction between a common language and commonality shows the relevance of the notion of commonality to my argument.

COMMONALITY

The basis of comparison on which I want to contrast the notion of a common language with the notion of commonality is the creating and sustaining of shared belief systems, mutual understandings, and intersubjective agreements. The substance of these shared understandings and agreements alters when selves are understood as selves-in-relation rather than as autonomous individuals and when the process of sharing understandings and agreements is described as seeing together rather than as seeing the same thing. In Chapter 3, I say that where the self is regarded as separate and autonomous, ethics and reason are required to function as the glue holding essentially unrelated individuals in relation. There I raise the possibility that when the theoretical emphasis is shifted away from autonomy toward connection, both reason and ethics might be revealed as projects of selves-in-relation. Selves-in-relation are constituted in and by relation; they are always and already positioned in relation interpersonally, contextually, and self-reflexively. With this discussion in mind I want to explore the contrasts between a common language, which enables separate and autonomous individuals to connect, and the commonality that describes the shared agreements and understandings of selves-in-relation.

The notion of a common language may, indeed, be applicable to aspects of the relational realities of selves-in-relation. What I question, however, is the assumption that we can share understandings and agreements only because, and insofar as, we share a common language.[60] Haraway expresses her reservation about this assumption in strong terms, asserting: "We do not need a totality to work well. The feminist dream of a common language, like all dreams for a perfectly true language, of a perfectly faithful naming of experience, is a totalizing and imperialist one."[61] The problem to which Haraway's accusation draws attention is that where the notion of a common language makes shared understandings contingent on a concept of truth as a universal and unitary regulatory ideal, the practical, concrete possibility that we might share understandings may be eclipsed by the logical, abstract possibility that language transcends particularity. In other words, the implicit association of a common language with truth (or a perfectly true language) propagates the assumption that any *failure* to arrive at shared understandings is a failure to perceive or to determine adequately the point at which our experiences translate "without remainder" into shared understandings of truth.[62]

I have said that the notions of a common language and commonality can be contrasted in terms of the way each notion accounts for the creation and sustenance of shared belief systems, mutual understandings, and intersubjective agreements. As well as making such shared understandings contingent on a problematic ideal of truth, the reliance on a common language may also implicitly endorse the concept of individuals as separate and autonomous. Here, shared understandings are the product of matching what is commensurable in individual accounts of reality, of establishing as homogeneous individual accounts of what is seen.

The emphasis on commensurability and homogeneity suggests that proponents of a common language[63] will resist the move toward partial reason I have described in this chapter. This resistance is generated, I have suggested, by the fear that to forgo the possibility of a common language is to endorse the kind of thoroughgoing relativism that would reduce philosophical talk of knowledge and reality to an incoherent babble. Such endorsements are assumed to celebrate incommensurability and heterogeneity for their own sake, much as attributing an epistemological imperative to partiality is assumed to endorse partiality as an end in itself. Like this assumption about partiality, I think that the necessary connection between rejecting the notion of common language and celebrating incommensurability and heterogeneity for their own sake can be refuted.

The notion of commonality arises from the possibility that shared belief systems, mutual understandings, and intersubjective agreements can be described as projects of selves-in-relation rather than products of autonomous individuals. Partiality, when it is understood not as a failure of impartiality but as the possibility that *enables* knowledge, shows us that *all* knowing, and *all* understanding, proceed from, and refer to, selves-in-relation. If the very idea of knowing involves knowing or seeing together, then the possibility that we might create and sustain shared understandings seems to depend not on transcending particularity but on identifying points of commonality. Proponents of a common language assume that, no matter how diverse our experiences, there will be some measure of commensurability, some sense in which we can say that our experiences are the same. This commensurability establishes the basis for the notion of a common language where shared understandings are contingent on a concept of truth as a universal and unitary regulatory ideal. Proponents of a common language risk propagating the assumption that we need a totality in order to work well and, in doing so, jeopardise the possibility of distinguishing between "seeing the same thing" and "seeing together." The notion of commonality, on the other hand, grows from an understanding that to reduce experiences to what is the same may be to remove them from the "life context" in which those experiences have meaning.

What I am talking about is the sense in which, when I grieve, for instance, no other grieving is like mine. When I give birth, neither my joy nor my pain is the same as others' joy and pain. What I do and the way I think about that doing in the ordinariness and the extraordinariness of everyday life—writing a thesis, forgetting birthdays, mending a fuse in the dark—are particular to me, not only in the trivial sense that my experiences involve my sense receptors (i.e., that you cannot feel my feelings) but also in the philosophically significant sense that my experiences constitute my reality. I am drawing here on a sense of particularity that is quite different from the radical individualism associated with separate, autonomous selves. The individualism associated with autonomy promotes the view that individuals share understandings to the extent that particularity is transcended. Emphasising the particularity of selves-in-relation, in contrast, reveals shared understandings as arising from the location of specific points of shared interest. By emphasising the particularity of selves-in-relation rather than promoting the individualism associated with autonomy, we can resist the reductive and coercive moves that separate shared understandings from the "life context" in which particular experiences are understood. The shared understandings of autonomous individuals may turn out to be more like hegemonic discourses, reconstructing and excluding particular experiences in the move toward universality.[64] The shared understandings of selves-in-relation, on the other hand, arise from the acknowledgment that in accounts of particular experiences, particular understandings lie the possibilities of establishing points of commonality. Establishing connections in this sense does not depend on highlighting what is matching or consistent. Rather, an awareness of points of commonality involves the sense that in the ambiguities, inconsistencies, and heterogeneity of particular accounts lie the possibilities of shared understandings. This is the awareness that, as selves-in-relation, we might share understandings *because* our experiences are particular rather than *despite* this particularity. When we seek out points of commonality, we accept that our experiences are different. This acceptance would only separate us, would only disconnect us if we understood our experiences as the experiences of individuals who are autonomous and separate. Where we understand our experiences as the experiences of selves-in-relation, however, it becomes apparent that what is particular to me might be the basis of what is shared between us. In other words, where I derive my understanding of experiences that are particular to me from my positioning in relation (relation to other selves, to context, and, self-reflexively, to myself), where I see my perspective as partial in the strong epistemological sense in which I have developed that term, I might cultivate shared understandings without losing sight of the sense in which those shared understandings are grounded on my particular experiences.

Despite the impression conveyed by the strength of Haraway's language, I do not want to suggest that a common language is *necessarily* coercive or reductive. Rather, my point is that our capacity to create and sustain shared belief systems, mutual understandings, and intersubjective agreements is much greater and much more philosophically interesting than its confinement to what is illuminated in a common language would indicate. To rely on a concept of a common language is to base our shared understandings on what we have in common. It is the aspect of "we-saying" that excludes or transcends difference.[65] Commonality, on the other hand, marks the capacity to see together while yet sustaining difference, the capacity to join with another without claiming to be another, noted by Haraway. What we share, then, is not necessarily the same experiences or even the same interpretative framework but our positioning as selves-in-relation.

I mean the distinction between approaches that promote the idea of a common language and those that promote the awareness of commonality to be of the most concrete relevance to the ways we create and sustain shared belief systems, mutual understandings, and intersubjective agreements. When I contrast the exclusion or transcendence of difference that marks the common language approach with the capacity to sustain difference that marks the awareness of commonality, I am not trying to use commonality to extend the boundaries of the knowing "we" so that those who were excluded as different can now be included as the same. Such a maneuver places "we-sayers" in the position of being able to identify the flaws in the perspectives of those who are excluded, thereby substantially negating my critique of the common language approach. Rather, what I am suggesting is that the concept of "we-saying" is radically altered by the move away from the idea that the sharing of understandings and agreements is contingent on the sharing of a common language. The seeing together that I associate with the process of identifying points of commonality does not involve the dropping away of difference so that everyone is included. Seeing together involves the recognition that, while we cannot speak from the perspectives of others, we *cannot but* speak as selves-in-relation. This insight marks the contrast between feminisms that essentialise the experiences of all women and feminisms that challenge the exclusions implied by essentialist concepts of woman.[66] It is involved in the contrast between ways of empathising which involve the loss of either self or other and ways of empathising that are attuned to resonances and affinities while yet acknowledging otherness, difference, and specificity.[67] In a concrete sense, the insight that we cannot but speak as selves-in-relation compels me to seek you out, to understand our speaking and listening to each other as a process that reveals the nature of the reality that is shared by us. This compulsion arises from the nature of partiality itself, which, as I will show in the next chapter, has both epistemological *and ethical* dimensions.

To base connection on commonality is to assume that what is particular to me is the basis of what is shared between us, that I come closer to sharing understandings with you as I locate myself in my particularity. Here, what is inexpressible in a common language is voiced in affinities and coalitions that take their meaning from the context in which they arise. It is in this sense that I use the term "commonality." Sometimes, these shared understandings are celebrated in temporary alliances or fleeting impressions of mutuality. At other times, they form the basis of lives spent in peace. Where shared understandings break down, as they frequently do, they are restored not through an appeal to what is consistent, homogeneous, and universal but through an appreciation of our particularity. Again, an example is provided by Seller's experiences in India.[68] Where attempts to establish relation by establishing a common language failed, Seller and the Indian women were yet able to cultivate a sense of commonality, of shared understandings. This sense began to develop at the moment at which Seller stopped trying to appeal to abstract and theoretical formulations (like self-expression, self-determination, self-identity), which built only "resounding silences," and started to understand that, for others as for herself, meaning depends on the "life context" in which it is generated. At first she was not prepared to lift her eyes from the map that distinguished this foreign terrain in terms of the differences between systems of thought and institutions.[69] What she eventually realised is that shared understandings depend not only on acknowledging other perspectives but on seeing the connections between those perspectives and our own. These connections begin to be established, for Seller, in the recognition that, despite the lack of a common language, she and the Indian women can share understandings of themselves and their world. But their shared understandings of, for example, the value of a commitment to gender equality can be conveyed neither in terms of abstract, theoretical formulations of how equality should be expressed nor in concrete, practical formulations of how equality should be lived out. Nevertheless, what Seller describes is a process in which the possibility of creating and sustaining shared belief systems, mutual understandings, and intersubjective agreements *increases* as she comes to appreciate the extent to which the Indian women do *not* think as she does. Far from establishing the content of a unitary and universal truth, what these shared understandings imply is that truth is constituted in the elaboration, the working out of the context of our knowing. Thus redefined, truth is not the elimination of what is particular but the mutual sustaining of what is ambiguous, heterogeneous, and inconsistent. In these shared understandings, then, there is a sense that Seller and the Indian women "share one world," even though this world is characterised by their radically discrepant understandings of it. As well as acknowledging other positions, they learned to see value in those positions and to understand their own positioning in relation to the positioning of others. Seller says: "My time in India sparkled with small acts of inclusion. . . . Perhaps at the end of the day, the most important gifts are those small acts of inclusion."[70] I think Seller underestimates the achievement of herself and the Indian women. After all, as Noddings remarks, if two parties with radically discrepant understandings of the world "maintain their regard and remain pledged to do one another no harm, a great moral victory has been won."[71] If small acts of inclusion generate the energy to rethink how I shall live the rest of my life within a context that includes those who have included me,[72] the achievement is, indeed, significant.

CONCLUSION

In Chapter 5, I present the extensionist version of partiality as bias in the form of responses to three alternatives: first, that either we retain the notion of truth as a regulatory ideal, or we restrict knowledge-claims to statements about personal perspectives; second, that either we endorse the separate, autonomous individual as the epistemic agent, or we concede the possibility of making authoritative knowledge-claims; third, that either we insist on a common language, or we sanction the lapse into an incoherent babble. I have associated this reading of the available alternatives with a failure to problematise anything other than "men's bias" in foundationalist accounts of truth and knowledge. A more critical basis for dissent from foundationalism is established, I suggested, by problematising any assumption that there is a world against which theories can be checked, by explicitly renouncing the premise of unpremisedness, and by objecting to the pejorative use of the notion of partiality. The alternatives that I draw out of this critique of foundationalism and for which I have argued in this chapter with the concept of partial reason are, first, that we might replace the notion of truth as a regulatory ideal by securing the notions of truth and knowledge in the universally operative requirement for the elaboration of the context in which we function as knowers[73]; second, that we might replace the insistence on the individual agent's epistemic authority with a concept of the authority of selves-in-relation; finally, that we might replace the notion of a totalising common language with the mutual understanding that is commonality.

In my final chapter I link the concept of partial reason with ethical care and show how the ethic of care is illuminated when it is understood in terms of the partial reason by which it is informed.

NOTES

1.   I emphasise that these judgments and arguments are philosophical to counter the response from nonfeminist philosophers that feminism is about politics and sociology rather than philosophy.   Ann Garry considers the "extraphilosophical" tag in 'A Minimally Decent Philosophical Method? Analytic Philosophy and Feminism,' 16.

2.   Fox Keller, 'The Gender/Science System,' 43.

3.   Longino, 'Can There Be a Feminist Science?,' 213.

4.   Harding, *The Science Question in Feminism,* 24.

5.   Code, 'Taking Subjectivity into Account,' 21.

6.   Seller, 'Realism versus Relativism: Towards a Politically Adequate Epistemology,' 170.

7.   My understanding of context and the link between context and care can be distinguished from the understandings that give rise to contextualism and situation ethics. Noddings, *Caring,* 28, argues that care is not like the act utilitarianism of situation ethics because care is not consequentialist. Held, 'Feminist Moral Inquiry and the Feminist Future,' 160, says feminist ethics generally is not like situation ethics because "it does not embrace a pure case-by-case approach." Sherwin, 'Feminist Ethics,' draws some crucial distinctions between the role of context in feminist and in other "context-specific" ethics.

8.   Malpas, 'Speaking the Truth,' 165.

9.   Ibid., 162.

10.   Quine, 'Two Dogmas of Empiricism,' 45.

11.   Malpas, 'Speaking the Truth,' 171.

12.   Fricker, 'Knowledge as Construct,' 96.

13.   Ibid., 107.

14.   See Malpas, 'Speaking the Truth,' 164 passim for the idea that "understanding the notion of truth itself" depends on "distinguish[ing] what is asserted in our speaking, what is *held true,* from what *is true.* "

15.   Gilligan, *In a Different Voice,* 140.

16.   Ibid., 149–150. Gilligan draws the metaphor from Margaret Drabble's *The Waterfall* (Harmondsworth: Penguin, 1969).

17.   See Chapter 3 for my discussion of three central aspects of the "relatedness" of selves-in-relation.

18. Addelson, 'Knower/Doers and Their Moral Problems,' 285: "In the conflict-of-rights analysis, abortion is removed from the life context in which it has its moral meaning."

19. Gilligan, *In a Different Voice*, 31.

20. My concept of the epistemic responses of selves-in-relation has a different focus from the concept of epistemological communities developed by Nelson in 'Epistemological Communities.' Her concern is to argue for the priority of communities, so that what we know as individuals derives from our membership of the community or communities of which we are a part and the knowledge that exists at the level of communities. What Nelson's concept suggests is that the differences between Jake's and Amy's understandings of the Heinz dilemma are attributable to the emergence of these understandings from different epistemological communities. There is obviously a close affinity between this idea and my concept of the epistemic responses of selves-in-relation. However, what I am interested in is the way that actual encounters are the precondition of understanding, the way that concrete relations are the enablers of knowledge. The concept of knowers as partial, where partiality is understood as carrying the strong epistemological and ethical imperatives that I develop in Chapter 7, focuses philosophical interest on knowers positioned in relation, while the concept of epistemological communities may leave this positioning in relation unexamined. My sense is that this is a difference of emphasis rather than a disagreement about the need to critique the concept of separate, autonomous knowers.

21. Gilligan, *In a Different Voice*, 31, describes Amy's interview as a dialogue and, by implication, Jake's as an interrogation. Without wanting to contradict Gilligan's point (which is about Amy's disruption of the interview process), I make a different one: both children attempt to engage the interviewer, but only Jake finds his responses confirmed.

22. Friedman, 'Care and Context in Moral Reasoning.'

23. I draw this concept from Addelson's title, 'Knower/Doers and Their Moral Problems.'

24. Gilligan, *In a Different Voice*, 26.

25. I make a comparable point in my discussion of the distinction to be drawn between institutional relations or social roles and relation at the level of lived experience in Chapter 7.

26. Cf. Code's point, 'Taking Subjectivity into Account,' 15, about the search for necessary and sufficient conditions "for justifying claims that 'S knows that p' across a range of 'typical' instances."

27. Seller, 'Should the Feminist Philosopher Stay at Home?'

28. Ibid., 231–239.

29. Addelson, 'Knower/Doers and Their Moral Problems,' 283, talks about "the descriptive core of a moral epistemology."

30. I note in Chapter 5 that this is not the only version of antifoundationalism.

31. As I set them out in Chapter 5 and develop them in this chapter, the other alternatives are that we either retain the notion of truth as a regulatory ideal or restrict knowledge-claims to statements about personal perspectives and that we either insist on a common or universal language or sanction the lapse into an incoherent babble.

32. This phrase is Rich's *The Dream of a Common Language: Poems 1974–1977.*

33. Fricker, 'Knowledge as Construct,' 102.

34. Ibid.

35. Antony, 'Quine as Feminist,' 190; emphasis added.

36. Fricker, 'Knowledge as Construct,' 102.

37. Where it is supposed that what is known can be dissociated from who knows and

how they know it.

38. See my discussion of Antony's argument in Chapter 5.

39. This is the approach that Gatens terms extensionist.

40. Harding, 'Rethinking Standpoint Epistemology: What Is "Strong Objectivity"?,' 59, makes this point: "Feminist thought is forced to 'speak as' and on behalf of the very notion it criticizes and tries to dismantle—women." Cf. Gatens, 'Feminism, Philosophy and Riddles without Answers,' 25, quoted in my introduction at note 12.

41. Haraway, 'Situated Knowledges,' 583.

42. Ibid., 584, 585.

43. Ibid., 585.

44. See my comments about humility in Chapter 4, note 87.

45. Gilligan, *In a Different Voice,* 172.

46. Haraway, 'Situated Knowledges,' 590.

47. Fricker, 'Knowledge as Construct,' 103.

48. This is Fricker's example, ibid., 96.

49. Fricker, ibid., 103, links "the political and methodological imperative not to eclipse others' perspectives" with the admission that "entertaining contradictory beliefs and viewpoints must comprise part of our methodology." Fricker could object to my use of the term "truth" at the political level, but I base the use of the term on her argument, 99, identifying political beliefs as "a set of beliefs . . . that, if true, . . . pick out real states of affairs in the world."

50. Of course, even claims about rain are problematic in cultures that distinguish, for example, between spitting, drizzling, showering, and pouring rain. This reinforces, rather than undermines, my point.

51. Seller, 'Should the Feminist Philosopher Stay at Home?,' 241, 242.

52. Haraway, 'Situated Knowledges,' 586.

53. Ibid.

54. Ibid.

55. This does point to another possibility: that I might want to maintain that critical positioning is not relevant to some domains of knowledge while simultaneously conceding that I cannot always determine where the edge of the system lies. It seems to me that such a claim does not undermine my point, which is that to make these discriminations, it is necessary to be critically positioned.

56. Haraway, 'Situated Knowledges,' 586.

57. Ibid., 593.

58. Ibid., 590.

59. As I explain in Chapter 3, I mean the concept of selves-in-relation not only to refer to the sense in which selves are always and already positioned in relation to other selves (which contrasts selves-in-relation with the autonomous individuals of liberal theory) but also to include the sense in which selves are always and already positioned in relation to context and are self-reflexive about their positioning in interpersonal and contextual relation.

60. "Language," of course, may be construed more broadly than verbal expression.

61. Haraway, 'A Manifesto for Cyborgs,' 215.

62. Code, *What Can She Know?*, 59, notes Donald Davidson's conviction that "it is logically possible for all linguistic utterances to be translated into any other language without remainder." In talking here of experience, I use that broad construal of "language" that I note in note 60.

63. By whom I mean those philosophers who make the possibility of shared understandings contingent on a concept of truth as a regulatory ideal. See my outline of

different sets of alternatives in Chapter 5, and Garry, 'A Minimally Decent Philosophical Method?,' 22, for the observation that "analytic philosophers probably wouldn't even bother with the term 'intersubjective agreement,' because they are willing to use the more forceful language of truth and objectivity." Garry cites Antony as an example of a philosopher who employs this forceful language.

64. Code, *What Can She Know?*, 59, notes: "The power of discourse to shape experiences, to reconstruct them so that their 'owners' can scarcely recognise them, or to exclude them from view is a palpable fact that arguments about logical possibilities cannot gainsay."

65. An aspect that Code, 'Taking Subjectivity into Account,' 24, acknowledges: "Naming ourselves as 'we' empowers us, but it always risks disempowering others."

66. This contrast is one of the foci of Spelman's *Inessential Woman*.

67. See my discussion of seeing together in Chapter 4.

68. Various ways in which people express their interests provide other examples of commonality. For example, the diverse range of women who come together to support a pro-choice stance on abortion may not find that their perspectives can be captured in a common language.

69. Seller makes use of the map metaphor in 'Should the Feminist Philosopher Stay at Home?'

70. Ibid., 246.

71. Noddings, 'Conversation as Moral Education,' 116.

72. Seller, 'Should the Feminist Philosopher Stay at Home?,' 246–247.

73. Again I emphasise that this replacement involves a *redescription* of the preconditions for truth and knowledge, not the identification of new norms or preconditions.

Chapter 7

Care: The Ethical Imperatives of Partiality

In preparing the ground for my elaboration of care and partial reason, I have described traditional liberal moral philosophy as constructing an ethics in the service of, or subservient to, reason.[1] I have depicted the reasoning of the liberal moral agent as bound to and by the constraints of a rationality that privileges abstract, universal, and impartial thinking. However, at the end of Chapter 3, I set the scene for my discussion about ethics and epistemology by distancing my approach from those that attempt to break the nexus between reason and ethics or attempt to loosen the bonds between what is rational and what is morally right, what is irrational and what is morally wrong. I have said that I do not locate the problem with liberal moral philosophy primarily in its linking of the rational and the ethical. The focus on breaking the nexus between reason and ethics leads to accounts of care constructed in opposition to reason, as irrational or unreasoned. By retaining the nexus between ethics and reason, I have established alternative accounts of ethics as caring and of reason as partial. In this final chapter I bring care and partial reason together to show how a feminist ethic of care transforms the nexus between ethics and reason so that each is mutually informing of the other.

For the autonomous selves of liberal moral theory, the epistemological injunction to be impartial means that the consideration of context is ruled out of both the epistemological and the ethical equation. I have shown that these autonomous selves are better described as selves-in-relation, both in terms of the inherently *contextual* nature of their thinking[2] and in terms of the inherently *relational* nature of their capacity to know, where this knowing is understood as seeing together rather than as seeing the same thing.[3] As selves-in-relation, the focus on elaborating the context in which we make knowledge- or truth-claims involves a process of self-reflection, a reflexive movement involving both the knower and the known in a process that moves beyond traditional distinctions between the subject and the object of knowledge. So, for example, what is revealed to Seller in the process of establishing the possibility that she and the Indian women might see together is not primarily some aspect of *their* reality but of her own. I have drawn a similar conclusion from Murdoch's example of M and D.[4] The "let me look again" that compels M to attend to D involves a self-reflexive move, in the sense both that M is prompted to try and change herself as a person who does not value D and that M comes to know herself as someone who values D.[5]

Self-reflexivity is not necessarily involved in the epistemological and ethical understandings of the autonomous selves of liberal moral theory. The philosophical paradigm that privileges abstract, universal, and impartial thinking is premised on the hierarchical oppositions that exonerate philosophy from any obligation to account for the concrete, particular, and partial. The important point here is that knowers—as knowers—are interchangeable. Indeed, for liberal theorists, this interchangeability is one of the crucial criteria that define knowledge. Subjectivity, then, is one of the things that knowers must supposedly transcend.[6] The process of abstraction means that differences between selves and others *as knowers* are not regarded as epistemologically or ethically relevant.[7] At least in the epistemological and the ethical sense, then, there is no self for the knower, as knower, to reflect upon or to engage in self-refection. So, as Michael Sandel has noted: "[The self that is] wholly without character, is incapable of self-knowledge in any morally serious sense. Where the self is unencumbered and essentially dispossessed, no person is left for *self-*reflection to reflect upon."[8]

Where knowledge is enabled by impartiality, then, knowers rule out the consideration of context and the need to be self-reflexive. What I have described, however, is a concept of knowledge that is enabled by strong epistemological partiality. Here knowledge is perspectival, in the double sense of being both partisan and incomplete. That knowledge might be understood in this way is the epistemological insight that shifts the emphasis from the content to the context of truth-claims, from knowers as autonomous individuals to knowers as selves-in-relation, and from a difference-suppressing common language to a difference-sustaining commonality.

My task in this chapter is to show that making these emphases entails an acknowledgment of certain imperatives that are of ethical as well as epistemological significance. As I introduce the idea of ethical imperatives, however, it is crucial to point out that I do not mean these imperatives to function as a series of necessary or sufficient conditions for the marshalling of moral thought.[9] Rather, I see them as guides to the tenor of the conversations that assist us to cultivate understandings and appreciations of relational realities, as signposts that help us to appreciate the responsibilities entailed in nurturing shared belief systems, mutual understandings, and intersubjective agreements. The contrast between this way of understanding moral imperatives and more traditional approaches is noted by other feminist philosophers. Walker, for example, says:

There is a way of looking at the understanding critical to and distinctive of full moral capacity on which this understanding is *not* really an *episteme*, not a nomologically ordered theory. On the alternative view moral understanding is a collection of perceptive, imaginative, appreciative, and expressive skills and capacities which put and keep us in unimpeded contact with the realities of ourselves and specific others.[10]

The epistemological and ethical imperatives that I associate with the concepts of care and partial reason link the epistemological and the ethical "I musts," thereby sustaining the nexus between reason and ethics. At the same time, however, these imperatives transform the reason-ethics nexus. Rather than ordering reason and ethics under the inflexible, impersonal, and abstract principles and rules that provide liberal moral theory with its substance, this transformed nexus opens up the possibility that we might more adequately understand and appreciate the concrete relational realities of human existence.

The imperatives I want to talk about here are drawn directly out of my discussions of care and partial reason and the examples I have used to illustrate various points in my arguments. My suggestion is that, for selves-in-relation, the imperatives associated with both care and partial reason can be presented as discrete, but interdependent, aspects of a process involving a self-reflexive elaboration of context. That this process comprises mainly concrete considerations about how we talk to each other rather than metaphysical abstractions is apparent from the nature of the responsibilities that are involved and emphasised in this process. As I have developed them, the several aspects of this process are intrinsically bound up with the three possibilities I explore in Chapter 6: that the notions of truth and of knowledge might involve emphasising the context, rather than the content, of truth, that knowers might be located as selves-in-relation, and that shared belief systems, mutual understandings, and intersubjective agreements might be grounded in a sense of commonality. From these possibilities, which arise from the recognition of strong epistemological partiality, I have developed epistemological and ethical imperatives that involve focusing on concrete relations rather than on abstract roles, emphasising the concrete and particular, rather than the universal and unitary in particular contexts, keeping relational possibilities open, seeking out others, seeing the connections between other perspectives and our own, and locating commonalities. In this final chapter I consider each of these imperatives as an aspect of the self-reflexive elaboration of context with the purpose of drawing together some different, but interconnected, insights that are characteristic of knowing and caring well.

FOCUSING ON CONCRETE RELATIONS

The possibility of focusing philosophical interest on the connections between individuals rather than on individuals' autonomy is not raised exclusively by a feminist ethic of care. In clarifying the nature of this focus on connection and its relevance to care, however, I want to make an important distinction between two ways in which relations might be conceived. My objective is to show that a focus on concrete relations is consonant with the critical stance I have associated with challenging philosophical axioms. This critical stance, however, may be undermined by theories that embed selves not in concrete relations but in abstract roles.

The approach from which I want to distinguish my focus on concrete relations is that taken by the communitarian philosophers MacIntyre and Sandel.[11] The kind of relatedness that is congruous with a communitarian "situated self"[12] is not what I want to associate with the concept of selves-in-relation. Let me explain this point by looking specifically at the notion of relation as it emerges from a system of thought that is grounded on communitarian concepts of social relationships and community.

Friedman has made some important observations about the antipathy to the interests of women of the particular institutions cited by communitarians as the sources of the situated self.[13] She sustains these criticisms by comparing "found communities" with "communities of choice," finding the latter to be more likely to yield models of relation that are compatible with women's interests.[14] Without pursuing this particular point here, I refer to Friedman's argument only because it draws attention to the potentially reactionary nature of communitarianism.[15] It seems to me that the notion of relation to which communitarianism gives rise needs to be read in the context of this reactionary tendency. Friedman's objection to the particular kinds of communities preferred by communitarians does not, of course, necessarily challenge the ontological priority accorded by communitarians to community. It may be that if the concept of community is remodeled so that it is more inclusive and egalitarian, the insights of MacIntyre and Sandel can be sustained.[16] My suggestion, however, is that communitarians might be challenged not only on the grounds of the particular kinds of communities they prefer but on the grounds of the concept of relation they promote.

Defending the communitarian emphasis on the common good against liberalism's rights-based politics, Sandel offers the image of a "confidently situated" self, saying that "intolerance flourishes most where forms of life are dislocated, roots unsettled, traditions undone."[17] For the communitarian, then, tolerance toward others is to be associated with a respect for the durability of established forms of life and the preservation of our social heritage and traditions.[18] But it seems that Sandel must face a predicament when he tries to account for those who are oppressed and exploited by the emphasis on maintaining and perpetuating established forms of life and roots and traditions. This possibility of being critical from within is directly related to my concern about how we might maintain the critical stance I have associated with the challenging of philosophical axioms.

If that in which the situated self is embedded is nothing other than the communal status quo, then people who are discriminated against on the basis of, say, sex, class, or race cannot be said to be confidently situated. Their interests are clearly not coextensive with the maintenance and perpetuation of the established way of life and its roots and traditions. In Chapter 2, I say that the project of feminist ethics is committed to taking the experience of all women seriously. If this is to be accomplished in an environment where the masculine has hegemonic status, it is hard to imagine a version of feminist thinking that leaves established forms of life intact and roots and traditions undisturbed.

The concept of relation that emerges from some communitarian models is fundamentally different from the one I associate with care and partial reason. Sandel's concept of the ontologically "situated self" is supposed to be an account of the fundamental embeddedness of persons in social context or community. But it does not necessarily account for the nature of concrete and particular relations themselves; the ontologically "situated self" is not necessarily embedded in concrete relation. That is why I think that it makes sense to distinguish a system of thought that is grounded on the idea of selves participating in social relations from a way of thinking that emphasises the concrete relatedness of particular persons. Let me elaborate on this point.[19]

As Rich shows in her study of motherhood, there can be high degrees of discrepancy between the experience of a social role and the way that role is institutionalised.[20]   In other words, the lived experiences of the mothering relation might be radically different from the ideal conveyed by the institution of motherhood.   The communitarian endeavour gains its momentum, at least in part, from the rejection of the notion of a self to whom everything other than the autonomy of that self is contingent.   To the extent that this is the case, communitarianism and feminism are certainly not contradictory projects.   But my suggestion is that the situated self of the communitarians is embedded not in concrete relations, in actual lived experiences of relation, but in the institutional framework that operates to regulate and control or, as Rich would say, constrain actual lived experiences.   What Rich's work draws attention to is the discontinuity between experience and institution. I believe that what Sandel and MacIntyre are referring to when they use terms like family, community, profession, city, tribe, and nation[21] is the "symbolic architecture . . . [the] invisible understandings . . . hidden collusions and connections"[22] that constitute the institutional framework structuring even the most intimate relationships.[23]

In making this assertion, I am not overlooking the emphasis placed by both Sandel and MacIntyre on *particular* relations. My point is that their notion of particularity has to be seen as part of their critique of the unencumbered self and their rejection of the assumption that the subject of moral theory is able, in some important philosophical sense, to transcend social contextualisation. The unencumbered self gets its sense of moral agency from a grasp of principles like universality and utility, principles that are not contingent in any sense on self-identification with the roles of, say, mother, philosopher, or nationalist. Set against these assumptions, the replacement of the transcendent moral self with a moral self whose dimensions include social coordinates is, indeed, a radical move.

But problems for critical feminist theory arise, I am suggesting, because the moral self is "encumbered" by communitarians like Sandel and MacIntyre only at the institutional level, not at the level of actual lived experience. The particularisation of the moral self that follows the establishment of social coordinates is, therefore, still too abstract to accommodate the observation that what is evident at the level of the institution may not only differ significantly from the experience of that institution but also conceal assumptions that systematically oppress and exploit certain groups and individuals. My proposition is that the references by Sandel and MacIntyre to specific relations are not intended to focus philosophical attention on, for example, the concrete details of my relation with my son but on my self-identification as a mother. In other words, what is of relevance to communitarian moral theory is not the lived experience of mothering relations but the maintenance and perpetuation of the relation between mothers and the institutions constraining the relations between mothers and children. Now this distinction is of crucial importance to my elaboration of the concepts of care and partial reason, where the approach I have taken focuses on the lived experience of concrete and particular relations. Implicit in the analyses of Sandel and MacIntyre is an emphasis not on how my actions are guided by my relations with this particular child but on the abstract principles dictating what the institutional role of mother entails.

It is important that the distinction between social roles and concrete relations to which I am drawing attention is not made by the communitarian philosophers with reference to whom I have drawn it. Indeed, their explicit comments frequently emphasise the particularity of relation. MacIntyre, for example, notes that "I am brother, cousin and grandson, member of this household, that village, this tribe."[24] He declares that "[i]t is to, for and with specific individuals that I must do what I ought, and it is to these same and other individuals, members of the same local community, that I am accountable."[25] My point, however, is that these references to particular relations do not necessarily situate moral deliberation in the concrete contexts established by lived experience. If the relations in which communitarians are interested appear to be concrete, then I suggest that this is so only in comparison with the highly abstract relational component of liberal moral theory. In comparison with the concreteness that is based on lived experience, however, this "social" relation remains detached from relational realities.

I can make this point clearer by comparing the deliberations of the communitarian individual who is located by the "boundaries provided by a social identity"[26] with the deliberations of the liberal man of reason that I elaborate in Chapter 1. For the latter, the question, "Ought I to do this to, for, or with x?" does not depend for its answer on whether x is a stranger or my son. The socially situated individual, on the other hand, says that it *is* relevant whether x is a stranger or my son; that is, the fact that x is my son is significant in determining my action. The question, "Ought I to do this to, for, or with x?" therefore involves consideration of social roles rather than only of an abstract principle or rule. By drawing the distinction between concrete relations and social roles, however, I am drawing attention to a third mode of deliberation, the mode I associate with care and partial reason. While agreeing with the communitarian that it is relevant whether x is my son, this third mode of deliberation sees the answer to the question, "Ought I to do this to, for, or with x?" as depending on the concrete reality of my relation with x. Admitting the relevance of social roles to my deliberations may leave moral thinking enframed in the terms established by the focus on institutional roles. In those terms, what I consider in deliberating the question, "Ought I to do this to, for, or with x?" where x is my son is how mothers ought to behave toward sons. In the third mode of deliberation, however, what I consider is where my son and I stand in terms of our lived experience of each other.[27]

Having said this, I must stress that the imperative to focus on concrete relation rather than on social roles does not translate into the imperative to ignore the moral implications of social and institutional constraints. This is Jaggar's concern about an ethic of care. Her view is that:

Despite the virtues of care thinking, its emphasis on the quality of individual relations seems to preclude its addressing the structural oppositions between the interests of social groups that make caring difficult or unlikely between members of those groups. Similarly, care's reliance on individual efforts to meet individual needs disregards the social structures that make this virtually impossible in many cases. Care thinking seems unable to focus on the social causes of many individual problems, such as widespread homelessness and hunger.[28]

As well as rejecting versions of care as irrational or nonrational, I have also shown that care cannot be understood solely in terms of the meeting of needs. Needs-based versions of care focus solely on care as action. With the concept of care as disposition I have introduced the possibility that the care relation is inherently valuable, in that it is expressive of a "mattering" that is not locatable in terms of needs or needs-meeting. The focus on context, which I have explored initially through the concept of care as disposition and subsequently developed as a central component of partial reason, portrays the "continual doing" of caring as an openness, a receptivity, to the realities of concrete and particular situations.[29] If, as a person who cares, what matters to me is your need not to be bullied or your need for food or housing, there may be a sense in which I can address your need by separating you from the bullies and providing you with a room and a meal. But in the broader sense of care as comprising both practical acts of care and care as disposition, what matters to me is relations of care, not, or not only, your need for care. It is by caring for you in this broader sense that I come to understand the wider context revealed by relations of care, a wider context that may not be evident when care is confined to the meeting of needs. It is, then, an aspect of my caring that widens the framework of care so that the focus on concrete relations is not limited in the way that the focus on the meeting of particular needs may be limited. But the focus on concrete relations means that my caring is always grounded in the context established by lived experience, not the context established by the abstract principles and rules governing institutional and social roles. Concrete relations of care may make a range of caring actions appropriate. Where what matters to me is not only the satisfaction of your needs but also the concrete caring relation itself, included in that range of appropriate actions will be attempts to reveal and alter the institutional, social, and political structures that compound the problems of bullying, homelessness, and starvation as well as actions that protect, shelter, and feed you.

CONSIDERING THE CONCRETE AND PARTICULAR

It seems fair to suggest that the emphasis on articulating what is unitary, what can be condensed into a single, integrated, self-consistent project, and what is universal, what applies to all knowers, is indicative of what the philosopher finds metaphysically interesting. Uncharitably, these interests have been identified with a concern for absolute stability, certainty, control, and predictability.[30] More generously, they might be characterised as the attempt to express that which is irreducible and fundamental to human being.[31] These interests may not necessarily imply that human existence is without ambiguity, heterogeneity, and inconsistency. They do, however, tend to cultivate the impression that what is consistent, homogeneous, and rational forms the core of the philosophical project. As well, they generate the ideals that "presuppose a universal, homogenous, and essential 'human nature'" and sustain the belief "that we have and thus think from unitary and coherent lives."[32]

A focus on the unitary and universal is problematic to feminist care theorists because, as Gilligan demonstrates, what care theorists are engaged in is the task of giving voice to the very notion they are critiquing.[33] As a feminist care theorist, I make myself visible as a woman, as female, in order to critique or dismantle the notions of woman and the feminine. There is no secure ground for this project; there is no consistent foundation for such philosophical practice. The notion of truth as unitary and universal, even when it rejects the templates of correspondence and representation or inserts the gap of underdetermination between "the world as we see it" and "the world as it is," is grounded on notions of consistency and compatibility that depend on the identity of the knower as autonomous individual. These knowing individuals are, at their core, stable and unified, sustained by the thought that, even if particular beliefs are false, their belief system is sound. Philosophers may insist that the soundness of our knowledge is provisional, that we can only ever be certain "that our beliefs are true 'in general and for the most part,'" and that truth depends on knowledge being intersubjectively confirmed.[34] These qualifications to the foundationalist position do not undermine my point, which is that truth that is intersubjectively confirmed may still be truth that is intersubjectively confirmed *for knowing individuals*. The self for whom truth is known "in conjunction with others" may still be the self who is isolated from others unless this intersubjective confirmation is forthcoming.

The focus on the universal and unitary diverts philosophical attention away from the significance of what is unique about particular situations and away from the realisation that judgments about consistency, judgments about the soundness of judgments, can be understood as aspects of relational processes rather than as products of the demand for truth. The focus on the universal and unitary and on the significance of the universal and unitary for generating philosophical understandings of the world implicitly locates the idea of a knowable world outside the relations of knowing. The suggestion that truth depends on knowledge being intersubjectively confirmed is not, it seems to me, necessarily anything more than a confirmation of the authority of autonomous individual knowers, each of whom cannot know that what he or she knows is true without confirming whether what he or she knows individually accords with what others know individually. Truth, then, might be regarded as "necessarily inter-subjective" in a sense that would be quite alien to the liberal man of reason, but the impression might yet be propagated that the knowing individual stands conceptually apart from the knowable world and other knowers. This is the version of knowledge that I associate with the idea that we see the same thing. What is of interest here, what is significant about knowing and knowledge-claims, is the connection between me and what I know, which, if what I know is true, maps onto the connection between you and what you know. What I picture here is a conceptual scheme in which separate individuals are each individually connected to one thing that is known, rather as the dancers around a maypole are each individually connected by a ribbon to the maypole.

My contrasting picture, which illustrates the notion of seeing together, is of knowers connected to each other by lines, as would be the case if the ribbons were detached from the maypole and used to connect the dancers to each other. The flaw in such a metaphorical picture is that it seems to suggest that interpersonal relations are determinative in the knowledge-seeking process: although it conveys the sense in which selves are always and already positioned in relation to other selves, it is not immediately obvious that it portrays selves-in-relation as always and already positioned in relation to context and as self-reflexive about their positioning in interpersonal and contextual relation.[35] My point, however, is that my contrasting picture reveals a shift of focus, an alteration in the perspective, a change of emphasis *away* from the connections of the dancers to the maypole and *toward* the connections between the dancers themselves. Emphasising the connections between selves, rather than the connections between the knowing individual and what is known, suggests that knowledge and truth do not consist of aggregates of what we know as individuals but are relational processes in which who knows and how they know are as significant as what is known.

The important point here is that the concepts of selves-in-relation and of seeing together, which are central to my account of care and partial reason, do not lend themselves to the kind of radical relativism that is constructed in dichotomous opposition to the insistence on the universal and unitary. Crucial to my metaphorical detachment of the dancers from the maypole is that their detachment from the maypole does not free the dancers from all constraint. What constrains them after the ribbons have been disconnected from the maypole, however, are their connections to each other: that is, they are constrained in that there are ribbons. In distinguishing seeing together from seeing the same thing, I do not mean to portray seeing together as a process in which anything goes. But the constraints on seeing together are not located in a knowable world that is external to the relations of knowing but in the context established by those relations. Let me explain what I mean by showing how the possibility of locating constraints in the context established by the knowing of selves-in-relation is linked with the concept of strong epistemological partiality.

Strong epistemological partiality is based on the understanding that the assumption that we can necessarily distinguish the epistemological from the nonepistemological aspects of knowledge-production is faulty. That this distinction *can* be upheld is an implicit assumption made by extensionist feminist philosophers who equate partiality with bias and an acknowledgment of the social and political coordinates of the knower. The crucial point I make is that what constitutes partiality or the partial perspective cannot necessarily be determined outside the context in which a knowledge-claim is made. The assumption that it can, that the coordinates that are epistemologically significant can be established as part of the necessary and sufficient conditions for knowledge, underpins the extensionist versions of epistemology that I consider in Chapter 5. There I suggest that if we respond to an account of the epistemic significance of location by interpreting it simply as a question of acknowledging bias, then we risk having to relinquish the *epistemological* content of partiality. Where the notion of partiality as bias has the effect of identifying partiality with, and limiting it to, sociopolitical location, strong epistemological partiality, while certainly *including* the social and political coordinates of the knower, situates the knower—as knower—in relations of knowing. Knowers, then, are selves-in-relation. Strong epistemological partiality sees knowledge as arising not only out of the biases of the knower but also out of the particular connections that both establish and are established by knowledge. The point is that these particular connections are *always* part of the process of knowing. Even straightforward empirical S-knows-that-p claims are known by knowers who know as selves-in-relation. What I know about flammability and gravity is what *we* know. This is a concept of partiality that arises not out of what the knower knows as an individual but out of the relational context in which the knower is situated.

This is not to suggest, of course, that there may not be domains of knowledge or at least certain kinds of knowledge-claims where what constitutes partiality *can* be determined apart from the context in which knowledge occurs or in which knowledge-claims are made. My point, however, is similar to the one I make in Chapter 6 when I talk about the potential ethical impact of simple empirical claims. There I suggest that *all* knowledge-claims can be pressed on the question of whether their epistemological interest is exhausted in its propositional content or whether we increase our understanding of a knowledge-claim by placing its propositional content in the context of who knows, what they know, and how they know it. It may be that there are certain kinds of knowledge-claims where the admission of bias *is* an adequate acknowledgment of partiality. Not all aspects of human reality are equally complex. Sometimes we *can* see clearly and be sure that what we see is unambiguously the case. Some knowledge-claims are less closely allied to contested human interests than others. Nevertheless, it is the province of feminist theorising to problematise the tendency to assume that what is relatively unproblematic epitomises the norm. What I mean is that, although in some cases we can be fairly sure that what is claimed is not dependent on who is claiming it, in other cases it seems that what is claimed is dependent on *far more* than the sociopolitical location of the knower. Sociopolitical positioning is, as I point out in Chapter 6, a way of accounting in a relatively abstract way for the location of knowers in the world. The *concrete* coordinates of the position of knowers, on the other hand, involve the characteristics, preferences, proclivities, expectations, needs, experiences, talents, strengths, weaknesses, and relationships that make us the particular persons we are. In the sense that these coordinates locate persons in their particularity, persons are not interchangeable.[36]

It seems to me that the suggestion that persons are not interchangeable is not an especially controversial idea. What *is* controversial is my identification of these persons in their particularity as *knowers*. But *not* to make this identification would be to endorse the confinement of knowing to what we do when, as persons, we *are* interchangeable or the confinement of knowledge to those claims whose epistemological interest is exhausted in their propositional content (i.e., where the particularity of S is not especially relevant).

In developing the concept of strong epistemological partiality, I distinguish that concept from two different understandings of partiality. The first is the foundationalist position; the second, the position I associate with feminists taking an extensionist approach. Without repeating the arguments put forward in Chapters 5 and 6, I want to draw out the sense in which strong epistemological partiality involves constraints that arise from the relatedness of selves-in-relation: relatedness that is interpersonal, contextual, and self-reflexive. That these constraints can be understood as ethical as well as epistemological becomes evident when we locate the constraints on knowledge in the contextual relations in which knowing is embedded.

As I have said, for the foundationalist, the idea that the location of the knower affects any knowledge-claim is not tenable. Only impartial claims are knowledge-claims, and, to the extent that it *is* possible to link what is known to the knower, the reliability of what is known deteriorates. On the other hand, for the extensionist, as for some nonfeminist antifoundationalists, all knowledge-claims are subject to the biases of the knower. However, for the extensionist, there remains a sense, a sense that I claim is very significant, in which knowledge can still be controlled for the biases of knowers. Partiality, here as in foundationalism, is understood as belonging to individuals. In foundationalism, the claim to know conceals the knower. Individuals, along with their worldly background, disappear behind their knowledge-claims. But it is crucial to understand *what* disappears or is concealed. My suggestion is that, in fact, for foundationalists, the individual is *deeply implicated* in the process of producing knowledge. This individual is the rational, autonomous epistemic and moral agent who legislates *for* himself and *by* himself according to the principles of rationality generated from *within* himself.[37] So "deeply presupposed" is the identification of foundationalist knowledge-claims with the impartial knower that the knower *qua* individual epistemic agent is submerged.[38] This is the individual whom extensionists (and some other antifoundationalists) retrieve. But the knowing individual who is made visible in the extensionist accounts with which I disagree is not necessarily located by the concrete coordinates I have identified. My suggestion is that this knowing individual may turn out to be only the epistemic agent of foundationalist epistemology, given a sociopolitical outline[39] but not necessarily deprived of the autonomy on which the authority of knowledge-claims is supposedly based.   This individual still legislates *for* himself and *by* himself, even though we can now see him doing it.

The third epistemological proposition about partiality, the proposition that I endorse in the concepts of strong epistemological partiality and partial reason, involves problematising not only the invisibility of the foundationalist knower but the very conception of knowledge and knowing presumed by the foundationalist account. Here the idea is that the location of knowers is what makes knowledge possible.   But the knowers thus located are not the autonomous knowers whose biases place at risk the possibility of making impartial knowledge-claims. Rather, these knowers know only to the extent that their knowing is the knowledge of selves-in-relation, so that we know what we know only because we can maintain connections across our differences.

When I discuss Kohlberg's theory of moral development in Chapter 5, I show that if we detach the constraints on what is known from the concrete context of who knows and how they know it, we may miss the substance of what might constitute a specifically critical or interrogative feminist critique. Such a critique does not only focus on establishing whether a theory does what it says it does: such a critical approach does not take theoretical frameworks or assumptions at face value. Rather, such an approach locates the constraints on knowledge in the relations that facilitate claims to know. Taking this approach, we can show that the problems in Kohlberg's theory of moral development stem from his failure to perceive the contextual relations in which all moral thinking is embedded. This failure accounts for his misrepresentation of both Amy's *and* Jake's interviews, his misdescription not only of thinking that lacks the criteria Kohlberg associates with mature reasoning but also of thinking in which such criteria are supposedly manifest.   The constraints that I associate with the concept of strong epistemological partiality are not applied to knowers whose perspectives are extricated from the partial. These constraints do not compel knowers to look toward what is claimed to check the validity of their claims. Rather, where these constraints are applied to knowers as selves-in-relation, they involve an evaluation of the relational context in which claims to know are established.[40] In the conventional terms of the maypole dance, the movements of the dancers are constrained by the maypole. When the dancers are joined to each other rather than the maypole, however, the dancers gauge their movements not by looking at the maypole but at each other and at the connections between each other.[41]

In examining the imperative to emphasise the concrete and particular rather than the universal and unitary, I show that the concepts of care and partial reason involve transforming our understanding not only of *how* knowledge is constrained and *where* constraints might be located but also of *who* is constrained. My conclusion is that, where focusing exclusively on the universal and unitary obscures the relational context by which care and partial reason are both enabled and constrained, focusing on the concrete and particular situates knowers as selves-in-relation, locates the constraints on knowing within this relational context, and identifies these constraints as determined by the possibilities of enhancing our capacities to see together.

KEEPING RELATIONAL POSSIBILITIES OPEN

In my discussion of care and partial reason, I identify relation as a crucial epistemological and ethical concept but establish that the basis of relation is our situatedness, our imperfectly-stitched-togetherness, rather than our (albeit social and sociable) individuality. I also talk about the inherent value of the caring relation for selves-in-relation and place the concept of selves-in-relation at the heart of a redescription of reason as partial reason.

I am suggesting that keeping relational possibilities open is one of the ethical imperatives associated with the exercise of partial reason. For me, this imperative is linked with an appreciation of the inherent value of the caring relation for selves-in-relation, whose concrete, practical understandings of particular situations I have described as seeing together. It is important to clarify what the assertion of this imperative involves and to establish the relevance of this imperative for the ethic of care. Three points contribute to this clarification.

The first point is that I mean the imperative to keep relational possibilities open to apply not as an abstract principle but as a concrete consideration of selves-in-relation. As a concrete consideration, it involves not the establishment of relation between individuals who are separate and autonomous but the acknowledgment of the relatedness of selves-in-relation. Because the imperative to keep relational possibilities open involves concrete considerations, it cannot be broken down into a series of specific injunctions or rules. I cannot, in other words, determine how relational possibilities might be kept open other than by cultivating an awareness of these possibilities in particular, concrete relations. In these particular, concrete contexts, what this imperative enjoins me to avoid is what Gilligan calls a "blindness to relationships,"[42] a blindness manifest in overlooking or ignoring or otherwise failing to acknowledge the relatedness of selves-in-relation. The injunction to keep relational possibilities open, then, does not generate anything like an ordering principle of relation. Rather, it is a commitment to consider particular relations, to ask how particular relations might be maintained, and to "take my cues . . . from the living other whom I encounter."[43]

The second point is that the commitment to keep relational possibilities open is not unconditional. It has seemed to some feminist care theorists that if care is associated with the imperative to keep relational possibilities open, as I am suggesting it is, then carers will be expected to maintain caring relationships even at the cost of the carer's integrity.[44] I think that this is a misreading of care that can be associated with the versions of care that confine care to needs-meeting.

When I set out the concept of care as disposition in Chapter 4, I link caring and mattering in a way that brings out the sense in which to care is to sustain particular kinds of relation that are not adequately understood in terms of an instrumental meeting of needs. It is when care is seen as entailing both caring action and the disposition to care that the qualitative aspects of care are revealed. A misreading of care occurs if it is assumed that the "cannot but" with which I link care as disposition relates to needs-meeting. If this assumption is correct, there may, indeed, be grounds to suspect that the exploitation of caring is not precluded by the terms of the ethic of care. The meeting of needs might be regarded as synonymous with keeping relational possibilities open, lest failing to meet needs closes off relational possibilities.

The assumption that the "cannot but" of care relates to needs-meeting, however, is not correct. The "cannot but" of care relates neither to needs-meeting nor to caring actions as such but to the relation of care itself, the caring about care that says that to care is to regard both what is cared about *and caring itself* as mattering. With this distinction between care as action and care as disposition in place, we can begin to see why the injunction to keep relational possibilities open is not an injunction to care at all costs. That I am a person disposed to care (i.e., a person to whom caring matters) means that I value relations of care. In particular caring relations, I value both the particular other and my caring for that particular other. But caring, here, is not a remote ethical construct. It is, as Murdoch notes with regard to M's endeavours, the patient, just, and loving regard of another. It is, as I have drawn out of Seller's account of her experiences, celebrated in small acts of inclusion as much as in larger commitments to peace. The injunction to keep relational possibilities open might, therefore, be characterised as a recognition that relation might be caring relation rather than as a commitment to maintain relation that is not caring.

The third point I want to consider involves the question of how we might distinguish between relations that thwart and relations that enhance relational possibilities. A consideration of this point draws my discussion together: if relational possibilities can be assessed only in the context of concrete, particular relations, then it seems to follow that the distinctions between relations are subject to the same restrictions. But at the same time, if the responsibility to keep relational possibilities open (which I claim is an imperative associated with partial reason) is to be kept distinct from an injunction to maintain relation that is not caring (which I claim is not an imperative associated with partial reason), it seems that I need to be able to do more than refer the assessment of each particular relation back to its context. The concept of seeing together, which adds an evaluative dimension to the caring of selves-in-relation, establishes a way in which I can talk about cultivating an understanding of the ways particular relation might be assessed as, for example, caring, indifferent, or abusive, while yet rejecting assessments formulated in abstract and universal terms.

Let me illustrate this point. As an autonomous, knowing individual, my knowledge-claims about, for example, domestic violence or incest are, at least to some degree, removed from the "life context" in which domestic violence or incest has moral meaning. The decontextualisation of the knowledge-claims of autonomous, knowing individuals risks removing knowledge both from particular contexts and, more significantly, from the *moral meaning* imparted in and by those contexts. In their search for explanations that lead to shared understandings, autonomous knowers overlook the shared understandings implicit in the particular contexts in which domestic violence or incest occurs. It is Haraway's insight that "there is no immediate vision from the standpoints of the subjugated."[45] The quest for immediate vision, which, for Haraway, is a metaphor for knowledge that is unmediated by context, may signify that "blindness to relationships" that results in a failure to acknowledge the relatedness of selves-in-relation.

Seeing together, by contrast, involves not only contextualising knowledge but ending the dissociation of knowledge from moral meaning. Seeing together is seeing as "full-blooded members of the social worlds for which we do our practical ethics."[46] Seeing together is to be part of a process of "we-saying"[47] by selves who know because they are selves-in-relation. As selves-in-relation, we might generate concrete, practical understandings of, for example, domestic violence or incest that yield richer accounts of human relatedness and its breakdown than understandings that confine themselves behind the boundaries of empirical or impartial claims. As autonomous knowers, we may treat domestic violence, incest, and, indeed, the myriad other forms in which humans abuse each other and their world as the result of our failure to keep out of each other's way. As selves-in-relation, we may instead reveal incest and domestic as well as other forms of violence as a failure of relation, where this is a breaking down of the very possibility that enables understanding.[48] The moral meaning pertaining to violence, then, may actually elude the autonomous knower whose seeing partly depends on being oblivious to the discourse of relation.

The blindness to relationships to which Gilligan refers is apparent in models of autonomous knowledge that factor relational contexts out of consideration. But this blindness also distorts the process of seeing together, which, in turn, distorts our understandings of relational possibilities. Thus, we find that a term like marital rape can be considered oxymoronic, while abusive adults "justify" their incestuous practices as caring, and spouses who are beaten interpret the violence of their partners as an expression of love. The key to restoring relational insight, however, is not to suspend judgment about whether particular relationships are caring, indifferent, or abusive but to link the cultivation of an understanding of the ways in which particular relationships might thwart or enhance relational possibilities with the capacity of selves-in-relation to see together.

SEEKING OUT OTHERS

Liberal moral theory keeps you out of my way; so, too, does feminist extensionism, where the confinement of partiality to bias issues the imperative not to eclipse others' points of view.   Strong epistemological partiality, on the other hand, compels me to seek you out, to understand our speaking and listening to each other as the only way of establishing our points of commonality and revealing the realities that are shared by us. This compulsion arises from the nature of partiality itself, where the concept of being positioned as selves-in-relation involves both voluntary decisions to seek you out and to attend to our relations as relations of care and the sense in which "I must" seek you out because, both ethically and epistemologically, I see to the extent that we see together.

Gilligan's critique of Kohlberg shows that care can be discerned only in a relational context.   Taken out of their relational context, the voices of care are not just philosophically unfathomable but actually inaudible.   In an important sense, then, I cannot care when nobody else is caring.   I do not mean that I cannot be placed in a position where I feel that nobody cares except me.   Rather, the observation borne out by Gilligan's work is that in order to recognise care, I must be situated within a relational framework.   It is in a relational framework, then, that the caring self emerges.   So it might be said that my caring *derives* from the relational context of care or at least that the relational context of care and my caring are mutually enabling (i.e., that the connection between the relational context of care and both my disposition to care about care and my practical acts of caring is one of mutual implication).

My caring, then, is inseparable from the relational context in which I care. Here is a vital difference between needs-based care and the caring that I want to associate with the ethic of care.[49]   Where care is only the response to a need for care, carers supply care where it is demanded.   In this version of care, what is involved in caring exists prior to any particular demand for care.   Carers are assumed to respond to particular demands for care by taking their caring skills into encounters where care is required, just as they might take, say, nursing or mediating skills into encounters with the sick or quarrelsome.   Another kind of caring, however, is generated in the encounter itself.   This caring is not confined to the response of an individual carer to a need for care but involves the recognition that the encounter between, or the engagement of, selves-in-relation is what creates and sustains care.[50]   I do not mean to imply that there is a particular temporal sequence of caring or that the care that is generated in the encounter itself is necessarily independent of previous caring experiences.   I certainly do not want to create the impression that concrete, particular acts of caring can be distinguished from an abstracted, universal care-in-itself.   I do, however, want to make a qualitative distinction between care that is a response to a particular demand and care that is generated in the engagement of selves-in-relation.   The first highlights what, in Chapter 4, I call the instrumental value of care.   The second enables us to appreciate the sense in which care is inherently valuable.   The first is a means to an end; the second, an end in itself.   In the context of lived experience, of course, the two may not be clearly distinguished. What I want to make clear, however, is that where needs-based care does not necessarily depend on the establishment of a relational context, care that is generated in the engagement of selves-in-relation is necessarily inseparable from this context. While we might imagine a computer being programmed to undertake the task of meeting needs, the engagement of selves-in-relation is fundamentally a noninstrumental process. My emphasis on the establishment of caring's relational context need not imply that this context is either an achievement of carers or a precondition of caring. In placing this emphasis on context, my intention is to underline the significance of the relational framework of caring as a aspect of care that both reveals and is revealed by the engagement of selves-in-relation.

The concepts of care and of partial reason that compel this seeking out of others are embedded in what Gilligan calls a "discourse of relationship."[51] I understand the idea of a discourse of relationship to be a way of drawing attention to a vital distinction between autonomous individuals (who, in Gilligan's terms, are "blind to relationships") and selves-in-relation.[52] Autonomous individuals have to construct relationships, have to contrive a sense of "feeling bound" to others. Where autonomy is theorised as primary, people are seen as primarily dissociated from each other: the self is dissociated from relation, and the relational world is dissociated from the world of individual autonomy. It is this construction of relationships as dissociated from the individual, autonomous self that Gilligan contrasts with a discourse of relationship, where this discourse "begins with connection, theorized as primary and seen as fundamental in human life."[53] Selves-in-relation are not autonomous selves that come together. The relational realities of selves positioned in relation acknowledge that "[p]eople live in connection with one another; human lives are interwoven in a myriad of subtle and not so subtle ways."[54]

The idea of a discourse of relationship, then, is to draw out the sense in which this living in connection, this interweaving, might inform our understandings of ourselves and our world. Embedding ethical and epistemological concepts of knowledge, truth, and reality in a discourse of relationship does not simply establish a relational framework for caring and knowing. What is more significant is the establishment of ethics and epistemology themselves as relational processes, processes that involve selves-in-relation seeing together rather than individual agents seeing the same thing. This is the point I link with strong epistemological partiality and the idea that we know not in spite of our partiality but because we are partial. I endorse Nelson's observation that "you or I *can* only know what *we know* (or could know), for some 'we'"[55] because it brings out the sense in which the processes of both care and partial reason are inextricably bound up with the relational context in which I am situated. We do not take our individual caring or knowing into relation. Rather, it is as selves-in-relation that we care or know, where our caring or knowing is both enabled by and enables positioning in relation.

When the imperative to seek out others is located within a discourse of relationship, it becomes apparent that this imperative does not establish a universal precondition for ethics and epistemology but rather promotes an understanding of ethics and epistemology as activities of selves-in-relation. I emphasise that ethical and epistemological processes involve the mutual implication of care and the relational framework of caring, the mutual implication of knowledge and the relational framework of knowing. What I am drawing attention to is that, although as selves-in-relation we are always and already in relation, and our perspectives can be only partial perspectives, the extent to which we *acknowledge* our positioning in relation and our partiality varies. Where this positioning in relation and partiality is unacknowledged, where we fail to take our ethical and epistemological cues from the "living others" we encounter, we move toward the stances stressing individualism, autonomy, and impartiality that I associate with liberal moral theory and foundational epistemology. When we acknowledge both our partiality and our relatedness, or, more precisely, when we acknowledge the *philosophical significance* of our partiality and our positioning in relation, we move toward the stances I characterise as care and partial reason.[56] Where autonomous and impartial individuals are supposed to ignore concrete and particular others in moving toward their ethical and epistemological objectives, selves who know themselves as partial and related seek others out in order to understand what those objectives might be and to realise those objectives in processes of seeing together.[57]

CONNECTING WITH OTHER PERSPECTIVES

According to the extensionist version of partiality as bias, the seeking out of others is an imperative only in the sense that I must acknowledge other points of view. This, I have said, links the concept of partiality with the political or methodological imperative not to silence your voice.

Where partiality is understood to refer to not only the partisan but also the incomplete nature of our theorising, however, I connect with others not only in order to acknowledge their perspectives but also to establish how their perspectives connect with my own. Here, the possibility of connecting with other positioned perspectives is one of the possibilities that enable both knowing and caring.[58] The concept of selves-in-relation challenges what Bowden calls "the universal validity of conceptions of persons as smoothly unified wholes, acting from a unitary centre of integrity."[59] This challenge takes two forms. In the sense emphasised by Bowden, it draws attention to a sense of "internal plurality," in which, given the non-existence of any "underlying I," several identities coexist in "ambiguous tension."[60] As well, however, it acknowledges that, in addition to an account of internal plurality, we need an account of "the *positioning* of knowing subjects."[61] What the concepts of care and partial reason contribute to an account of positioning is the idea that caring selves and knowing selves are selves-in-relation. Care does not exist prior to the relation of care. Care is created and sustained in the "continual doing" of the relation of care.[62] Similarly, knowledge-claims and the constraints on those claims are located in the relation of knowers to each other rather than in the relation between knowers and what is known. Conceiving knowledge and care as active, relational processes leads to the idea that the positioning of knowing and caring subjects is the positioning of selves-in-relation. By this I do not mean that selves-in-relation are constituted in relations of caring and knowing. This understanding would leave open the possibility that relations of caring and knowing are relations between otherwise separate individuals: that "the positioning of selves-in-relation" is "the positioning in relation of individual knowing and caring subjects." But a crucial aspect of my concept of selves-in-relation is that selves are always positioned in relation, are always partial. The shift of philosophical emphasis away from separation and impartiality toward partial and positioned selves transforms the ethics and epistemology of separate, impartial individuals into the moral understandings of care and partial reason. Seen in this light, the imperative to establish how other perspectives connect with my own does not imply that either care or knowledge is an amalgam of our individual caring or knowing. Rather, it suggests that it is in the process of connecting with other perspectives (perspectives that, like mine, are the partial perspectives of selves-in-relation) that care and knowledge are established.

This is a complex point, which can be made clearer by drawing on other metaphorical accounts of positioning. One that I find particularly pertinent, providing it draws on concepts of commonality rather than of a common language, is the comparison of the caring relation to conversation or dialogue. While not all dialogical models take account of the potential for inequalities in conversational input and response,[63] others offer fertile ground for feminist theorising. For example, Noddings' concept of "ordinary conversation," in which "all parties speak, listen and respond to one another," makes apparent the emptiness of the notion of the individual as the determinant of understanding. What matters in "ordinary conversation" are the establishment and maintenance of relation between conversational partners, rather than, or as well as, "the topic, the conclusion or the argument."[64] This, of course, need not be interpreted as meaning that the topic, the conclusion, or the argument is irrelevant or unimportant. Neither need the model of ordinary conversation be understood as applicable only in "easy cases" where speakers feel some degree of trust and affection for each other. Rather, I understand Noddings' point to be that, where the relation between speakers is not secondary to the topic, the conclusion, or the argument, even people who disagree or who dislike or distrust each other might "come to have positive regard for one another."[65] Positioning, here, does not involve a progression toward a point of resolution or closure but a cultivation of the shared interpretations and mutual understandings that might sustain further conversations.

There are resonances here with Haraway's notion of the knowing self, to which I make reference in Chapter 6. This "split and contradictory" self, which is "partial in all its guises, . . . always constructed and stitched together imperfectly," knows itself in "shared conversations." Haraway talks about the "partial views and halting voices" that join in the "power-charged social relation of 'conversation.'"[66]

Conversation or dialogue has always been a significant aspect of Gilligan's theorising, too. The notion of different voices and the way these different voices are constrained or enabled by the contexts in which they are positioned are developed in her 'Letter to Readers, 1993.'[67] There she describes how she has learned:

[to] hear the difference between a voice that is an open channel—connected physically with breath and sound, psychologically with feelings and thoughts, and culturally with a rich resource of language—and a voice that is impeded or blocked. I have also learned . . . to pick up relational resonances and follow the changes in people's voices that occur when they speak in places where their voices are resonant with or resounded by others, and when their voices fall into a space where there is no resonance, or where the reverberations are frightening, where they begin to sound dead or flat.[68]

In her latest writing, Gilligan refers to conversation as the "talking cure" that repairs the damage done "by not speaking, not listening, not knowing, not seeing, not caring and ultimately not feeling."[69]

What I detect in these references to conversation might be expressed, in the terms of my argument, as a subtle shifting of emphasis away from the interconnection of individuals toward the mutuality of selves-in-relation. I associate this move with a shift in focus from unitary individuals to selves-in-relation. Unitary individuals, as I show in my critique of liberal moral theory, connect with other individuals to the extent that they reason impartially, where the objective of connection is to see the same thing. Selves-in-relation are always and already positioned in relation, so that connecting with other perspectives is a process undertaken together, a process in which partial perspectives, which are irreducibly particular, come together in processes of seeing together, which are irreducibly communal.

I am describing a move away from unitary toward positioned individuals, away from autonomous, separate selves who come together in order to know, or whose knowing facilitates their coming together, toward selves-in-relation. Again I emphasise that this move is better characterised as a redescription of aspects of thought and activity than as the replacement of one set of norms with another. So, for example, developing the concept of connecting with other perspectives involves redescribing rather than discarding the concept of autonomy. To assert, as I have done, that, as moral and epistemic subjects, individuals are more appropriately described as selves-in-relation than as autonomous, separate selves is not necessarily to imply that selves-in-relation are selves stripped of their autonomy. Rather, it is to redescribe individuals as selves whose capacity for autonomous thought and action is properly understood in the context of their capacity to connect with other perspectives, where this connection is enabled by the constitution of individuals as selves-in-relation.

LOCATING AND CULTIVATING COMMONALITIES

Both care and partial reason are shaped by the imperative to be critically positioned, where this involves an awareness of both self and others as selves-in-relation. The imperative to be critically positioned is the imperative to accept responsibility for our knowing and caring practices by locating and cultivating the commonalities or shared interests that enable us to see together. There are, I think, two aspects to the cultivation of shared interests on which seeing together is grounded.

First, by identifying relation as a crucial epistemological and ethical concept, but establishing the basis of relation in our concrete situatedness, the shared beliefs, mutual understandings, and intersubjective agreements of ethical carers and partial reasoners can be understood to be enabled by our concrete particularity. Partial reasoners and ethical carers operate in terms that are neither exclusively abstract and universal nor exclusively concrete and particular. Rather, as ethical carers and partial reasoners, our interest is in discovering the ways in which we might see and do together, where this means seeing our particularity and concreteness not as isolating one from another but as furnishing the grounds of our relation. In our specificity lies the possibility of the move beyond our specificity. Our agreements, our shared understandings, do not transcend this specificity. Rather, they are grounded in the context in which agreement and understanding are sought.

Second, where care informs and is informed by partial reason, caring locates truth and knowledge in the universally operative requirement for the elaboration of context. What is true, what constitutes knowledge, is established as part of, not prior to, our doing and thinking. Knowledge and truth, then, issue from the particular encounter. Not all encounters, of course, are accounted for in these terms. It may be that there is no reality that is shared by us, in which case we cannot share beliefs systems, mutual understandings, and intersubjective agreements. It may be that one of us has imposed a reality on the other, that one of us has talked without listening, or that neither of us has both talked *and* listened. Importantly, though, what the idea of strong epistemological and ethical partiality allows is that where we both talk and listen from the basis of our own particularity and concreteness, we might reach a point at which we can, together, see further than our own particularity and concreteness. From specificity comes the possibility of going beyond specificity. As Haraway says, "The only way to find a larger vision is to be somewhere in particular."[70]

These two aspects of cultivating shared interests or locating commonalities need some kind of concrete illustration in order to ensure that certain misunderstandings are avoided. The first misunderstanding is that the concept of seeing together might be supposed to be operating at the normative level, as the moral injunction to cultivate shared interests. The second and associated misunderstanding is that the relatedness of selves-in-relation is a neutral ontological condition that may be either fostered, giving rise to care, or neglected, giving rise to individualism. I think that elements of these misunderstandings are evident in Seller's account of her experiences in India and that her dawning realisation about the complexity of her relation with the Indian women provides an insight into how the process of locating commonalities might be understood in a way that avoids these misunderstandings. Seller says that she arrived in India determined not to judge or at least determined that "[a]s a Briton I have no right to judge Indian ways."[71] But in forcing her determination to withhold judgment on the women, she effectively eliminates the possibility that the women might remain *un*judged. In her determination not to replay the role of coloniser, she effectively repeats the coloniser's assumption that *we*, and not *they*, know what is best for *them*. Her assumption, then, is that she can forge *shared* understandings out of understandings that are *hers*. What she expects is that the preconditions for sharing interests can be put in place by her effective predetermination of how these interests should be constituted.

What Seller gradually realises is that both her assumption of impartiality and her assumption about establishing the conditions for dialogue are mistaken. The point is that she may not have realised that her assumptions were mistaken if she had simply failed to cultivate shared interests. Such a failure may have been attributed to a failure to remain sufficiently impartial or to establish sufficiently clear conditions for dialogue. What happens, though, and what makes her account such a poignant illustration of the processes I am describing as care and partial reason, are that when she *does* discover shared interests, they arise in what, for her, are completely unexpected places. Where she fails to cultivate shared interests is precisely in the places she had contrived those interests to coincide.

The point is that, as I have drawn them out of the concepts of care and partial reason, the possibility of seeing together and locating points of commonality encompasses a range of responses. Even forms of "separatism," where we withdraw from those who have harmed us or where those whom we have harmed withdraw from us, might be conceived as processes of seeing together. What these conceptions of seeing together depend on, though, is a second consideration, which is that selves-in-relation are partial selves. Partial selves see from partial perspectives. As selves-in-relation, we might be able to neglect our relatedness, but we cannot be neutral or impartial in the sense that Seller expected. We may be unsure about the grounds of our judgments or even about what we are judging. But, as Seller discovers, such doubts and disputes about the grounds or appropriateness of judging should not divert us from "the fact that judgement cannot be avoided":

[B]eing who I was, doing things in the way I knew, meant that I judged, even when I didn't intend to. Further, the friendships I made, my engagement in and responsiveness to others' lives necessarily involved my emotions and concerns, my values. . . . The only way to avoid judgement is to totally lose identity, and to be completely unresponsive to the world around you.[72]

Seller's insight, then, is not that she failed to remain impartial and therefore failed to establish shared understandings but that she established shared understandings *to the extent that* she failed to remain impartial.

Were relation a neutral ontological condition, partial and impartial perspectives might be conceived as two aspects of understanding or two ways of responding to the world around us. Reasoning impartially would be reasoning that is independent of who I am, of my emotions and concerns and my values, while partial reason would necessarily involve these considerations. What can be drawn out of Seller's story, however, is the emptiness of the concept of impartial reason. Impartial reason is reason that is *devoid* of perspective, devoid of the sense in which I am always and already a self positioned in relation to other selves and to the world around me, and knowing myself, self-reflexively, as both sustaining and sustained by my positioning in interpersonal and contextual relation. Impartial *a*perspectivity affords no insight into the knowing self: *who* knows is not relevant to the impartial reasoner. But neither does impartial *a*perspectivity afford insight into the world. The world revealed to the impartial reasoner is the world of "resounding silences."[73] It is the world constructed in the image of a knower who is without identity.

What I want to say, then, is not that Seller's initial assumption that impartiality would lay down the preconditions for establishing shared understandings gives way to a realisation that partiality lays down those preconditions. Rather, her realisation is that to share understandings, it is necessary to see whom one is sharing with. She realises that where impartiality or aperspectivity blinds us to the particular identities of those who might share understandings, to be partial is to consider "what I should say to . . . how I should respond to" those particular others, together with whom I might see.[74] Here the focus is on "my relationships to the people that I am with,"[75] rather than on the interests and understandings I assume we might share. In my terms, then, Seller provides a concrete example of the way shared understandings arise out of considering the *context* in which we might share, rather than the *content* of what might be shared.

What Seller's story illustrates is that the relatedness of selves-in-relation might be conceived not as a neutral ontological condition but as imbued with possibilities that turn resounding silences into shared understandings and mutual agreements. Where the focus is on relation in this concrete sense, there can be no moral injunction to cultivate shared interests, no universal preconditions for ensuring that selves-in-relation see together. The imperative to locate commonalities, to cultivate shared interests, when it is seen to be an epistemological and ethical imperative associated with partial reason and ethical care, is more like a guide to the responsibilities entailed in the self-reflexive elaboration of context than a normative injunction. The small acts of inclusion in which Seller celebrates her seeing together with the Indian women are an achievement in terms of her increased awareness of these responsibilities, not in terms of the satisfaction of preconditions or the heeding of an injunction.

CONCLUSION

The connection I have established between the ethic of care and partial reason is a strong one. I have built a sturdy link between the two partly so that are they are understood as mutually informing. But I also want to suggest that the concept of selves-in-relation can be seen as sustaining practices of caring and knowing that help us develop more subtle understandings of our concerns and responsibilities than are available when ethics and reason are made subservient to the impartial ideals of autonomy. For autonomous selves, the injunction to be impartial functions as both an epistemological and an ethical imperative. For selves-in-relation, the imperatives associated with both care and partial reason engage ethical and epistemic subjects in a self-reflexive elaboration of context. In this chapter, I explain what this self-reflexive elaboration of context might entail by associating it with the responsibility to focus on lived experience, rather than on social roles, to emphasise the concrete and particular, rather than the universal and unitary in particular contexts, to keep open relational possibilities, to seek out others, to see the connections between other perspectives and our own and to locate and cultivate commonalities. These imperatives do not supply the content of care. Neither do they equate care with the fulfillment of the necessary and sufficient conditions for caring. Rather, they describe the parameters of the partial reason by which care is informed.

The ethical and epistemological imperatives and responsibilities associated with care and partial reason involve concrete considerations about how we talk to each other, rather than metaphysical abstractions: they are aids to understanding, rather than rules of engagement. This is a crucial point, the grasping of which sheds light on why the philosophical elaboration of the ethic of care consists less in describing the *content* of care and more in describing the *reason* by which care might be informed and constrained. It is noticeable, I think, that one of the places where care appears to founder when it is presented in philosophical forums is where questions about the content of care are posed. It is here that the inherently contextual nature of caring responses seems to commit the ethic of care to a relativism or an irrationalism, an unreasoned responsiveness or a strictly instrumental, self-justifying rationality. These are commitments that do not adequately account for care. With the concept of partial reason we can account philosophically for care without necessarily being able to specify what the content of care might be. Where care informs and is informed by partial reason and where partial reason is understood as entailing the epistemological and ethical imperatives I outline in the last two chapters, it becomes apparent that the judgment about whether, or how well, I am caring is to be made not through the eyes of a detached arbitrator but through the eyes of an engaged participant. So, for Seller, the process of reaching the stage at which she has the sense that she and the Indian women are seeing together involves cultivating an understanding of a set of unique criteria that foster the appreciation of small acts of inclusion as well as larger-scale acts of mutual consideration.[76] In Gilligan's framework, what care "means" depends on particular ways of responding to the demands of partial reason.[77] Where caring fails, we have a sense of the breakdown of the carer herself, the breakdown of the self as a self-in-relation. Such breakdowns, or "encounters with defeat," are not defined as the absence of what might constitute the specific content of care, although they result in the loss of care.[78] Rather, what we hear when care fails are accounts of people sapped of the energy to respond to the demands of partial reason, where heeding these demands might have grounded the activities of care.[79] For the mother who, rather than remain alone with the baby she has been tempted to kill, rides public transport with the baby all night, the association of her thinking with care and the positive evaluation of herself as caring are made only sometime later, when she realises that "what she did was enough."[80]

The point illustrated by these examples is that even though I cannot necessarily specify the content of care, I can have an understanding of the reasoning by which care is informed and of the emphases and considerations to which this reasoning gives rise. The fact that care may not be amenable to evaluation by a detached arbitrator does not mean that care is not subject to evaluation or is self-justifying. Where care is associated with mattering, as I suggest in Chapter 5, partial reason establishes the parameters that link our dispositions to care with our actions as carers. Partial reason, entailing the ethical responsibilities or imperatives I consider in this chapter, provides us with the measure of our caring. Unlike the evaluative processes of impartial reason as applied to duty, utility, or contract, partial reason does not detach the measure of morality from the context of the moral response. Partial reason is to be understood as acknowledging not only the partisan nature of our thinking but also the inherently incomplete or fragmentary nature of our thinking and the *awareness* of our perspectivity. This suggests that the measure of care, and, indeed, of the workings of partial reason itself, lies in the sustaining of selves-in-relation, selves whose shared belief systems, mutual understandings, and intersubjective agreements are enabled by their awareness of their inherent partiality (in the complex sense of being partisan and incomplete). What partial reason suggests is not that incomplete selves find completion in relation (at least if completion involves a closure to the self-reflexive elaboration of context) but that it is as selves-in-relation that partial selves come to know themselves and their world. The measure of care, then, is the measure not of the content of care but of whether my caring is guided by the ethical imperatives of partial reason. Such considerations might not be a measure of the "true care" sought after by those who understand care solely in terms of the meeting of needs.[81] They do, however, show that care reasoning is both directed and shaped by an acceptance of specific responsibilities and that we shoulder these responsibilities not as selves "standing alone before some tribunal"[82] but as selves-in-relation who can *be* in-relation *because of* our inherent partiality.

In my account of knowing and caring, of partial reason and of the ethic of care, I have shown that the axiomatic status of autonomous knowing subjects obscures the possibility of conceptualising knowing subjects as selves-in-relation, just as the axiomatic status of autonomous moral subjects obscures the possibility of conceptualising moral subjects as selves-in-relation. Autonomous individuals are sustained in their autonomy by ethical and epistemological practices that privilege separation. With different understandings of ethical and epistemological practices in place, we can see that the idea of subjects positioned in relation does not supplement or complement the idea of the autonomous, impartial subject. It redescribes this subject, revealing autonomy and impartiality to be an epistemological and moral fantasy.

For selves-in-relation, care is inherently valuable. As I show in Chapter 4, the notion of care as disposition highlights the inadequacy of an instrumental version of care. Care understood as the meeting of needs does not capture the sense in which my caring reflects the fact that you matter to me. The value of care in the needs-based version is expressed quantitatively. My version of care, which depends on understanding care in terms of both practical acts of caring and the disposition to care about care, expresses care not quantitatively but qualitatively.

For selves-in-relation, care is also inherently rational. My version of care shows that care is to be understood neither as irrational nor as unreasoned nor in terms of the strictly instrumental or self-justifying rationality associated with needs-meeting. The epistemological imperatives that I have associated with partial reason are also ethical imperatives. Both partial reason and care are self-reflexive and contextual, where this involves cultivating understandings of the different, but interrelated, possibilities I draw together in this chapter.

Where the understanding of care is grounded on the inherent *value* and the inherent *rationality* of care for selves-in-relation, the ethic of care emerges as both an alternative moral system and a critical feminist epistemology. The philosophical articulation of care involves a refusal to take the epistemological and ethical premises of liberal philosophy at face value. In the redescription of knowers and carers as selves-in-relation, in the reworking of the concept of partiality that proves so troubling when its sense is restricted to bias, we can discern a version of care that entails a critique of liberal approaches to ethics and epistemology and a suggestion about how we might yet provide more constructive accounts of both. This version of care is, as I have said, a transformative project. True to Gatens' critical-interrogative approach, it shows that neither ethics nor epistemology is immutable and that both can be held to account for the possibilities open to us as knowers and doers.

At the beginning of Chapter 5, I question whether it is helpful to describe moral philosophy as having reached an impasse. There I suggest that the dilemma that seems to arise when care is constructed in epistemological terms antithetical to foundationalism fails to arise when we give a different meaning to partiality. Once partiality is understood as entailing not only a political or methodological but also an epistemological imperative, we can see that what the ethic of care establishes is not a competing paradigm but an opportunity to question whether what once appeared to be philosophically plausible is still viable. In other words, rather than opposing the accounts of deontologists, utilitarians, and contractarian theorists, the ethic of care shows where and how these accounts are deficient and describes alternative ways of arriving at philosophical understanding.[83]

By re-presenting the alternatives so that the dilemma associated with antithetical accounts is avoided, it seems to me that we also avoid creating an impasse. There might, indeed, be no way out of the debate about care and traditional moral philosophy if care merely filled in the spaces left vacant by traditional accounts. My belief is that care cannot be confined in this way. Care, when it is understood as sustaining the nexus between ethics and reason, points to the implausibility of traditional accounts of morality. Care develops the critique of liberalism into accounts of reason, selves-in-relation, truth, knowledge, and reality in which the legitimacy of axiomatic claims and assumptions is thrown into question. The objective of this questioning is not to instate other axioms but to ensure that we think philosophically in ways that do not obscure the relations that sustain our capacity to know and to care well.

NOTES

1. In Chapter 1.
2. See my discussion in Chapters 1 and 3.
3. See my discussion in Chapters 4 and 6.
4. Although my reservation about Murdoch's account is that, without the inclusion of something like critical positioning, attention may end up describing the product of seeing the same thing rather than the process of seeing together. See my discussion of this point in Chapter 4.
5. I do not see the idea of self-reflection as solipsistic. I mean it to *add* a dimension to our understanding of the process of knowing by making the knower as well as the known epistemologically active.
6. Code, 'Taking Subjectivity into Account,' 16, notes the assumption that "[i]f one cannot transcend subjectivity and the particularities of its 'location,' then there is no knowledge worth analyzing."
7. This recalls my discussion of Benhabib in Chapter 3.
8. Sandel, *Liberalism and the Limits of Justice*, 180. Sandel is referring specifically to the deontological self. I think this point is also relevant in the broader context of my critique.
9. Cf. the point I emphasise in Chapter 6 about the epistemological imperatives associated with partiality involving a *redescription* of the preconditions for truth and knowledge, not the identification of new epistemological norms or preconditions or necessary and sufficient conditions.
10. Walker, 'Moral Understandings,' 21. The dissent from nomologically ordered theoretical approaches, to ethics if not to epistemology, is expressed by nonfeminist philosophers, too. See, for example, the references I give in Chapter 5, note 31.
11. MacIntyre, *After Virtue;* Sandel, *Liberalism.*
12. Sandel, *Liberalism,* 6. Friedman, 'Feminism and Modern Friendship,' 89, in her critique of MacIntyre and Sandel, refers to the "social self." A version of this paper appears as Chapter 9 in Friedman, *What are Friends For?*
13. Friedman, 'Feminism and Modern Friendship.' Poole, *Morality and Modernity,* 149, makes a similar point to Friedman: "[T]he communities which [MacIntyre] applauds are hierarchical and exclusive, intolerant of deviation and deeply and systematically oppressive of women."
14. Friedman, 'Feminism and Modern Friendship,' 92 passim.
15. I leave open the possibility that communitarianism may not necessarily entail this fundamentally reactionary understanding of established forms of life while agreeing with Friedman that it is certainly implied in the accounts of Sandel and MacIntyre.
16. This remodeling is, at least in part, what Friedman does with the notion of "communities of choice." The point I am making here applies equally to Poole's criticisms of communitarianism.
17. Sandel, *Liberalism,* 7.
18. For a critique of MacIntyre's concept of practice and its failure to account for evil and oppressive practices, see Frazer and Lacey, 'MacIntyre, Feminism and the Concept of Practice.'

19. In Chapter 3 I say that my interest is in considering the way ethics and epistemology might be transformed by the presumption that individuals can be understood as selves-in-relation rather than with the direct explication of relation in the realm of metaphysics. That point is relevant to the distinction I want to make here, which is founded primarily not on differences between the concepts of situated selves and selves-in-relation at the level of ontology but on the difference between accounts of human connectedness in terms of institutional coordinates and in terms of the lived experience of concrete and particular relations.

20. Rich, *Of Woman Born.*

21. Sandel, *Liberalism,* 179; MacIntyre, *After Virtue,* 204–205.

22. Rich, *Of Woman Born,* 274.

23. As Eisenstein notes, *Contemporary Feminist Thought,* 72. Rich actually thinks that the institution of motherhood lacks this symbolic architecture. It seems to me, however, that Madonna images and the mass portrayal of idealised mother–child relations establish for motherhood the metaphorical equivalent of a symbolic monument like the Vatican or Parliament House.

24. MacIntyre, *After Virtue,* 33.

25. Ibid., 126.

26. Ibid., 34.

27. For an extreme, but telling, example of the way a mother might relinquish abstract accounts of "how mothers ought to behave toward sons" in order to discover what she ought to do in the context of the concrete realities of her relation with her son, see Anne Deveson's *Tell Me I'm Here.*

28. Jaggar, 'Caring as a Feminist Practice of Moral Reason,' 196–7. Kathleen League, 'Individualism, Class, and the Situation of Care,' 79, expresses similar concerns, charging Gilligan with "[s]upporting prevailing conditions by deflecting attention away from them to individual attitudes."

29. The phrase "continual doing" is Seller's, 'Realism versus Relativism,' 180: "Neither knowledge *nor* political solutions are final, they consist rather in continual doing."

30. See, for example, the interpretation of Cartesian methodology as representing "the efforts of a paranoid to free himself forever from the insecurity of doubt." The words are Antony's, 'Quine as Feminist,' 199. She disputes this interpretation. She is, presumably, referring to accounts like Bordo's, 'The Cartesian Masculinization of Thought'; Scheman's, 'Othello's Doubt/Desdemona's Death'; and Bernstein's, *Beyond Objectivism and Relativism.*

31. These are the terms in which philosophy is often introduced to students. See, for example, Hospers' comments about how philosophers "cut through the confusions" and experience "feelings of mastery" (*An Introduction to Philosophical Analysis,* 7).

32. Code, 'Taking Subjectivity into Account,' 16; Harding, 'Rethinking Standpoint Epistemology,' 66.

33. As I point out in Chapter 6, note 40, with references to Harding and Gatens.

34. Malpas, 'Speaking the Truth,' 172–173.

35. I have generally avoided an approach that seeks to exemplify relational concepts like care, responsibility, positioning, attentiveness, empathy, and mattering by elaborating them in concrete metaphorical contexts like mothering (Ruddick, *Maternal Thinking),* friendship (Code, *What Can She Know?),* or the relationships based on nurturing practices (Whitbeck, 'A Different Reality'). Too frequently, critics of these approaches miss or at least overlook the point that such accounts are only elaborations of metaphors. I think that it undermines the potential explanatory power of such accounts

to accuse their authors of trying to establish paradigmatic models or to observe that some mothering (or friendship or nurturing) practices do not embody these concepts (and most mothering-friendship-nurturing practices do not always embody them). For an example of such a critique, see Grimshaw, *Feminist Philosophers*, especially Chapter 8. This, however, is not the reason I have, in general, avoided metaphorical examples. Rather, what concerns me about metaphorical models is that they tend to be situated by critics in the adversarial tradition (even though, at least in the cases of Code, Ruddick, and Whitbeck, their authors' intent might be to dissent from such tradition), where the most effective way to demolish the argument of opponents is to construct examples and counterexamples in the terms defined by the opponents' argument. As Moulton explains, 'A Paradigm of Philosophy,' 159, this process involves abstracting the essential features of a problem and finding an analogy "that has those features but which is different enough and clear enough to be considered dispassionately apart from the issue in question." This has not seemed to me to be a productive path, particularly as many of the ideas I am exploring in this discussion involve the attempt to fill terms and concepts with new meanings and to hold open questions about what is given, what is natural, and what is contingent.

36. This discussion of interchangeability recalls my critique of liberal moral theory in Chapter 1. There I say that, because liberal moral theory confines morality to the public realm, the assumption is that the particularity of the other is irrelevant: when I encounter the other ethically, it does not matter whom I am encountering.

37. See, for example, Addelson, 'What Do Women Do?,' 209, for a critique of the assumption that "a single individual can guarantee that his decisions are morally proper by reasoning all by himself"; and Blum, 'Gilligan and Kohlberg,' 51–52, for an account of "the individual rational being legislating for himself and obeying laws and principles generated solely from within himself (i.e. from within his own reason)."

38. As Addelson says, 'Knower/Doers and Their Moral Problems,' 270–272, the unit of a person or individual is "so deeply presupposed" in traditional epistemology of science that it is submerged: "Persons . . . dropped into the deep background as objects of analysis, because it was self-evident to the reigning materialist/reductionists that it is individual persons who exist and know. The 'norm of universalism' in science also rationalized forgetting about persons; it makes no difference who discovers or states the truth, because scientific knowledge is not relative to personal idiosyncrasy or political or cultural context." She cites R. K. Merton, *Social Theory and Social Structure* (Glencoe, IL: Free Press, 1949), at the end of this quotation. The variety of metaphors describing the disappeared, forgotten, and submerged knowing individual indicates how successful the vanishing trick is and, perhaps, how close are the links between the submerged knower and the transcendency of impartial knowledge.

39. Or, as Bordo, 'Feminism, Postmodernism, and Gender-Scepticism,' 137, says, "brought down to earth, given a pair of pants, and reminded that it was not the only player in town."

40. Something like the relational context of constraints is implied, I think, by Haraway's assertion that "[p]ositioning implies responsibility for our enabling practices. . . . How to see? Where to see from? What limits to vision? What to see for? Whom to see with? Who gets to have more than one point of view? Who gets blinded? Who wears blinders? Who interprets the visual field? What other sensory powers do we wish to cultivate besides vision?" ('Situated Knowledges,' 587).

41. Where such interpersonal looking is both contextual and self-reflective.

42. Gilligan, 'Hearing the Difference,' 122.

43. Noddings, *Philosophy of Education,* 188.

44. This is the concern, for example, of Hoagland and Houston, whom I citie in Chapter 2, note 16.

45. Haraway, 'Situated Knowledges,' 586.

46. Addelson, 'Knower/Doers and Their Moral Problems,' 286.

47. Code, 'Taking Subjectivity into Account,' 24, 25.

48. Conventional ways of understanding knowledge-claims may also see domestic violence as a breakdown of whatever enables understanding but may cite this enabling factor as autonomy rather than relation.

49. I discuss needs-based caring in more detail in Chapter 4.

50. The engagement of selves-in-relation does not refer to the engagement of otherwise-separate selves in relation. Selves-in-relation are already engaged in a relational sense; it is selves who are always and already in relation who are engaged in care.

51. Gilligan, 'Hearing the Difference,' 122.

52. It is significant that Gilligan, ibid., 121, contrasts the discourse of relationship associated with care not with other discourses of relationship but with what she calls "the prevailing discourse of individual rights and freedom." As I understand it, the latter entails the "blindness to relationships" signified by the separation of the autonomous self from relation.

53. Ibid., 122. I base the title of Chapter 3 on this quotation.

54. Ibid.

55. Nelson, 'Epistemological Communities,' 124. I first quote this passage in Chapter 5.

56. While admitting that the extent to which we acknowledge our positioning in relation and our partiality vary, I do not accept the suggestion that the relatedness of selves-in-relation is a neutral ontological condition that different philosophical approaches might either foster or neglect. I develop this point later in this chapter.

57. Although she uses very different language and is pursuing a different argument, I think Noddings, *Philosophy of Education,* 190, makes a similar point to mine when she says: "In contrast to the individualism of Kantian ethics wherein every moral agent is wholly responsible for his or her own moral perfection, the ethic of care requires each of us to recognize our own frailty and to bring out the best in one another. It recognizes that we are dependent on each other (and to some degree on good fortune) for our moral goodness. How good I can be depends at least in part on how you treat me."

58. The other factors are those which I identify in this chapter as the epistemological and ethical imperatives associated with care and partial reason.

59. Bowden, 'Ethical Attention,' 21.

60. Ibid., 22. Bowden is drawing on Lugones, 'Playfulness, "World"-Traveling, and Loving Perception' and 'Hispaneando y Lesbiando. For another discussion of internal plurality and a caution about "taking splitting and internal multiplicity as the hallmarks of liberatory subjectivity," see Scheman, 'Though This Be Method,' 102.

61. This phrase is used by Yeatman, 'Postmodern Epistemological Politics and Social Science,' 190.

62. See my reference to Seller in note 29.

63. See, for example, Spender's account of women's conversational disadvantages in *Man Made Language,* especially the section 'Who Does the Talking?,' 41–50.

64. Noddings, 'Conversation as Moral Education,' 114–116.

65. Ibid., 115.

66. Haraway, 'Situated Knowledges,' 584–593.

67. Preface to the 1993 edition of Gilligan, *In a Different Voice,* ix–xxvii.

68. Ibid., xvi.
69. Gilligan, 'Hearing the Difference,' 125.
70. Haraway, 'Situated Knowledges,' 590.
71. Seller, 'Should the Feminist Philosopher Stay at Home?,' 245.
72. Ibid.
73. See Seller, quoted in Chapter 6, note 28.
74. Seller, Should the Feminist Philosopher Stay at Home?,' 246. In this passage, Seller says that those who "don't judge" are *blind* "to the question of who the subjects and objects of their sentences might be." I think that Gilligan's "blindness to relationships" (see note 42) marks a similar use of the metaphor.
75. Ibid.
76. See my discussion at the end of Chapter 6.
77. In her 'Letter to Readers, 1993,' xviii, Gilligan commends Toni Morrison's novel *Beloved* for exploring the question "what does care mean, or what could it potentially mean or entail, for a woman who loves her children and is living in a racist and violent society?"
78. See Gilligan, *In a Different Voice,* especially Chapter 4, 'Crisis and Transition,' 106–127, where Gilligan considers the responses of those women "for whom . . . pregnancy precipitated a crisis and led to an encounter with defeat" (108).
79. For another account of a failure of care that I take to illustrate my point about the breakdown of the carer as partial reasoner, see Manning's account of her own experience, *Speaking from the Heart,* 146.
80. Ruddick, *Maternal Thinking,* 67.
81. I have associated Tronto, in particular, with the needs-based version of care.
82. Noddings, *Caring,* 95.
83. In Chapter 1, I show that liberal deontological, utilitarian, and contractarian theories are both ethical and epistemological projects.

Bibliography

Addelson, Kathryn Pyne. *Impure Thoughts: Essays in Philosophy, Feminism, and Ethics.* Philadelphia: Temple University Press, 1991

Addelson, Kathryn Pyne. 'What Do Women Do? Some Radical Implications of Carol Gilligan's Ethics 1985.' In *Impure Thoughts: Essays in Philosophy, Feminism, and Ethics.* Kathryn Pyne Addelson. 188–211. Philadelphia: Temple University Press, 1991.

Addelson, Kathryn Pyne. 'Knower/Doers and Their Moral Problems.' In *Feminist Epistemologies.* Ed. Linda Alcoff and Elizabeth Potter. 265–294. New York and London: Routledge, 1993.

Addelson, Kathryn Pyne. *Moral Passages: Toward a Collectivist Moral Theory.* New York and London: Routledge, 1994.

Alcoff, Linda and Elizabeth Potter, eds. *Feminist Epistemologies.* New York and London: Routledge, 1993.

Andolsen, Barbara Hilkert. 'Agape in Feminist Ethics.' *Journal of Religious Ethics* 9 (1981): 69–83.

Antony, Louise M. 'Quine as Feminist: The Radical Import of Naturalized Epistemology.' In *A Mind of One's Own: Feminist Essays on Reason and Objectivity.* Ed. Louise M. Antony and Charlotte Witt. 185–225. Boulder, CO: Westview Press, 1993.

Antony, Louise M. and Charlotte Witt, eds. *A Mind of Own's Own: Feminist Essays on Reason and Objectivity.* Boulder, CO: Westview Press, 1993.

Auerbach, Judy, Linda Blum, Vicki Smith, and Christine Williams. 'Commentary on Gilligan's *In a Different Voice.*' *Feminist Studies* 11, no. 1 (Spring 1985): 149–161.

Austin, Nancy K. 'The Death of Hierarchy.' *Working Woman* (July 1990): 22–25.

Baier, Annette C. 'Caring about Caring: A Reply to Frankfurt.' *Synthese* 53 (1982): 273–290.

Baier, Annette C. 'Cartesian Persons.' In *Postures of the Mind: Essays on Mind and Morals.* Annette C. Baier. 74–92. Minneapolis: University of Minnesota Press, 1985.

Baier, Annette C. *Postures of the Mind: Essays on Mind and Morals.* Minneapolis: University of Minnesota Press, 1985.

Baier, Annette. 'Trust and Antitrust.' *Ethics* 96 (1986): 231–260.

Baier, Annette. 'The Need for More than Justice.' In *Science, Morality and Feminist Theory*. Ed. Marsha Hanen and Kai Nielsen. 41–56. Calgary: University of Calgary Press, 1987.

Baier, Annette. 'What Do Women Want in a Moral Theory?' In *An Ethic of Care: Feminist and Interdisciplinary Perspectives*. Ed. Mary Jeanne Larrabee. 19–32. New York: Routledge, 1993.

Baier, Annette. 'A Note on Justice, Care, and Immigration Policy.' *Hypatia* 10, no. 2 (Spring 1995): 150–152.

Baier, Kurt. *The Moral Point of View*. Ithaca, NY: Cornell University Press, 1958.

Baron, Marcia. 'The Alleged Moral Repugnance of Acting from Duty.' *The Journal of Philosophy* 81 (1984): 197– 220.

Bartky, Sandra Lee. 'Feeding Egos and Tending Wounds: Deference and Disaffection in Women's Emotional Labor.' In *Femininity and Domination: Studies in the Phenomenology of Oppression*. Sandra Lee Bartky. 99–119. New York and London: Routledge, 1990.

Bateson, Gregory, Don D. Jackson, Jay Haley, and John H. Weakland. 'Toward a Theory of Schizophrenia.' In *Steps to an Ecology of Mind: Collected Essays in Anthropology, Psychiatry, Evolution and Epistemology*. Gregory Bateson. 173–198. London: Granada, 1973.

Benhabib, Seyla. 'The Generalized and the Concrete Other: The Kohlberg-Gilligan Controversy and Moral Theory.' In *Women and Moral Theory*. Ed. Eva Feder Kittay and Diana T. Meyers. 154–177. Totowa, NJ: Rowman and Littlefield, 1987.

Bernstein, Richard. *Beyond Objectivism and Relativism: Science, Hermeneutics, and Praxis*. Philadelphia: University of Philadelphia Press, 1983.

Bernstein, Richard. *The New Constellation: The Ethical-Political Horizons of Modernity/Postmodernity*. Cambridge: MIT Press, 1992.

Blum, Lawrence A. 'Gilligan and Kohlberg: Implications for Moral Theory.' In *An Ethic of Care: Feminist and Interdisciplinary Perspectives*. Ed. Mary Jeanne Larrabee. 49–68. New York: Routledge, 1993.

Blustein, Jeffrey. *Care and Commitment: Taking the Personal Point of View*. New York and Oxford: Oxford University Press, 1991.

Bock, Gisela and Sue James. *Beyond Equality and Difference*. London and New York: Routledge, 1992.

Bordo, Susan. 'The Cartesian Masculinization of Thought.' *Signs: Journal of Women in Culture and Society* 11 (1986): 439–456.

Bordo, Susan. 'Feminism, Postmodernism, and Gender-Scepticism.' In *Feminism/Postmodernism*. Ed. Linda J. Nicholson. 133–156. New York and London: Routledge, 1990.

Bowden, Peta. 'Ethical Attention.' Paper presented to the Australian Association of Philosophers (New Zealand Branch) Conference. Auckland. May 1994.

Bowden, Peta. *Caring: Gender-Sensitive Ethics*. London: Routledge, 1997.

Braidotti, Rosi. 'The Politics of Ontological Difference.' In *Between Feminism and Psychoanalysis*. Ed. Teresa Brennan. 89–105. London and New York: Routledge, 1989.

Braidotti, Rosi. *Patterns of Dissonance: A Study of Women in Contemporary Philosophy*. Cambridge: Polity Press, 1991.

Braidotti, Rosi. 'On the Female Feminist Subject, or: From "She-self" to "She-other".' In *Beyond Equality and Difference*. Ed. Gisela Bock and Sue James. 177–192. London and New York: Routledge, 1992.

Braidotti, Rosi. 'Embodiment, Sexual Difference, and the Nomadic Subject.' *Hypatia* 8, no. 1 (Winter 1993): 1–13.

Brennan, Samantha. 'Review of *Women and Evil* by Nel Noddings,' *Hypatia* 7, no. 1 (Winter 1992): 142–146.

Brennan, Teresa, ed. *Between Feminism and Psychoanalysis.* London and New York: Routledge, 1989.

Brian's Wife, Jenny's Mum. A collection of writings by Australian 'suburban' women presented by Gwen Wesson. Victoria: Dove Communications, 1975.

Burgess-Jackson, Keith. 'The Problem with Contemporary Moral Theory.' *Hypatia* 8, no. 3 (Summer 1993): 160–166.

Butler, Judith. 'Gender Trouble, Feminist Theory and Psychoanalytic Discourse.' In *Feminism/Postmodernism.* Ed. Linda J. Nicholson. 324–340. New York and London: Routledge, 1990.

Calhoun, Cheshire. 'Justice, Care, Gender Bias.' *Journal of Philosophy* 85 (1988): 451–463.

Card, Claudia. 'Caring and Evil.' *Hypatia* 5, no. 1 (Spring 1990): 101–108.

Card, Claudia. 'Gender and Moral Luck.' In *Identity, Character, and Morality.* Ed. Owen Flanagan and Amélie Oksenberg Rorty. 199–218. Cambridge: MIT Press, 1990.

Card, Claudia. 'The Feistiness of Feminism.' In *Feminist Ethics.* Ed. Claudia Card. 3–31. Lawrence: University Press of Kansas, 1991.

Card, Claudia, ed. *Feminist Ethics.* Lawrence: University Press of Kansas, 1991.

Code, Lorraine. 'Is the Sex of the Knower Epistemologically Significant?' *Metaphilosophy* 12 (July–October 1981): 267–276.

Code, Lorraine. 'Experience, Knowledge, and Responsibility.' In *Feminist Perspectives in Philosophy.* Ed. Margaret Whitford and Morwenna Griffiths. 187–204. Bloomington: Indiana University Press, 1988.

Code, Lorraine. *What Can She Know? Feminist Theory and the Construction of Knowledge.* Ithaca, NY: Cornell University Press, 1991.

Code, Lorraine. 'Taking Subjectivity into Account.' In *Feminist Epistemologies.* Ed. Linda Alcoff and Elizabeth Potter. 15–48. New York and London: Routledge, 1993.

Code, Lorraine. 'I Know Just How You Feel: Empathy and the Problem of Epistemic Authority.' In *Rhetorical Spaces: Essays on Gendered Locations.* Lorraine Code. 120–143. New York and London: Routledge, 1995.

Code, Lorraine. 'Responsibility and Rhetoric.' In *Rhetorical Spaces: Essays on Gendered Locations.* Lorraine Code. 1–22. New York and London: Routledge, 1995.

Code, Lorraine. *Rhetorical Spaces: Essays on Gendered Locations.* New York and London: Routledge, 1995.

Code, Lorraine. 'What Is Natural about Epistemology Naturalized?' *American Philosophical Quarterly* 33, no. 1 (1996): 1–22.

Code, Lorraine, Sheila Mullett, and Christine Overall, eds. *Feminist Perspectives: Philosophical Essays on Method and Morals.* Toronto: University of Toronto Press, 1988.

Cole, Eve Browning and Susan Coultrap-McQuin. 'Toward a Feminist Conception of Moral Life.' In *Explorations in Feminist Ethics: Theory and Practice.* Ed. Eve Browning Cole and Susan Coultrap-McQuin. 1–11. Bloomington and Indianapolis: Indiana University Press, 1992.

Cole, Eve Browning and Susan Coultrap-McQuin, eds. *Explorations in Feminist Ethics: Theory and Practice.* Bloomington and Indianapolis: Indiana University Press, 1992.

Cornell, Drucilla. *Beyond Accommodation: Ethical Feminism, Deconstruction, and the Law.* New York: Routledge, 1991.

Cox, Eva. *Leading Women: Tactics for Making the Difference.* Sydney: Random House, 1996.

C.W.A. Cookery Book and Household Hints. Perth, Western Australia: Wigg, 1978.

Davis, Kathy. 'Toward a Feminist Rhetoric: The Gilligan Debate Revisited.' *Women's Studies International Forum* 15, no. 2 (1992): 219–231.

Deveaux, Monique. 'Shifting Paradigms: Theorizing Care and Justice in Political Theory.' *Hypatia* 10, no. 2 (Spring 1995): 115–119.

Deveson, Anne. *Tell Me I'm Here.* Ringwood, Vic.: Penguin Books, 1991.

Dillon, Robin S. 'Care and Respect.' In *Explorations in Feminist Ethics: Theory and Practice.* Ed. Eve Browning Cole and Susan Coultrap-McQuin. 69–81. Bloomington and Indianapolis: Indiana University Press, 1992.

Diprose, Rosalyn. *The Bodies of Women: Ethics, Embodiment and Sexual Difference.* London and New York: Routledge, 1994.

Diprose, Rosalyn and Robyn Ferrell, eds. *Cartographies: Poststructuralism and the Mapping of Bodies and Spaces.* Sydney: Allen and Unwin, 1991.

Eisenstein, Hester. *Contemporary Feminist Thought.* London and Sydney: Unwin Paperbacks, 1984.

Elshtain, Jean Bethke. *Public Man, Private Woman.* Princeton: Princeton University Press, 1981.

Feinberg, Mortimer R. 'A Few Kind Words about Fear.' *Working Woman* (August 1990): 20.

Flanagan, Owen and Kathryn Jackson. 'Justice, Care, and Gender: The Kohlberg-Gilligan Debate Revisited.' In *An Ethic of Care: Feminist and Interdisciplinary Perspectives.* Ed. Mary Jeanne Larrabee. 69–84. New York: Routledge, 1993.

Flax, Jane. 'Why Epistemology Matters.' *Journal of Politics* 43 (November 1981): 1006–1024.

Flax, Jane. 'Postmodernism and Gender Relations.' In *Feminism/Postmodernism.* Ed. Linda J. Nicholson. 133–156. New York and London: Routledge, 1990.

Foucault, Michel. *Power/Knowledge: Selected Interviews and Other Writings by Michel Foucault 1972–1977.* Ed. Colin Gordon. New York: Pantheon Books, 1980.

Fox Keller, Evelyn. *Reflections on Gender and Science.* New Haven, CT: Yale University Press, 1985.

Fox Keller, Evelyn. 'The Gender/Science System: or, Is Sex to Gender as Nature Is to Science?.' In *Feminism and Science.* Ed. Nancy Tuana. 33–44. Bloomington and Indianapolis: Indiana University Press, 1989.

Fox Keller, Evelyn and Christine Grontkowski. 'The Mind's Eye.' In *Discovering Reality: Feminist Perspectives on Epistemology, Metaphysics, Methodology, and Philosophy of Science.* Ed. Sandra Harding and Merrill Hintikka. 207–224. Dordrecht: Reidel, 1983.

Frankfurt, Harry. 'The Importance of What We Care About.' *Synthese* 53 (1982): 257–272.

Frazer, Elizabeth and Nicola Lacey. 'MacIntyre, Feminism and the Concept of Practice.' In *After MacIntyre: Critical Perspectives on the Work of Alasdair MacIntyre.* Ed. John Horton and Susan Mendus. 265–282. Cambridge: Polity Press, 1994.

French, Marilyn. *The Women's Room.* London: Sphere, 1978.

Fricker, Miranda. 'Knowledge as Construct: Theorizing the Role of Gender in Knowledge.' In *Knowing the Difference: Feminist Perspectives in Epistemology.* Ed. Kathleen Lennon and Margaret Whitford. 95–109. London and New York: Routledge, 1994.

Friedman, Marilyn. 'Care and Context in Moral Reasoning.' In *Women and Moral Theory*. Ed. Eva Feder Kittay and Diana T. Meyers. 190–204. Totowa, NJ: Rowman and Littlefield, 1987.

Friedman, Marilyn. 'The Impracticality of Impartiality.' *Journal of Philosophy* 86 (1989): 645–656.

Friedman, Marilyn. 'The Practice of Partiality.' *Ethics* 101 (July 1991): 818–835.

Friedman, Marilyn. 'Feminism and Modern Friendship: Dislocating the Community.' In *Explorations in Feminist Ethics: Theory and Practice*. Ed. Eve Browning Cole and Susan Coultrap McQuin. 89–97. Bloomington and Indianapolis: Indiana University Press, 1992.

Friedman, Marilyn. 'Beyond Caring: The De-Moralization of Gender.' In *An Ethic of Care: Feminist and Interdisciplinary Perspectives*. Ed. Mary Jeanne Larrabee. 258–273. New York: Routledge, 1993.

Friedman, Marilyn. *What Are Friends For? Feminist Perspectives on Personal Relationships and Moral Theory*. Ithaca, NY, and London: Cornell University Press, 1993.

Frye, Marilyn. 'In and Out of Harm's Way.' In *The Politics of Reality: Essays in Feminist Theory*. Marilyn Frye. Trumansburg, NY: Crossing Press, 1983.

Garry, Ann. 'A Minimally Decent Philosophical Method? Analytic Philosophy and Feminism.' *Hypatia* 10, no. 3 (Summer 1995): 7–30.

Garry, Ann and Marilyn Pearsall, eds. *Women, Knowledge, and Reality: Explorations in Feminist Philosophy*. Boston: Unwin Hyman, 1989.

Gatens, Moira. 'Feminism, Philosophy and Riddles without Answers.' In *Feminist Challenges: Social and Political Theory*. Ed. Carole Pateman and Elizabeth Gross. 13–29. Sydney: Allen and Unwin, 1986.

Gatens, Moira. 'Corporeal Representation in/and the Body Politic.' In *Cartographies: Poststructuralism and the Mapping of Bodies and Spaces*. Ed. Rosalyn Diprose and Robyn Ferrell. 79–87. Sydney: Allen and Unwin, 1991.

Gatens, Moira. *Feminism and Philosophy: Perspectives on Difference and Equality*. Cambridge, U.K.: Polity Press, 1991.

Gilligan, Carol. *In a Different Voice: Psychological Theory and Women's Development*. Cambridge and London: Harvard University Press, 1982, 1993.

Gilligan, Carol. 'Letter to Readers, 1993.' Preface to 1993 Edition of *In a Different Voice*.

Gilligan, Carol. 'Reply to Critics.' In *An Ethic of Care: Feminist and Interdisciplinary Perspectives*. Ed. Mary Jeanne Larrabee. 207–214. New York: Routledge, 1993.

Gilligan, Carol. 'Hearing the Difference: Theorizing Connection.' *Hypatia* 10, no. 2 (Spring 1995): 120–127.

Gilligan, Carol. 'Moral Orientation and Moral Development.' In *Justice and Care: Essential Readings in Feminist Ethics*. Ed. Virginia Held. 31–46. Boulder, CO, and Oxford: Westview Press, 1995.

Gorham, Geoffrey. 'The Concept of Truth in Feminist Sciences.' *Hypatia* 10, no. 3 (Summer 1995): 99–116.

Gould, Carol C, ed. *Beyond Domination: New Perspectives on Women and Philosophy*. Totowa, NJ: Rowman and Allenheld, 1983.

Gould, Carol C. and Max W. Wartofsky, eds. *Women and Philosophy: Toward a Theory of Liberation*. New York: Putnam, 1976.

Grimshaw, Jean. *Feminist Philosophers: Women's Perspectives on Philosophical Traditions*. Brighton: Harvester Wheatsheaf, 1986.

Habermas, Jürgen. 'Technology and Science as "Ideology".' In *Toward a Rational Society: Student Protest, Science, and Politics.* Jürgen Habermas. 81–122. Boston: Beacon Press, 1970.

Habermas, Jürgen. *Moral Consciousness and Communicative Action.* Cambridge: Polity Press, 1990.

Hampton, Jean. 'Feminist Contractarianism.' In *A Mind of One's Own: Feminist Essays on Reason and Objectivity.* Ed. Louise M. Antony and Charlotte Witt. 227–255. Boulder, CO: Westview Press, 1993.

Hanen, Marsha and Kai Nielsen, eds. *Science, Morality and Feminist Theory.* Calgary: University of Calgary Press, 1987.

Haraway, Donna J. 'Situated Knowledges: The Science Question in Feminism and the Privilege of Partial Perspective.' *Feminist Studies* 14, no. 3 (1988): 575–599.

Haraway, Donna J. 'A Manifesto for Cyborgs: Science, Technology and Social Feminism in the 1980s.' In *Feminism/Postmodernism.* Ed. Linda J. Nicholson. 190–233. New York and London: Routledge, 1990.

Harding, Sandra. 'The Instability of the Analytical Categories of Feminist Theory.' *Signs: Journal of Women in Culture and Society* 11, no. 4 (1986): 645–664.

Harding, Sandra. *The Science Question in Feminism.* Milton Keynes, U.K.: Open University Press, 1986.

Harding, Sandra. 'Feminism, Science, and the Anti-Enlightenment Critiques.' In *Feminism/Postmodernism.* Ed. Linda J. Nicholson. 83–106. New York and London: Routledge, 1990.

Harding, Sandra. *Whose Science? Whose Knowledge? Thinking from Women's Lives.* Milton Keynes, U.K.: Open University Press, 1991.

Harding, Sandra. 'Rethinking Standpoint Epistemology: What is "Strong Objectivity?"' In *Feminist Epistemologies.* Ed. Linda Alcoff and Elizabeth Potter. 49–82. New York and London: Routledge, 1993.

Harding, Sandra and Merrill Hintikka, eds. *Discovering Reality: Feminist Perspectives on Epistemology, Metaphysics, Methodology, and Philosophy of Science.* Dordrecht: Reidel, 1983.

Hekman, Susan J. *Gender and Knowledge: Elements of a Postmodern Feminism.* Cambridge: Polity Press, 1990.

Hekman, Susan J. *Moral Voices, Moral Selves: Carol Gilligan and Feminist Moral Theory.* Cambridge: Polity Press, 1995.

Held, Virginia. *Rights and Goods: Justifying Social Action.* New York: Free Press, 1984.

Held, Virginia. *Feminist Morality: Transforming Culture, Society, and Politics.* Chicago: University of Chicago Press, 1993.

Held, Virginia. 'Feminist Moral Inquiry and the Feminist Future.' In *Justice and Care: Essential Readings in Feminist Ethics.* Ed. Virginia Held. 153–176. Boulder, CO, and Oxford: Westview Press, 1995.

Held, Virginia. 'The Meshing of Care and Justice.' *Hypatia* 10, no. 2 (Spring 1995): 128–132.

Held, Virginia, ed. *Justice and Care: Essential Readings in Feminist Ethics.* Boulder, CO, and Oxford: Westview Press, 1995.

Herman, Barbara. 'Integrity and Impartiality.' *Monist* 66 (1983): 233–250.

Hilgard, Ernest R., Richard C, Atkinson, and Rita L. Atkinson, eds. *Introduction to Psychology.* 6th Ed. New York: Harcourt Brace Jovanovich, 1975.

Hoagland, Sarah Lucia. *Lesbian Ethics: Toward New Value.* Palo Alto, CA: Institute of Lesbian Studies, 1988.

Hoagland, Sarah Lucia. 'Some Thoughts about *Caring.*' In *Feminist Ethics.* Ed. Claudia Card. 246–263. Lawrence: University Press of Kansas, 1991. A shortened version is published as 'Some Concerns about Nel Noddings' Caring.' *Hypatia* 5, no. 1 (Spring 1990): 109–114.

Hoffman, Martin L. 'Sex Differences in Empathy and Related Behaviours.' *Psychological Bulletin* 84 (1977): 712–722.

Horton, John and Susan Mendus. *After MacIntyre: Critical Perspectives on the Work of Alasdair MacIntyre.* Cambridge: Polity Press, 1994.

Hospers, John. *An Introduction to Philosophical Analysis.* 3rd ed. London: Routledge, 1990.

Houston, Barbara. 'Rescuing Womanly Virtues: Some Dangers of Moral Reclamation.' In *Science, Morality and Feminist Theory.* Ed. Marsha Hanen and Kai Nielsen. 237–262. Calgary: University of Calgary Press, 1987.

Houston, Barbara. 'Gilligan and the Politics of a Distinctive Women's Morality.' In *Feminist Perspectives: Philosophical Essays on Method and Morals.* Ed. Lorraine Code, Sheila Mullett, and Christine Overall. 168–189. Toronto: University of Toronto Press, 1988.

Houston, Barbara. 'Prolegomena to Future Caring.' In *A Reader in Feminist Ethics.* Ed. Debra Shogan. 109–128. Toronto: Canadian Scholars' Press, 1992.

Irigaray, Luce. *Speculum of the Other Woman.* Tr. Gillian C. Gill. Ithaca, NY: Cornell University Press, 1985.

Irigaray, Luce. *This Sex Which Is Not One.* Tr. Catherine Porter. Ithaca, NY: Cornell University Press, 1985.

Jaggar, Alison M. *Feminist Politics and Human Nature.* Totowa, NJ: Rowman and Allanheld, 1983.

Jaggar, Alison M. 'Feminist Ethics: Some Issues for the Nineties.' *Journal of Social Philosophy* 20, nos. 1–2 (Spring–Fall 1989): 91–107.

Jaggar, Alison M. 'Feminist Ethics: Projects, Problems, Prospects.' In *Feminist Ethics.* Ed. Claudia Card. 78–104. Lawrence: University Press of Kansas, 1991.

Jaggar, Alison M. 'Caring as a Feminist Practice of Moral Reason.' In *Justice and Care: Essential Readings in Feminist Ethics.* Ed. Virginia Held. 179–202. Boulder, CO, and Oxford: Westview Press, 1995.

Jaggar, Alison M. and Susan R. Bordo, eds. *Gender/Body/Knowledge: Feminist Reconstructions of Being and Knowing.* New Brunswick, NJ: Rutgers University Press, 1989.

Jay, Nancy. 'Gender and Dichotomy.' *Feminist Studies* 7, no. 1 (1981): 35–56.

Kant, Immanuel. *Groundwork of the Metaphysic of Morals.* Tr. and analysed by H. J. Paton. New York: Harper Torchbooks, 1964.

Kaufman, Frederik. 'Warren on the Logic of Domination.' *Environmental Ethics* 16 (1994): 333–334.

Kittay, Eva Feder and Diana Tietjens Meyers, eds. *Women and Moral Theory.* Totowa, NJ: Rowman and Littlefield, 1987.

Kohlberg, Lawrence. 'Stages of Moral Development as a Basis for Moral Education.' In *Moral Education: Interdisciplinary Approaches.* Ed. Clive M. Beck, Brian S. Crittenden, and Edmund V. Sullivan. 23–92. New York: Newman Press, 1971.

Kohlberg, Lawrence. 'Moral Stages and Moralization: The Cognitive-Developmental Approach.' In *Moral Development and Behaviour: Theory, Research and Social Issues.* Ed. Thomas Lickona. 31–53. New York: Holt, Rinehart, and Winston, 1976.

Kohlberg, Lawrence. *The Philosophy of Moral Development: Moral Stages and the Idea of Justice.* Vol. 1. San Francisco: Harper and Row, 1981.

Kohlberg, Lawrence. 'A Reply to Owen Flanagan and Some Comments on the Puka-Goodpaster Exchange.' *Ethics* 92 (1982): 513–528.

Kohlberg, Lawrence. *The Psychology of Moral Development: Moral Stages and the Life Cycle.* Vol. 2. San Francisco: Harper and Row, 1984.

Kohlberg, Lawrence. 'A Current Statement on Some Theoretical Issues.' In *Lawrence Kohlberg: Consensus and Controversy.* Ed. Sohan Modgil and Celia Modgil. 485–546. Philadelphia and London: Falmer Press, 1986.

Kohlberg, Lawrence and Robert Kramer. 'Continuities and Discontinuities in Childhood and Adult Moral Development.' *Human Development* 12 (1969): 93–120.

Kohlberg, Lawrence, Charles Levine, and Alexandra Hewer. *Moral Stages: A Current Formulation and a Response to Critics.* New York: Karger, 1983.

Kornblith, Hilary. *Naturalizing Epistemology.* 2nd ed. Cambridge: MIT Press, 1994.

Kuhn, Thomas S. *The Structure of Scientific Revolutions.* 2nd ed. Chicago: University of Chicago Press, 1970.

Larrabee, Mary Jeanne, ed. *An Ethic of Care: Feminist and Interdisciplinary Perspectives.* New York: Routledge, 1993.

de Lauretis, Teresa. *Alice Doesn't: Feminism, Semiotics, Cinema.* Bloomington: Indiana University Press, 1984.

League, Kathleen. 'Individualism, Class, and the Situation of Care: An Essay on Carol Gilligan.' *Journal of Social Philosophy* 24, no. 3 (1993): 69–79.

Lennon, Kathleen and Margaret Whitford, eds. *Knowing the Difference: Feminist Perspectives in Epistemology.* London and New York: Routledge, 1994.

Levinas, Emmanuel. 'Philosophy and the Idea of Infinity.' In *Collected Philosophical Papers.* Tr. Alphonso Lingis. 47–59. Dordrecht: Martinus Nijhoff, 1987.

Levinas, Emmanuel. 'Ethics as First Philosophy.' In *The Levinas Reader.* Ed. Sean Hand. 75–87. Oxford: Blackwell, 1989.

Lindgren, J. Ralph. 'Beyond Revolt: A Horizon for Feminist Ethics.' *Hypatia* 5, no. 1 (Spring 1990): 145–150.

Lloyd, Genevieve. *The Man of Reason: 'Male' and 'Female' in Western Philosophy.* London: Methuen, 1984.

Lloyd, Genevieve. 'Maleness, Metaphor, and the "Crisis" of Reason.' In *A Mind Of One's Own: Feminist Essays on Reason and Objectivity.* Ed. Louise M. Antony and Charlotte Witt. 69–83. Boulder, CO: Westview Press, 1993.

Locke, Don. 'A Psychologist among the Philosophers: Philosophical Aspects of Kohlberg's Theories.' In *Lawrence Kohlberg: Consensus and Controversy.* Ed. Sohan Modgil and Celia Modgil. 21–38. Philadelphia and London: Falmer Press, 1986.

Longino, Helen E. 'Can There Be a Feminist Science?' In *Women, Knowledge, and Reality: Explorations in Feminist Philosophy.* Ed. Ann Garry and Marilyn Pearsall. 203–216. Boston: Unwin Hyman, 1989.

Lorde, Audre. *Sister Outsider: Essays and Speeches.* London: Crossing Press, 1984.

Lovibond, Sabina. 'Feminism and Postmodernism.' *New Left Review* 178 (November–December 1989): 5–28.

Lugones, María. 'Playfulness, "World"-Traveling, and Loving Perception.' In *Women, Knowledge, and Reality: Explorations in Feminist Philosophy.* Ed. Ann Garry and Marilyn Pearsall. 275–290. Boston: Unwin Hyman, 1989.

Lugones, María. 'Hispaneando y Lesbiando: On Sarah Hoagland's *Lesbian Ethics.*' *Hypatia* 5, no. 3 (Fall 1990): 138–144.

MacIntyre, Alasdair. 'Comments on Frankfurt.' *Synthese* 53 (1982): 291–294.

MacIntyre, Alasdair. *After Virtue: A Study in Moral Theory.* 2nd ed. Notre Dame, IN: University of Notre Dame Press, 1984.

MacIntyre, Alasdair. *Whose Justice? Which Rationality?* Notre Dame, IN: University of Notre Dame Press, 1988.

Malpas, Jeff. 'Speaking the Truth.' *Economy and Society* 25, no. 2 (May 1996): 156–177.

Manning, Rita C. *Speaking from the Heart.* Lanham, MD: Rowman and Littlefield, 1992.

Mason Mullett, Sheila. 'Inclusive Philosophy: Feminist Strategies for the Recovery of Persons.' In *A Reader in Feminist Ethics.* Ed. Debra Shogan. 69–88. Toronto: Canadian Scholars' Press, 1992.

Meyers, Diana Tietjens. 'Moral Reflection: Beyond Impartial Reason.' *Hypatia* 8, no. 3 (Summer 1993): 21–47.

Mill, John Stuart. 'Utilitarianism.' In *Utilitarianism, on Liberty and Considerations on Representative Government.* Ed. H. B. Acton. 1–67. London: J. M. Dent and Sons, 1972.

Modgil, Sohan and Celia Modgil, eds. *Lawrence Kohlberg: Consensus and Controversy.* Philadelphia and London: Falmer Press, 1986.

Moody-Adams, Michele M. 'Feminist Inquiry and the Transformation of the "Public" Sphere in Virginia Held's *Feminist Morality.'* *Hypatia* 11, no. 1 (Winter 1996): 155–167.

Mortimer, Lorraine. 'What If I Talked like a Woman Right Here in Public?' *Arena* 92 (1990): 43–65.

Moulton, Janice. 'A Paradigm of Philosophy: The Adversary Method.' In *Women, Knowledge, and Reality: Explorations in Feminist Philosophy.* Ed. Ann Garry and Marilyn Pearsall. 5–20. Boston: Unwin Hyman, 1989.

Murdoch, Iris. 'The Idea of Perfection.' In *The Sovereignty of Good.* Iris Murdoch. 1–45. London: Routledge and Kegan Paul, 1970.

Murdoch, Iris. *The Sovereignty of Good.* London: Routledge and Kegan Paul, 1970.

Murdoch, Iris. *Metaphysics as a Guide to Morals.* London: Chatto and Windus, 1992.

Nagel, Thomas. *The View from Nowhere.* New York: Oxford University Press, 1986.

Nagel, Thomas. *Equality and Partiality.* New York: Oxford University Press, 1991.

Narayan, Uma. 'Colonialism and Its Others: Considerations on Rights and Care Discourses.' *Hypatia* 10, no. 2 (Spring 1995): 133–140.

Nelson, Lynn Hankinson. *Who Knows? From Quine to a Feminist Empiricism.* Philadelphia: Temple University Press, 1990.

Nelson, Lynn Hankinson. 'Epistemological Communities.' In *Feminist Epistemologies.* Ed. Linda Alcoff and Elizabeth Potter. 121–159. New York and London: Routledge, 1993.

Nelson, Lynn Hankinson. 'A Question of Evidence.' *Hypatia* 8, no. 2 (Spring 1993): 172–189.

Nicholson, Linda, ed. *Feminism/Postmodernism.* New York and London: Routledge, 1990.

Noddings, Nel. *Caring: A Feminine Approach to Ethics and Moral Education.* Berkeley: University of California Press, 1984.

Noddings, Nel. *Women and Evil.* Berkley and London: University of California Press, 1989.

Noddings, Nel. 'Conversation as Moral Education.' *Journal of Moral Education* 23, no. 2 (1994): 107–118.

Noddings, Nel. *Philosophy of Education.* Boulder, CO, and Oxford: Westview Press, 1995.

Nunner-Winkler, Gertrud. 'Two Moralities? A Critical Discussion of an Ethic of Care and Responsibility versus an Ethic of Rights and Justice.' In *An Ethic of Care: Feminist and Interdisciplinary Perspectives*. Ed. Mary Jeanne Larrabee. 143–156. New York: Routledge, 1993.

Nussbaum, Martha. *The Fragility of Goodness*. New York: Cambridge University Press, 1986.

Nussbaum, Martha. 'Feminists and Philosophy.' *New York Review of Books* (October 20, 1994).

Okin, Susan Moller. *Women in Western Political Thought*. Princeton: Princeton University Press, 1979.

Okin, Susan Moller. *Justice, Gender, and the Family*. New York: Basic Books, 1989.

Okin, Susan Moller. 'Reason and Feeling in Thinking about Justice.' *Ethics* 99 (January 1989): 229–249.

O'Neill, Onora. *Acting on Principle*. New York: Columbia University Press, 1975.

O'Neill, Onora. 'Kant after Virtue.' *Inquiry* 26 (1984): 387–405.

Pateman, Carole. *The Sexual Contract*. Cambridge: Polity Press, 1988.

Pateman, Carole. '"The Disorder of Women": Women, Love, and the Sense of Justice.' In *The Disorder of Women*. Carole Pateman. 17–32. Cambridge: Polity Press, 1989.

Pateman, Carole. *The Disorder of Women*. Cambridge: Polity Press, 1989.

Pateman, Carole and Elizabeth Gross, eds. *Feminist Challenges: Social and Political Theory*. Sydney: Allen and Unwin, 1986.

Poole, Ross. *Morality and Modernity*. London and New York: Routledge, 1991.

Porter, Elisabeth J. *Women and Moral Identity*. Sydney: Allen and Unwin, 1991.

Pratt, Minnie Bruce. 'Identity: Skin Blood Heart.' In *Rebellion: Essays 1980–1991*. Minnie Bruce Pratt. 27–81. Ithaca, NY: Firebrand Books, 1991.

Quine, W.V.O. 'Two Dogmas of Empiricism.' In *From a Logical Point of View: Nine Logico-Philosophical Essays*. W.V.O. Quine. 20–46. Cambridge: Harvard University Press, 1953.

Quine, W. V. O. 'Epistemology Naturalized.' In *Naturalizing Epistemology*. 2nd ed. Ed. Hilary Kornblith. 15–31. Cambridge: MIT Press, 1994.

Rawls, John. *A Theory of Justice*. Cambridge: Harvard University Press, 1971.

Rawls, John. *Political Liberalism*. New York: Columbia University Press, 1993.

Rich, Adrienne. *Of Woman Born: Motherhood as Experience and Institution*. London: Virago, 1977.

Rich, Adrienne. *The Dream of a Common Language: Poems 1974–1977*. New York: Norton, 1978.

Richards, Eulalia S. *Ladies' Handbook of Home Treatment*. Victoria: Signs, 1945.

Romain, Dianne. 'Care and Confusion.' In *Explorations in Feminist Ethics: Theory and Practice*. Ed. Eve Browning Cole and Susan Coultrap-McQuin. 27–37. Bloomington and Indianapolis: Indiana University Press, 1992.

Rorty, Richard. *Philosophy and the Mirror of Nature*. Princeton: Princeton University Press, 1982.

Ruby, Lionel, *The Art of Making Sense: A Guide to Logical Thinking*. 2nd ed. London: Angus and Robertson, 1969.

Ruddick, Sara. 'Remarks on the Sexual Politics of Reason.' In *Women and Moral Theory*. Ed. Eva Fedder Kittay and Diana T. Meyers. 237–260. Totowa, NJ: Rowman and Littlefield, 1987.

Ruddick, Sara. *Maternal Thinking: Towards a Politics of Peace*. London: Women's Press, 1989.

Ruggiero, Vincent Ryan. *The Art of Thinking: A Guide to Critical and Creative Thought.* 4th ed. New York: HarperCollins, 1995.

Sandel, Michael. *Liberalism and the Limits of Justice.* Cambridge: Cambridge University Press, 1982.

Scheman, Naomi. *Engenderings: Constructions of Knowledge, Authority, and Privilege.* New York and London: Routledge, 1993.

Scheman, Naomi. 'Othello's Doubt/Desdemona's Death: The Engendering of Scepticism.' In *Engenderings: Constructions of Knowledge, Authority, and Privilege.* Naomi Scheman. 57–74. New York and London: Routledge, 1993.

Scheman, Naomi. 'Though This Be Method, Yet There Is Madness in It: Paranoia and Liberal Epistemology.' In *Engenderings: Constructions of Knowledge, Authority, and Privilege.* Naomi Scheman. 75–105. New York and London: Routledge, 1993.

Seller, Anne. 'Realism versus Relativism: Towards a Politically Adequate Epistemology.' In *Feminist Perspectives in Philosophy.* Ed. Margaret Whitford and Morwenna Griffiths. 169–186. Bloomington: Indiana University Press, 1988.

Seller, Anne. 'Should the Feminist Philosopher Stay at Home?.' In *Knowing the Difference: Feminist Perspectives in Epistemology.* Ed. Kathleen Lennon and Margaret Whitford. 230–248. London and New York: Routledge, 1994.

Sher, George. 'Other Voices, Other Rooms? Women's Psychology and Moral Theory.' In *Women and Moral Theory.* Ed. Eva Feder Kittay and Diana T. Meyers. 178–189. Totowa, NJ: Rowman and Littlefield, 1987.

Sherwin, Susan. 'Feminist Ethics and Medical Ethics: Two Different Approaches to Contextual Ethics.' In *A Reader in Feminist Ethics.* Ed. Debra Shogan. 39–56. Toronto: Canadian Scholars' Press, 1992.

Shogan, Debra, ed. *A Reader in Feminist Ethics.* Toronto: Canadian Scholars' Press, 1992.

Shrage, Laurie. *Moral Dilemmas of Feminism: Prostitution, Adultery, and Abortion.* New York and London: Routledge, 1994.

Singer, Peter. *Animal Liberation: A New Ethics for Our Treatment of Animals.* New York: Avon Books, 1975.

Spelman, Elizabeth V. *Inessential Woman: Problems of Exclusion in Feminist Thought.* London: Women's Press, 1990.

Spender, Dale. *Man Made Language.* 2nd ed. London: Pandora Press, 1990.

Spivak, Gayatri Chakravorty. *In Other Worlds: Essays in Cultural Politics.* New York: Methuen, 1987.

Sullivan, Roger J. *Immanuel Kant's Moral Theory.* Cambridge: Cambridge University Press, 1989.

Taylor, Charles. 'Cross-Purposes: The Liberal-Communitarian Debate.' In *Liberalism and the Moral Life.* Ed. Nancy L. Rosenblum. 159–182. Cambridge: Harvard University Press, 1989.

Taylor, Charles. *Sources of the Self: The Making of the Modern Identity.* Cambridge: Harvard University Press, 1989.

Taylor, Charles. 'Leading a Life.' Paper delivered at Murdoch University, Perth, Western Australia. April 1994.

Tomm, Winnie. 'Ethics and Self-knowing: The Satisfaction of Desire.' In *Explorations in Feminist Ethics: Theory and Practice.* Ed. Eve Browning Cole and Susan Coultrap McQuin. 101–110. Bloomington and Indianapolis: Indiana University Press, 1992.

Tronto, Joan C. 'Women and Caring: What Can Feminists Learn about Morality from Caring?' In *Gender/Body/Knowledge: Feminist Reconstructions of Being and*

Knowing. Ed. Alison M. Jaggar and Susan R. Bordo. 172–187. New Brunswick, NJ: Rutgers University Press, 1989.

Tronto, Joan C. 'Beyond Gender Difference to a Theory of Care.' In *An Ethic of Care: Feminist and Interdisciplinary Perspectives.* Ed. Mary Jeanne Larrabee. 240–257. New York: Routledge, 1993.

Tronto, Joan C. *Moral Boundaries: A Political Argument for an Ethic of Care.* New York and London: Routledge, 1993.

Tronto, Joan C. 'Care as a Basis for Radical Political Judgements.' *Hypatia* 10, no. 2 (Spring 1995): 141–149.

Tuana, Nancy, ed. *Feminism and Science.* Bloomington and Indianapolis: Indiana University Press, 1989.

Walker, Margaret Urban. 'Moral Understandings: Alternative "Epistemology" for a Feminist Ethics.' In *Explorations in Feminist Ethics: Theory and Practice.* Ed. Eve Browning Cole and Susan Coultrap-McQuin. 165–175. Bloomington and Indianapolis: Indiana University Press, 1992.

Walker, Margaret Urban. 'Partial Consideration.' *Ethics* 101 (July 1991): 758–774.

Walker, Margaret Urban. 'Feminism, Ethics, and the Question of Theory.' *Hypatia* 7, no. 3 (Summer 1992): 23–38.

Walzer, Michael. *Spheres of Justice.* New York: Basic Books, 1983.

Warren, Karen J. 'Feminism and Ecology: Making Connections.' *Environmental Ethics* 9 (1987): 3–21.

Warren, Karen J. 'The Power and the Promise of Ecological Feminism.' *Environmental Ethics* 12 (1990): 125–146.

Whitbeck, Caroline. 'A Different Reality: Feminist Ontology.' In *Beyond Domination: New Perspectives on Women and Philosophy.* Ed. Carol C. Gould. 64–88. Totowa, NJ: Rowman and Allenheld, 1983.

Whitford, Margaret and Morwenna Griffiths, ed. *Feminist Perspectives in Philosophy.* Bloomington: Indiana University Press, 1988.

Williams, Bernard. *Moral Luck: Philosophical Papers 1973–1980.* Cambridge: Cambridge University Press, 1981.

Williams, Bernard. 'Persons, Character and Morality.' In *Moral Luck: Philosophical Papers 1973–1980.* Bernard Williams. 1–19. Cambridge: Cambridge University Press, 1981.

Williams, Bernard. *Ethics and the Limits of Philosophy.* London: Collins, 1985.

Witt, Charlotte. 'Feminist Metaphysics.' In *A Mind of One's Own: Feminist Essays on Reason and Objectivity.* Ed. Louise M. Antony and Charlotte Witt. 273–288. Boulder, CO, and Oxford: Westview Press, 1993.

Yeatman, Anna. 'Postmodern Epistemological Politics and Social Science.' In *Knowing the Difference: Feminist Perspectives in Epistemology.* Ed. Kathleen Lennon and Margaret Whitford. 187–202. London and New York: Routledge, 1994.

Young, Iris Marion. 'The Ideal of Community and the Politics of Difference.' In *Feminism/Postmodernism.* Ed. Linda J. Nicholson. 300–323. New York and London: Routledge, 1990.

Index

Absolutism, 123, 130. *See also*
Foundationalism; Positivism
Addelson, Kathryn Pyne, 26, 35 n.74,
126, 151 nn.28, 34, 153 n.62, 184
nn.18, 23, 29, 215 n.37, 38
Anthony, Louise M., 123, 124, 130–
149, 150 n.8, 151 n.39, 167–68, 186
n.63, 214 n.30
Antifoundationalism, 127, 142, 143,
145, 148, 151 n.39, 154 n. 83, 166,
170, 184 n.30
Attention, 104–113, 116 n.58, 213 n.4

Baier, Annette C., 34 n.62, 87 n.28, 115
nn.32, 41, 116 nn.46, 48, 118–19
n.101, 150 n.1
Bartky, Sandra Lee, 44, 45, 61 n.62,
116 n.63
Benhabib, Seyla, 58 n.18, 59 n.38, 60
n.52, 64–66, 68–71, 87 n.29, 213 n.7
Bias paradox, 131, 140
Binary thinking. *See* Dichotomies;
Dualism; Logic of domination
Bordo, Susan, 150 n.13, 214 n.30, 215
n.39
Bowden, Peta, 44–45, 107, 204
Burgess-Jackson, Keith, 24

Card, Claudia, 29 n.2, 33 n.47, 53, 58
n.17, 116 n.62

Care: and evaluation, 109–113, 121,
124, 200, 211; and instrumental
reason, 4, 9, 38, 108, 200, 210, 211–
12; as action, 4, 94, 99–103, 106,
108, 114 n.16, 193, 200; as
alternative moral theory, 44, 124,
212; as complement to other ethics
(filling the gaps), 4, 38–41, 43, 44,
51, 57, 93, 149–50 n.1; as
disposition, 4, 94, 101–104, 106, 109,
121, 193, 200, 202, 212; as distinct
from ethics, 17, 63, 83–84, 94–96,
111–113; as inferior (devalued) moral
response, 44–45, 46, 47, 50, 92; as
irrational, 41–43; as "mattering",
103; as rational, 102, 104; confined to
private realm, 17, 18, 39, 41, 44, 50,
59 n.28, 92; instrumental value of,
94, 102–103, 117 nn.69, 72, 202;
necessary and sufficient conditions
of, 4–5, 103, 121, 210; needs-based,
102–103, 117 nn. 68, 70, 71, 202–3,
211, 212; practical acts of, 113, 121,
193
Categorical imperative, 10–11, 14, 16,
19, 95, 96, 114 n.27, 128. *See also*
Deontology; Kant
Code, Lorraine, 33 n.52, 60 n.59, 61
n.70, 125, 126, 127, 129, 137, 144,
151 nn.32, 35, 153 n.77, 158, 184
n.26, 185 n.62, 186 nn.64, 65, 213

n.6, 214–15 n.35

Common language, 27, 28, 57, 124, 131, 149, 157, 167, 178–182, 183, 188, 205. *See also* Seeing the same thing

Commonality, 4, 28, 69, 131, 149, 157, 167, 177, 178–82, 183, 188, 189, 202, 205, 206–209. *See also* Seeing together

Communitarianism, 34 n.58, 96–97, 190–93

Conversation, 170, 177, 205–206

Cox, Eva, 51, 60 n.58

Critical positioning, 76, 107, 168–72, 175–77, 206, 213 n.4

Deontology, 9, 10, 18, 51, 78, 79, 85, 88 n.43, 92, 98, 112, 127, 211, 212, 213 n.8; as both ethical and epistemological project, 27; care as complement to, 40–41, 44. *See also* Categorical imperative; Kant

Deveaux, Monique, 1, 150 n.5

Deveson, Anne, 214 n.27

Dichotomies, 3, 18, 25–26, 29, 53, 55, 64, 108, 122–24, 167, 195. *See also* Dualism; Logic of domination

Dualism, 42–43, 45–46, 53, 55. *See also* Dichotomies; Logic of domination

Empathy, 51–57, 64, 214 n.35

Ethic of contract, 3, 4, 9, 12–22 passim., 51, 78, 79, 88 n.43, 92, 112, 114 n.28, 211, 212; as both ethical and epistemological project, 27; care as complement to, 40–41, 44; moral subjects of, 10. *See also* Rawls

Ethics: and reason as "glue," 63, 79–83, 178; conflation with reason, 24–27; liberal, exclusion of private realm, 15–18; liberal, failure in public realm, 19–24

Ethics and reason, nexus between, 9, 10, 15, 17, 28, 43, 62 n.85, 85, 121, 122, 125, 187, 189, 212

Feminist theory: critical, 2, 3, 5, 6, 9, 10, 28, 38, 51, 91, 93, 130, 141, 145, 149, 166, 168–70, 176, 189–90, 198, 212; extensionist, 2, 3, 43, 52, 91,

130–148 passim., 154 n.83, 166, 176, 196, 197–98, 201–202, 204; separatist, 2, 3, 40, 41, 43, 91. *See also* Gatens

Foundationalism, 93, 127, 131, 137, 140–149, 157, 158, 182–83, 194, 197, 212; critique of, 140. *See also* Absolutism; Antifoundationalism; Positivism

Foundationalist epistemology, 125–26, 131–32, 198, 204

Foundationalist moral theory, 137

Foundationalist-relativist dichotomy, 123, 129, 130

Fox Keller, Evelyn, 158

Fox Keller, Evelyn and Christine Grontkowski, 117 n.80

Frankfurt, Harry, 84, 94–103, 106, 108, 109, 110–113

Franklin, Ursula, 129

Fricker, Miranda, 123–124, 130, 141–49, 159, 167, 172–74

Friedman, Marilyn, 34 n.57, 35 n.62, 42, 58 n.11; and communitarianism, 190, 213 n.12; and Heinz dilemma, 66–71, 73–74, 75, 89 n.48, 161–162

Gatens, Moira, 2–3, 5, 28, 38, 43, 49, 52, 58 n.25, 130, 170, 185 nn.39, 40, 212, 214 n.33

Generalized and concrete other, 64–66, 68–71, 74, 75, 82. *See also* Benhabib

Gilligan, Carol, 1, 2, 7 nn.18, 19, 29 nn.1, 2, 35 n.71, 42, 85, 91–93, 116 nn.61, 63, 150 nn.4, 6, 152 nn.57, 58, 160, 170–71, 184 n.21, 194, 202, 210; "blindness to relationships," 73, 199, 201, 217 n.74; care-justice relation, 58–59 n.27, 59 n.33, 93; conversation, 205–206; ethic-care distinction, 83–84; debate with Kohlberg, 24, 37, 139–140; "discourse of relationship," 203; selflessness, 76–77

Haraway, Donna J., 7 n.21, 49, 53, 61 n.72, 107, 151 n.32, 168, 170–172, 175, 176–77, 178, 180, 201, 205, 207, 215 n.40

Harding, Sandra, 58 n.19, 151 n.31, 152 n.44, 154 n.92, 158, 185 n.40

Heinz dilemma, 37, 71, 73–74, 76, 79–81, 139, 161, 163, 165; Amy's responses, 37, 139, 161–62, 164, 165, 198; Jake's responses, 35 n.71, 86 n.16, 161–62, 198
Hekman, Susan J., 1, 29, 116 n.63
Held, Virginia, 3, 59 n.28, 116 n.63, 150 n.1, 183 n.7
Hoagland, Sarah Lucia, 60 n.61, 61 n.71, 62 n.84, 86 n.3, 116 nn.62, 63, 216 n.44
Hoffman, Martin L., 61 nn.78, 80, 62 n.82

Impartiality, critique of, 124–27, 140–49

Jaggar, Alison M., 7 n.20, 38, 117 n.68, 149–50 n.1, 193

Kant, Immanuel, 10–19 passim., 24, 26, 86 n.11, 92, 114 n.27, 117 n.83; and Constant, 10, 11, 87 n.24. See also Categorical imperative; Deontology
Knowledge, fields of, 127–29, 196–97
Knowledge: and epistemic relation, 160–162; and interchangeability, 163, 188, 197; as aperspectival, 145, 209; enabled by partiality, 130, 166, 168, 179, 188; fields of, 127–29, 196–97; matching reality, 141–45, 159–160; neutrality of, 25, 26, 122, 128, 141, 144, 147–148. See also Minimal realism; Reason; Seeing the same thing; Seeing together; Truth
Kohlberg, Lawrence, 7 n.19, 24, 25–26, 37, 54, 61 n.80, 66, 67, 68, 72, 74, 80, 86 n.16, 87 n.24, 88–89 n.47, 89 nn.48, 49, 92–93, 134–40, 142, 145, 149, 161, 162, 165, 198, 202. See also Heinz dilemma

Locke, Don, 81, 87 n.30, 88 nn.44, 46
Logic of domination, 46–51. See also Dichotomies; Dualism
Longino, Helen, 138, 158

MacIntyre, Alasdair, 34 n.58, 96, 116 n.59, 118 n.99, 190, 191, 192
Malpas, Jeff, 150 n.11, 183 n.14

Manning, Rita C., 34 n.61, 116 n.63, 149–50 n.1, 217 n.79
Mason Mullett, Sheila, 58 n.26, 86 n.3
Mill, John Stuart, 10, 15, 17, 20, 24–25, 26. See also Utilitarianism
Minimal realism, 142, 143, 158–59, 167
Moody-Adams, Michele M., 78
Moral point of view, 72, 79–83
Moulton, Janice, 5, 215 n.35
Murdoch, Iris, 31 n.20, 93, 98, 101, 104–107, 110, 116 n.66, 118 n.93, 188, 200

Nelson, Lynn Hankinson, 126
Noddings, Nel, 1, 2, 7 n.18, 29 n.2, 34 n.61, 37, 42, 51, 58 n.13, 60 n.61, 68, 87 n.24, 114 n.16, 116 n.63, 118 nn.97, 100, 119 n.102, 150 n.1, 182, 183 n.7, 205, 216 n.57

Okin, Susan Moller, 54

Partiality: as bias, 129–40; as irrationality, 148–49; as perspectivity, 129–30; for its own sake, 166–68, 177; pejorative use of, 147–49; strong epistemological partiality, 130–31, 157, 166–67, 168, 172, 177–78, 180, 188, 189, 196, 197, 198, 202, 203, 207
Poole, Ross, 16, 30 n.11, 58 n.23, 213 nn.13, 16
Porter, Elisabeth J., 45–46, 49
Positivism, 126. See also Foundationalism; Absolutism
Pratt, Minnie Bruce, 6
"Premise of unpremisedness," 145–46

Quine, W. V. O., 137–38, 151 n.27, 159

Rawls, John, 7 n.9, 10, 12–20 passim., 24, 25, 26, 54, 61 n.80, 112. See also Ethic of contract
Rawsian deliberators, 15, 16, 19, 54, 65, 87 n.29
Reason: and concrete particularity, 4, 13, 14, 21, 22, 26, 28, 29, 44, 45, 65–74, 77, 78, 82, 83, 93, 112, 123, 124, 148, 163, 171; and emotion, 17, 18,

42–43, 123–24, 150 n.9; and ethics as "glue," 63, 79–83, 178; and the moral point of view, 72, 82, 83; as consistency, 10–11, 16, 19, 96, 159, 194; conflation with ethics, 24–27; dichotomous modes of, 122–23; ethics in the service of, 10–13, 17, 25, 26, 27, 122; instrumental, 14, 15, 32 n.31, 102, 212

Reasoners, impartial, 9, 10, 13, 18, 27, 38, 41, 53, 55, 72–73, 150 n.1

Relativism, 93, 123, 129, 130, 144, 151 n.36, 167, 179, 195, 210

Rich, Adrienne, 119 n.108, 184 n.32

Ruby, Lionel, 59–60 n.40, 191

Ruddick, Sara, 6, 7 n.20, 60 n.42, 99, 122–23, 214–15 n.35

Sandel, Michael, 34 n.58, 188, 190, 191, 192

Seeing the same thing, 4, 82, 107, 160–61, 167, 172, 178, 179, 187, 195, 203, 213 n.4. *See also* Common language

Seeing together, 4, 5, 28, 57, 82, 104–108, 109, 110, 112, 113, 124, 160–61, 163, 164, 167, 172, 177, 178, 179, 180, 181, 187–88, 195–96, 199–210 passim., 213 n.4. *See also* Commonality

Seller, Anne, 158, 164, 174–75, 181–82, 188, 200, 207–209, 210, 214 n.29

Self-reflexiveness, 13, 176, 212; and critical positioning, 168–70; and elaboration of context, 209–210, 211; and selves-in-relation, 76, 77, 106, 163, 177, 178, 187–89, 195, 197, 208–9

Selves-in-relation, 75–78, 165–78

Tomm, Winnie, 53

Tronto, Joan C., 4, 7 nn.18, 20, 38, 54, 59 nn.29, 32, 104, 116 nn.63, 68, 70, 71, 217 n.61

Truth: and contradiction, 172–75; and minimal realism, 158; as aperspectival, 125; as normative constraint, 143, 144; as product, 160; as relational process, 160, 195, 203; as universal and unitary regulatory ideal, 27, 28, 56, 127, 129, 131, 145,

157, 159, 160, 172, 178; associated with common language, 178, 179; checked against "how the world is," 140, 141–145, 146, 159–60; content of, 146, 162–63, 164, 173, 174; context of, 4, 28, 131, 145, 157, 159–165, 167, 174, 182, 183, 187, 207; dichotomous construction of, 123–24, 129, 130, 165, 182; empirical determinants of, 133, 135, 138, 145; foundational account of, 13, 125, 126, 194–95; nexus with knowing individual, 167, 170; partiality as criterion of, 167–68

Utilitarianism, 9, 11–12, 14–15, 16, 17, 18, 21, 24–25, 51, 78, 88 n.43, 96, 112, 114 n.28, 127–128, 191, 211, 212; as both ethical and epistemological project, 27; Benthamite, 20; care as complement to, 40–41, 44; moral subjects of, 10; particularity of the other, 20. *See also* Mill

Walker, Margaret Urban, 22, 23, 29 n.3, 31 n.20, 115 n.35, 123, 127, 150 n.1, 151 n.34, 188–189

Warren, Karen J., 47, 48, 59 n.39, 60 nn.41, 44. *See also* Logic of domination

Whitbeck, Caroline, 86 n.3, 214–15 n.35

Yeatman, Anna, 216 n.61

About the Author

SALLY E. TALBOT is Honorary Visiting Research Fellow at the Centre for Research in Culture and Communication of Murdoch University, Western Australia. She teaches philosophy at the university and is also assistant to various Labor Members of Parliament including the Federal Leader of the Opposition.